CLYMER®

KAWASAKI

ZX500 & 600 NINJA • 1985-1997

The world's finest publisher of mechanical how-to manuals

INTERTEC PUBLISHING
P.O. Box 12901, Overland Park, Kansas 66282-2901

Copyright ©1997 Intertec Publishing

FIRST EDITION
First Printing September, 1987
Second Printing May, 1989
Third Printing July, 1991

SECOND EDITION
First Printing May, 1993
Second Printing April, 1995

THIRD EDITION
First Printing March, 1997
Second Printing June, 1998
Third Printing May, 2000

Printed in U.S.A.

CLYMER and colphon are registered trademarks of Intertec Publishing.

ISBN: 0-89287-696-4

Library of Congress: 97-70698

MEMBER

 MOTORCYCLE INDUSTRY COUNCIL, INC.

Technical illustrations by Steve Amos.

Technical assistance by Action Fours, Inc., Santa Ana, California.

COVER: Photographed by Mark Clifford, Mark Clifford Photography, Los Angeles, California. Motorcycle courtesy of Burbank Kawasaki, Burbank, California.

INTERTEC BOOK DIVISION

President Cameron Bishop
Executive Vice President of Operations/CFO Dan Altman
Senior Vice President, Book Division Ted Marcus

EDITORIAL

Director of Price Guides
Tom Fournier

Senior Editor
Mark Jacobs

Editors
Mike Hall
Frank Craven
Paul Wyatt

Associate Editors
Robert Sokol
Carl Janssens
James Grooms

Technical Writers
Ron Wright
Ed Scott
George Parise
Mark Rolling
Michael Morlan
Jay Bogart
Ronney Broach

Inventory and Production Manager
Shirley Renicker

Editorial Production Supervisor
Dylan Goodwin

Editorial Production Coordinator
Sandy Kreps

Editorial Production Assistants
Greg Araujo
Dennis Conrow
Shara Meyer
Susan Hartington

Technical Illustrators
Steve Amos
Robert Caldwell
Mitzi McCarthy
Michael St. Clair
Mike Rose

MARKETING/SALES AND ADMINISTRATION

General Manager, Technical and Specialty Books
Michael Yim
General Manager, AC-U-KWIK
Randy Stephens
Advertising Production Coordinator
Kim Sawalich
Advertising Coordinator
Jodi Donohoe
Advertising/Editorial Assistant
Janet Rogers
Advertising & Promotions Manager
Elda Starke
Senior Art Director
Andrew Brown
Marketing Assistant
Melissa Abbott
Associate Art Director
Chris Paxton
Sales Manager/Marine
Dutch Sadler
Sales Manager/Manuals
Ted Metzger
Sales Manager/Motorcycles
Matt Tusken
Sales Coordinator
Paul Cormaci
Telephone Sales Supervisor
Joelle Stephens
Telemarketing Sales Representative
Susan Kay
Customer Service/Fulfillment Manager
Caryn Bair
Fulfillment Coordinator
Susan Kohlmeyer
Customer Service Supervisor
Terri Cannon
Customer Service Representatives
Ardelia Chapman
Donna Schemmel
Dana Morrison
April LeBlond

The following books and guides are published by Intertec Publishing.

CLYMER SHOP MANUALS
Boat Motors and Drives
Motorcycles and ATVs
Snowmobiles
Personal Watercraft

ABOS/INTERTEC/CLYMER BLUE BOOKS AND TRADE-IN GUIDES
Recreational Vehicles
Outdoor Power Equipment
Agricultural Tractors
Lawn and Garden Tractors
Motorcycles and ATVs
Snowmobiles and Personal Watercraft
Boats and Motors

AIRCRAFT BLUEBOOK-PRICE DIGEST
Airplanes
Helicopters

AC-U-KWIK DIRECTORIES
The Corporate Pilot's Airport/FBO Directory
International Manager's Edition
Jet Book

I&T SHOP SERVICE MANUALS
Tractors

INTERTEC SERVICE MANUALS
Snowmobiles
Outdoor Power Equipment
Personal Watercraft
Gasoline and Diesel Engines
Recreational Vehicles
Boat Motors and Drives
Motorcycles
Lawn and Garden Tractors

CONTENTS

QUICK REFERENCE DATA

CAMSHAFT SPROCKET POSITION

MEASURE VALVES

Exhaust valves

Intake valves

Measure valves marked in black

CAMSHAFT SPROCKET POSITION

MEASURE VALVES

Exhaust valves

Intake valves

Measure valves marked in black

GENERAL TORQUE SPECIFICATIONS

Thread diameter	N•m	ft.-lb.
5 mm	3.4-4.9	30-43 in.-lb.
6 mm	5.9-7.8	52-69 in.-lb.
8 mm	14-19	10.0-13.5
10 mm	25-39	19-25
12 mm	44-61	33-45
14 mm	73-98	54-72
16 mm	115-155	83-115
18 mm	165-225	125-165
20 mm	225-325	165-240

TIRES AND TIRE PRESSURE *

Model/tire size	Pressure	Tire wear limit
Front-110/90 V 16	32 psi (2.25 kg/cm²)	1 mm (1/32 in.)
Rear-130/90 V 16	36 psi (2.50 kg/cm²)	3 mm (1/8 in.)

* Check tire pressure when cold.

RECOMMENDED LUBRICANTS AND FUEL

Engine oil	SAE 10W40, 10W50, 20W50, 20W50, rated SE or SF
Front fork oil	SAE 10W20
Brake fluid	DOT 3
Fuel	87 pump octane (RON + MON)/2
	91 research octane (RON)
Battery	Distilled water
Cooling system	Permanent type antifreeze compounded for aluminum engines and radiator

ENGINE OIL CAPACITY

	Liter	U.S. qt.
Without filter change	2.6	2.7
With filter change	3.0	3.2

FRONT FORK OIL CAPACITY

Fork leg	Change	Rebuild	Oil level
1985-1987 models			
Both right	273 cc	317-325 cc	332-336 mm
and left	(9.23 oz.)	(10.72-11.00 oz.)	(13.07-13.228 in.)
1988-on models			
Right-hand	305 cc	352-360 cc	152-156 mm
	(10.31 oz.)	(11.90-12.17 oz.)	(5.9-6.1 in.)
Left-hand	265 cc	307-315 cc	180-184 mm
	(8.96 oz.)	(10.38-10.65 oz.)	(7.0-7.2 in.)
1994-on Non-U.S. models			
Both fork legs	300 cc	345-353 cc	124-128 cc
	(10.14 oz.)	(11.66-11.93 oz.)	(4.8-5.0 in.)

COOLING SYSTEM SPECIFICATIONS

Capacity	2.0 L (2.1 qts.)
Coolant ratio	57 percent water/43 percent coolant
Radiator cap	14-18 psi (0.95-1.25 kg/cm²)
Thermostat	
Opening temperature	157.1-163.0 F (69.5-72.5 C)
Valve opening lift	Not less than 8 mm (5/16 in.)
	@ 203° F (95° C)

FRONT FORK AIR PRESSURE

	kg/cm^2	psi
1985-1987 models		
Standard	0.6	8.5
Usable range	0.5-0.7	7.1-10.0
Maximum	2.50	36
1988-on models		
Standard*	0	0

* Kawasaki recommends that the front forks be left at atmospheric pressure with no air added for best all around riding results.

REAR SHOCK ABSORBER AIR PRESSURE

Road/load conditions	kg/cm^2	psi
1985-1987 models		
Good/light	0	0
Bad/hard	2.5	35
1988-on models		
Good/light	0	0
Bad/hard	2.0	28

FRONT FORK REBOUND DAMPING ADJUSTMENT

Adjuster position	Load	Road	Speed
1985-1987 models			
1 and 2	Light	Good	Slow
3 and 4	Heavy	Rough	High
1988-on models			
1	Light	Good	Slow
2	Medium	Semi-rough	Moderate
3	Heavy	Rough	High

SPARK PLUGS

	Standard riding	High speed riding	Low speed riding
U.S.	NGKD9EA	NGK D9EA	NGKD8EA
	ND X27ES-U	ND X27ES-U	ND X24EX-U
Canada	NGK DR8ES	NGK DR8ES	NGKDR8ES-L
	ND X27ESR-U	ND X27ESR-U	ND X24ESR-U
Italy	NGK D9EA	NGK D9EA	NGK D8EA
	ND X27ES-U	ND X27ES-U	ND X24ES-U
All Europe	NGK DR8ES	NGK DR8ES	NGK DR8ES-L
except Italy	ND X27ES-U	ND X27ES-U	ND X24ES-U

TUNE-UP SPECIFICATIONS

Spark plug gap	0.6-0.7 mm (0.024-0.028 in.)
Valve clearance (cold)	
Intake	0.13-0.18 mm (0.005-0.007 in.)
Exhaust	0.18-0.23 mm (0.007-0.009 in.)
Idle speed	
ZX500	1,150-1,700 rpm
ZX600 (49-state and European)	1,000-1,100 rpm
ZX600 (California)	1,250-1,800 rpm
Compression	
1985-1987 models	7.7-12.0 kg/cm^2 (109-171 psi)
1988 and later	
ZX500R	9.5-14.5 kg/cm^2 (135-206 psi)
ZX600R	9.8-15.0 kg/cm^2 (139-213 psi)

CYLINDER POSITION

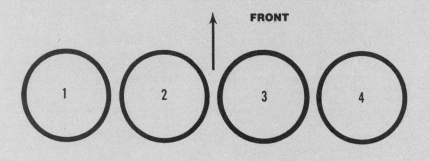

CLYMER®

KAWASAKI

ZX500 & 600 NINJA • 1985-1997

INTRODUCTION

This detailed, comprehensive manual covers 1985-on Kawasaki ZX500 and 600 Ninja models. The expert text gives complete information on maintenance, repair and overhaul. Hundreds of photos and drawings guide you through every step. The book includes all you need to know to keep your bike running right.

Where repairs are practical for the owner/mechanic, complete procedures are given. Equally important, difficult jobs are pointed out. Such operations are usually more economically performed by a dealer or independent garage.

A shop manual is a reference. You want to be able to find information fast. As in all Clymer books, this one is designed with this in mind. All chapters are thumb tabbed. Important items are indexed at the end of the book. All the most frequently used specifications and capacities are summarized on the *Quick Reference Data* pages at the beginning of the book.

Keep the book handy. It will help you better understand your Kawasaki, lower repair and maintenance costs and generally improve your satisfaction with your bike.

CHAPTER ONE

GENERAL INFORMATION

This detailed, comprehensive manual covers Kawasaki ZX500 and ZX600 Ninja models.

Troubleshooting, tune-up, maintenance and repair are not difficult if you know what tools and equipment to use and what to do. Anyone of average intelligence and with some mechanical ability can perform most of the procedures in this manual.

The manual is written simply and clearly enough for owners who have never worked on a motorcycle, but is complete enough for use by experienced mechanics.

Some of the procedures require the use of special tools. Using an inferior substitute tool for a special tool is not recommended as it can be dangerous to you and may damage the part.

Metric and U.S. standards are used throughout this manual. Metric to U.S. conversion is given in Table 1.

MANUAL ORGANIZATION

This chapter provides general information and discusses equipment and tools useful both for preventive maintenance and troubleshooting.

Chapter Two provides methods and suggestions for quick and accurate diagnosis and repair of problems. Troubleshooting procedures discuss typical symptoms and logical methods to pinpoint the trouble.

Chapter Three explains all periodic lubrication and routine maintenance necessary to keep your Kawasaki operating well. Chapter Three also includes recommended tune-up procedures, eliminating the need to constantly consult other chapters on the various assemblies.

Subsequent chapters describe specific systems such as the engine, clutch, transmission, fuel, exhaust, suspension, steering, brakes and fairing. Each chapter provides disassembly, repair, and assembly procedures in simple step-by-step form. If a repair is impractical for a home mechanic, it is so indicated. It is usually faster and less expensive to take such repairs to a dealer or competent repair shop. Specifications concerning a particular system are included at the end of the appropriate chapter.

NOTES, CAUTIONS AND WARNINGS

The terms NOTE, CAUTION and WARNING have specific meanings in this manual. A NOTE provides additional information to make a step or procedure easier or clearer. Disregarding a NOTE could cause inconvenience, but would not cause damage or personal injury.

A CAUTION emphasizes areas where equipment damage could occur. Disregarding a CAUTION could cause permanent mechanical damage; however, personal injury is unlikely.

A WARNING emphasizes areas where personal injury or even death could result from negligence. Mechanical damage may also occur. WARNINGS *are to be taken seriously.* In some cases, serious injury and death has resulted from disregarding similar warnings.

SAFETY FIRST

Professional mechanics can work for years and never sustain a serious injury. If you observe a few rules of common sense and safety, you can enjoy many safe hours servicing your own machine. If you ignore these rules you can hurt yourself or damage the equipment.

1. Never use gasoline as a cleaning solvent.
2. Never smoke or use a torch in the vicinity of flammable liquids, such as cleaning solvent, in open containers.
3. If welding or brazing is required on the machine, remove the fuel tank and rear shock to a safe distance, at least 50 feet away. Welding on a gas tank requires special safety precautions and must be performed by someone skilled in the process. Do not attempt to weld or braze a leaking gas tank.
4. Use the proper sized wrenches to avoid damage to fasteners and injury to yourself.
5. When loosening a tight or stuck nut, be guided by what would happen if the wrench should slip. Be careful; protect yourself accordingly.
6. When replacing a fastener, make sure to use one with the same measurements and strength as the old one. Incorrect or mismatched fasteners can result in damage to the vehicle and possible personal injury. Beware of fastener kits that are filled with cheap and poorly made nuts, bolts, washers and cotter pins. Refer to *Fasteners* in this chapter for additional information.
7. Keep all hand and power tools in good condition. Wipe greasy and oily tools after using them. They are difficult to hold and can cause injury. Replace or repair worn or damaged tools.
8. Keep your work area clean and uncluttered.
9. Wear safety goggles during all operations involving drilling, grinding, the use of a cold chisel or anytime you feel unsure about the safety of your eyes. Safety goggles should also be worn anytime compressed air is used to clean a part.
10. Keep an approved fire extinguisher nearby. Be sure it is rated for gasoline (Class B) and electrical (Class C) fires.
11. When drying bearings or other rotating parts with compressed air, never allow the air jet to rotate the bearing or part; the air jet is capable of rotating them at speeds far in excess of those for

which they were designed. The bearing or rotating part is very likely to disintegrate and cause serious injury and damage.

SERVICE HINTS

Most of the service procedures covered are straightforward and can be performed by anyone reasonably handy with tools. It is suggested, however, that you consider your own capabilities carefully before attempting any operation involving major disassembly of the engine or transmission.

1. "Front," as used in this manual, refers to the front of the motorcycle; the front of any component is the end closest to the front of the motorcycle. The "left-" and "right-hand" sides refer to the position of the parts as viewed by a rider sitting on the seat facing forward. For example, the throttle control is on the right-hand side. These rules are simple, but confusion can cause a major inconvenience during service.
2. Whenever servicing the engine or transmission, or when removing a suspension component, the bike should be secured in a safe manner. If the bike is to be parked on its sidestand, check the stand to make sure it is secure and not damaged. Block the front and rear wheels if they remain on the ground. A small hydraulic jack and a block of wood can be used to raise the chassis. If the transmission is not going to be worked on and the drive chain is connected to the rear wheel, shift the transmission into first gear.
3. Disconnect the negative battery cable when working on or near the electrical, clutch or starter systems and before disconnecting any wires. On most batteries, the negative terminal will be marked with a minus (-) sign and the positive terminal with a plus (+) sign.
4. When disassembling a part or assembly, it is a good practice to tag the parts for location and mark all parts which mate together. Small parts, such as bolts, can be identified by placing them in plastic sandwich bags. Seal the bags and label them with masking tape and a marking pen. When reassembly will take place immediately, an accepted practice is to place nuts and bolts in a cupcake tin or egg carton in the order of disassembly.
5. Finished surfaces should be protected from physical damage or corrosion. Keep gasoline and brake fluid off painted surfaces.
6. Use penetrating oil on frozen or tight bolts, then strike the bolt head a few times with a hammer and punch (use a screwdriver on screws). Avoid the use of heat where possible, as it can warp, melt or affe

the temper of parts. Heat also ruins finishes, especially paint and plastics.

7. Keep flames and sparks away from a charging battery or flammable fluids and do not smoke near them. It is a good idea to have a fire extinguisher handy in the work area. Remember that many gas appliances in home garages (water heater, clothes drier, etc.) have pilot lights.

8. No parts removed or installed (other than bushings and bearings) in the procedures given in this manual should require unusual force during disassembly or assembly. If a part is difficult to remove or install, find out why before proceeding.

9. Cover all openings after removing parts or assemblies to prevent dirt, small tools, etc. from falling in.

10. Read each procedure *completely* while looking at the actual parts before starting a job. Make sure you *thoroughly* understand what is to be done and then carefully follow the procedure, step by step.

11. Recommendations are occasionally made to refer service or maintenance to a Kawasaki dealer or a specialist in a particular field. In these cases, the work will be done more quickly and economically than if you performed the job yourself.

12. In procedural steps, the term "replace" means to discard a defective part and replace it with a new or exchange unit. "Overhaul" means to remove, disassemble, inspect, measure, repair, reassemble and install major assemblies or parts.

13. Some operations require the use of a hydraulic press. It would be wiser to have these operations performed by a shop equipped for such work, rather than to try to do the job yourself with makeshift equipment that may damage your machine.

14. Repairs go much faster and easier if your machine is clean before you begin work. There are many special cleaners on the market, like Bel-Ray Degreaser, for washing the engine and related parts. Follow the manufacturer's directions on the container for the best results. Clean all oily or greasy parts with cleaning solvent as you remove them.

WARNING
Never use gasoline as a cleaning agent. It presents an extreme fire hazard. Be sure to work in a well-ventilated area when using cleaning solvent. Keep a fire extinguisher, rated for gasoline fires, handy in any case.

15. Much of the labor charged for by dealers is for the time involved in removal, disassembly, assembly, and installation of other parts in order to reach the defective part. It is frequently possible to perform the preliminary operations yourself and then take the defective unit to the dealer for repair at considerable savings.

16. If special tools are required, make arrangements to get them before you start. It is frustrating and time-consuming to get partly into a job and then be unable to complete it.

17. Make diagrams (or take a Polaroid picture) wherever similar-appearing parts are found. For instance, crankcase bolts are often not the same length. You may think you can remember where everything came from—but mistakes are costly. There is also the possibility that you may be sidetracked and not return to work for days or even weeks—in which time carefully laid out parts may have become disturbed.

18. When assembling parts, be sure all shims and washers are replaced exactly as they came out.

19. Whenever a rotating part butts against a stationary part, look for a shim or washer. Use new gaskets if there is any doubt about the condition of the old ones. A thin coat of oil on non-pressure type gaskets may help them seal more effectively.

20. If it is necessary to make a gasket, and you do not have a suitable old gasket to use as a guide, apply engine oil to the gasket surface of the part. Then place the part on the new gasket material and press the part slightly. The oil will leave a very accurate outline on the gasket material that can be cut around.

21. Heavy grease can be used to hold small parts in place if they tend to fall out during assembly. However, keep grease and oil away from electrical and brake components.

22. A carburetor is best cleaned by disassembling it and soaking the parts in a commercial carburetor cleaner. Never soak gaskets and rubber parts in these cleaners. Never use wire to clean out jets and air passages. They are easily damaged. Use compressed air to blow out the carburetor only if the float has been removed first.

23. Take your time and do the job right. Do not forget that a newly rebuilt engine must be broken in just like a new one.

TORQUE SPECIFICATIONS

Torque specifications throughout this manual are given in Newton-meters (N•m) and foot-pounds (ft.-lb.).

Table 2 lists general torque specifications for nuts and bolts that are not listed in the respective chapters. To use the table, first determine the size of the nut or bolt. **Figure 1** and **Figure 2** show how this is done.

FASTENERS

The materials and designs of the various fasteners used on your Kawasaki are not arrived at by chance or accident. Fastener design determines the type of tool required to work the fastener. Fastener material is carefully selected to decrease the possibility of physical failure.

Threads

Nuts, bolts and screws are manufactured in a wide range of thread patterns. To join a nut and bolt, the diameter of the bolt and the diameter of the hole in the nut must be the same. It is just as important that the threads on both be properly matched.

The best way to tell if the threads on 2 fasteners are matched is to turn the nut on the bolt (or the bolt into the threaded hole in a piece of equipment) with fingers only. Be sure both pieces are clean. If much force is required, check the thread condition on each fastener. If the thread condition is good but the fasteners jam, the threads are not compatible. A thread pitch gauge can also be used to determine pitch. Kawasaki motorcycles are manufactured with metric standard fasteners. The threads are cut differently than those of American fasteners (**Figure 3**).

Most threads are cut so that the fastener must be turned clockwise to tighten it. These are called right-hand threads. Some fasteners have left-hand threads; they must be turned counterclockwise to be tightened. Left-hand threads are used in locations where normal rotation of the equipment would tend to loosen a right-hand threaded fastener.

Machine Screws

There are many different types of machine screws. **Figure 4** shows a number of screw heads requiring different types of turning tools. Heads are also designed to protrude above the metal (round) or to be slightly recessed in the metal (flat). See **Figure 5**.

Bolts

Commonly called bolts, the technical name for these fasteners is cap screw. Metric bolts are described by the diameter, pitch (or the distance between each thread) and length. For example, a M8—1.25 × 130 bolt is one that has a diameter of 8 millimeters with a distance of 1.25 millimeters between each thread and a length of 130 mm. The measurement across 2

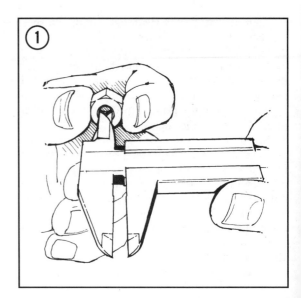

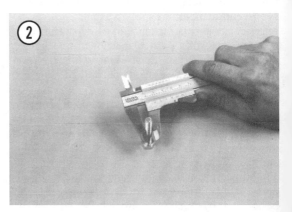

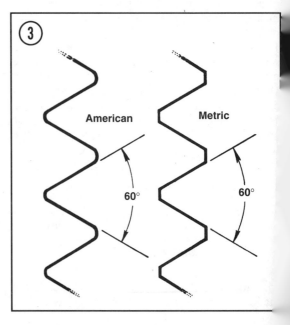

American   Metric

60°   60°

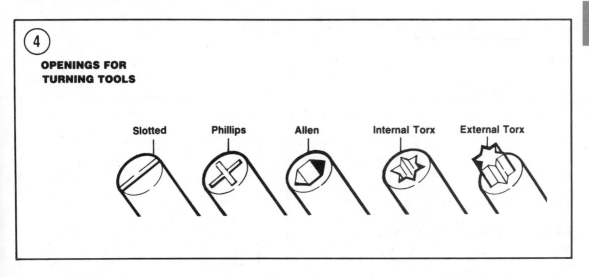

④ OPENINGS FOR TURNING TOOLS

Slotted   Phillips   Allen   Internal Torx   External Torx

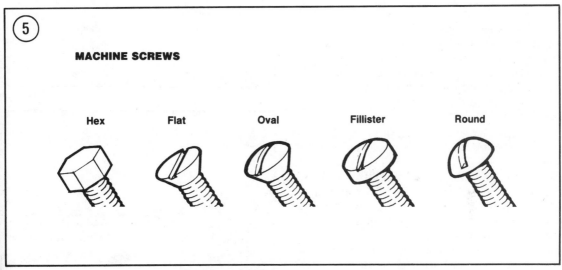

⑤ MACHINE SCREWS

Hex   Flat   Oval   Fillister   Round

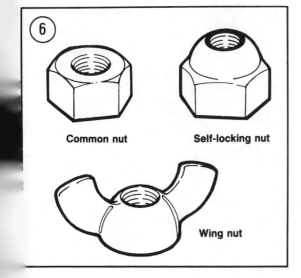

⑥

Common nut   Self-locking nut

Wing nut

flats on the head of the bolt indicates the proper wrench size to be used. **Figure 2** shows how to determine bolt diameter.

Nuts

Nuts are manufactured in a variety of types and sizes. Most are hexagonal (6-sided) and fit on bolts, screws and studs with the same diameter and pitch.

Figure 6 shows several types of nuts. The common nut is generally used with a lockwasher. Self-locking nuts have a nylon insert which prevents the nut from loosening; no lockwasher is required. Wing nuts are designed for fast removal by hand. Wing nuts are used for convenience in non-critical locations.

To indicate the size of a nut, manufacturers specify the diameter of the opening and the threads per inch. This is similar to bolt specifications, but without the length dimension. The measurement of the inside bore (**Figure 1**) indicates the proper wrench size to be used.

Self-Locking Fasteners

Several types of bolts, screws and nuts incorporate a system that develops an interference between the bolt, screw, nut or tapped hole threads. Interference is achieved in various ways: by distorting threads, coating threads with dry adhesive or nylon, distorting the top of an all-metal nut, using a nylon insert in the center or at the top of a nut, etc.

Self-locking fasteners offer greater holding strength and better vibration resistance. Some prevailing torque fasteners can be reused if in good condition. Others, like the nylon insert nut, form an initial locking condition when the nut is first installed; the nylon forms closely to the bolt thread pattern, thus reducing any tendency for the nut to loosen. When the nut is removed, its locking efficiency is greatly reduced. For greatest safety, it is recommended that you install new self-locking fasteners whenever they are removed.

Washers

There are 2 basic types of washers: flat washers and lockwashers. Flat washers are simple discs with a hole to fit a screw or bolt. Lockwashers are designed to prevent a fastener from working loose due to vibration, expansion and contraction. **Figure 7** shows several types of washers. Washers are also used in the following functions:

    a. As spacers.
    b. To prevent galling or damage of the equipment by the fastener.
    c. To help distribute fastener load during torquing.
    d. As seals.

Note that flat washers are often used between a lockwasher and a fastener to provide a smooth bearing surface. This allows the fastener to be turned easily with a tool.

Cotter Pins

Cotter pins (**Figure 8**) are used to secure special kinds of fasteners. The threaded stud must have a hole in it; the nut or nut lock piece has castellations around which the cotter pin ends wrap. Cotter pins should not be reused after removal.

Snap Rings

Snap rings can be internal or external design. They are used to retain items on shafts (external type) or within tubes (internal type). In some

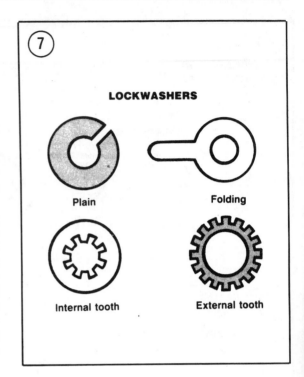

⑦

LOCKWASHERS

Plain   Folding

Internal tooth   External tooth

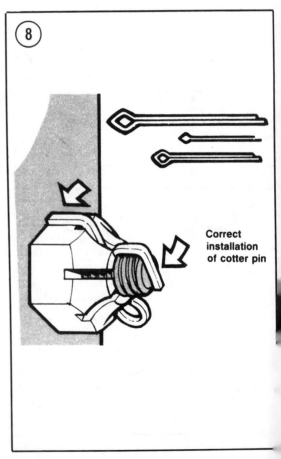

⑧

Correct installation of cotter pin

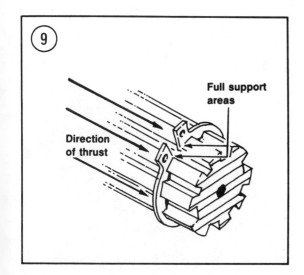

Full support areas

Direction of thrust

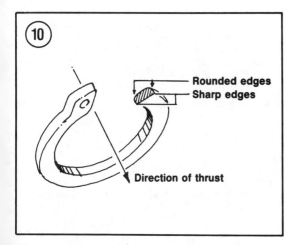

Rounded edges
Sharp edges

Direction of thrust

LUBRICANTS

Periodic lubrication assures long life for any type of equipment. The *type* of lubricant used is just as important as the lubrication service itself, although in an emergency the wrong type of lubricant is better than none at all. The following paragraphs describe the types of lubricants most often used on motorcycle equipment. Be sure to follow the manufacturer's recommendations for lubricant types.

Generally, all liquid lubricants are called "oil." They may be mineral-based (including petroleum bases), natural-based (vegetable and animal bases), synthetic-based or emulsions (mixtures). "Grease" is an oil to which a thickening base has been added so that the end product is semi-solid. Grease is often classified by the type of thickener added; lithium soap is commonly used.

Engine Oil

Oil for motorcycle and automotive engines is graded by the American Petroleum Institute (API) and the Society of Automotive Engineers (SAE) in several categories. Oil containers display these ratings on the top or label.

API oil grade is indicated by letters; oils for gasoline engines are identified by an "S." The engines covered in this manual require SE or SF graded oil.

Viscosity is an indication of the oil's thickness. The SAE uses numbers to indicate viscosity; thin oils have low numbers while thick oils have high numbers. A "W" after the number indicates that the viscosity testing was done at low temperature to simulate cold-weather operation. Engine oils fall into the 5W-30 and 20W-50 range.

Multi-grade oils (for example 10W-40) are less viscous (thinner) at low temperatures and more viscous (thicker) at high temperatures. This allows the oil to perform efficiently across a wide range of engine operating conditions. The lower the number, the better the engine will start in cold climates. Higher numbers are usually recommended for engine running in hot weather conditions.

Grease

Greases are graded by the National Lubricating Grease Institute (NLGI). Greases are graded by number according to the consistency of the grease; these range from No. 000 to No. 6, with No. 6 being the most solid. A typical multipurpose grease is NLGI No. 2. For specific applications,

applications, snap rings of varying thicknesses are used to control the end play of parts assemblies. These are often called selective snap rings. Snap rings should be replaced during installation, as removal weakens and deforms them.

Two basic styles of snap rings are available: machined and stamped snap rings. Machined snap rings (**Figure 9**) can be installed in either direction (shaft or housing) because both faces are machined, thus creating two sharp edges. Stamped snap rings (**Figure 10**) are manufactured with one sharp edge and one rounded edge. When installing stamped snap rings in a thrust situation (transmission shafts, fork tubes, etc.), the sharp edge must face away from the part producing the thrust. When installing snap rings, observe the following:

a. Compress or expand snap rings only enough to install them.

b. After the snap ring is installed, make sure it is completely seated in its groove.

equipment manufacturers may require grease with an additive such as molybdenum disulfide (MOS2).

PARTS REPLACEMENT

Kawasaki makes frequent changes during a model year, some minor, some relatively major. When you order parts from the dealer or other parts distributor, always order by engine number (**Figure 11**) and frame number (**Figure 12**). Write the numbers down and carry them with you. Compare new parts to old before purchasing them. If they are not alike, have the parts manager explain the difference to you.

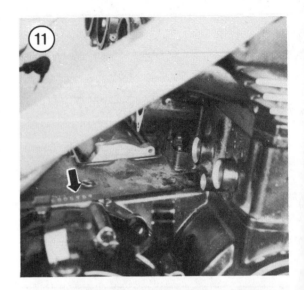

BASIC HAND TOOLS

Many of the procedures in this manual can be carried out with simple hand tools and test equipment familiar to the average home mechanic. Keep your tools clean and in a tool box. Keep them organized with the sockets and related drives together, the open-end and combination wrenches together, etc. After using a tool, wipe off dirt and grease with a clean cloth and return the tool to its correct place.

Top quality tools are essential; they are also more economical in the long run. If you are now starting to build your tool collection, stay away from the "advertised specials" featured at some parts houses, discount stores and chain drug stores. These are usually a poor grade tool that can be sold cheaply and that is exactly what they are—*cheap*. They are usually made of inferior material, and are thick, heavy and clumsy. Their rough finish makes them difficult to clean and they usually don't last very long. If it is ever your misfortune to use such tools, you will probably find out that the wrenches do not fit the heads of bolts and nuts correctly and damage fasteners.

Quality tools are made of alloy steel and are heat treated for greater strength. They are lighter and better balanced than cheap ones. Their surface is smooth, making them a pleasure to work with and easy to clean. The initial cost of good quality tools may be more but they are cheaper in the long run. Don't try to buy everything in all sizes in the beginning; do it a little at a time until you have the necessary tools. To sum up tool buying, "...the bitterness of poor quality lingers long after the sweetness of low price has faded."

The following tools are required to perform virtually any repair job. Each tool is described and

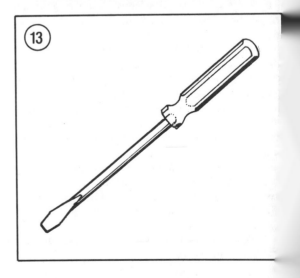

the recommended size given for starting a tool collection. Additional tools and some duplicates may be added as you become familar with the vehicle. Kawasaki motorcycles are built with metric standard fasteners—so if you are starting your collection now, buy metric sizes.

Screwdrivers

The screwdriver is a very basic tool, but if used improperly it will do more damage than good. The slot on a screw has a definite dimension and shape. A screwdriver must be selected to conform with that shape. Use a small screwdriver for small

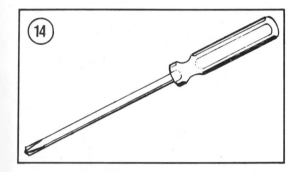

screws and a large one for large screws or the screw head will be damaged.

Two basic types of screwdriver are required: common (flat-blade) screwdrivers (**Figure 13**) and Phillips screwdrivers (**Figure 14**).

Screwdrivers are available in sets which often include an assortment of common and Phillips blades. If you buy them individually, buy at least the following:

a. Common screwdriver—5/16×6 in. blade.
b. Common screwdriver—3/8×12 in. blade.
c. Phillips screwdriver—size 2 tip, 6 in. blade.

Use screwdrivers only for driving screws. Never use a screwdriver for prying or chiseling metal. Do not try to remove a Phillips or Allen head screw with a common screwdriver (unless the screw has a combination head that will accept either type); you can damage the head so that the proper tool will be unable to remove it.

Keep screwdrivers in the proper condition and they will last longer and perform better. Always keep the tip of a common screwdriver in good condition. **Figure 15** shows how to grind the tip to the proper shape if it becomes damaged. Note the symmetrical sides of the tip.

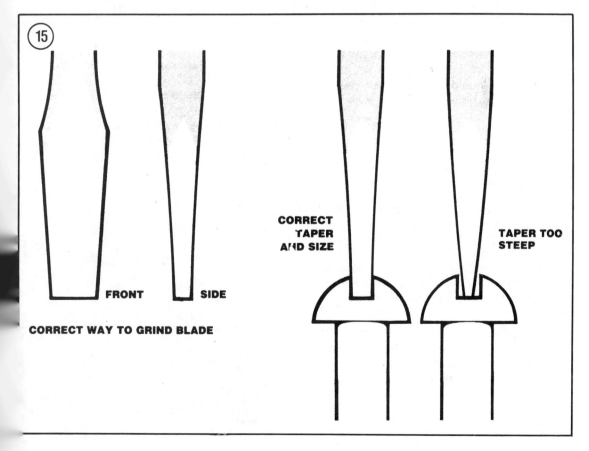

Pliers

Pliers come in a wide range of types and sizes. Pliers are useful for cutting, bending and crimping. They should never be used to cut hardened objects or to turn bolts or nuts. **Figure 16** shows several pliers useful in motorcycle repairs.

Each type of pliers has a specialized function. Gas pliers are general purpose pliers and are used mainly for holding things and for bending. Locking pliers, such as Vise-grips, are used as pliers or to hold objects very tightly like a vise. Needlenose pliers are used to hold or bend small objects. Channel lock pliers can be adjusted to hold various sizes of objects; the jaws remain parallel to grip around objects such as pipe or tubing. There are many more types of pliers.

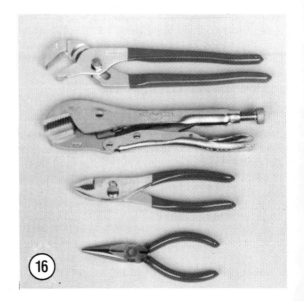

Box and Open-end Wrenches

Box and open-end wrenches are available in sets or separately in a variety of sizes. The size number stamped near the end refers to the distance between 2 parallel flats on the hex head bolt or nut.

Box wrenches are usually superior to open-end wrenches (**Figure 17**). Open-end wrenches grip the nut on only 2 flats. Unless a wrench fits well, it may slip and round off the points on the nut. The box wrench grips on all 6 flats. Both 6-point and 12-point openings on box wrenches are available. The 6-point gives superior holding power; the 12-point allows a shorter swing.

Combination wrenches which are open on one side and boxed on the other are also available. Both ends are the same size. See **Figure 18**.

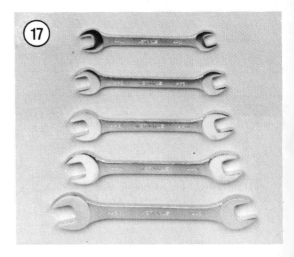

Adjustable Wrenches

An adjustable wrench can be adjusted to fit a variety of nuts or bolt heads (**Figure 19**). However, it can loosen and slip, causing damage to the nut and injury to your knuckles. Use an adjustable wrench only when other wrenches are not available.

Adjustable wrenches come in sizes ranging from 4-18 in. overall. A 6 or 8 in. wrench is recommended as an all-purpose wrench.

Socket Wrenches

This type is undoubtedly the fastest, safest and most convenient to use. Sockets which attach to a ratchet handle (**Figure 20**) are available with 6-point or 12-point openings and 1/4, 3/8, 1/2 and 3/4 inch drives. The drive size indicates the size of the square hole which mates with the ratchet handle.

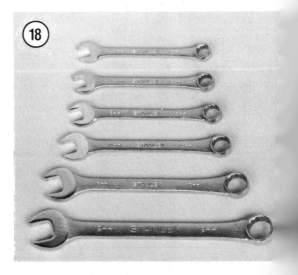

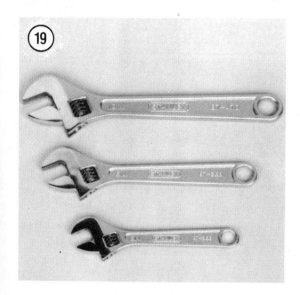

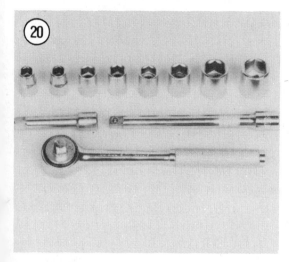

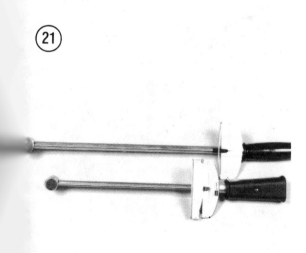

Torque Wrench

A torque wrench (**Figure 21**) is used with a socket to measure how tightly a nut or bolt is installed. They come in a wide price range and with either 3/8 or 1/2 in. square drive. The drive size indicates the size of the square drive which mates with the socket.

Impact Driver

This tool makes removal of tight fasteners easy and eliminates damage to bolts and screw slots. Impact drivers and interchangeable bits (**Figure 22**) are available at most large hardware and motorcycle dealers. Sockets can also be used with a hand impact driver. However, make sure the socket is designed for impact use. Do not use regular hand type sockets, as they may shatter.

Hammers

The correct hammer is necessary for repairs. Use only a hammer with a face (or head) of rubber or plastic or the soft-faced type that is filled with buckshot. These are sometimes necessary in engine teardowns. *Never* use a metal-faced hammer, as severe damage will result in most cases. You can always produce the same amount of force with a soft-faced hammer.

Feeler Gauge

This tool has both flat and wire measuring gauges and is used to measure spark plug gap. See

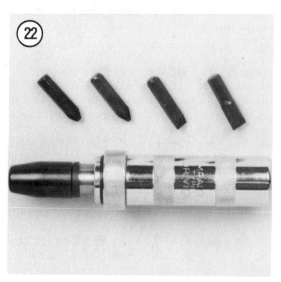

Figure 23. Wire gauges are used to measure spark plug gap; flat gauges are used for all other measurements.

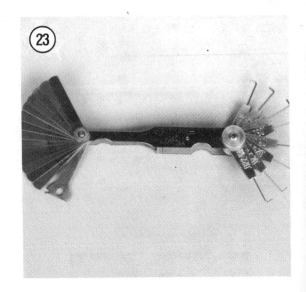

Vernier Caliper

This tool is invaluable when reading inside, outside and depth measurements to close precision. The vernier caliper can be purchased from large dealers or mail order houses. See **Figure 24.**

Special Tools

A few special tools may be required for major service. These are described in the appropriate chapters and are available either from Kawasaki dealers or other manufacturers as indicated.

TEST EQUIPMENT

Voltmeter, Ammeter and Ohmmeter

A good voltmeter is required for testing ignition and other electrical systems. Voltmeters are available with analog meter scales or digital readouts. An instrument covering 0-20 volts is satisfactory. It should also have a 0-2 volt scale for testing points or individual contacts where voltage drops are much smaller. Accuracy should be $\pm 1/2$ volt.

An ohmmeter measures electrical resistance. This instrument is useful in checking continuity (for open and short circuits) and testing lights. A self-powered 12-volt test light can often be used in its place.

The ammeter measures electrical current. These are useful for checking battery starting and charging currents.

Some manufacturers combine the 3 instruments into one unit called a multimeter or VOM. See **Figure 25.**

Compression Gauge

An engine with low compression cannot be properly tuned and will not develop full power. A compression gauge measures the amount of pressure present in the engine's combustion chambers during the compression stroke. This indicates general engine condition.

The Kawasaki models described in this manual require the use of a screw-in compression gauge that threads into the spark plug holes (**Figure 26**).

Dial Indicator

Dial indicators (**Figure 27**) are precision tools used to check dimension variations on machined parts such as transmission shafts and axles and to

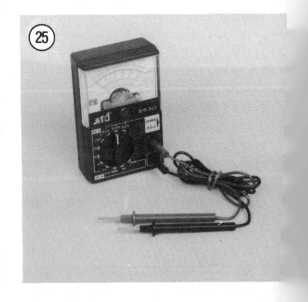

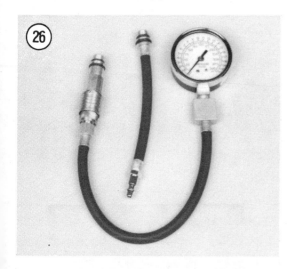

check crankshaft and axle shaft end play. Dial indicators are available with various dial types for different measuring requirements.

Strobe Timing Light

This instrument is necessary for checking ignition timing. By flashing a light at the precise instant the spark plug fires, the position of the timing mark can be seen. The flashing light makes a moving mark appear to stand still opposite a stationary mark.

Suitable lights range from inexpensive neon bulb types to powerful xenon strobe lights. See **Figure 28**. A light with an inductive pickup is recommended to eliminate any possible damage to ignition wiring.

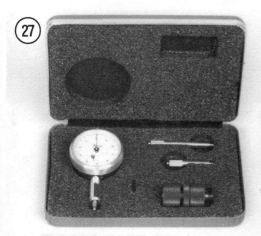

Portable Tachometer

A portable tachometer is necessary for tuning. See **Figure 29**. Ignition timing and carburetor adjustments must be performed at the specified idle speed. The best instrument for this purpose is one with a low range of 0-1,000 or 0-2,000 rpm and a high range of 0-4,000 rpm. Extended range (0-6,000 or 0-8,000 rpm) instruments lack accuracy at lower speeds. The instrument should be capable of detecting changes of 25 rpm on the low range.

Expendable Supplies

Certain expendable supplies are also required. These include grease, oil, gasket cement, shop rags and cleaning solvent. Ask your dealer for the

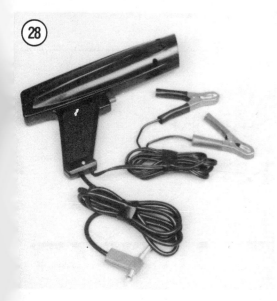

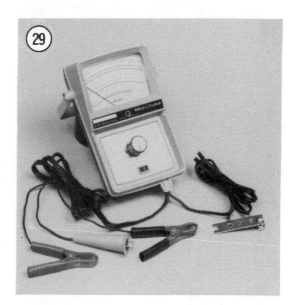

special locking compounds, silicone lubricants and lube products which make vehicle maintenance simpler and easier. Cleaning solvent is available at some service stations.

MECHANIC'S TIPS

Removing Frozen Nuts and Screws

When a fastener rusts and cannot be removed, several methods may be used to loosen it. First, apply penetrating oil such as Liquid Wrench or WD-40 (available at hardware or auto supply stores). Apply it liberally and let it penetrate for 10-15 minutes. Rap the fastener several times with a small hammer; do not hit it hard enough to cause damage. Reapply the penetrating oil if necessary.

For frozen screws, apply penetrating oil as described, then insert a screwdriver in the slot and rap the top of the screwdriver with a hammer. This loosens the rust so the screw can be removed in the normal way. If the screw head is too chewed up to use this method, grip the head with locking pliers and twist the screw out.

Avoid applying heat unless specifically instructed, as it may melt, warp or remove the temper from parts.

Remedying Stripped Threads

Occasionally, threads are stripped through carelessness or impact damage. Often the threads can be cleaned up by running a tap (for internal threads on nuts) or die (for external threads on bolts) through the threads. See **Figure 30**. To clean or repair spark plug threads, a spark plug tap can be used (**Figure 31**).

Removing Broken Screws or Bolts

When the head breaks off a screw or bolt, several methods are available for removing the remaining portion.

If a large portion of the remainder projects out, try gripping it with locking pliers. If the projecting portion is too small, file it to fit a wrench or cut a slot in it to fit a screwdriver. See **Figure 32**.

If the head breaks off flush, use a screw extractor. To do this, centerpunch the exact center of the remaining portion of the screw or bolt. Drill a small hole in the screw and tap the extractor into the hole. Back the screw out with a wrench on the extractor. See **Figure 33**.

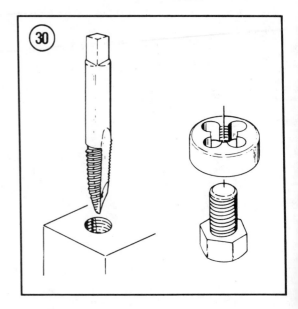

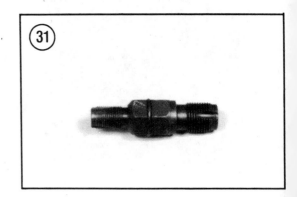

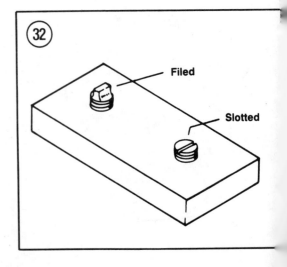

Filed

Slotted

**REMOVING BROKEN SCREWS
AND BOLTS**

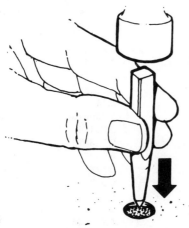

1. Center punch broken stud

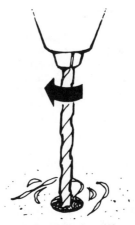

2. Drill hole in stud

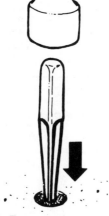

3. Tap in screw extractor

4. Remove broken stud

Table 1 DECIMAL AND METRIC EQUIVALENTS

Fractions	Decimal in.	Metric mm	Fractions	Decimal in.	Metric mm
1/64	0.015625	0.39688	33/64	0.515625	13.09687
1/32	0.03125	0.79375	17/32	0.53125	13.49375
3/64	0.046875	1.19062	35/64	0.546875	13.89062
1/16	0.0625	1.58750	9/16	0.5625	14.28750
5/64	0.078125	1.98437	37/64	0.578125	14.68437
3/32	0.09375	2.38125	19/32	0.59375	15.08125
7/64	0.109375	2.77812	39/64	0.609375	15.47812
1/8	0.125	3.1750	5/8	0.625	15.87500
9/64	0.140625	3.57187	41/64	0.640625	16.27187
5/32	0.15625	3.96875	21/32	0.65625	16.66875
11/64	0.171875	4.36562	43/64	0.671875	17.06562
3/16	0.1875	4.76250	11/16	0.6875	17.46250
13/64	0.203125	5.15937	45/64	0.703125	17.85937
7/32	0.21875	5.55625	23/32	0.71875	18.25625
15/64	0.234375	5.95312	47/64	0.734375	18.65312
1/4	0.250	6.35000	3/4	0.750	19.05000
17/64	0.265625	6.74687	49/64	0.765625	19.44687
9/32	0.28125	7.14375	25/32	0.78125	19.84375
19/64	0.296875	7.54062	51/64	0.796875	20.24062
5/16	0.3125	7.93750	13/16	0.8125	20.63750
21/64	0.328125	8.33437	53/64	0.828125	21.03437
11/32	0.34375	8.73125	27/32	0.84375	21.43125
23/64	0.359375	9.12812	55/64	0.859375	21.82812
3/8	0.375	9.52500	7/8	0.875	22.22500
25/64	0.390625	9.92187	57/64	0.890625	22.62187
13/32	0.40625	10.31875	29/32	0.90625	23.01875
27/64	0.421875	10.71562	59/64	0.921875	23.41562
7/16	0.4375	11.11250	15/16	0.9375	23.81250
29/64	0.453125	11.50937	61/64	0.953125	24.20937
15/32	0.46875	11.90625	31/32	0.96875	24.60625
31/64	0.484375	12.30312	63/64	0.984375	25.00312
1/2	0.500	12.70000	1	1.00	25.40000

TABLE 2 GENERAL TORQUE SPECIFICATIONS

Thread diameter	N·m	ft.-lb.
5 mm	3.4-4.9	30-43 in.-lb.
6 mm	5.9-7.8	52-69 in.-lb.
8 mm	14-19	10.0-13.5
10 mm	25-39	19-25
12 mm	44-61	33-45
14 mm	73-98	54-72
16 mm	115-155	83-115
18 mm	165-225	125-165
20 mm	225-325	165-240

CHAPTER TWO

TROUBLESHOOTING

Every motorcycle engine requires an uninterrupted supply of fuel and air, proper ignition and adequate compression. If any of these are lacking, the engine will not run.

Diagnosing mechanical problems is relatively simple if you use orderly procedures and keep a few basic principles in mind.

The troubleshooting procedures in this chapter analyze typical symptoms and show logical methods of isolating causes. These are not the only methods. There may be several ways to solve a problem, but only a systematic approach can guarantee success.

Never assume anything. Do not overlook the obvious. If you are riding along and the bike suddenly quits, check the easiest, most accessible problem spots first. Is there gasoline in the tank? Has a spark plug wire fallen off?

If nothing obvious turns up in a quick check, look a little further. Learning to recognize and describe symptoms will make repairs easier for you or a mechanic at the shop. Describe problems accurately and fully. Saying that "it won't run" isn't the same thing as saying "it quit at high speed and won't start," or that "it sat in my garage for 3 months and then wouldn't start."

Gather as many symptoms as possible to aid in diagnosis. Note whether the engine lost power gradually or all at once. Remember that the more complicated a machine is, the easier it is to troubleshoot because symptoms point to specific problems.

After the symptoms are defined, areas which could cause problems are tested and analyzed. Guessing at the cause of a problem may provide the solution, but it can easily lead to frustration, wasted time and a series of expensive, unnecessary parts replacements.

You do not need fancy equipment or complicated test gear to determine whether repairs can be attempted at home. A few simple checks could save a large repair bill and lost time while the bike sits in a dealer's service department. On the other hand, be realistic and don't attempt repairs beyond your abilities. Service departments tend to charge heavily for putting together a disassembled engine that may have been abused. Some won't even take on such a job—so use common sense and don't get in over your head.

OPERATING REQUIREMENTS

An engine needs 3 basics to run properly: correct fuel/air mixture, compression and a spark at the correct time. If one or more are missing, the engine will not run. Four-stroke engine operating principles are described under *Engine Principles* in Chapter Four. The electrical system is the weakest link of the 3 basics. More problems result from electrical breakdowns than from any other source. Keep that in mind before you begin tampering with carburetor adjustments and the like.

If the machine has been sitting for any length of time and refuses to start, check and clean the spark plugs and then look to the gasoline delivery system. This includes the fuel tank, fuel shutoff valve and fuel line to the carburetor. Gasoline deposits may have formed and gummed up the carburetor jets and air passages. Gasoline tends to lose its potency after standing for long periods. Condensation may contaminate the fuel with water. Drain the old fuel (fuel tank, fuel lines and carburetors) and try starting with a fresh tankful.

TROUBLESHOOTING INSTRUMENTS

Chapter One lists the instruments needed and instruction on their use.

EMERGENCY TROUBLESHOOTING

When the bike is difficult to start, or won't start at all, it doesn't help to wear down the battery using the electric starter. Check for obvious problems even before getting out your tools. Go down the following list step by step. Do each one; you may be embarrassed to find the engine stop switch off, but that is better than wearing down the battery. If the bike still will not start, refer to the appropriate troubleshooting procedures which follow in this chapter.
1. Is there fuel in the tank? Open the filler cap and rock the bike. Listen for fuel sloshing around.

WARNING
Do not use an open flame to check in the tank. A serious explosion is certain to result.

2. Is the fuel supply valve in the ON position? Turn the valve to the RES position to be sure you get the last remaining gas.
3. Make sure the engine stop switch (**Figure 1**) is not stuck in the OFF position or that the wire is broken and shorting out. Test the switch as described under *Switches* in Chapter Eight.
4. Are the spark plug wires on tight? Remove the fuel tank as described in Chapter Seven. Push all 4 spark plugs on and slightly rotate them to clean the electrical connection between the plug and the connector.
5. Is the choke lever (**Figure 2**) in the right position?

ENGINE STARTING

An engine that refuses to start or is difficult to start is very frustrating. More often than not, the

problem is very minor and can be found with a simple and logical troubleshooting approach.

The following items will help isolate engine starting problems.

Engine Fails to Start

Perform the following spark test to determine if the ignition system is operating properly.
1. Remove the fuel tank as described in Chapter Seven.
2. Remove one of the spark plugs.
3. Connect the spark plug wire and connector to the spark plug and touch the spark plug base to a good ground like the engine cylinder head. Position the spark plug so you can see the electrodes.

WARNING
During the next step, do not hold the spark plug, wire or connector with fingers or a serious electrical shock may result. If necessary, use a pair of insulated pliers to hold the spark plug or wire. The high voltage generated by the ignition system could produce serious or fatal shocks.

4. Crank the engine over with the starter. A fat blue spark should be evident across the spark plug electrodes.

NOTE
*If the starter does not operate or if the starter motor rotates but the engine does not turn over, refer to **Engine Will Not Crank** in this section.*

5. If the spark is good, check for one or more of the following possible malfunctions:

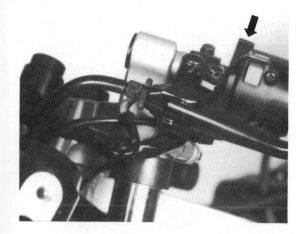

2

a. Obstructed fuel line or fuel filter.
b. Leaking head gasket.
c. Low compression.

6. If the spark is not good, check for one or more of the following:

a. Loose electrical connections.
b. Dirty electrical connections.
c. Loose or broken ignition coil ground wire.
d. Broken or shorted high tension lead to the spark plug(s).
e. Discharged battery.
f. Disconnected or damaged battery connection.
g. IC igniter malfunction.
h. Neutral, starter lockout or side stand switch malfunction.
i. Ignition or engine stop switch malfunction.
j. Blown fuse.

Engine is Difficult to Start

Check for one or more of the following possible malfunctions:

a. Fouled spark plug(s).
b. Improperly adjusted choke.
c. Intake manifold air leak.
d. Contaminated fuel system.
e. Improperly adjusted carburetor.
f. Weak ignition unit.
g. Weak ignition coil(s).
h. Poor compression.
i. Engine and transmission oil too heavy.

Engine Will Not Crank

Check for one or more of the following possible malfunctions:

a. Blown fuse.
b. Discharged battery.
c. Defective starter motor.
d. Seized piston(s).
e. Seized crankshaft bearings.
f. Broken connecting rod.
g. Starter lockout or neutral switch malfunction.
h. Engine stop switch malfunction.
i. Defective starter motor button and contact.

ENGINE PERFORMANCE

In the following checklist, it is assumed that the engine runs, but is not operating at peak performance. This will serve as a starting point from which to isolate a performance malfunction.

Engine Will Not Idle

a. Carburetor incorrectly adjusted.
b. Fouled or improperly gapped spark plug(s).
c. Leaking head gasket.
d. Obstructed fuel line or fuel shutoff valve.
e. Obstructed fuel filter.
f. Ignition timing incorrect due to defective ignition component(s).
g. Valve clearance incorrect.

Engine Misses at High Speed

a. Fouled or improperly gapped spark plugs.
b. Improper carburetor main jet selection.
c. Ignition timing incorrect due to defective ignition component(s).
d. Weak ignition coil(s).
e. Obstructed fuel line or fuel shutoff valve.
f. Obstructed fuel filter.
g. Clogged carburetor jets.
h. Dirty air cleaner.
i. Air suction valve malfunction (U.S. models).

Engine Overheating

a. Incorrect carburetor adjustment or jet selection.
b. Ignition timing retarded due to defective ignition component(s).
c. Improper spark plug heat range.
d. Cooling system malfunction (see below).
e. Incorrect coolant level.
f. Oil level low.
g. Oil not circulating properly.
h. Valves leaking.

i. Heavy engine carbon deposits.
j. Dragging brake(s).
k. Clutch slipping.

Engine Overheating (Cooling System Malfunction)

Note the above, then proceed with the following items:

a. Clogged radiator.
b. Damaged thermostat.
c. Worn or damaged radiator cap.
d. Water pump worn or damaged.
e. Fan relay malfunction.
f. Thermostatic fan switch malfunction.
g. Damaged fan blade(s).

Smoky Exhaust and Engine Runs Roughly

a. Clogged air filter element.
b. Carburetor adjustment incorrect—mixture too rich.
c. Choke not operating correctly.
d. Water or other contaminants in fuel.
e. Clogged fuel line.
f. Spark plugs fouled.
g. Ignition coil defective.
h. IC igniter or pickup coil defective.
i. Loose or defective ignition circuit wire.
j. Short circuit from damaged wire insulation.
k. Loose battery cable connection.
l. Valve timing incorrect.
m. Intake manifold or air cleaner air leak.

Engine Loses Power at Normal Riding Speed

a. Carburetor incorrectly adjusted.
b. Engine overheating.
c. Ignition timing incorrect due to defective ignition component(s).
d. Incorrectly gapped spark plugs.
e. Obstructed muffler.
f. Dragging brake(s).

Engine Lacks Acceleration

a. Carburetor mixture too lean.
b. Clogged fuel line.
c. Ignition timing incorrect due to defective ignition component(s).
d. Dragging brake(s).
e. Slipping clutch.

ENGINE NOISES

Often the first evidence of an internal engine problem is a strange noise. That knocking, clicking or tapping sound which you never heard before may be warning you of impending trouble.

While engine noises can indicate problems, they are difficult to interpret correctly; inexperienced mechanics can be seriously misled by them.

Professional mechanics often use a special stethoscope (which looks like a doctor's stethoscope) for isolating engine noises. You can do nearly as well with a "sounding stick" which can be an ordinary piece of doweling, a length of broom handle or a section of small hose. By placing one end in contact with the area to which you want to listen and the other end near your gear, you can hear sounds emanating from that area. The first time you do this, you may be horrified at the strange sounds coming from even a normal engine. If you can, have an experienced friend or mechanic help you sort out the noises.

Consider the following when troubleshooting engine noises:

1. *Knocking or pinging during acceleration*—Caused by using a lower octane fuel than recommended. May also be caused by poor fuel. Pinging can also be caused by a spark plug of the wrong heat range or carbon build-up in the combustion chamber. Refer to *Correct Spark Plug Heat Range* and *Compression Test* in Chapter Three.

2. *Slapping or rattling noises at low speed or during acceleration*—May be caused by piston slap, i.e., excessive piston-cylinder wall clearance.

3. *Knocking or rapping while decelerating*—Usually caused by excessive rod bearing clearance.

4. *Persistent knocking and vibration*—Usually caused by worn main bearing(s).

5. *Rapid on-off squeal*—Compression leak around cylinder head gasket or spark plug(s).

6. *Valve train noise*—Check for the following:

   a. Valves adjusted incorrectly.
   b. Loose valve adjuster.
   c. Valve sticking in guide.
   d. Low oil pressure.
   e. Damaged rocker arm or shaft. Rocker arm may be binding on shaft.

ENGINE LUBRICATION

An improperly operating engine lubricatio system will quickly lead to engine seizure. Th engine oil level should be checked weekly an

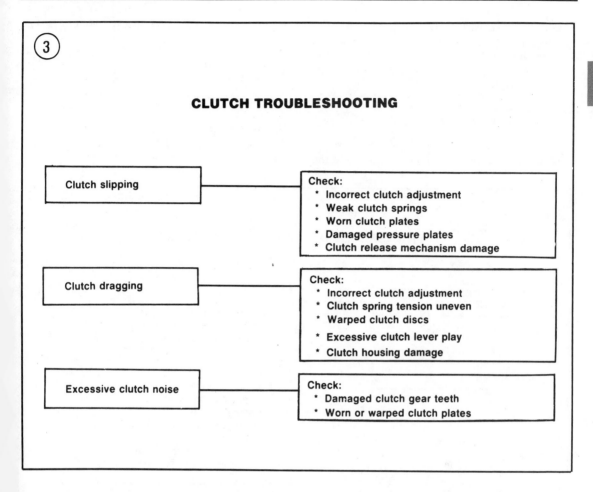

③

CLUTCH TROUBLESHOOTING

Clutch slipping
Check:
* Incorrect clutch adjustment
* Weak clutch springs
* Worn clutch plates
* Damaged pressure plates
* Clutch release mechanism damage

Clutch dragging
Check:
* Incorrect clutch adjustment
* Clutch spring tension uneven
* Warped clutch discs
* Excessive clutch lever play
* Clutch housing damage

Excessive clutch noise
Check:
* Damaged clutch gear teeth
* Worn or warped clutch plates

2

topped up, as described in Chapter Three. Oil pump service is described in Chapter Four.

**Oil Consumption High or
Engine smokes excessively**

  a. Worn valve guides.
  b. Worn or damaged piston rings.

Excessive Engine Oil Leaks

  a. Clogged air cleaner breather hose.
  b. Loose engine parts.
  c. Damaged gasket sealing surfaces.

Black Smoke

  a. Clogged air cleaner.
  b. Incorrect carburetor fuel level (too high).
  c. Choke stuck open.
  d. Incorrect main jet (too large).

White Smoke

  a. Worn valve guide.
  b. Worn valve oil seal.

  c. Worn piston ring oil ring.
  d. Excessive cylinder and/or piston wear.

CLUTCH

The three basic clutch troubles are:
  a. Clutch noise.
  b. Clutch slipping.
  c. Improper clutch disengagement or dragging.
All clutch troubles, except adjustments, require partial clutch disassembly to identify and cure the problem. The troubleshooting chart in **Figure 3** lists clutch troubles and checks to make. Refer to Chapter Five for clutch service procedures.

TRANSMISSION

The basic transmission troubles are:
  a. Excessive gear noise.
  b. Difficult shifting.
  c. Gears pop out of mesh.
  d. Incorrect shift lever operation.
Transmission symptoms are sometimes hard to distinguish from clutch symptoms. The

troubleshooting chart in **Figure 4** lists transmission troubles and checks to make. Refer to Chapter Six for transmission service procedures. Be sure that the clutch is not causing the trouble before working on the transmission.

CHARGING SYSTEM

Before beginning any charging system tests, be sure that the battery is in good condition and that it is at or near full charge. See *Battery* in Chapter Three.

Regulator/Rectifier
Output Voltage Check

Refer to **Figure 5**.
1. Start the bike and allow to warm to normal operating temperature.
2. Turn the engine off and remove the left-hand side cover.

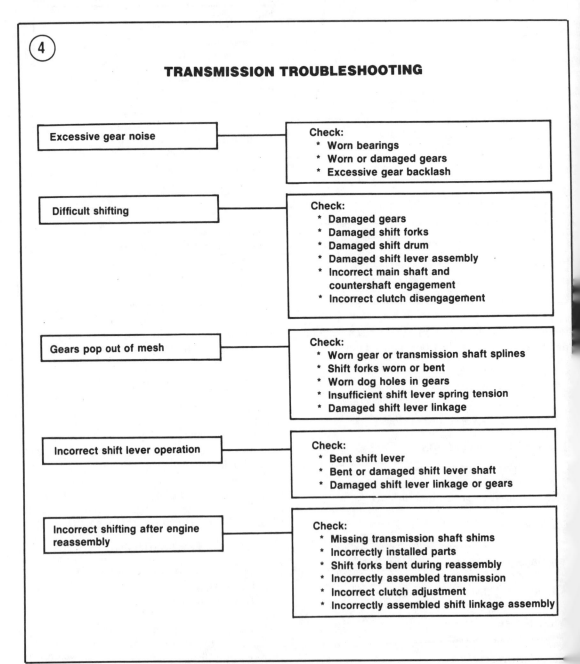

④

TRANSMISSION TROUBLESHOOTING

Excessive gear noise

Check:
* Worn bearings
* Worn or damaged gears
* Excessive gear backlash

Difficult shifting

Check:
* Damaged gears
* Damaged shift forks
* Damaged shift drum
* Damaged shift lever assembly
* Incorrect main shaft and countershaft engagement
* Incorrect clutch disengagement

Gears pop out of mesh

Check:
* Worn gear or transmission shaft splines
* Shift forks worn or bent
* Worn dog holes in gears
* Insufficient shift lever spring tension
* Damaged shift lever linkage

Incorrect shift lever operation

Check:
* Bent shift lever
* Bent or damaged shift lever shaft
* Damaged shift lever linkage or gears

Incorrect shifting after engine reassembly

Check:
* Missing transmission shaft shims
* Incorrectly installed parts
* Shift forks bent during reassembly
* Incorrectly assembled transmission
* Incorrect clutch adjustment
* Incorrectly assembled shift linkage assembly

3. Disconnect the white/red (connector 4) and black/yellow (connector 6) connectors identified in **Figure 5**.

CAUTION
The white/red connector is connected directly to the battery positive terminal. When attaching the voltmeter lead to the white/red connector, make sure the lead does not touch any part of the chassis.

4. Set a voltmeter to the 25 DC volt range. Attach the red voltmeter lead to the white/red connector and the black lead to the black/yellow connector.

NOTE
To turn the headlight off on U.S. models when performing Step 4, disconnect the black/yellow connector in the upper fairing.

5. Start the engine and and allow to idle. Record the voltage readings at various engine speeds and with the headlight turned on and off. The readings should be approximately 12 volts at low rpm and increase to but not exceed 15 volts at higher rpm's.
6. Turn off the engine and interpret results as follows:

  a. If the voltage is correct as tested in Step 4, the charging system is working correctly.

  b. If the voltage did not rise as the engine speed was increased in Step 4, the regulator/rectifier is defective or the alternator output is insufficient.

  c. If the voltage exceeded 15 volts in Step 4, the regulator/rectifier is damaged or the regulator/rectifier leads are loose or disconnected.

  d. Perform the alternator and regulator/rectifier checks as described in this chapter to determine the defective component.

Alternator Checks

1. Turn the ignition switch to the OFF position and remove the seat.
2. Remove the sprocket cover as described under *Sprocket Cover Removal/Installation* in Chapter Six.
3. Disconnect connector 1 (**Figure 5**) from the alternator. It contains 6 wires: 3 yellow and 3 black. See **Figure 6**.

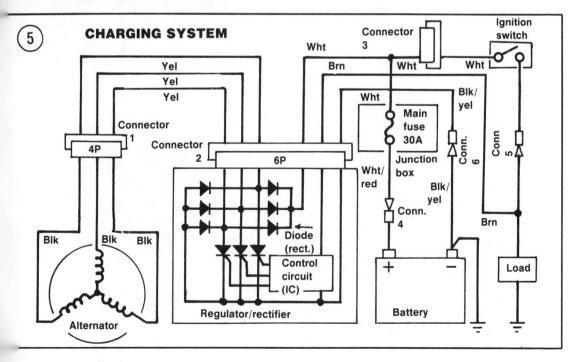

CHARGING SYSTEM

4. Connect the positive terminal of a 250 AC-volt voltmeter to one yellow lead and the negative voltmeter lead to another yellow lead.

5. Start the engine and run it at 4,000 rpm.

6. Observe the voltmeter. If it indicates approximately 45 volts, the alternator is operating correctly and the regulator/rectifier is damaged. If the reading is appreciably lower than 60 volts, the stator is defective.

7. Turn the engine off.

8. Repeat Steps 4-7 for each of the 3 yellow wires.

9. Remove the stator as described under *Stator Removal/Installation* in Chapter Eight.

Stator Test

Use an ohmmeter, set at $R \times 1$, and measure the resistance between the 3 yellow leads from the alternator (**Figure 5**). The valve should be about 0.1-0.8 ohms. If the resistance is greater than specified or no meter reading (infinity), the stator has an open and must be replaced.

Change the ohmmeter setting to the highest range and measure the resistance between each yellow lead and the chassis (ground). The meter should read infinity; if it doesn't, this indicates a short and the stator must be replaced.

Replace the stator as described under *Stator Removal/Installation* in Chapter Eight.

> *NOTE*
> *If the stator winding resistance is within the specified range, but the voltage output is incorrect, the rotor has probably lost some of its magnetism and must be replaced. See **Rotor Removal/Installation** in Chapter Eight.*

Rectifier/Regulator Inspection

Before making any voltage regulator test, be sure that the battery is in good condition and is at or near full charge.

1. Remove the seat.

2. Disconnect connector 2 (**Figure 5**) and remove the regulator (**Figure 7**). It has 6 wires—one white, one brown, one black/yellow and 3 yellow.

3. Measure and record resistance at the regulator terminals (**Figure 8**) as indicated in **Figure 9**.

4. Reverse ohmmeter leads, then Repeat Step 3. Each pair of measurements must be high with the ohmmeter connected one way and low when the ohmmeter leads are connected the other way. It is not possible to specify exact meter readings, but each pair of measurements should differ by a factor of not less than 10.

5. Replace the rectifier if it fails any check in Step 3 or Step 4. See *Rectifier/Regulator Removal/Installation* in Chapter Eight.

STARTING SYSTEM

The basic starter-related troubles are:

a. The starter does not crank.

b. The starter spins, but the engine does not crank.

Testing

Starting system problems are relatively easy to find. In most cases, the trouble is a loose or dirty electrical connection.

Starter does not crank

1. Turn on the headlight and push the starter button. Check for one of the following conditions.

2. *Starter does not crank and headlight does not come on:* The battery is dead or there is a loose battery connection. Check the battery charge as described under *Battery* in Chapter Three. If the battery is okay, check the starter connections at the battery, solenoid and at the starter switch.

3. *Headlight comes on, but goes out when the starter button is pushed:* There may be a bad connection at the battery. Wiggle the battery terminals and recheck. If the starter starts cranking you've found the problem. Remove and clean the battery terminal clamps. Clean the battery posts also. Reinstall the clamps and tighten securely. Refer to *Battery* in Chapter Three.

4. *Headlight comes on, but dims slightly when the starter button is pushed:* The problem is probably in the starter. Remove and test the starter as described in Chapter Eight.

5. *Headlight comes on, but dims severely when the starter button is pushed:* Either the battery is nearly dead or the starter or engine is partially seized. Check the battery as described in Chapter Three. Check the starter as described in Chapter Eight before checking for partial engine seizure.

6. *Headlight comes on and stays bright when the starter button is pushed:* The problem is in the starter button-to-solenoid wiring or in the starter itself. Check the starter switch, engine stop switch, starter relay and the starter lockout switch. Check each switch as described under *Switches* in Chapter Eight. Check the starter as described in Chapter Eight. Check the starter relay as described under *Starter Relay Testing* in Chapter Eight.

Starter spins but engine does not crank

If the starter spins at normal or high speed speed but the engine fails to crank, the problem is in the starter drive mechanism.

NOTE
Depending upon battery condition, the battery will eventually run down as the starter button is continually pressed. Remember that if the starter cranks normally, but the engine fails to start, the starter is working properly. It's time to start checking other engine systems. Don't wear the battery down.

ELECTRICAL PROBLEMS

If bulbs burn out frequently the cause may be excessive vibration loose connections that permit sudden current surges, or the installation of the wrong type of bulb.

Most light and ignition problems are caused by loose or corroded ground connections. Check these before replacing a bulb or electrical component.

IGNITION SYSTEM

The ignition system (**Figure 10**) is a breakerless type. See Chapter Eight. Most problems involving failure to start, poor driveability or rough running are caused by trouble in the ignition system.

Note the following symptoms:
a. Engine misses.
b. Stumbles on acceleration (misfiring).
c. Loss of power at high speed (misfiring).
d. Hard starting (or failure to start).
e. Rough idle.

Most of the symptoms can also be caused by a carburetor that is worn or improperly adjusted. But considering the law of averages, the odds are far

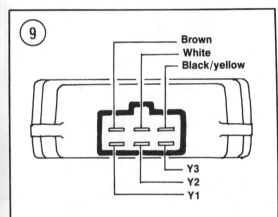

Brown
White
Black/yellow

Y3
Y2
Y1

Rectifier circuit inspection

No.	Connection		Reading	Meter range
	Meter (+) to	Meter (−) to		
1	Y$_1$			
2	Y$_2$	White	∞	
3	Y$_3$			
4	Y$_1$			
5	Y$_2$	Black/yellow		× 10 Ω or × 100 Ω
6	Y$_3$		½ scale	
7		Y$_1$		
8	White	Y$_2$		
9		Y$_3$		
10		Y$_1$		
11	Black/yellow	Y$_2$	∞	
12		Y$_3$		

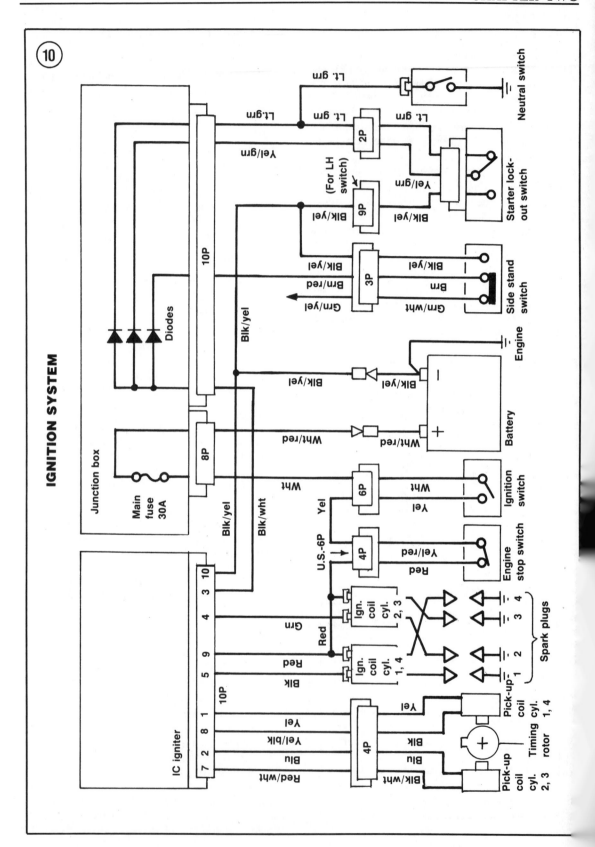

better that the source of the problem will be found in the ignition system rather than the fuel system.

Troubleshooting

The following basic tests are designed to quickly pinpoint and isolate problems in the ignition system.

Ignition Spark Test

Perform the following spark test to determine if the ignition system is operating properly.
1. Remove the fuel tank as described in Chapter Seven.
2. Remove one of the spark plugs.
3. Connect the spark plug wire and connector to the spark plug and touch the spark plug base to a good ground like the engine cylinder head. Position the spark plug so you can see the electrodes.

> *WARNING*
> *During the next step, do not hold the spark plug, wire or connector with fingers or a serious electrical shock may result. If necessary, use a pair of insulated pliers to hold the spark plug or wire. The high voltage generated by the ignition system could produce serious or fatal shocks.*

4. Crank the engine over with the starter. A fat blue spark should be evident across the spark plug electrodes.
5A. If a spark is obtained in Step 4, the problem is not in the breakerless ignition or coil. Check the fuel system and spark plugs.
5B. If no spark is obtained, proceed with the following tests.

Testing

Test procedures for troubleshooting the ignition system are found in the diagnostic chart in **Figure 11**. A multimeter, as described in Chapter One, is required to perform the test procedures.
Before beginning actual troubleshooting, read the entire test procedure (**Figure 11**). When required, the diagnostic chart will refer you to a certain procedure for testing.

Pick-Up Coil
Testing

1. Remove the right-hand side cover.
2. Disconnect the pick-up coil connector (**Figure 12**).
3. Use an ohmmeter on R×100 to measure the pick-up coil resistance between the following terminals:
   a. Pick-up coil for No. 1 and No. 4 cylinders: Black/white to blue.
   b. Pick-up coil for No. 2 and No. 3 cylinders: Black to yellow.
4. The correct resistance is 360-440 ohms.
5. Replace the pick-up coil(s) if it does not meet the test specifications. Refer to *Pick-up Coil Removal/Installation* in Chapter Eight.

Ignition Coil Testing

Refer to **Figure 13** for this procedure.
1. Remove the ignition coils as described in Chapter Eight.
2. Measure the coil primary resistance using an ohmmeter set at R×1. Measure between the coil's primary terminals as shown in **Figure 13**. The correct primary resistance is 1.8-2.8 ohms.
3. Measure the secondary resistance using an ohmmeter set at R×100. Measure between the coil's secondary spark plug leads (**Figure 13**). The correct secondary resistance is 10,000-16,000 (10-16 K) ohms.
4. Replace the ignition coil(s) if it doesn't test within the specifications in Steps 2 or Step 3. See *Ignition Coil Removal/Installation* in Chapter Eight.

Switches

Test the following switches as described under *Switches* in Chapter Eight:
   a. Neutral switch.
   b. Starter lockout switch.
   c. Side stand switch.
   d. Ignition switch.
   e. Engine stop switch.

IC Igniter Check

A special Kawasaki tester is necessary to check out the IC igniter. Refer the IC igniter to your Kawasaki dealer or a qualified specialist for this testing.

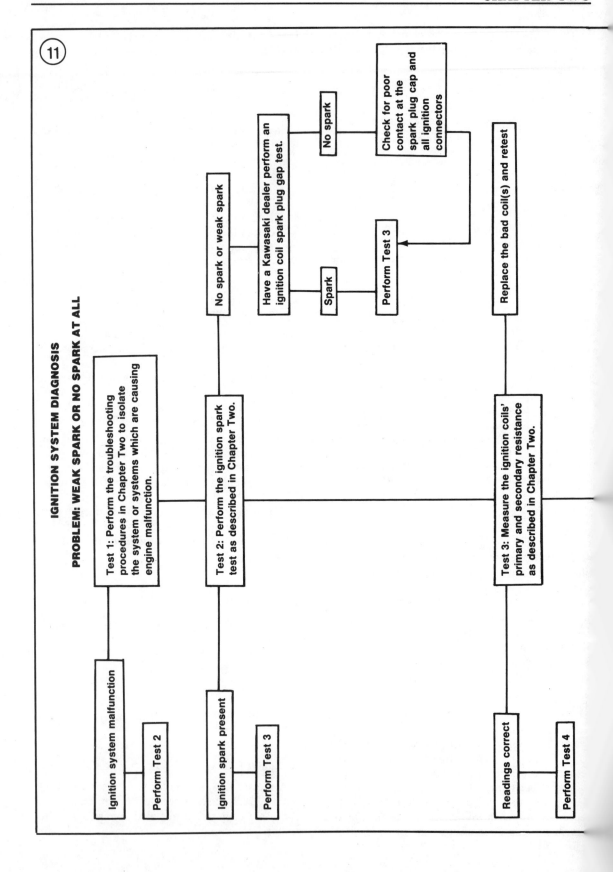

⑪

IGNITION SYSTEM DIAGNOSIS

PROBLEM: WEAK SPARK OR NO SPARK AT ALL

Test 1: Perform the troubleshooting procedures in Chapter Two to isolate the system or systems which are causing engine malfunction.

Ignition system malfunction

Perform Test 2

Test 2: Perform the ignition spark test as described in Chapter Two.

Ignition spark present

Perform Test 3

No spark or weak spark

Have a Kawasaki dealer perform an ignition coil spark plug gap test.

No spark

Check for poor contact at the spark plug cap and all ignition connectors

Spark

Perform Test 3

Test 3: Measure the ignition coils' primary and secondary resistance as described in Chapter Two.

Readings correct

Perform Test 4

Replace the bad coil(s) and retest

2

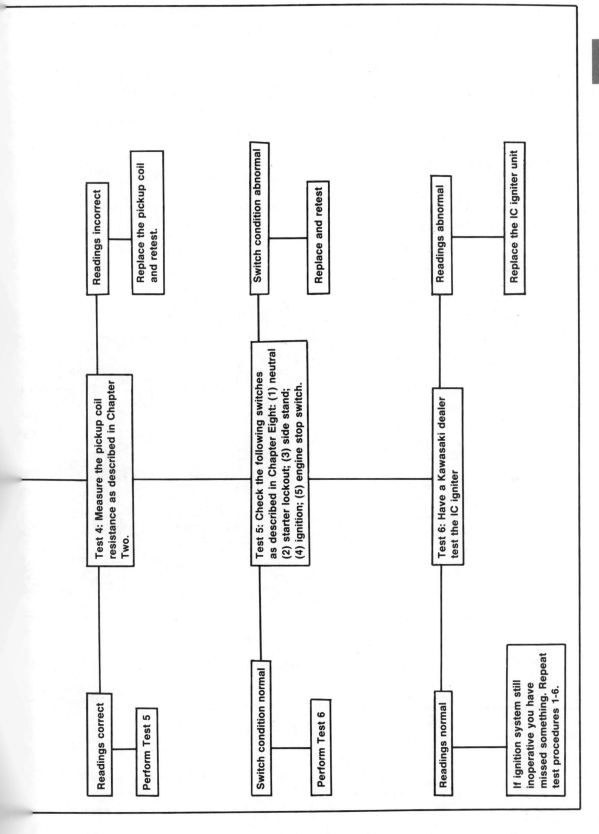

Test 4: Measure the pickup coil resistance as described in Chapter Two.

Readings incorrect → Replace the pickup coil and retest.

Readings correct → Perform Test 5

Test 5: Check the following switches as described in Chapter Eight: (1) neutral (2) starter lockout; (3) side stand; (4) ignition; (5) engine stop switch.

Switch condition abnormal → Replace and retest

Switch condition normal → Perform Test 6

Test 6: Have a Kawasaki dealer test the IC igniter

Readings abnormal → Replace the IC igniter unit

Readings normal → If ignition system still inoperative you have missed something. Repeat test procedures 1-6.

EXCESSIVE VIBRATION

Usually this is caused by loose engine mounting hardware. If not, it can be difficult to find without disassembling the engine. High speed vibration may be due to a bent axle shaft or loose or faulty suspension components. Vibration can also be caused by the following conditions:

a. Broken frame.
b. Worn drive chain.
c. Improperly balanced wheels.
d. Defective or damaged wheels.
e. Defective or damaged tires.
f. Internal engine wear or damage.

CARBURETOR TROUBLESHOOTING

Basic carburetor troubleshooting procedures are found in **Figure 14**.

FRONT SUSPENSION AND STEERING

Poor handling may be caused by improper tire pressure, a damaged or bent frame or front steering components, worn wheel bearings or dragging brakes. Possible causes of suspension and steering malfunctions are listed below.

Irregular or Wobbly Steering

a. Loose wheel axle nuts.
b. Loose or worn steering head bearings.
c. Excessive wheel hub bearing play.
d. Damaged wheel.
e. Unbalanced wheel assembly.
f. Worn hub bearings.
g. Incorrect wheel alignment.
h. Bent or damaged steering stem or frame (at steering neck).
i. Tire incorrectly seated on rim.
j. Excessive front end loading from non-standard equipment.

k. Damaged fairing assembly.
l. Loose fairing mounts or brackets.

Stiff Steering

a. Low front tire air pressure.
b. Bent or damaged steering stem or frame (at steering neck).
c. Loose or worn steering head bearings.

Stiff or Heavy Fork Operation

a. Incorrect fork springs.
b. Incorrect fork oil viscosity.
c. Excessive amount of fork oil.
d. Bent fork tubes.
e. Anti-dive incorrectly adjusted.
f. Anti-dive unit malfunction.

Poor Fork Operation

a. Worn or damage fork tubes.

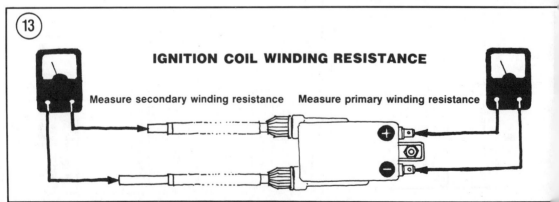

IGNITION COIL WINDING RESISTANCE

Measure secondary winding resistance   Measure primary winding resistance

b. Fork oil level low due to leaking fork seals.

c. Bent or damaged fork tubes.

d. Contaminated fork oil.

e. Worn fork springs.

f. Heavy front end loading from non-standard equipment.

g. Anti-dive unit malfunction.

Poor Rear Shock Absorber Operation

a. Damper unit leaking.

b. Incorrect rear shock adjustment.

c. Heavy rear end loading from non-standard equipment.

d. Incorrect loading.

BRAKE PROBLEMS

Sticking disc brakes may be caused by a stuck piston(s) in a caliper assembly, warped pad shim(s) or improper rear brake adjustment. See **Figure 15** for disc brake troubles and checks to make.

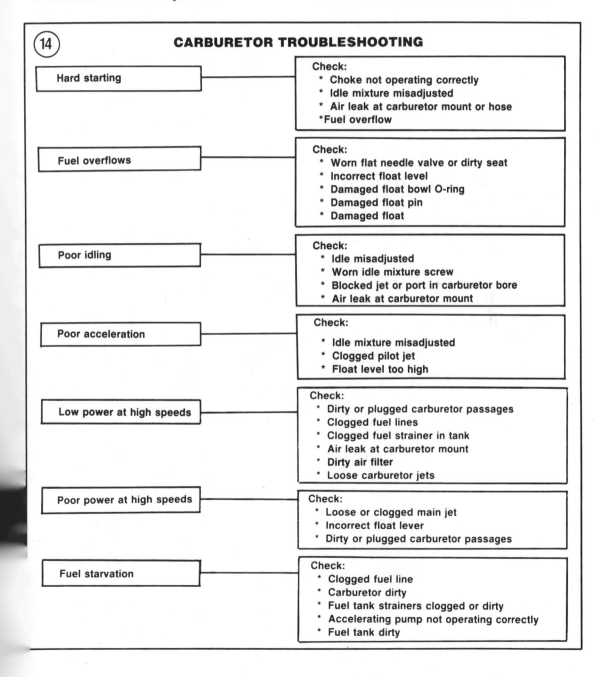

(14) CARBURETOR TROUBLESHOOTING

Hard starting
Check:
* Choke not operating correctly
* Idle mixture misadjusted
* Air leak at carburetor mount or hose
* Fuel overflow

Fuel overflows
Check:
* Worn flat needle valve or dirty seat
* Incorrect float level
* Damaged float bowl O-ring
* Damaged float pin
* Damaged float

Poor idling
Check:
* Idle misadjusted
* Worn idle mixture screw
* Blocked jet or port in carburetor bore
* Air leak at carburetor mount

Poor acceleration
Check:
* Idle mixture misadjusted
* Clogged pilot jet
* Float level too high

Low power at high speeds
Check:
* Dirty or plugged carburetor passages
* Clogged fuel lines
* Clogged fuel strainer in tank
* Air leak at carburetor mount
* Dirty air filter
* Loose carburetor jets

Poor power at high speeds
Check:
* Loose or clogged main jet
* Incorrect float lever
* Dirty or plugged carburetor passages

Fuel starvation
Check:
* Clogged fuel line
* Carburetor dirty
* Fuel tank strainers clogged or dirty
* Accelerating pump not operating correctly
* Fuel tank dirty

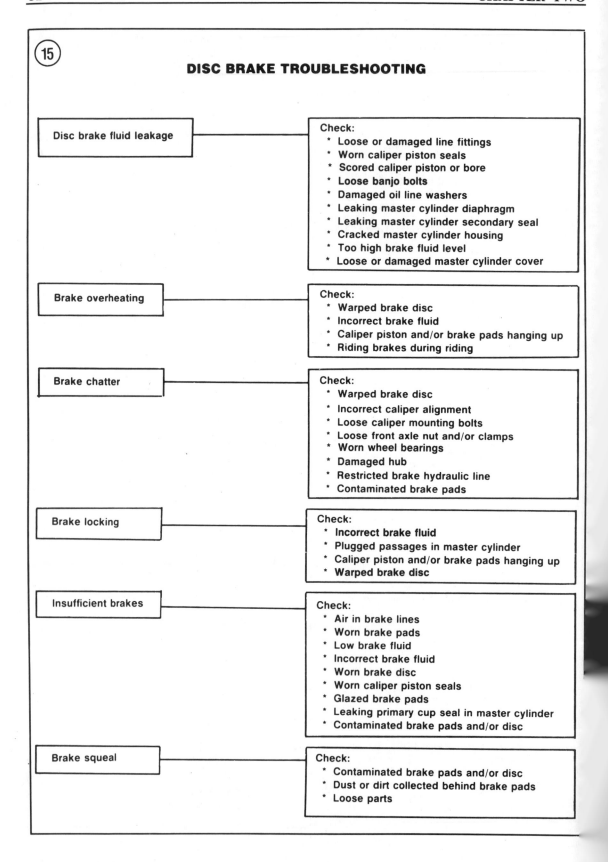

⑮

DISC BRAKE TROUBLESHOOTING

Disc brake fluid leakage

Check:
* Loose or damaged line fittings
* Worn caliper piston seals
* Scored caliper piston or bore
* Loose banjo bolts
* Damaged oil line washers
* Leaking master cylinder diaphragm
* Leaking master cylinder secondary seal
* Cracked master cylinder housing
* Too high brake fluid level
* Loose or damaged master cylinder cover

Brake overheating

Check:
* Warped brake disc
* Incorrect brake fluid
* Caliper piston and/or brake pads hanging up
* Riding brakes during riding

Brake chatter

Check:
* Warped brake disc
* Incorrect caliper alignment
* Loose caliper mounting bolts
* Loose front axle nut and/or clamps
* Worn wheel bearings
* Damaged hub
* Restricted brake hydraulic line
* Contaminated brake pads

Brake locking

Check:
* Incorrect brake fluid
* Plugged passages in master cylinder
* Caliper piston and/or brake pads hanging up
* Warped brake disc

Insufficient brakes

Check:
* Air in brake lines
* Worn brake pads
* Low brake fluid
* Incorrect brake fluid
* Worn brake disc
* Worn caliper piston seals
* Glazed brake pads
* Leaking primary cup seal in master cylinder
* Contaminated brake pads and/or disc

Brake squeal

Check:
* Contaminated brake pads and/or disc
* Dust or dirt collected behind brake pads
* Loose parts

NOTE: If you own a 1988 or later model, first check the Supplement at the back of this book for any new service information.

CHAPTER THREE

PERIODIC LUBRICATION, MAINTENANCE AND TUNE-UP

Your bike can be cared for by two methods: preventive and corrective maintenance. Because a motorcycle is subjected to tremendous heat, stress and vibration—even in normal use—preventive maintenance prevents costly and unexpected corrective maintenance. When neglected, any bike becomes unreliable and actually dangerous to ride. When properly maintained, your Kawasaki is one of the most reliable bikes available and will give many miles and years of dependable, fast and safe riding. By maintaining a routine service schedule as described in this chapter, costly mechanical problems and unexpected breakdowns can be prevented.

The procedures presented in this chapter can be easily performed by anyone with average mechanical skills. **Table 1** is a suggested factory maintenance schedule. **Tables 1-12** are located at the end of this chapter.

ROUTINE CHECKS

The following simple checks should be carried out at each fuel stop.

Engine Oil Level

Refer to *Engine Oil Level Check* under *Periodic Lubrication* in this chapter.

Coolant Level

Check the coolant level when the engine is cool.
1. Park the motorcycle on the centerstand.
2. Check the level through the level gauge in the coolant reserve tank. The level should be between the FULL and LOW marks (**Figure 1**). If necessary, add coolant to the reserve tank (not to the radiator) so the level is to the FULL mark.

General Inspection

1. Examine the engine for signs of oil or fuel leakage.
2. Check the tires for embedded stones. Pry them out with your ignition key.
3. Make sure all lights work.

NOTE
At least check the brake light. It can burn out anytime. Motorists cannot stop as quickly as you and need all the warning you can give.

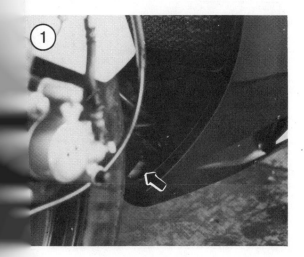

Tire Pressure

Tire pressure must be checked with the tires cold. Correct tire pressure depends on the load you are carrying. See **Table 2**.

Battery

The battery must be removed to check the electrolyte level. For complete details see *Battery Removal/Installation and Electrolyte Level Check* in this chapter.

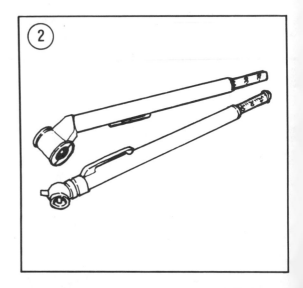

Lights and Horn

With the engine running, check the following.
1. Pull the front brake lever and check that the brake light comes on.
2. Push the rear brake pedal and check that the brake light comes on soon after you have begun depressing the pedal.
3A. *U.S. and Canadian models:* With the engine running, check to see that the headlight and taillight are on.
3B. *All non-U.S. and Canadian models:* With the engine running, check the headlight and taillight operation by operating the headlight switch.
4. Move the dimmer switch up and down between the high and low positions, and check to see that both headlight elements are working.
5. Push the turn signal switch to the left position and the right position and check that all 4 turn signal lights are working.
6. Push the horn button and note that the horn blows loudly.
7. If the horn or any light failed to work properly, refer to Chapter Eight.

MAINTENANCE INTERVALS

The services and intervals shown in **Table 1** are recommended by the factory. Strict adherence to these recommendations will insure long life from your Kawasaki. If the bike is run in an area of high humidity, the lubrication services must be done more frequently to prevent possible rust damage.

For convenience when maintaining your motorcycle, most of the services shown in **Table 1** are described in this chapter. Those procedures which require more than minor disassembly or adjustment are covered elsewhere in the appropriate chapter. The *Table of Contents* and *Index* can help you locate a particular service procedure.

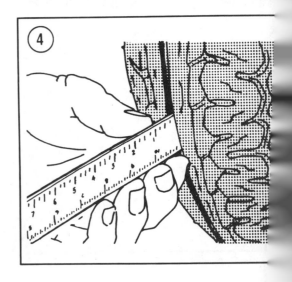

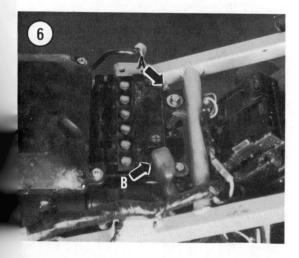

failures occur during the last 10 percent of usable tread wear. Check tire tread for excessive wear, deep cuts, embedded objects such as stones, nails, etc. Check also for high spots that indicate internal tire damage. Replace tires that show high spots or swelling. If you find a nail in a tire, mark its location with a light crayon before pulling it out. This will help locate the hole for repair. Refer to *Tubeless Tires* and *Tubeless Tire Changing* in Chapter Ten.

Measure tread wear at the center of the tire with a tread depth gauge (**Figure 4**) or small ruler. Because tires sometimes wear unevenly, measure wear at several points. **Table 2** lists tread wear limits for stock tires.

3

Rim Inspection

Frequently inspect the wheel rims. If a rim has been damaged it might have been knocked out of alignment. Improper wheel alignment can cause severe vibration and result in an unsafe riding condition. If the rim portion of an alloy wheel is damaged, the wheel must be replaced as it cannot be repaired.

BATTERY

CAUTION
If it becomes necessary to remove the battery vent tube when performing any of the following procedures, make sure to route the tube correctly during installation to prevent acid from spilling on parts.

TIRES

Tire Pressure

Tire pressure should be checked and adjusted to accommodate rider and luggage weight. A simple, accurate gauge (**Figure 2**) can be purchased for a few dollars and should be carried in your motorcycle tool kit. The appropriate tire pressures are shown in **Table 2**.

NOTE
After checking and adjusting the air pressure, make sure to reinstall the air valve cap (Figure 3). The cap prevents small pebbles and dirt from collecting in the valve stem; this could allow air leakage or result in incorrect tire pressure readings.

Tire Inspection

The likelihood of tire failure increases with tread wear. It is estimated that the majority of all tire

Removal/Installation and Electrolyte Level Check

The battery is the heart of the electrical system. It should be checked and serviced as indicated in **Table 1**. Most electrical system troubles can be attributed to neglect of this vital component.

In order to correctly service the electrolyte level it is necessary to remove the battery from the frame. The electrolyte level should be maintained between the two marks on the battery case (**Figure 5**). If the electrolyte level is low, it's a good idea to completely remove the battery so that it can be thoroughly cleaned, serviced and checked.
1. Remove the seat.
2. Remove the battery cover.
3. Disconnect the negative battery cable (A, **Figure 6**) from the battery.
4. Disconnect the positive battery cable (B, **Figure 6**).
5. Disconnect the battery vent tube.

6. Lift the battery (**Figure 7**) out of the battery box and remove it.

WARNING
Protect your eyes, skin and clothing. If electrolyte gets into your eyes, flush your eyes thoroughly with clean water and get prompt medical attention.

CAUTION
Be careful not to spill battery electrolyte on painted or polished surfaces. The liquid is highly corrosive and will damage the finish. If it is spilled, wash it off immediately with soapy water and thoroughly rinse with clean water.

7. Remove the caps (**Figure 8**) from the battery cells and add distilled water. Never add electrolyte (acid) to correct the level. Fill only to the upper battery level mark (**Figure 5**).

8. After the level has been corrected and the battery allowed to stand for a few minutes, check the specific gravity of the electrolyte in each cell with a hydrometer (**Figure 9**). Follow the manufacturer's instructions for reading the instrument. See *Battery Testing* in this chapter.

9. After the battery has been refilled, recharged or replaced, install it by reversing these removal steps.

Testing

Hydrometer testing is the best way to check battery condition. Use a hydrometer with numbered graduations from 1.100 to 1.300 rather than one with just color-coded bands. To use the hydrometer, squeeze the rubber ball, insert the tip into the cell and release the ball. Draw enough electrolyte to float the weighted float inside the hydrometer. Note the number in line with the electrolyte surface; this is the specific gravity for this cell. Return the electrolyte to the cell from which it came. See **Figure 9**.

The specific gravity of the electrolyte in each battery cell is an excellent indication of that cell's condition (**Table 3**). A fully charged cell will read 1.275-1.280 while a cell in good condition reads from 1.225-1.250 and anything below 1.125 is practically dead.

NOTE
Specific gravity varies with temperature. For each 10° that electrolyte temperature exceeds 80° F, add 0.004 to reading indicated on hydrometer. Subtract 0.004 for each 10° below 80° F.

If the cells test in the poor range, the battery requires recharging. The hydrometer is useful for checking the progress of the charging operation. **Table 3** shows approximate state of charge.

Charging

CAUTION
Always remove the battery from the motorcycle before connecting charging equipment.

WARNING
During charging, highly explosive hydrogen gas is released from the battery. The battery should be charged only in a well-ventilated area, and open flames and cigarettes should be kept away. Never check the charge of the battery by arcing across the terminals; the resulting spark can ignite the hydrogen gas.

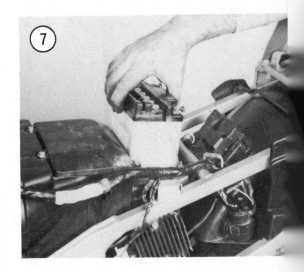

1. Remove the battery from the motorcycle as described in this chapter.

2. Connect the positive (+) charger lead to the positive battery terminal and the negative (-) charger lead to the negative battery terminal.

3. Remove all vent caps from the battery, set the charger at 12 volts, and switch it on. If the output of the charger is variable, it is best to select a low setting—1 1/2 to 2 amps.

CAUTION
The electrolyte level must be maintained at the upper level during the charging cycle; check and refill as necessary.

4. After battery has been charged for about 8 hours, turn the charger off, disconnect the leads and check the specific gravity. It should be within the limits specified in **Table 3**. If it is, and remains stable for one hour, the battery is charged.

5. To ensure good electrical contact, cables must be clean and tight on the battery's terminals. If the cables' terminals are badly corroded, even after performing the above cleaning procedures, the cables should be disconnected, removed from the bike and cleaned separately with a wire brush and a baking soda solution. After cleaning, apply a very thin coating of petroleum jelly (Vaseline) to the battery terminals before reattaching the cables. After connecting the cables, apply a light coating to the connections also—this will delay future corrosion.

New Battery Installation

When replacing the old battery with a new one, be sure to charge it completely (specific gravity, 1.260-1.280) before installing it in the bike. Failure to do so, or using the battery with a low electrolyte level, will permanently damage the battery.

PERIODIC LUBRICATION

Engine Oil Level Check

Engine oil level is checked through the inspection window located at the bottom of the clutch cover (**Figure 10**).

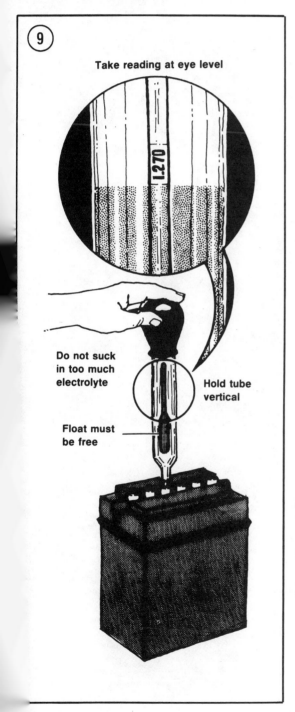

(9)

Take reading at eye level

1.270

Do not suck in too much electrolyte

Hold tube vertical

Float must be free

(10)

1. Start the engine and let it reach normal operating temperature.

2. Stop the engine and allow the oil to settle.

3. Park the bike so that it is off the centerstand and level.

4. The oil level should be between the maximum and minimum window marks (**Figure 10**). If necessary, remove the oil fill cap (**Figure 11**) and add the recommended oil (**Table 4**) to raise the oil to the proper level. Do not overfill.

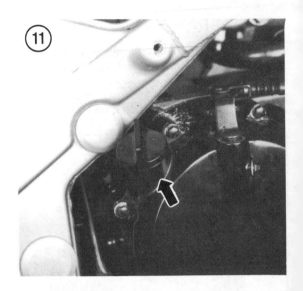

Engine Oil and Filter Change

The factory-recommended oil and filter change interval is specified in **Table 1**. This assumes that the motorcyle is operated in moderate climates. The time interval is more important than the mileage interval because combustion acids, formed by gasoline and water vapor, will contaminate the oil even if the motorcycle is not run for several months. If a motorcycle is operated under dusty conditions, the oil will get dirty more quickly and should be changed more frequently than recommended.

Use only a detergent oil with an API rating of SE or SF. The quality rating is stamped on top of the can (**Figure 12**). Try always to use the same brand of oil. Use of oil additives is not recommended. Refer to **Table 4** for correct weight of oil to use under different temperatures.

To change the engine oil and filter you will need the following:

    a. Drain pan.
    b. Funnel.
    c. Can opener or pour spout.
    d. Wrench or socket to remove drain plug.
    e. Oil (see **Table 5**).
    f. Oil filter element.

There are a number of ways to discard the used oil safely. The easiest way is to pour it from the drain pan into a gallon plastic bleach, juice or milk container for disposal.

NOTE
Never dispose of motor oil in the trash or pour it on the ground, or down a storm drain. Many service stations accept used motor oil. Many waste haulers provide curbside used motor oil collection. Do not combine other fluids with motor oil to be recycled. To find a recycling location contact the American Petroleum Institute (API) at www.recycleoil.org.

1. Place the motorcycle on the centerstand.

2. Remove the lower fairing as described under *Lower Fairing Removal/Installation* in Chapter Thirteen.

3. Start the engine and run it until it is at normal operating temperature, then turn it off.

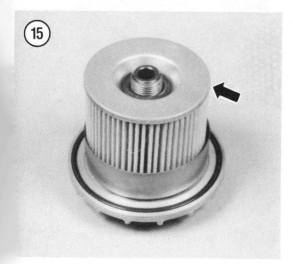

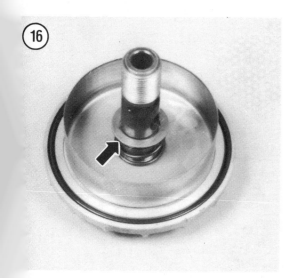

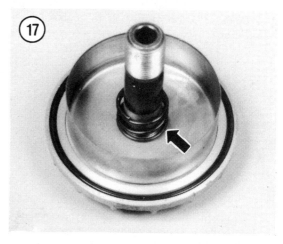

4. Place a drip pan under the crankcase and remove the drain plug (**Figure 13**).

> *NOTE*
> ***Figure 13*** *shows the drain pan removed for clarity.*

> *NOTE*
> *Do not remove the primary chain tensioner bolt (**Figure 14**) located at the front of the engine.*

5. Replace the oil filter as follows:

> *CAUTION*
> *The oil filter mounting bolt is made of soft material. To prevent damaging the bolt head, always loosen the bolt with a socket or box-end wrench. Do not use an adjustable wrench.*

a. Unscrew the filter mounting bolt from underneath the engine and lower the filter assembly.

b. Hold the filter and turn the mounting bolt to remove the filter (**Figure 15**). Discard the oil filter.

c. Remove the washer (**Figure 16**), spring (**Figure 17**) and oil fence (**Figure 18**).

3

d. Pull the mounting bolt (A, **Figure 19**) out of the filter cover.

e. Inspect the filter cover (B, **Figure 19**) and mounting bolt O-rings. Replace the O-rings if deformed, cracked or if the filter cover leaked previously.

f. Clean the filter cover and oil fence of all oil residue.

g. The oil filter bypass valve is located in the mounting bolts. Clean the mounting bolt in solvent and check bypass valve assembly for damage. Check the mounting bolt hex head for damage that could make further removal of the bolt difficult. Replace the bolt if necessary.

h. Wipe the crankcase gasket surface with a clean, lint-free cloth.

i. With the mounting bolt and filter cover O-rings installed, insert the bolt through the filter cover.

j. Slide the oil fence (**Figure 18**), spring (**Figure 17**) and washer (**Figure 16**) over the mounting bolt.

k. Install the oil filter (**Figure 15**) by turning it onto the mounting bolt. Make sure the rubber grommets on both sides of the oil filter do not dislodge or tear.

l. Install the oil filter assembly into the oil pan. Tighten the mounting bolt to 20 N•m (14.5 ft.-lb.).

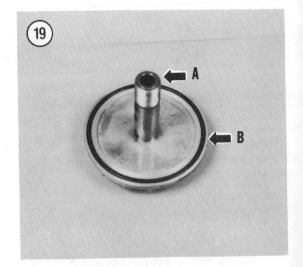

> *CAUTION*
> *The mounting bolt is made of soft material. To prevent damaging the hex head, always tighten the bolt with a socket or box-end wrench. Do not use an adjustable wrench.*

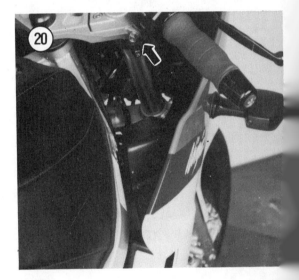

6. Replace the oil drain plug gasket if deformed.

7. Install the oil drain plug and gasket and tighten to 20 N•m (14.5 ft.-lb.).

8. Remove the oil filler cap (**Figure 11**) and fill the crankcase with the correct weight (**Table 4**) and quantity of oil (**Table 5**).

9. Screw in the oil fill plug securely.

10. After completing Step 9, start the engine and allow it to idle. Check for leaks.

11. Turn the engine off and allow the oil to settle. Then check for correct oil level as described under *Engine Oil Level Check* in this chapter. Adjust if necessary.

12. Reinstall the lower fairing assembly as described in Chapter Thirteen.

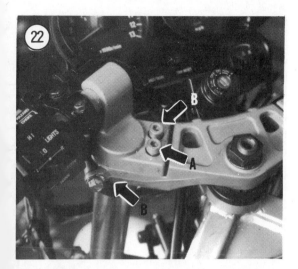

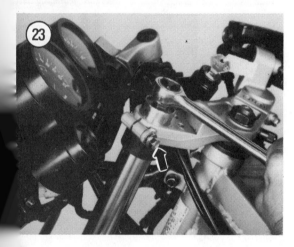

3

Front Fork Oil Change

. Place the bike on the centerstand. Support the front end so that the front tire is clear of the ground.

. Remove the air valve cap from the right-hand fork tube and depress the valve stem (**Figure 20**) with a screwdriver to release all air from the fork tubes.

Place a drip pan beside one fork tube and remove the drain screw (**Figure 21**). Allow the oil to drain until it stops. Then with both of the bike's wheels on the ground, apply the front brake and push down on the front end and allow it to return. Repeat to remove as much oil as possible.

WARNING
Do not allow the fork oil to come in contact with any of the brake components.

Install the drain screw (**Figure 21**).

5. Repeat Steps 3 and 4 for the opposite side.

6. Place the bike onto its centerstand.

7. Remove the handlebar Allen bolts (A, **Figure 22**) and lift the left- and right-hand handlebar (B, **Figure 22**) off of the steering stem. It is not necessary to disconnect the control cables.

8. Working on one fork tube only, perform the following:

   a. Loosen the top steering stem pinch bolt (**Figure 23**).

   b. Loosen the fork cap with the drive portion of a 1/2 in. socket (**Figure 23**).

   c. Slowly loosen and remove the fork cap.

   d. Lift the fork spring out of the fork tube.

9. Fill the fork tube with slightly less than the specified quantity of oil (**Table 6**). **Table 4** lists the recommended fork oil to use.

NOTE
In order to measure the correct amount of fluid, use a baby bottle. These bottles have measurements in cubic centimeters (cc) and fluid ounces (oz.) imprinted on the side.

NOTE
The amount of oil poured in is not as accurate a measurement as the actual level of the oil. You may have to add more oil later in this procedure.

10. After filling the fork tube, slowly pump the forks up and down to distribute the oil throughout the fork damper.

NOTE
Step 11 is performed with the fork tubes fully extended.

11. Measure the distance from the top of the fork tube to the surface of the oil (**Figure 24**) with an oil level gauge or ruler.

12. Add oil, if required, to bring the level up to specifications (**Table 6**). Do not overfill.

CAUTION
An excessive amount of oil can cause a hydraulic locking of the forks during compression, destroying the oil seals.

13. Reinstall the fork spring and fork cap. Tighten the fork cap securely.

14. Repeat Steps 8-13 for the opposite side.

15. Fill the forks with air as described under *Front Fork Air Adjustment* in this chapter.

16. Install the left- and right-hand handlebars onto the steering stem. Install the Allen bolts (A, **Figure 22**) and tighten to 23 N•m (16.5 ft.-lb.).

17. Road test the bike and check for oil and air leaks.

Control Cables

The control cables should be lubricated at the intervals specified in **Table 1**. At this time they should also be inspected for fraying and the cable sheath should be checked for chafing. The cables are relatively inexpensive and should be replaced when found to be faulty.

They can be lubricated with a cable lubricant and a cable lubricator available at most motorcycle dealers.

> *NOTE*
> *The main cause of cable breakage or cable stiffness is improper lubrication. Maintaining the cables as described in this section will assure long service life.*

1. Disconnect the clutch and choke cables from the left-hand handlebar. Label and then disconnect the throttle cables from the throttle grip.

> *NOTE*
> *To service the throttle cables, it is necessary to remove the screws that clamp the housing together to gain access to the cable ends.*

2. Attach a cable lubricator (**Figure 25**) to the cable following the manufacturer's instructions.
3. Insert the nozzle of the lubricant can into the lubricator, press the button on the can and hold it down until the lubricant begins to flow out of the other end of the cable.

> *NOTE*
> *Place a shop cloth at the end of the cable(s) to catch all excess lubricant that will flow out.*

> *NOTE*
> *If lubricant does not flow out the end of the cable, check the entire cable for fraying, bending or other damage.*

4. Remove the lubricator, then reconnect and adjust the cable(s) as described in this chapter. Refer to:
    a. *Throttle Cable Adjustment.*
    b. *Clutch Lever Adjustment.*
    c. *Choke Cable Adjustment.*

Swing Arm Bearing Lubrication

The rear swing arm needle bearings should be cleaned in solvent and lubricated with a molybdenum disulfide grease at the intervals specified in **Table 1**. The swing arm must be removed to service the needle bearings. Refer to

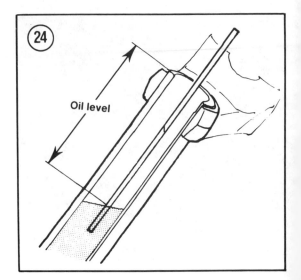

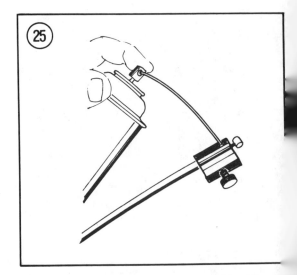

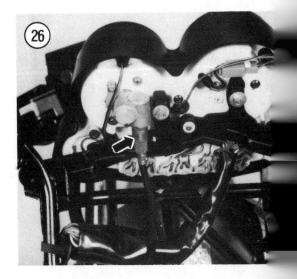

Rear Swing Arm Removal/Installation in Chapter Eleven.

Uni-trak Linkage
Lubrication

The Uni-trak tie-rod and connecting rod needle bearings should be cleaned in solvent and lubricated with molybdenum disulfide grease at the intervals specified in **Table 1**. The Uni-trak linkage must be removed to service the needle bearings. Refer to *Tie-Rod Removal/Installation* and *Connecting Rod Removal/Installation* in Chapter Eleven.

Speedometer
Cable Lubrication

Lubricate the speedometer cable every year or whenever needle operation is erratic.
1. Unscrew the end of the speedometer cable (**Figure 26**) at the instrument cluster.
2. Pull the cable from the sheath.
3. If the grease is contaminated, thoroughly clean off all old grease.
4. Thoroughly coat the cable with a good grade of multi-purpose grease and reinstall into the sheath.
5. Make sure the cable is correctly seated into the speedometer drive unit.

> *NOTE*
> *If the cable does not seat into the drive unit, it will be necessary to disconnect the cable at its lower connection (**Figure 27**).*

Wheel Bearings
Inspection/Lubrication

Worn wheel bearings cause excessive wheel play that results in vibration and other steering troubles. At the intervals specified in **Table 1**, the bearing should be inspected and lubricated with wheel bearing grease. Refer to *Front Hub* in Chapter Ten and *Rear Hub* in Chapter Eleven.

Speedometer Gear Lubrication

Refer to *Speedometer Gear Lubrication* in Chapter Ten.

Steering Stem Lubrication

Refer to *Steering Head* in Chapter Ten.

Drive Chain Lubrication

Kawasaki recommends SAE 90 gear oil for chain lubrication; it is less likely to be thrown off the chain than lighter oils. Many commercial drive chain lubricants are also available and will do an excellent job.

> *NOTE*
> *If the drive chain is obviously dirty, remove and clean it as described under Drive Chain Cleaning in Chapter Eleven before lubricating it as described in this procedure.*

> *CAUTION*
> *The factory drive chain is equipped with O-rings between the side plates (**Figure 28**) that seal lubricant between the pins and bushings. To prevent damaging these O-rings, use only kerosene or diesel oil for cleaning. Do not use gasoline or other solvents that will cause the O-rings to swell or deteriorate. Refer to cleaning procedures in Chapter Eleven.*

1. Place the bike on the centerstand.
2. Oil the bottom chain run with SAE 90 gear oil or a commercial chain lubricant. Concentrate on getting the oil down between the side plates of the chain links (**Figure 28**).
3. Rotate the chain and continue until the entire chain has been lubricated.

PERIODIC MAINTENANCE

Drive Chain Adjustment

> *NOTE*
> *As drive chains stretch and wear in use, the chain will become tighter at one point. The chain must be checked and adjusted at this point.*

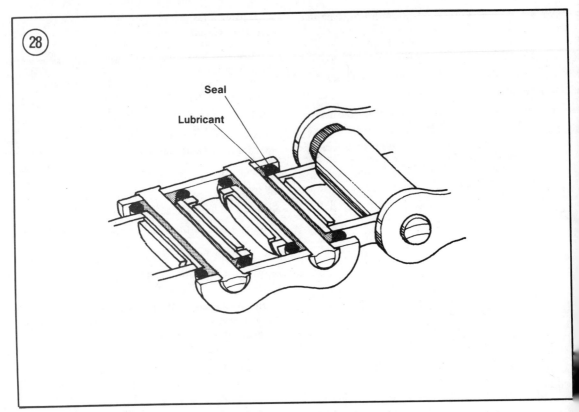

Seal

Lubricant

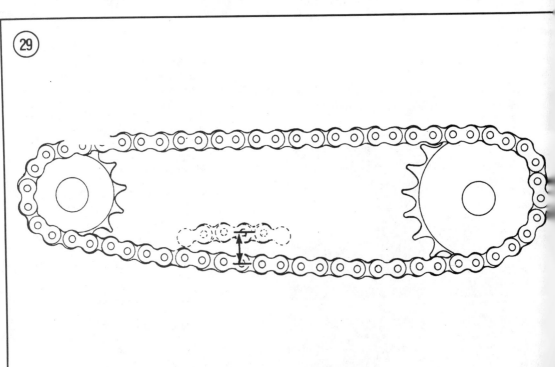

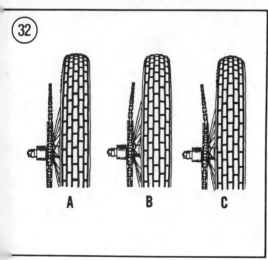

A   B   C

1. Place the motorcycle on the centerstand.
2. Turn the rear wheel and check the chain for its tightest point. Mark this spot and turn the wheel so that the mark is located on the chain's lower run, midway between both drive sprockets. Check and adjust the drive chain as follows.
3. With thumb and forefinger, lift up and press down the chain at that point, measuring the distance the chain moves vertically.
4. The drive chain should have approximately 35-40 mm (1 3/8-1 9/16 in.) of vertical travel at midpoint (**Figure 29**). If necessary, adjust the chain as follows.
5. Loosen the rear torque link nut (**Figure 30**).
6. Remove the rear axle cotter pin and loosen the axle nut.
7. Loosen the axle adjuster locknut (A, **Figure 31**) on both sides of the wheel.
8. Turn each adjuster bolt (B, **Figure 31**) clockwise to take up slack in the chain. To loosen the chain, turn each adjuster bolt counterclockwise. Be sure to turn each adjuster stud equally to maintain rear wheel alignment. Alignment is checked by observing the swing arm marks (C, **Figure 31**) on both sides of the swing arm. Adjust the chain until the correct amount of free play is obtained (Step 4). See **Figure 29**.
9. Check rear wheel alignment by sighting along the chain as it runs over the rear sprocket. It should not appear to bend sideways. See **Figure 32**.
10. Tighten the rear axle nut to 110 N•m (80 ft.-lb.). Tighten the torque link nut securely.
11. Install a new cotter pin through the rear axle and bend the ends over to lock it.
12. Recheck chain play.
13. Perform the *Rear Brake Light Switch Adjustment* in this chapter.

Disc Brake Inspection

The hydraulic brake fluid in the disc brake master cylinders should be checked every month. The disc brake pads should be checked at the intervals specified in **Table 1**. Replacement is described under *Brake Pad Replacement* in Chapter Twelve.

Disc Brake Fluid Level Inspection

1. Place the bike on its centerstand.
2. Turn the handlebars so that the front master cylinder is level.

3. Make sure the brake fluid is above the lower level lines. See **Figure 33** (front) or **Figure 34** (rear). If it is low, add brake fluid as described in this chapter.

NOTE
A very low fluid level may indicate worn brake pads. Inspect as described in this chapter. If the pads are good, check for a fluid leak.

Adding Brake Fluid

1. Clean the outside of the reservoir cap thoroughly with a dry rag and remove the reservoir cap. Remove the diaphragm under the cap.
2. The fluid level in the reservoir should be up to the upper level line. Add fresh DOT 3 brake fluid as required.

WARNING
Use brake fluid clearly marked DOT 3 only and specified for disc brakes. Others may vaporize and cause brake failure.

CAUTION
Be careful not to spill brake fluid on painted or plated surfaces as it will destroy the surface. Wash immediately with soapy water and thoroughly rinse it off.

3. Reinstall all parts. Make sure the cap is tightly secured.

NOTE
*If the brake fluid was so low as to allow air in the hydraulic system, the brakes will have to be bled. Refer to **Bleeding the System** in Chapter Twelve.*

Disc Brake Lines and Seals

Check brake lines between the master cylinder and the brake caliper. If there is any leakage, tighten the connections and bleed the brakes as described in Chapter Twelve. If this does not stop the leak or if a line is obviously damaged, cracked or chafed, replace the line and seals and bleed the brake.

Disc Brake Pad Inspection

Inspect the disc brake pads for wear according to the maintenance schedule.
1. Apply the front brake.

2. Shine a light between the caliper and the disc (from in front of the fork leg) and inspect the brake pads.

3. If either pad measures 1 mm (1/32 in.) or less, replace both pads as a set.

NOTE
*If it is difficult to observe the thickness and condition of the brake pads, remove them as described under **Brake Pad Replacement** in Chapter Twelve.*

4. Replace brake pads as described in Chapter Twelve.

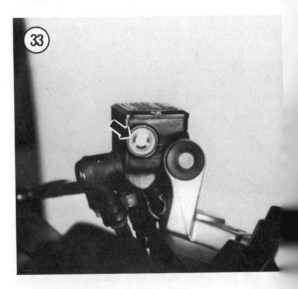

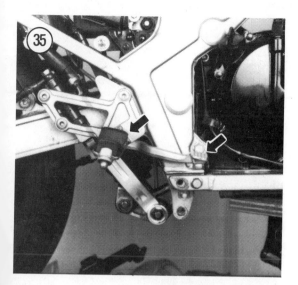

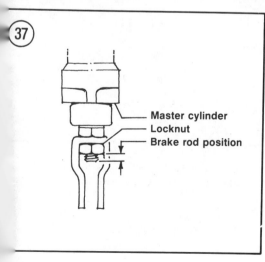

Master cylinder
Locknut
Brake rod position

Disc Brake Fluid Change

Every time you remove the reservoir cap, a small amount of dirt and moisture enters the brake fluid. The same thing happens if a leak occurs or when any part of the hydraulic system is loosened or disconnected. Dirt can clog the system and cause unnecessary wear. Water in the fluid vaporizes at high temperatures, impairing the hydraulic action and reducing brake performance.

To change brake fluid, drain the master cylinders as described under *Front Master Cylinder Removal/Installation* or *Rear Master Cylinder Removal/Installation* in Chapter Twelve. Add new fluid to the master cylinder and bleed at the caliper until the fluid leaving the caliper is clean and free of contaminants and air bubbles. Refer to *Bleeding the System* in Chapter Twelve.

> *WARNING*
> *Use brake fluid clearly marked DOT 3 only. Others may vaporize and cause brake failure. DOT 4 brake fluid can also be safely used.*

Front Brake Lever Adjustment

Periodic adjustment of the front disc brake is not required because disc pad wear is automatically compensated. If there is excessive play in the front brake lever, check the front brake lever pivot hole and bolt for excessive wear. Replace worn parts.

Rear Brake Pedal Height Adjustment

1. Place the motorcycle on the centerstand.
2. Check to be sure the brake pedal is in the at-rest position.
3. The correct height position below the top of the foot peg (**Figure 35**) is approximately 40 mm (1 9/16 in.). To adjust, proceed to Step 4.
4. Referring to **Figure 36**, perform the following:
   a. Loosen the master cylinder locknut (**Figure 37**).
   b. Remove the clevis pin (A) and disconnect the brake pedal from the master cylinder.
   c. Remove the master cylinder mounting bolts (B) and lift the master cylinder (C) off the frame. Do not disconnect the hydraulic hose.
   d. Turn the master cylinder adjusting nut (**Figure 37**) until the pushrod protrudes 3.5-5.5 mm (9/64-7/32 in.) below the adjusting nut.
   e. Reinstall the master cylinder and tighten the bolts to 32 N•m (24 ft.-lb.). Attach the brake pedal. Install the old clevis pin but do not lock it at this time.
   f. Recheck the brake pedal height and readjust if necessary.

g. Install a *new* clevis pin and bend the ends to lock it.

Rear Brake Light Switch
Adjustment

1. Turn the ignition switch to the ON position.
2. Depress the brake pedal. The brake light should come on after the brake pedal is depressed. If necessary, adjust as follows.
3. Remove the right-hand side cover.
4. To make the light come on earlier, hold the switch body (**Figure 38**) and turn the adjusting locknut to move the switch body *up*. Move the switch body *down* to delay the light. Tighten the locknut.
5. Reinstall the side cover.

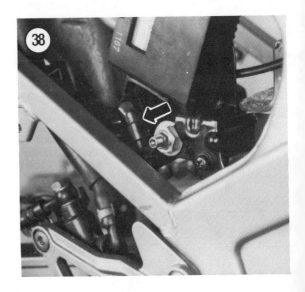

Clutch Lever Adjustment

1. Pull the clutch lever until resistance is felt. Then measure the distance between the adjuster locknut and the clutch lever (**Figure 39**). This is clutch cable free play. The clutch cable should have about 2-3 mm (1/8 in.) free play. Minor adjustment can be made at the hand lever. Loosen the locknut, turn the adjuster as required and tighten the locknut.

> *NOTE*
> *If sufficient free play cannot be obtained at the hand lever, additional adjustment can be made at the engine clutch cable adjuster as follows.*

2. Remove the right-hand lower fairing stay as described in Chapter Thirteen.
3. Loosen the clutch cable adjuster nuts (**Figure 40**) at the crankcase as far as they will go.
4. At the clutch lever, loosen the locknut (**Figure 39**) and turn the adjuster until 5-6 mm (3/16-1/4 in.) of threads are showing between the locknut and the adjuster body (**Figure 41**).
5. At the crankcase, pull the clutch cable forward and tighten the adjuster nuts (**Figure 40**) to lock the cable.
6. At the clutch lever, turn the adjuster as required to get about 2-3 mm (1/8 in.) of cable play at the clutch lever.
7. Tighten all locknuts.
8. Start the engine and make sure the clutch operates correctly.
9. Reinstall the right-hand rear fairing stay.

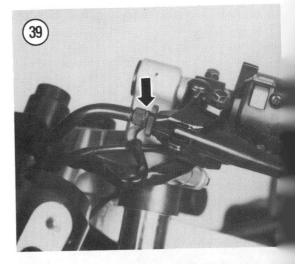

Throttle Cable Adjustment

Always check the throttle cables before you make any carburetor adjustments. Too much free

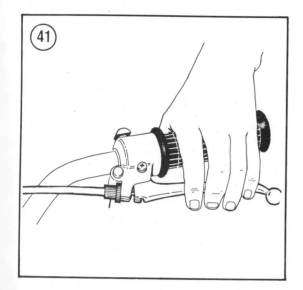

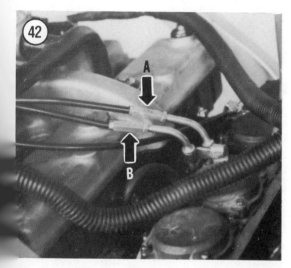

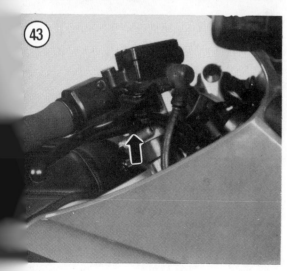

3

play causes delayed throttle response. Too little free play will cause unstable idling.

Check the throttle cable from grip to carburetors. Make sure they are not kinked or chafed. Replace them if necessary.

Make sure that the throttle grip rotates smoothly from fully closed to fully open. Check at center, full left, and full right position of steering.

Check free play at the throttle grip flange. Kawasaki specifies about 2-3 mm (1/8 in.). If adjustment is required proceed as follows.

WARNING
If idle speed increases when the handlebar is turned to right or left, check throttle cable routing. Do not ride the motorcycle in this unsafe condition.

NOTE
*All models use a dual throttle cable arrangement. These are identified as accelerator (A, **Figure 42**) and decelerator (B, **Figure 42**) cables.*

1. Loosen the accelerator cable (outer) locknut at the handlebar (**Figure 43**) and turn the adjuster until the correct amount of free play at the throttle grip is obtained. Tighten the locknut.
2. If the correct throttle grip free play cannot be obtained by performing Step 1, proceed with Step 3.
3. Remove the fuel tank as described in Chapter Seven.
4. Loosen both cable locknuts at the carburetors (**Figure 42**) to obtain as much slack in the throttle grip as possible.
5. Close the throttle grip and lengthen the decelerator cable adjusting nut (B, **Figure 42**) until its inner cable becomes tight. Tighten the locknut.
6. Lengthen the accelerator adjusting nut (A, **Figure 42**) until the correct free play is obtained at the throttle grip. Tighten the locknut.
7. Operate the throttle grip a few times. Then check that the throttle linkage rests against the idle adjusting screw when the throttle grip is closed.
8. The throttle grip should now be adjusted correctly. If not, the throttle cables may be stretched and should be replaced.
9. Reinstall the fuel tank after completing the adjustment.
10. Park the motorcycle on its centerstand. Sit on the seat and start the engine. Then lean back so that the front wheel clears the ground. Turn the

handlebars from right to left to check for abnormal idle speed variances due to improper cable routing.

WARNING
If idle speed increases when the handlebar is turned to right or left, check throttle cable routing. Do not ride the motorcycle in this unsafe condition.

Choke Cable Adjustment

1. Check for correct choke cable free play at the choke lever as follows:
   a. Pull the choke lever until the starter lever contacts the starter plunger at the carburetor. See **Figure 44**. The distance the choke lever traveled is choke cable play.
   b. The correct amount of choke lever play is 2-3 mm (1/8 in.).
   c. If the choke lever play is incorrect, proceed to Step 2.
2. Remove the fuel tank as described in Chapter Seven.
3. Locate the choke cable midline adjuster (**Figure 45**) and loosen the locknut. Turn the adjuster until the correct amount of choke lever play is obtained in Step 1. Tighten the locknut and recheck the adjustment.
4. Reinstall the fuel tank.

Fuel Valve/Filter

At the intervals specified in **Table 1**, remove and drain the fuel tank. Remove the fuel shutoff valve and clean it of all dirt and debris. Replace worn or damaged O-rings and gaskets. Refer to *Fuel Valve* in Chapter Seven.

Fuel and Vacuum Line Inspection

Inspect the condition of all fuel and vacuum lines for cracks or deterioration. Replace if necessary. Make sure the hose clamps are in place and holding securely.

Exhaust System

Check for leakage at all fittings. Tighten all bolts and nuts. Replace any gaskets if necessary. Refer to *Exhaust System* in Chapter Seven.

Air Cleaner
Removal/Installation

A clogged air cleaner can decrease the efficiency and life of the engine. Never run the bike without the air cleaner installed. Even minute particles of dust can cause severe internal engine wear.

The service intervals specified in **Table 1** should be followed with general use. However, the air

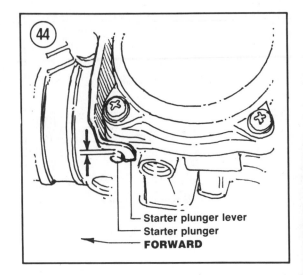

Starter plunger lever
Starter plunger
FORWARD

3

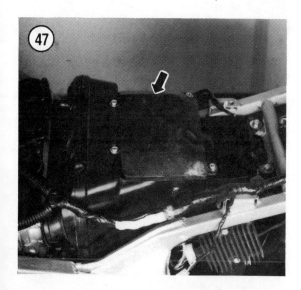

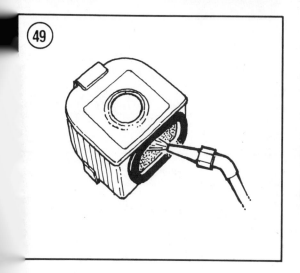

cleaner should be serviced more often if the bike is ridden in dusty areas.

1. Remove the fuel tank.

2. Remove the fuel tank bracket bolts and remove the bracket (**Figure 46**).

3. Remove the air filter cover screws and remove the cover (**Figure 47**).

4. Remove the air filter element (**Figure 48**).

5. Clean the air filter element with compressed air from the inside of the element as shown in **Figure 49**.

6. Inspect the air filter element for tears or other damage that would allow unfiltered air to pass into the engine. Check the sponge gasket on the element for tears. Replace the element if necessary.

7. Install by reversing these steps.

8. Route the wiring harness as shown in **Figure 50** when installing the fuel tank bracket.

Air Suction Valve
(U.S. Models)

Refer to *Air Suction System (U.S. Models)* in Chapter Seven for complete inspection and service procedures.

Steering Play

The steering head should be checked for looseness at the intervals specified in **Table 1** or whenever the following symptoms or conditions exist:

    a. The handlebars vibrate more than normal.

    b. The front forks make a clicking or clunking noise when the front brake is applied.

    c. The steering feels tight or slow.

    d. The motorcycle does not want to steer straight on level road surfaces.

Inspection

1. Prop up the motorcycle so that the front tire clears the ground.
2. Remove the upper and lower fairings. See Chapter Thirteen.
3. Center the front wheel. Push lightly against the left handlebar grip to start the wheel turning to the right, then let go. The wheel should continue turning under its own momentum until the forks hit their stop.
4. Center the wheel, and push lightly against the right handlebar grip.
5. If, with a light push in either direction, the front wheel will turn all the way to the stop, the steering adjustment is not too tight.
6. If the front wheel will not turn all the way to the stop, the steering is too tight. Adjust the steering as described in this chapter.
7. Center the front wheel and kneel in front of it. Grasp the bottoms of the 2 front fork slider legs. Try to pull the forks toward you, and then try to push them toward the engine. If no play is felt, the steering adjustment is not too loose.
8. If the steering adjustment is too tight or too loose, adjust it as described in this chapter.

Adjustment

1. Prop up the motorcycle so that the front tire clears the ground.
2. Remove the upper and lower fairings. See Chapter Thirteen.
3. Remove the fuel tank.
4. Loosen the lower front fork steering stem bolts (**Figure 51**).
5. Loosen the steering stem nut (A, **Figure 52**).
6. Loosen or tighten the steering stem locknut (B, **Figure 52**) less than 1/8 turn at a time.
7. Tighten the steering stem nut to 39 N•m (29 ft.-lb.).
8. Tighten the lower front fork clamp bolts to 21 N•m (15 ft.-lb.).
9. Recheck the steering as described under *Inspection* in this chapter.
10. Perform Steps 4-9 until the adjustment is correct.
11. Install the fuel tank and fairings.

Cooling System Inspection

At the intervals indicated in **Table 1**, the following items should be checked. If you do not

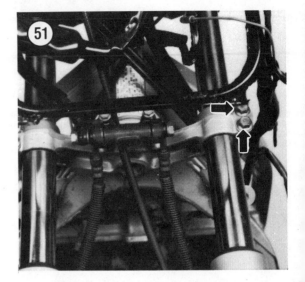

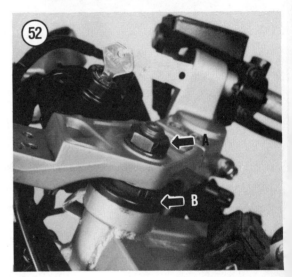

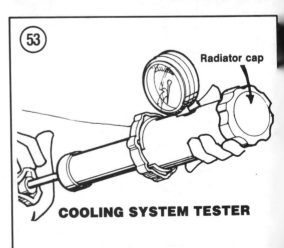

Radiator cap

COOLING SYSTEM TESTER

have the test equipment, the tests can be done by a Kawasaki dealer, radiator shop or service station.

WARNING
Do not remove the radiator cap when the engine is hot.

1. Have the radiator cap pressure tested (**Figure 53**). The specified radiator cap relief pressure is 0.95-1.25 kg/cm² (14-18 psi). The cap must be able to sustain this pressure for 6 seconds. Replace the radiator cap if it does not hold pressure or if the relief pressure is too high or too low.

2. Leave the radiator cap off and have the entire cooling system pressure tested (**Figure 54**). The entire cooling system should be pressurized up to, but not exceeding, 1.25 kg/cm² (18 psi). The system must be able to sustain this pressure for 6 seconds. Replace or repair any components that fail this test.

CAUTION
If test pressures exceed specifications, the radiator may be damaged.

3. Test the specific gravity of the coolant with an antifreeze tester (**Figure 55**) to ensure adequate temperature and corrosion protection. Never let the mixture become less than 40 percent antifreeze or corrosion protection will be impaired.

4. Check all cooling system hoses for damage or deterioration. Replace any hose that is questionable. Make sure all hose clamps are tight.

5. Carefully clean any road dirt, bugs, mud, etc. from the radiator core. Use a whisk broom, compressed air or low-pressure water. If the radiator has been hit by a small rock or other item, *carefully* straighten out the fins with a screwdriver.

Coolant Change

The cooling system should be completely drained and refilled at the interval indicated in **Table 1**.

CAUTION
Use only a high quality ethylene glycol antifreeze specifically labeled for use with aluminum engines. Do not use an alcohol-based antifreeze.

In areas where freezing temperatures occur, add a higher percentage of antifreeze to protect the system to temperatures far below those likely to occur. **Table 7** lists the recommended amount of antifreeze for protection. The following procedure must be performed when the engine is cool.

CAUTION
Be careful not to spill antifreeze on painted surfaces as it will destroy the surface. Wash immediately with soapy water and rinse thoroughly with clean water.

1. Place the bike on the centerstand.
2. Remove the lower fairing. See Chapter Thirteen.

WARNING
Do not remove the radiator cap when the engine is hot.

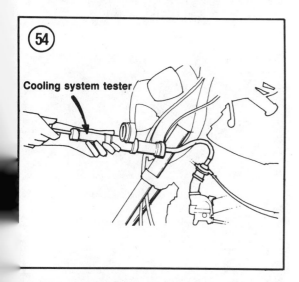

(54) Cooling system tester

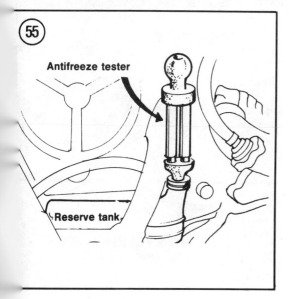

(55) Antifreeze tester

Reserve tank

3. Remove the radiator cap (**Figure 56**).

4. Place a drain pan under the frame on the right-hand side of the bike under the water pump. Remove the drain screw (**Figure 57**) and sealing washer on the water pump.

> *WARNING*
> *Antifreeze is poisonous and may attract animals. Do not leave the drained coolant where it is accessible to children or pets.*

5. Reinstall the drain screw and sealing washer on the water pump cover.

6. Drain the reservoir tank (**Figure 58**) located in the lower fairing.

> *NOTE*
> *It will be necessary to remove the lower fairing to drain the reservoir tank. See Chapter Thirteen. Reinstall the lower fairing.*

7. Refill the radiator. Add the coolant through the radiator filler neck (**Figure 56**). Use the recommended mixture of antifreeze and distilled water (**Table 7**). Fill to the radiator filler neck (just below the reservoir tank tube opening).

8. Install the radiator cap. Turn the radiator cap clockwise to the first stop. Then push the cap down and turn it clockwise until it stops.

9. Start the engine and let it run at idle speed until the engine reaches normal operating temperature. Make sure there are no air bubbles in the coolant and that the coolant level stabilizes at the correct level. Add coolant as necessary.

10. Add coolant to the reservoir tank (**Figure 59**) to correct the level.

11. Test ride the bike and readjust the coolant level in the reservoir tank if necessary.

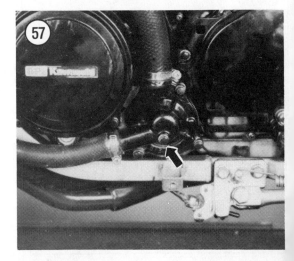

Front Suspension Check

1. Apply the front brake and pump the fork up and down as vigorously as possible. Check for smooth operation and check for any oil leaks.

2. Make sure the upper and lower steering stem bolts are tight.

3. Check that the front axle pinch bolt is tight.

4. Check that the front axle nut cotter pin is in place and that the axle nut is tight.

> *WARNING*
> *If any of the previously mentioned bolts and nuts are loose, refer to Chapter Ten for correct procedures and torque specifications.*

Rear Suspension Check

1. Place the bike on the centerstand.

2. Push hard on the rear wheel sideways to check for side play in the rear swing arm bearings.

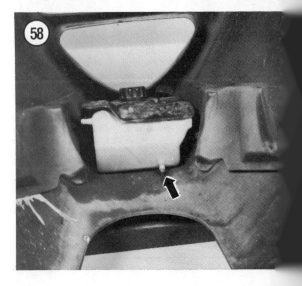

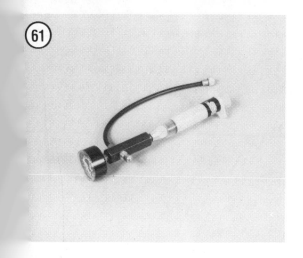

3. Check the tightness of the shock absorber mounting nuts and bolts.

4. Check the tightness of the rear brake torque arm bolts.

5. Make sure the rear axle nut is tight and the cotter pin is still in place.

> *WARNING*
> *If any of the previously mentioned nuts or bolts are loose, refer to Chapter Eleven for correct procedures and torque specifications.*

Nuts, Bolts, and Other Fasteners

Constant vibration can loosen many fasteners on a motorcycle. Check the tightness of all fasteners, especially those on:
  a. Engine mountng hardware.
  b. Engine crankcase covers.
  c. Handlebars and front forks.
  d. Gearshift lever.
  e. Sprocket bolts and nuts.
  f. Brake pedal and lever.
  g. Exhaust system.
  h. Lighting equipment.

SUSPENSION ADJUSTMENT

Front Fork Air Adjustment

Both the fork springs and air pressure support the motorcycle and rider. Air pressure should be measured with the forks at normal room temperature.

The air pressure can be varied to suit the load and your ride preference. Don't use a high-pressure hose or bottle to pressurize the forks. A tire pump is a lot closer to the scale you need. Note the following when adjusting the front fork air pressure:
  a. Increase air pressure for heavy loads.
  b. If the suspension is too hard, reduce air pressure.
  c. If the suspension is too soft, increase air pressure.

1. Support the bike with the front wheel off the ground.

2. Remove the air valve cap (**Figure 60**).

> *CAUTION*
> *In the next step, do not exceed 36 psi or the fork seals will be damaged.*

3. Connect a pump (**Figure 61**) to the valve and pump the forks to about 20 psi.

4. Slowly bleed off the pressure to reach the desired value. The standard pressure is listed in **Table 8**.

> *NOTE*
> *Each application of a pressure gauge bleeds off some air pressure in the process of applying and removing the gauge.*

5. Install the valve cap.

Anti-Dive Adjustment

The anti-dive system can be adjusted for different road and riding conditions by turning the adjuster ring (**Figure 62**) at the bottom of the anti-dive unit. The anti-dive adjusters on each fork tube can be set to one of the following positions:

  a. Position 1: Weak.
  b. Position 2: Moderate.
  c. Position 3: Strong.

When adjusting the anti-dive, note the following:

  a. The numbers on the adjuster (**Figure 63**) indicate the different numbered positions.
  b. Align the desired adjuster number with the triangle index mark on the fork tube (**Figure 63**).
  c. Turn the adjuster until it clicks into position.
  d. Turn both adjusters to the same numbered position.

> *WARNING*
> *If the anti-dive adjusters are not set to the same numbered position, front suspension operation may become uncertain and result in a hazardous condition.*

Rear Shock Absorber Adjustment

The Uni-trak rear shock absorber is equipped with air pressure and damping adjustments.

Air pressure adjustment

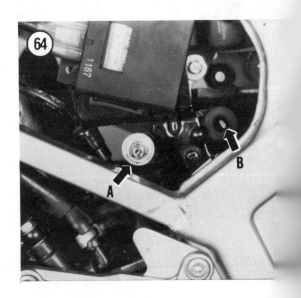

Air pressure should be measured with the shock at normal room temperature.

The air pressure can be varied to suit the load and your ride preference. Don't use a high-pressure hose or bottle to pressurize the shock. A tire pump is a lot closer to the scale you need. Note the following when adjusting the rear shock air pressure:

  a. Increase air pressure for heavy loads.
  b. If the suspension is too hard, reduce air pressure.
  c. If the suspension is too soft, increase air pressure.

1. Support the bike on the centerstand with the rear wheel off the ground.
2. Remove the left-hand side cover.
3. Remove the air valve cap.

> *CAUTION*
> *In the next step, do not exceed 71 psi or the oil seal will be damaged.*

4. Connect a pump to the valve (A, **Figure 64**) and pump the shock to about 50 psi.
5. Slowly bleed off the pressure to reach the desired value. Suggested pressure ranges with varying load settings are listed in **Table 9**.

> *NOTE*
> *Each application of a pressure gauge bleeds off some air pressure in the process of applying and removing the gauge.*

6. Install the valve cap.

Damping adjustment

The damping can be adjusted to 4 different positions to best suit riding, load and speed conditions. **Table 10** lists adjuster positions in relation to various road and riding conditions.

The damping is changed by pushing or pulling the shock absorber damper stick (B, **Figure 64**) to the desired numbered position that corresponds to the adjuster positions in **Table 10**.

> *NOTE*
> *The factory recommended setting for average riding with no accessories is adjuster position No. 2.*

TUNE-UP

A complete tune-up restores performance and power that is lost due to normal wear and deterioration of engine parts. Because engine wear occurs over a combined period of time and mileage, the engine tune-up should be performed at the intervals specified in **Table 1**. More frequent tune-ups may be required if the bike is ridden primarily in stop-and-go traffic.

Table 11 lists tune-up specifications.

Before starting a tune-up procedure, make sure to have all the necessary new parts on hand.

Because different systems in an engine interact, the procedures should be done in the following order:

  a. Clean or replace the air cleaner element.
  b. Adjust valve clearances.
  c. Check engine compression.
  d. Check or replace the spark plugs.
  e. Check the ignition timing.
  f. Synchronize carburetors and set idle speed.

Tools

To perform a tune-up on your Kawasaki, you will need the following tools:

  a. Spark plug wrench.
  b. Socket wrench and assorted sockets.
  c. Flat feeler gauge.
  d. Compression gauge.
  e. Spark plug wire feeler gauge and gapper tool.
  f. Ignition timing light.
  g. Carburetor synchronization tool—to measure manifold vacuum.

Air Cleaner Element

The air cleaner element should be cleaned or replaced before doing other tune-up procedures. Refer to *Air Cleaner Removal/Installation* in this chapter.

Valve Clearance

> *CAUTION*
> *Valve clearance check and adjustment must be performed with the engine cold.*

1. Place the motorcycle on the centerstand.
2. Remove the cylinder head cover. Refer to *Cylinder Head Cover Removal/Installation* in Chapter Four.
3. Remove the spark plugs as described in this chapter. This will make it easier to turn the engine by hand.
4. Remove the pickup coil cover (**Figure 65**) from the right-hand side.

NOTE
The pistons are numbered 1-4, starting with the left piston and counting left to right.

5. Position the No. 1 piston at top dead center (TDC) on its compression stroke. To do this, turn the crankshaft clockwise with the bolt on the end of the crankshaft (**Figure 66**) until the No. 1 piston TDC mark on the rotor is aligned with the crankcase timing mark (**Figure 67**). When the No. 1 piston is at top dead center on its compression stroke, the camshaft sprockets (**Figure 68** and **Figure 69**) will be positioned as shown in **Figure 70** and the camshaft lobes indicated in **Figure 71** will be facing away from the rocker arms.

NOTE
Camshaft sprocket positioning is viewed from the right-hand side.

6. Insert a feeler gauge between the following intake and exhaust valve stems and rocker arms:
    a. No. 1 piston: Intake and exhaust valves.
    b. No. 2 piston: Exhaust valves only.
    c. No. 3 piston: Intake valves only.
The correct valve clearance is listed in **Table 11**. The clearance is measured correctly when there is a slight drag on the feeler gauge when it is inserted and withdrawn. If the clearance is within tolerance, go on to Step 8. If adjustment is required, continue with Step 7.

7. Adjust by loosening the adjuster locknut (**Figure 72**) and turning the adjuster as required to get the proper clearance. Hold the adjuster steady and tighten the locknut securely. Check that the locknut is tightened securely.

8. Turn the crankshaft clockwise until the No. 4 piston "T" mark on the rotor is aligned with the

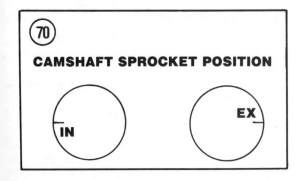

CAMSHAFT SPROCKET POSITION

IN EX

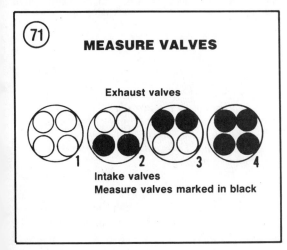

MEASURE VALVES

Exhaust valves

1 2 3 4

Intake valves
Measure valves marked in black

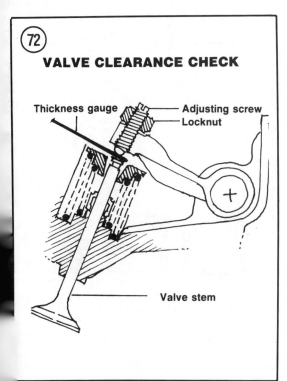

VALVE CLEARANCE CHECK

Thickness gauge

Adjusting screw
Locknut

Valve stem

crankcase timing mark (**Figure 67**). When the No. 4 piston is at top dead center on its compression stroke, the camshaft sprockets will be positioned as shown in **Figure 73** and the camshaft lobes indicated in **Figure 74** will be facing away from the rocker arms.

9. Insert a feeler gauge between the following intake and exhaust valve stems and rocker arms:

    a. No. 2 piston: Intake valves only.

    b. No. 3 piston: Exhaust valves only.

    c. No. 4 piston: Intake and exhaust valves.

The correct valve clearance is listed in **Table 11**. The clearance is measured correctly when there is a slight drag on the feeler gauge when it is inserted and withdrawn. If the clearance is within tolerance, go on to Step 10. If adjustment is required, adjust as described in Step 7.

10. Reinstall the spark plugs.

11. Reinstall the pickup coil cover so that the notch in the cover faces down.

12. Install the cylinder head cover. Refer to *Cylinder Head Cover Removal/Installation* in Chapter Four.

3

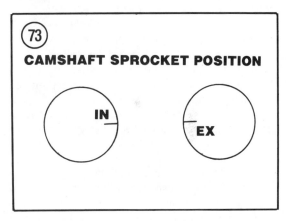

CAMSHAFT SPROCKET POSITION

IN EX

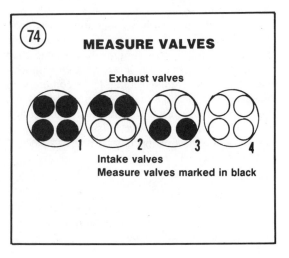

MEASURE VALVES

Exhaust valves

1 2 3 4

Intake valves
Measure valves marked in black

Compression Test

At every tune-up, check cylinder compression. Record the results and compare them at the next check. A running record will show trends in deterioration so that corrective action can be taken before complete failure.

The results, when properly interpreted, can indicate general cylinder, piston ring and valve condition.

NOTE
The valves must be properly adjusted to correctly interpret the results of this test.

1. Warm the engine to normal operating temperature. Ensure that the choke valve and throttle valve are completely open.
2. Remove the spark plugs as described in this chapter.

NOTE
A screw-in type compression tester will be required for this procedure.

3. Connect the compression tester to one cylinder following manufacturer's instructions.
4. Have an assistant crank the engine over until there is no further rise in pressure.
5. Remove the tester and record the reading.
6. Repeat Steps 3-5 for the other cylinders.
7. When interpreting the results, actual readings are not as important as the difference between the readings. Standard compression pressure is specified in **Table 11**. Greater differences indicate worn or broken rings, leaky or sticky valves, blown head gasket or a combination of all.

If compression reading does not differ between cylinders by more than 10 psi, the rings and valves are in good condition.

If a low reading (10 percent or more) is obtained on one of the cylinders, it indicates valve or ring trouble. To determine which, pour about a teaspoon of engine oil through the spark plug hole onto the top of the piston. Turn the engine over once to clear some of the excess oil, then take another compression test and record the reading. If the compression increases significantly, the valves are good but the rings are defective on that cylinder. If compression does not increase, the valves require servicing. A valve could be hanging open or burned, or a piece of carbon could be on a valve seat.

NOTE
If the compression is low, the engine cannot be tuned to maximum performance. The worn parts must be replaced and the engine rebuilt.

Correct Spark Plug Heat Range

Spark plugs are available in various heat ranges that are hotter or colder than the spark plugs originally installed at the factory.

Select plugs in a heat range designed for the loads and temperature conditions under which the engine will operate. Using incorrect heat ranges however, can cause piston seizure, scored cylinder walls or damaged piston crowns.

In general, use a hotter plug for low speeds, low loads and low temperatures. Use a colder plug for high speeds, high engine loads and high temperatures.

NOTE
In areas where seasonal temperature variations are great, the factory recommends a "two-plug system"—a cold plug for hard summer riding and a hot plug for slower winter operation. This may prevent spark plug and engine problems.

The reach (length) of a plug is also important. A longer than normal plug could interfere with the valves and pistons, causing permanent and severe damage (**Figure 75**). Factory suggested spark plugs are listed in **Table 12**.

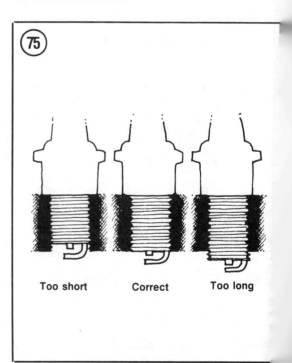

Too short   Correct   Too long

3

Spark Plug Removal/Cleaning

1. Remove the fuel tank as described in Chapter Seven.

2. Remove the ignition coils as described in Chapter Eight.

3. Grasp the spark plug leads as near to the plug as possible and pull them off the plugs.

4. Blow away any dirt that has accumulated in the spark plug wells.

CAUTION
The dirt could fall into the cylinders when the plugs are removed, causing serious engine damage.

5. Remove the spark plugs with a spark plug wrench.

NOTE
If plugs are difficult to remove, apply penetrating oil, such as WD-40 or Liquid Wrench, around base of plugs and let it soak in (about 10-20 minutes).

6. Inspect spark plugs carefully. Look for plugs with broken center porcelain, excessively eroded electrodes and excessive carbon or oil fouling. Replace such plugs. See **Figure 76**.

CAUTION
Spark plug cleaning with the use of a sand-blast type device is not recommended. While this type of cleaning is thorough, the plug must be perfectly free of all abrasive cleaning material when done. If not, it is possible for the cleaning material to fall into the engine during operation and cause damage.

Gapping and Installing the Plugs

New plugs should be carefully gapped to ensure a reliable, consistent spark. You must use a special spark plug gapping tool with a wire gauge.

1. Remove the new plugs from the box. Do *not* screw in the small pieces that are loose in each box (**Figure 77**). They are not used.

2. Insert a wire gauge between the center and the side electrode of each plug (**Figure 78**). The correct gap is found in **Table 11**. If the gap is correct, you will feel a slight drag as you pull the wire through. If there is no drag, or the gauge won't pass through, bend the side electrode *with the gapping tool* (**Figure 79**) to set the proper gap (**Table 11**).

3. Put a small drop of oil on the threads of each spark plug.

4. Screw each spark plug in by hand until it seats. Very little effort is required. If force is necessary, you have the plug cross-threaded; unscrew it and try again.

NOTE
If a spark plug is difficult to install, the cylinder head threads may be dirty or slightly damaged. To clean the threads, apply grease to the threads of a spark plug tap and screw it carefully into the cylinder head. Turn the tap slowly until it is completely installed. If the tap cannot be installed, the threads are severely damaged. Damaged threads can be replaced with a heli-coil insert.

5. Tighten the spark plugs to a torque of 20 N•m (14 ft.-lb.). If you don't have a torque wrench, an additional 1/4 to 1/2 turn is sufficient after the gasket has made contact with the head. If you are reinstalling old, regapped plugs and are reusing the old gasket, tighten only an additional 1/4 turn.

CAUTION
Do not overtighten. Besides making the plug difficult to remove, the excessive torque will squash the gasket and destroy its sealing ability.

6. Install each spark plug wire. Make sure it goes to the correct spark plug.

Reading Spark Plugs

Much information about engine and spark plug performance can be determined by careful examination of the spark plugs. This information is valid only after performing the following steps.

1. Ride bike a short distance at full throttle in any gear.

2. Turn off kill switch before closing throttle and, simultaneously, pull in clutch and coast to a stop. Do *not* downshift transmission in stopping.

3. Remove spark plugs and examine them. Compare them to **Figure 76**.

If the insulator tip is white or burned, the plug is too hot and should be replaced with a colder one.

A too-cold plug will have sooty deposits ranging in color from dark brown to black. Replace with a hotter plug and check for too-rich carburetion or evidence of oil blow-by at the piston rings.

If any one plug is found unsatisfactory, replace all 4.

SPARK PLUG CONDITION

OIL FOULED
- Identified by wet black deposits on the insulator shell bore and electrodes.
- Caused by excessive oil entering combustion chamber through worn rings and pistons, excessive clearance between valve guides and stems, or worn or loose bearings. Can be cleaned. If engine is not repaired, use a hotter plug.

NORMAL
- Identified by light tan or gray deposits on the firing tip.
- Can be cleaned.

GAP BRIDGED
- Identified by deposit buildup closing gap between electrodes.
- Caused by oil or carbon fouling. If deposits are not excessive, the plug can be cleaned.

CARBON FOULED
- Identified by black, dry fluffy carbon deposits on insulator tips, exposed shell surfaces and electrodes.
- Caused by too cold a plug, weak ignition, dirty air cleaner, too rich a fuel mixture or excessive idling. Can be cleaned.

LEAD FOULED
- Identified by dark gray, black, yellow or tan deposits or a fused glazed coating on the insulator tip.
- Caused by highly leaded gasoline. Can be cleaned.

WORN
- Identified by severly eroded or worn electrodes.
- Caused by normal wear. Should be replaced.

PREIGNITION
- Identified by melted electrodes and possibly blistered insulator. Metallic deposits on insulator indicate engine damage.
- Caused by wrong type of fuel, in correct ignition timing or advance, too hot a plug, burned valves or engine overheating. Replace the plug.

OVERHEATING
- Identified by a white or light gray insulator with small black or gray brown spots and with bluish-burnt appearance of electrodes.
- Caused by engine overheating, wrong type of fuel, loose spark plugs, too hot a plug or incorrect ignition timing. Replace the plug.

FUSED SPOT DEPOSIT
- Identified by melted or spotty deposits resembling bubbles or blisters
- Caused by sudden acceleration. Can be cleaned.

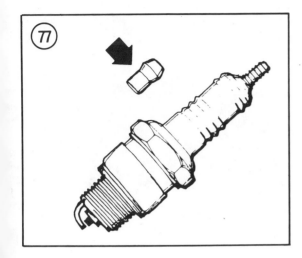

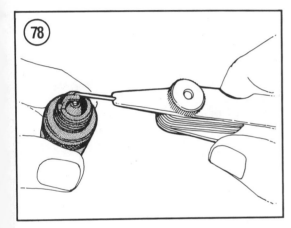

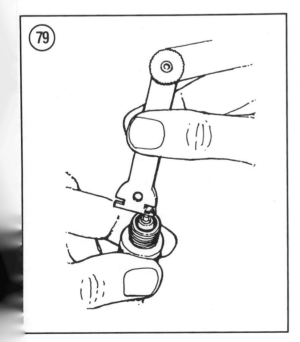

ELECTRONIC IGNITION

The ignition system on these models is completely electronic. No mechanical advance unit is used. The ignition timing is fixed and no adjustment is provided. If the engine is running poorly and the trouble has been traced to the ignition system, refer to Chapter Two for troubleshooting procedures.

CARBURETOR

Idle Speed

Proper idle speed setting is necessary to prevent stalling and to provide adequate engine compression braking, but you can't set it perfectly with the bike's tachometer—it's not accurate at the low rpm range. A portable tachometer is required for this procedure.

1. Place the bike on its centerstand.
2. Attach a portable tachometer, following the manufacturer's instructions.
3. Start the engine and warm it to normal operating temperature.
4. Sit on the seat while the engine is idling and adjust your weight to raise the front wheel off the ground. Turn the front wheel from side to side without touching the throttle grip. If the engine speed increases when the wheel is turned, the throttle cable(s) may be damaged or incorrectly adjusted. Perform the *Throttle Cable Adjustment* described in this chapter.
5. Turn the throttle stop screw (**Figure 80**) to set the idle speed as specified in **Table 11**.
6. Rev the engine a couple of times to see if it settles down to the set speed. Readjust, if necessary.

Carburetor Synchronization

Synchronizing the carburetors makes sure that one cylinder doesn't try to run faster than the others, cutting power and gas mileage. You can check for a rough balance by listening to the exhaust noise at idle and feeling pressure at the mufflers, but the only accurate way to synchronize the carburetors is to use a set of vacuum gauges that measure the intake vacuum of both cylinders at the same time.

1. Start the engine and warm it up fully.
2. Adjust the idle speed as described in this chapter.
3. Remove the fuel tank as described in Chapter Seven.
4. Install an auxiliary fuel tank onto the motorcycle and attach its fuel hose to the carburetor.

> *NOTE*
> *Carburetor synchronization cannot be performed with the stock fuel tank in place because of the lack of room required to install the gauges and make adjustments. An auxiliary fuel tank is required to supply fuel to the carburetors during this procedure.*

> *NOTE*
> *Fuel tanks from small displacement motorcycles and ATV's make excellent auxiliary fuel tanks. Make sure the tank is mounted securely and positioned so that connecting fuel hose is not kinked or obstructed.*

> *WARNING*
> *When supplying fuel by temporary means, make sure the fuel tank is secure and that all fuel lines are tight with no leaks.*

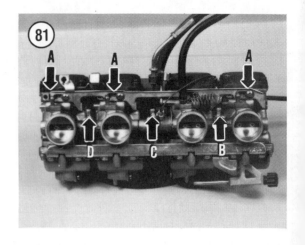

5. Remove the vacuum port plugs. A, **Figure 81** shows the vacuum ports with the carburetors removed for clarity.
6. Start the engine and check that the difference between the cylinders is less than 2 cm Hg. Identical readings are desirable.
7. If the difference is greater, perform the following:
    a. The carburetor adjusting screws are identified in **Figure 81**.
    b. With the engine at idle, synchronize the No. 1 and No. 2 carburetors by turning the left-hand adjusting screw (B, **Figure 81**).
    c. Then synchronize the No. 3 and No. 4 carburetors by turning the right-hand adjusting screw (D, **Figure 81**).
    d. Finally synchronize the No. 1 and No. 2 carburetors to the No. 3 and No. 4 carburetors by turning the middle adjusting screw (C, **Figure 81**).
8. Reset the idle speed, stop the engine and install the vacuum plugs.
9. Install the fuel tank.

Tables are on the following pages.

Table 1 MAINTENANCE SCHEDULE

Weekly/gas stop	• Check tire pressure cold; adjust to suit load and speed • Check brakes for a solid feel • Check brake lever play; adjust if necessary • Check brake pedal play; adjust if necessary • Check throttle grip for smooth opening and return • Check clutch lever play; adjust if necessary • Check for smooth but not loose steering • Check axles, suspension, controls and linkage nuts, bolts and fasteners; tighten if necessary • Check engine oil level; add oil if necessary • Check lights and horn operation, especially brake light • Check for any abnormal engine noise and leaks • Check coolant level • Check kill switch operation • Lubricate drive chain
Monthly/500 miles (800 km)	• Check battery electrolyte level (more frequently in hot weather); add distilled water if necessary • Check disc brake fluid level; add if necessary • Check drive chain tension; adjust if necessary
6 months/3,000 miles (5,000 km)	• All above checks and the following: • Check carburetor synchronization; adjust if necessary • Check carburetor idle speed; adjust if necessary • Check spark plugs, set gap; replace if necessary • Check air suction valve • Check evaporative emission control system * • Check brake pad wear • Check brake light switch operation; adjust if necessary • Check rear brake pedal free play; adjust if necessary • Adjust clutch • Check steering play; adjust if necessary • Check drive chain wear • Change engine oil and filter • Check tire wear • Lubricate all pivot points • Check and tighten all nuts, bolts and fasteners • Clean air filter element
Yearly/6,000 miles (10,000 km)	• Check throttle free play; adjust if necessary • Check valve clearance; adjust if necessary • Lubricate swing arm pivot shaft • Lubricate Uni-trak linkage • Check radiator hoses • Check fuel system hoses, clamps and all fittings
2 years/12,000 miles 20,000 km)	• Change front fork oil • Change brake fluid • Change coolant • Lubricate steering stem bearings • Replace master cylinder cups and seals • Replace caliper piston seal and dust seal • Replace anti-dive brake plunger parts • Lubricate wheel bearings • Lubricate speedometer gear
Every 4 years	• Replace fuel hoses

* California models.

Table 2 TIRES AND TIRE PRESSURE *

Model/tire size	Pressure	Tire wear limit
Front-110/90 V 16	32 psi (2.25 kg/cm²)	1 mm (1/32 in.)
Rear-130/90 V 16	36 psi (2.50 kg/cm²)	3 mm (1/8 in.)

* Check tire pressure when cold

Table 3 STATE OF CHARGE

Specific Gravity	State of Charge
1.110-1.130	Discharged
1.140-1.160	Almost discharged
1.170-1.190	One-quarter charged
1.200-1.220	One-half charged
1.230-1.250	Three-quarters charged
1.260-1.280	Fully charged

Table 4 RECOMMENDED LUBRICANTS AND FUEL

Engine oil	SAE 10W40, 10W50, 20W50, 20W50, rated SE or SF
Front fork oil	SAE 10W20
Brake fluid	DOT 3
Fuel	87 pump octane (RON + Mon)/2
	91 research octane (RON)
Battery	Distilled water
Cooling system	Permanent type antifreeze compounded for aluminum engines and radiator

Table 5 ENGINE OIL CAPACITY

	Liter	U.S. qt.
Without filter change	2.6	2.7
With filter change	3.0	3.2

Table 6 FRONT FORK OIL CAPACITY

Change	Rebuild	Oil level
273 cc	317-325 cc	332-336 mm
(9.23 oz.)	(10.72-11.00 oz)	(13.071-13.228 in.)

Table 7 COOLING SYSTEM SPECIFICATIONS

Capacity	2.0 L (2.1 qts.)
Coolant ratio	57 percent water/43 percent coolant
Radiator cap	14-18 psi (0.95-1.25 kg/cm²)
Thermostat	
Opening temperature	157.1-163.0 F (69.5-72.5 C)
Valve opening lift	Not less than 8 mm (5/16 in.)
	@ 203° F (95° C)

Table 8 FRONT FORK AIR PRESSURE

	kg/cm²	psi
Standard	0.6	8.5
Usable range	0.5-0.7	7.1-10.0
Maximum	2.50	36

Table 9 REAR SHOCK ABSORBER AIR PRESSURE

Road/load conditions	kg/cm²	psi
Good/light	0	0
Bad/hard	3.5	35

Table 10 DAMPING ADJUSTMENT

Adjuster position	Load	Road	Speed
1	Light	Good	Slow
2			
3			
4	Heavy	Rough	High

Table 11 TUNE-UP SPECIFICATIONS

Spark plug gap	0.6-0.7 mm (0.024-0.028 in.)
Valve clearance (cold)	
Intake	0.13-0.18 mm (0.005-0.007 in.)
Exhaust	0.18-0.23 mm (0.007-0.009 in.)
Idle speed	
ZX500	1,150-1,700 rpm
ZX600 (except California)	1,000-1,100 rpm
ZX600 California	1,250-1,800 rpm
Compression	7.7-12.0 kb/cm² (109-171 psi)

Table 12 SPARK PLUGS

	Standard riding	High speed riding	Low speed riding
U.S.	NGKD9EA	NGK D9EA	NGKD8EA
	ND X27ES-U	ND X27ES-U	ND X24EX-U
Canada	NGK DR8ES	NGK DR8ES	NGKDR8ES-L
	ND X27ESR-U	ND X27ESR-U	ND X24ESR-U
Italy	NGK D9EA	NGK D9EA	NGK D8EA
	ND X27ES-U	ND X27ES-U	ND X24ES-U
All Europe	NGK DR8ES	NGK DR8ES	NGK DR8ES-L
except Italy	ND X27ES-U	ND X27ES-U	ND X24ES-U

NOTE: If you own a 1988 or later model, first check the Supplement at the back of this book for any new service information.

CHAPTER FOUR

ENGINE

The engine is a liquid-cooled double overhead cam eight-valve parallel four. Valves are operated by two chain-driven overhead camshafts.

This chapter provides complete service and overhaul procedures, including information for disassembly, removal, inspection, service and reassembly of the engine.

Before starting any work, read the service hints in Chapter One. You will do a better job with this information fresh in your mind.

Table 1 lists engine specifications. **Tables 1-4** are at the end of the chapter.

SERVICING ENGINE IN FRAME

Many components can be serviced while the engine is mounted in the frame:

  a. Cylinder head.
  b. Cylinders and pistons.
  c. Gearshift mechanism.
  d. Clutch.
  e. Carburetors.
  f. Starter motor.
  g. Alternator and electrical systems.

ENGINE PRINCIPLES

Figure 1 explains how the engine works. This will be helpful when troubleshooting or repairing your engine.

ENGINE

Removal/Installation

1. Place the motorcycle on its centerstand.
2. Remove the fairing assembly. See Chapter Thirteen.
3. Disconnect the negative battery terminal (**Figure 2**).
4. Remove the fuel tank and seat.
5. Drain the engine oil as described in Chapter Three.
6. Drain the cooling system as described in Chapter Three.
7. Disconnect the spark plug wires. Then disconnect the ignition coil electrical connector and remove the coils (A, **Figure 3**).
8. *U.S. models:* Disconnect the hoses and remove the air suction valve (B, **Figure 3**).
9. Remove the following as described in Chapter Nine:
   a. Radiator.
   b. Thermostat housing.
10. Remove the exhaust system as described in Chapter Seven.
11. Remove the carburetors as described in Chapter Seven.
12. Remove the oil cooler as described in this chapter.

①

4-STROKE PRINCIPLES

4

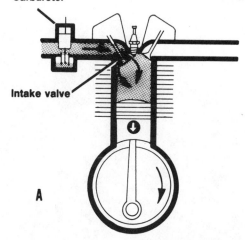

Carburetor

Intake valve

A

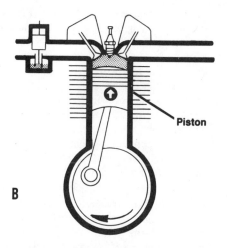

Piston

B

As the piston travels downward, the exhaust valve is closed and the intake valve opens, allowing the new air-fuel mixture from the carburetor to be drawn into the cylinder. When the piston reaches the bottom of its travel (BDC), the intake valve closes and remains closed for the next 1 1/2 revolutions of the crankshaft.

While the crankshaft continues to rotate, the piston moves upward, compressing the air-fuel mixture.

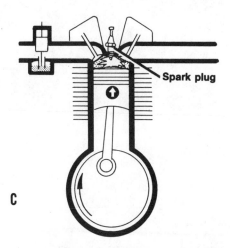

Spark plug

C

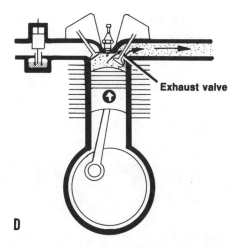

Exhaust valve

D

As the piston almost reaches the top of its travel, the spark plug fires, igniting the compressed air-fuel mixture. The piston continues to top dead center (TDC) and is pushed downward by the expanding gases.

When the piston almost reaches BDC, the exhaust valve opens and remains open until the piston is near TDC. The upward travel of the piston forces the exhaust gases out of the cylinder. After the piston has reached TDC, the exhaust valve closes and the cycle starts all over again.

13. Loosen the clutch cable at the hand grip. Then disconnect the clutch cable at the crankcase.

14. Disconnect the crankcase breather hose.

15. Remove the front and rear screws (**Figure 4**) and slide the gear shift lever off of the shift shaft and pivot stud.

16. Remove the engine sprocket cover (**Figure 5**).

17. Remove the engine sprocket as described under *Engine Sprocket Removal/Installation* in Chapter Six.

18. Disconnect the following wiring connectors:
   a. Neutral switch (**Figure 6**).
   b. Starter motor connector.
   c. Alternator wiring connector (**Figure 7**).
   d. Side stand switch connector (A, **Figure 8**).
   e. Pick-up coil connector (**Figure 9**).
   f. Oil pressure switch connector (underneath engine at oil filter housing).

19. *Engine disassembly:* If the engine requires disassembly, it will be easier to remove many of the large sub-assembles while the engine is mounted in the frame. Remove the following as described in this chapter unless otherwise noted:
   a. Cylinder head.
   b. Cylinder block.
   c. Pistons.
   d. Alternator and pickup coil (Chapter Eight).
   e. Starter (Chapter Eight).
   f. Clutch (Chapter Five).
   g. External external shift mechanism (Chapter Six).

20. Place wooden blocks under the crankcase to support the engine once the mounting bolts are removed.

NOTE
If the engine is being removed as a complete assembly, the down tubes (A, Figure 10) can be left mounted to the engine to serve as a grab point.

21. Remove the left- and right-hand frame down tube mounting bolts and remove the down tubes (A, **Figure 10**). See B, **Figure 10** (front) and B, **Figure 8** (rear).

22. Remove the front engine mounting bolts (**Figure 11**).

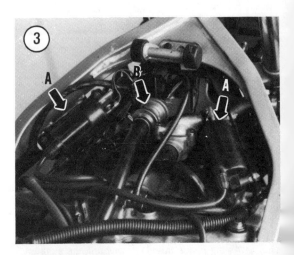

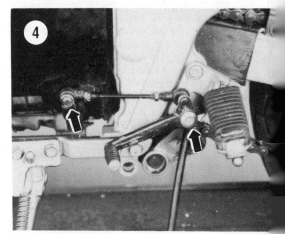

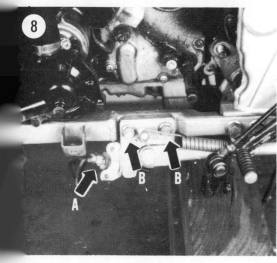

4

23. Remove the 2 rear engine mounting nuts (**Figure 12**). **Figure 13** shows how to remove the top nut.

> *WARNING*
> *One or more assistants will be required to remove the engine from the frame. Do not attempt engine removal by yourself.*

24. Support the engine with wood blocks or a small jack and remove the rear engine mounting bolts from the right-hand side. Remove the spacer from the lower mounting bolt on the right-hand side.

25. Lower the engine and remove it from the frame. See **Figure 14** or **Figure 15**.

26. While the engine is removed for service, check all of the frame engine mounts for cracks or other damage. See **Figure 16** (front) and **Figure 17** (rear). If any cracks are detected, take the chassis assembly to a Kawasaki dealer for further examination.

27. Install by reversing the removal steps. Note the following.

28. Install the spacer onto the lower engine mount bolt.

29. Tighten the engine mount nuts and bolts as follows:
  a. Front engine mount bolts (**Figure 11**): 34 N•m (25 ft.-lb.).
  b. All other bolts: 25 N•m (18 ft.-lb.).

30. Fill the crankcase with the recommended type and quantity of engine oil. Refer to *Engine Oil and Filter Change* in Chapter Three.

31. Refill the cooling system. See *Coolant Change* in Chapter Three.

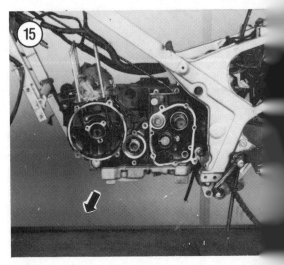

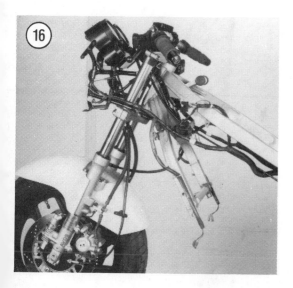

32. Adjust the following as described in Chapter Three:
    a. Clutch.
    b. Drive chain.
    c. Rear brake.
    d. Throttle cables.
    e. Choke cable.
33. Start the engine and check for leaks.
34. Install the fairing assembly. See Chapter Thirteen.

CYLINDER HEAD COVER AND CAMSHAFTS

This section describes removal, inspection and installation procedures for the camshaft components.

Cylinder Head Cover Removal/Installation

1. Park the bike on the centerstand.
2. Drain the engine coolant as described under *Coolant Change* in Chapter Three.
3. Remove the upper and lower fairings. See Chapter Thirteen.
4. Remove the fuel tank. See Chapter Seven.
5. Remove the ignition coils and brackets. See Chapter Eight.
6. Remove the thermostat housing as described in Chapter Nine.
7. Remove the vacuum switch as described under *Vacuum Switch Removal/Installation* in Chapter Seven.
8. Remove the baffle plate mounting bolts and slide the baffle plate (**Figure 18**) out of the frame.
9. Remove the cylinder head cover bolts and remove the cover (**Figure 19**).

NOTE
*A cam chain guide is installed in the cylinder head cover (**Figure 20**).*

10. Rem ɔve the 4 cylinder head cover dowel pins from the middle of the cylinder head. **Figure 21** shows the dowel pins for the right-hand side.

11. Installation is the reverse of these steps, noting the following.

12. Replace the cylinder head cover gasket if necessary. Note the following:
   a. Remove all residue from the head cover and cylinder head mating surfaces.
   b. Apply a non-hardening gasket sealer (such as RTV) to the 4 cylinder head cavities. **Figure 22** shows one of the cavities.
   c. Apply a coat of liquid gasket to the cylinder head cover and install the new gasket onto the cover (**Figure 23**).

13. Install the 4 dowel pins (**Figure 21**).

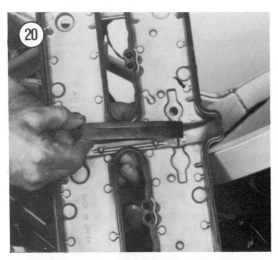

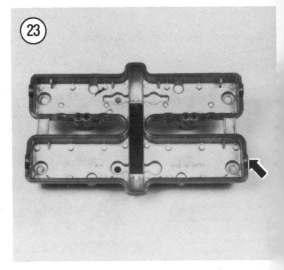

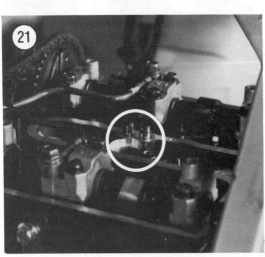

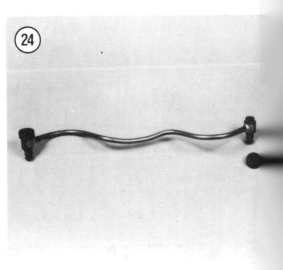

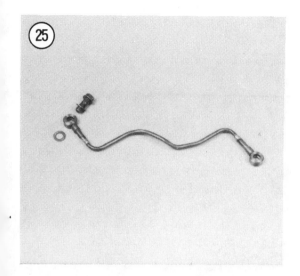

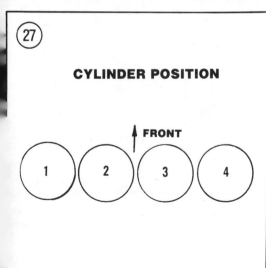

CYLINDER POSITION

↑ FRONT

1 2 3 4

14. Make sure the cam chain guide is installed in the cylinder head cover (**Figure 20**) before installing the cover.

> *CAUTION*
> *On late models, the camshaft oil pipes are no longer secured with banjo bolts and washers. Instead, 2 one-piece oil pipes with 4 rubber caps are used. **Figure 24** shows the new style oil pipes with rubber caps. **Figure 25** shows the old style with banjo bolts and washers. When installing the cylinder head cover, the late style rubber cap(s) can be easily knocked off one or more of the oil pipes. If this should happen the oil pipe(s) will loosen in their camshaft caps and cause loss of oil pressure and severe engine damage. When installing the cylinder head cover on these models, work the cover into position carefully and make sure all 4 rubber caps are in place.*

15. Install the cylinder head cover and tighten the bolts to the specifications in **Table 2**.
16. Refill the engine coolant as described under *Coolant Change* in Chapter Three.

Camshaft Removal

1. Remove the cylinder head cover as described in this chapter.
2. Disconnect the battery ground cable.
3. Remove the spark plugs. This will make it easier to turn the engine by hand.
4. Remove the pick-up coil cover (**Figure 26**).

> *NOTE*
> *Figure 27 identifies cylinder numbering.*

5. Use a wrench on the crankshaft nut (**Figure 28**) and rotate the engine clockwise until the top dead

center (TDC) rotor mark for the No. 1 and No. 4 cylinders aligns with the fixed pointer on the crankcase (**Figure 29**). No. 1 and 4 cylinders are now at top dead center (TDC) on the compression stroke.

6. Remove the camshaft chain tensioner as described in this chapter.

7A. *Early models:* Loosen the oil pipe bolts and remove the bolts, copper washers and oil pipes. See **Figure 30**.

7B. *Late models:* Remove the oil pipe rubber caps and lift the oil pipes out of the camshaft caps. **Figure 24** shows an oil pipe with its rubber caps.

> *CAUTION*
> *The oil pipes can be easily damaged.*
> *Place them in a box until reassembly.*

8. Loosen the valve adjuster locknuts and loosen the adjusters.

> *NOTE*
> *Each camshaft cap is marked with an arrow (pointing forward) and with a letter representing position. See **Figure 31** and **Figure 32**. If the camshaft cap markings on your bike differ from those in **Figure 32** or there are no marks, label them for direction and position before performing Step 9.*

> *NOTE*
> *The 2 caps (with arrows only) installed on the left-hand side of the intake and exhaust cam sprockets are not camshaft caps. See **Figure 33**.*

9. Remove the camshaft cap bolts and remove the caps (**Figure 34**).

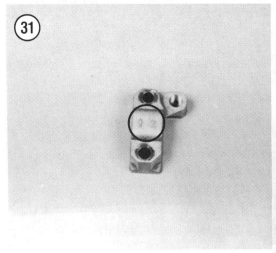

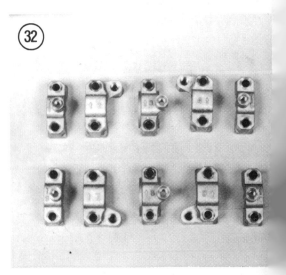

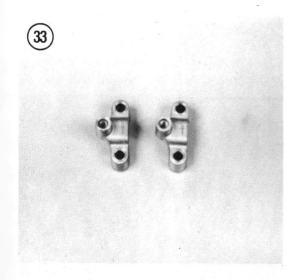

(33)

10. Secure the camshaft chain with wire. Then remove both camshafts with their sprockets (**Figure 35**). Remove the camshafts slowly to prevent damaging any cam lobe or bearing surface.

> *CAUTION*
> *The crankshaft can be turned with the camshafts removed. However, pull the camshaft chain tight to prevent it from binding at the crankshaft sprocket.*

Camshaft Inspection

1. Check cam lobes (A, **Figure 36**) for wear. The lobes should not be scored and the edges should be square. Slight damage may be removed with a silicon caride oilstone. Use No. 100-120 grit initially, then polish with a No. 280-320 grit.

2. Even though the cam lobe surfaces appear to be satisfactory, with no visible signs of wear, they must be measured with a micrometer as shown in **Figure 37**. Replace the shaft(s) if worn beyond the

4

(34)

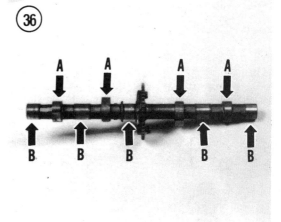

(36)

(35)

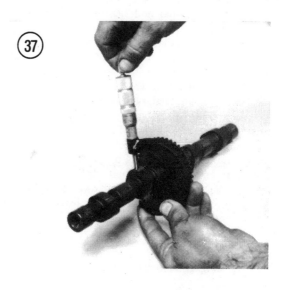

(37)

service limits (if measurements are less than those given in **Table 1**).

3. Check the camshaft bearing journals (B, **Figure 36**) for wear and scoring.

4. Even though the camshaft bearing journal surfaces appear satisfactory, with no visible signs of wear, the camshaft bearing journals must be measured with a micrometer (**Figure 38**). Replace the shaft(s) if worn beyond the service limits (if measurements are less than those given in **Table 1**).

5. Place the camshaft on a set of V-blocks and check its runout with a dial indicator. Replace the camshaft if runout exceeds specifications in **Table 1**. Repeat for the opposite camshaft.

6. Inspect the camshaft sprockets (**Figure 39**) for wear. Replace if necessary.

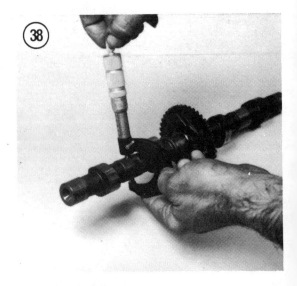

NOTE
If the camshaft sprockets are worn, also check the camshaft chain, chain guides and chain tensioner as described in this chapter.

7. Check the camshaft bearing bores in the cylinder head (**Figure 40**) and camshaft caps (**Figure 41**) for wear and scoring. They should not be scored or excessively worn. If they are, replace the cylinder head and camshaft caps as a matched set.

Camshaft Bearing Clearance Measurement

This procedure requires the use of a Plastigage set. The camshaft must be installed into the head. Before installation, wipe all oil residue from each cam bearing journal and bearing surface in the head and all camshaft caps.

1. Install the camshafts into the cylinder head.

2. Install all locating dowels into their camshaft caps.

3. Wipe all oil from the cam bearing journals before using the Plastigage material.

4. Place a strip of Plastigage material on top of each cam bearing journal (**Figure 42**), parallel to the cam.

5. Place the camshaft cap into position.

6. Install all camshaft cap bolts. Install finger-tight at first, then tighten in a crisscross pattern (**Figure 43**) to the final torque specification listed in **Table 2**.

CAUTION
Do not rotate the camshaft with the Plastigage material in place.

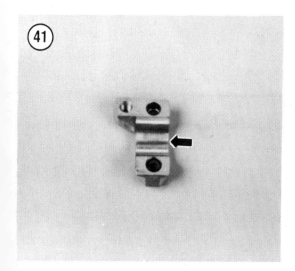

7. Gradually remove the camshaft cap bolts in a crisscross pattern. Remove the camshaft caps carefully.

8. Measure the width of the flattened Plastigage according to manufacturer's instructions (**Figure 44**).

9. If the clearance exceeds the wear limits in **Table 1**, measure the camshaft bearing journals (**Figure 38**) with a micrometer and compare to the limits in **Table 1**. If the camshaft bearing journal is less than dimension specified, replace the cam. If the cam is within specifications, the cylinder head and camshaft caps must be replaced as a matched set.

> *CAUTION*
> *Remove all particles of Plastigage from all camshaft bearing journals and the camshaft holder. Be sure to clean the camshaft holder groove. This material must not be left in the engine as it can plug up an oil control orifice and cause severe engine damage.*

Oil Pipe
Cleaning/Inspection

1. Examine the oil pipes for damage. Check the brazed joints for cracking or other abnormal

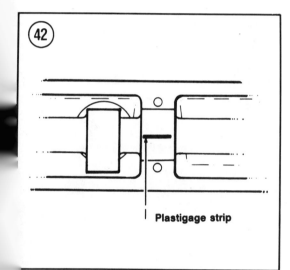

Plastigage strip

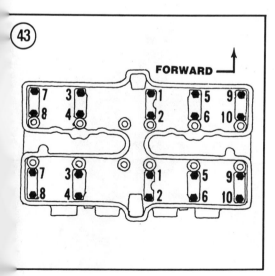

FORWARD

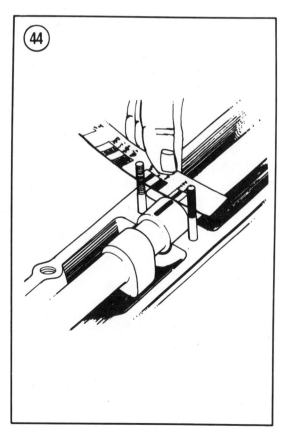

conditions. On late models, replace the oil pipe O-rings (**Figure 45**) if deformed or damaged.

2. Flush the oil pipes and bolts with solvent and allow to dry before installation.

Camshaft Chain and Sprockets Inspection/Replacement

1. Examine the camshaft sprockets (**Figure 39**) for any signs of wear, cracks or tooth damage. If the camshaft sprockets are worn, also check the camshaft chain and the crankshaft drive sprocket for wear. See *Crankshaft Inspection* in this chapter. Severe wear of one component will require the replacement of both sprockets and chain.

2. Check camshaft chain stretch as follows:
   a. Lay the chain on a workbench and stretch a 21-pin segment as shown in **Figure 46**.
   b. Measure 21 pins with a vernier caliper (**Figure 46**) at several points around the chain.
   c. Replace the camshaft chain if the length of 21 pins exceeds the service limit listed in **Table 1**.

3. The intake and exhaust sprockets are identical. If the sprockets were removed from the camshafts, note the following before installation:
   a. Install the sprockets onto each camshaft so that the sprocket sides marked IN and EX face to the left-hand side (**Figure 47**).
   b. There are 4 holes drilled into each sprocket. Two sprocket holes are marked IN and the other two holes are marked EX. Align the sprocket holes marked IN with the intake camshaft bolt holes. Align the sprocket holes marked EX with the exhaust camshaft bolt holes. See **Figure 47**.
   c. Apply Loctite 242 (blue) to the sprocket bolts and tighten to the torque specifications in **Table 2**.

Camshaft Installation

1. If camshaft bearing clearance was checked, make sure all Plastigage material has been removed from the camshaft and bearing cap surfaces.

> *CAUTION*
> *When rotating the crankshaft in Step 2, lift the cam chain tightly on the exhaust side (front) to prevent it from binding on the crankshaft sprocket.*

2. Use a wrench on the large crankshaft nut and rotate the engine clockwise until the top dead center (TDC) rotor mark for the No. 1 and 4 cylinders aligns with the fixed pointer on the crankcase (**Figure 48**). No. 1 and 4 cylinders are

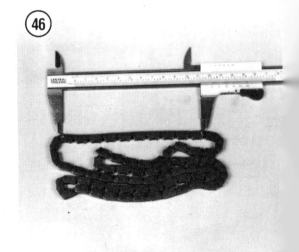

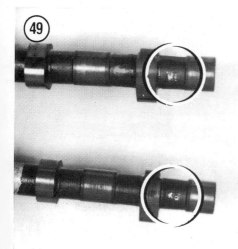

now at top dead center (TDC) on the compression stroke.

3. Coat all camshaft lobes and bearing journals with molybdenum disulfide grease or assembly oil.

4. Also coat the bearing surfaces in the cylinder head and camshaft bearing caps.

NOTE
*Identification marks are cast into each camshaft. The exhaust camshaft is marked with EX and the intake camshaft with IN. See **Figure 49**.*

5. Lift the cam chain and slide the exhaust camshaft through and set it in the front bearing blocks (**Figure 35**). Install the intake camshaft through the cam chain and set it in the rear bearing blocks.

6. Without turning the crankshaft, align the EX line on the exhaust cam sprocket and the IN on the intake cam sprocket with the upper cylinder head surface as viewed from the right-hand side of the engine (**Figure 50**). If the cam chain has been set onto the sprockets, it may be necessary to lift the cam chain off the sprockets and reposition the camshafts.

7. Refer to **Figure 50**. Locate the first cam chain link pin that aligns with the exhaust sprocket EX mark. Beginning with this mark, count off 42 cam chain link pins toward the intake sprocket. The 42nd pin must align with the intake camshaft IN mark. If the pin count is incorrect, recount and reposition the intake or exhaust camshaft as required.

8. Check that the cam chain is properly seated in the front and rear cam chain guides.

9. Check that the camshaft cap dowel pins are in place and loosely install the camshaft caps (**Figure 51**) in their original positions. The arrow on each

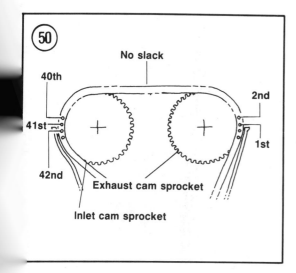

No slack

40th

41st

42nd

2nd

1st

Exhaust cam sprocket

Inlet cam sprocket

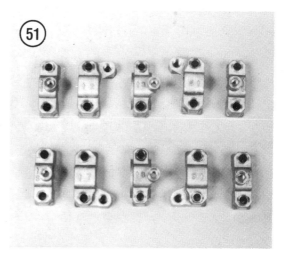

cap (**Figure 52**) must face to the front of the bike and the location numbering on the cap must correspond to the numbering (**Figure 53**) cast into the cylinder head.

> *CAUTION*
> *The camshaft caps were machined with the cylinder head at the time of manufacturer. If the caps are not installed in their original positions, camshaft seizure may result.*

10. Tighten the camshaft cap bolts marked No. 1 and 2 (**Figure 43**) for the exhaust and intake cams. This will seat the camshafts in position. Then tighten all bolts in a crisscross pattern (**Figure 43**) to the torque specification in **Table 2**.

11. Slowly turn the crankshaft clockwise 2 full turns, using the large crankshaft bolt (**Figure 54**). Check that all timing marks again align as shown in **Figure 50** when the No. 1 and 4 cylinder TDC mark on the rotor aligns with the crankcase timing mark (**Figure 48**). **Figure 55** and **Figure 56** show sprocket alignment with the No. 1 and 4 cylinder at TDC. If all marks align as indicated, cam timing is correct.

> *CAUTION*
> *If there is any binding while turning the crankshaft, **stop**. Recheck the camshaft timing marks. Improper timing can cause valve and piston damage.*

12. If the cam timing is incorrect, remove the camshaft caps and reposition the camshafts as described in Steps 5-11.

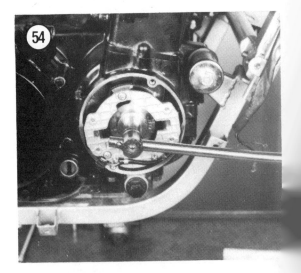

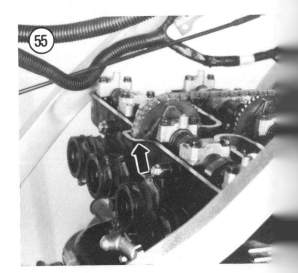

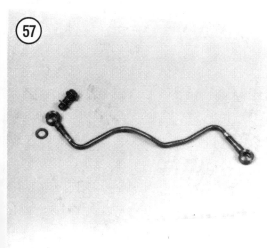

13A. *Early models:* Position the oil pipes into the cylinder head. Then install the banjo bolts with a copper washer placed on both sides of the pipe bolt fittings. See **Figure 57**.

13B. *Late models:* Make sure each oil pipe shaft is equipped with an O-ring (**Figure 45**). Then align the pipe shafts with the oil gallery holes in the camshaft caps and insert the oil pipe shafts into them. Install a rubber cap onto each pipe bolt (**Figure 58**).

14. Install the cam chain tensioner as described in this chapter.

15. Adjust the valves as described under *Valve Adjustment* in Chapter Three.

16. Install the cylinder head cover as described in this chapter.

> *CAUTION*
> *Make sure to read the CAUTION listed under* **Cylinder Head Cover Removal/Installation** *to prevent camshaft seizure on late models.*

CAM CHAIN TENSIONER

The automatic tensioner is continually self-adjusting. The tensioner pushrod is free to move inward, but can't move out. Whenever the cam chain tensioner bolts are loosened, the tensioner assembly must be completely removed and reset as described in this section.

Removal/Installation

1. Remove the fuel tank and carburetors. See Chapter Seven.

2. Loosen the front cam chain tensioner cap bolt (**Figure 59**) and remove the following:

　　a. Cap bolt (**Figure 59**).

4

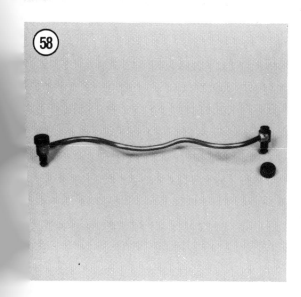

   b. Spring (**Figure 60**).
   c. Pushrod stop (**Figure 61**).
3. Remove the 2 tensioner mounting bolts and pull
the tensioner housing (**Figure 62**) away from the
engine.
4. Clean the tensioner assembly as follows:
   a. Pull the pin (**Figure 63**) out of the tensioner
      body and remove the pushrod (A, **Figure 64**)
      and spring (B, **Figure 64**).
   b. Clean the tensioner assembly (**Figure 65**) in
      solvent and dry thoroughly.
   c. Replace the tensioner housing O-ring (**Figure
      66**) if cracked, damaged or if the tensioner
      leaked oil.
   d. Apply molybdenum disulfide grease to all
      tensioner component sliding surfaces.
5. Align the slot in the pushrod (C, **Figure 64**) with
the pin hole (**Figure 63**) in the tensioner housing.
Then slide the spring on the pushrod (**Figure 64**)
and insert the pushrod into the tensioner body
(**Figure 63**).
6. Push the pushrod to compress the spring. Then
align the hole in the tensioner body with the slot on
the pushrod and install the pin (**Figure 63**) through
the tensioner body and engage with the pushrod
slot.
7. Align the tensioner housing with the cylinder
head and place it in position. Install the tensioner
bolts and tighten securely.
8. Align the pushrod and pushrod stop sliding
surfaces (tapered portion) and install the pushrod
stop (**Figure 61**). When the pushrod stop is
installed correctly, the end of the stop will extend
through the end of the tensioner body
approximately 5 mm (3/16 in.). See **Figure 67**.

NOTE
If the pushrod stop extends through the
end of the tensioner body by more than
5 mm (3/16 in.), the camshaft chain
slack has not been taken up. Rotate the
crankshaft clockwise until the pushrod
measurement is correct. If the pushrod
sticks out much more or less after
rotating the engine, the cam chain,
guides or sprockets may be excessively
worn.

9. Slide the spring (**Figure 60**) onto the pushrod
stop.
10. Install the tensioner cap bolt (**Figure 59**) and
tighten securely.
11. Install the carburetors and fuel tank. See
Chapter Seven.

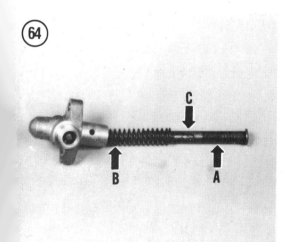

ROCKER ARM ASSEMBLIES

The rocker arms are identical (same Kawasaki part number), but they will develop different wear patterns during use. All parts should be marked during removal so they can be assembled in their original positions.

Removal

1. Remove the camshafts as described in this chapter.
2. Remove the rocker arm shafts as follows:
    a. Remove one of the rocker arm shaft plugs with an Allen wrench (**Figure 68**).

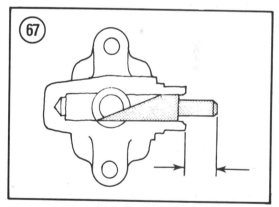

b. Pull the rocker arm locating pin (**Figure 69**) out of the cylinder head.

c. Thread a M8×1.25 bolt (approximately 30 mm long) into the end of the rocker arm and pull the rocker arm out of the cylinder head (**Figure 70**).

3. Lift the rocker arm and spring (**Figure 71**) out of the cylinder head.

4. Repeat Step 2 and Step 3 for the remaining rocker arms.

Inspection

1. Wash all parts (**Figure 72**) in cleaning solvent and dry thoroughly.

2. Check each rocker arm spring for fatigue, cracks or other damage. Replace if necessary.

3. Inspect the rocker arm pad (A, **Figure 73**) where it rides on the cam lobe and where the adjusters (**Figure 74**) ride on the valve stems. If the pad is scratched or unevenly worn, inspect the cam lobe for scoring, chipping or flat spots. Replace the rocker arm if defective.

> *NOTE*
> *If the rocker arm pad (A, **Figure 73**) is worn, also check the mating cam lobe for wear or damage.*

4. Measure the inside diameter of the rocker arm bore (A, **Figure 75**) with an inside micrometer and check against dimension in **Table 1**. Replace if worn to the service limit or greater.

5. Inspect the rocker arm shaft for wear or scoring. Measure the outside diameter (B, **Figure 75**) with a micrometer and check against dimension in **Table 1**. Replace if worn to the service limit or greater.

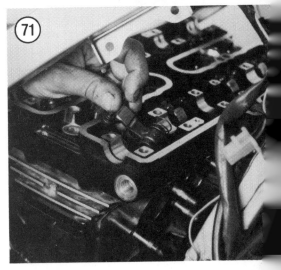

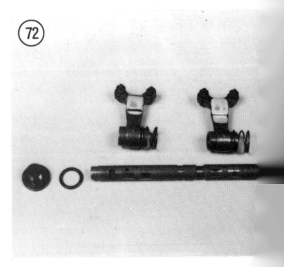

Installation

1. Coat the rocker arm shaft and rocker arm bore with assembly oil.

2. Assemble the spring (B, **Figure 73**) onto each rocker arm so that the spring will face to the inside of the engine after installation. See **Figure 76**.

3. Place the rocker arms and springs into the cylinder head (**Figure 71**). The valve adjusters will rest on the valves when the rocker arms are installed correctly.

> *CAUTION*
> *If the rocker arm shafts are installed backwards in Step 4, they will be difficult to remove.*

4. Thread the bolt onto the rocker arm as used during rocker arm shaft removal. Then insert the rocker arm through the cylinder head, rocker arms and springs.

5. Turn the rocker arm shaft to align the notch in the shaft (**Figure 77**) with the locating pin hole in the cylinder head. Then insert the locating pin (**Figure 69**) through the cylinder head hole and engage it with the rocker arm. Make sure the pin is pushed all the way in.

6. Remove the bolt from the rocker arm shaft.

7. Install the rocker arm shaft plugs (**Figure 68**) and tighten securely. Make sure an O-ring is installed on each plug.

8. Install the camshafts as described in this chapter.

4

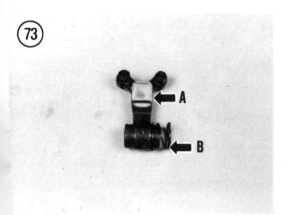

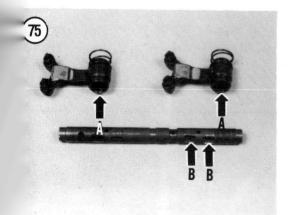

CYLINDER HEAD

Removal

1. Remove the cylinder head cover as described under *Cylinder Head Cover Removal/Installation* in this chapter.

2. Remove the camshafts as described in this chapter.

3. Remove the 2 cylinder head oil line banjo bolts (**Figure 78**) and copper washers.

4. Remove the front and rear cylinder head nuts and bolts (**Figure 79**).

5. Loosen the cylinder head nuts in a crisscross pattern (**Figure 80**) and remove the nuts and washers.

6. Loosen the cylinder head by tapping around the perimeter with a rubber or plastic mallet.

7. Remove the cylinder head by pulling straight up and off the cylinder. Place a clean shop rag into the cam chain tunnel in the cylinder to prevent the entry of foreign matter.

NOTE
After removing the cylinder head, check the top and bottom mating surfaces for any indications of leakage. Also check the head and base gaskets for signs of leakage. A blown gasket could indicate possible cylinder head warpage or other damage.

8. Remove the 2 dowel pins (A, **Figure 81**) and the cylinder head gasket.

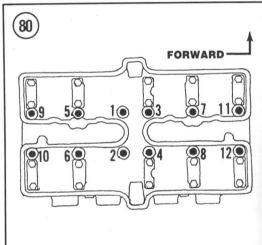

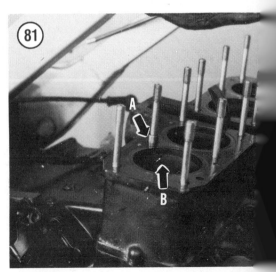

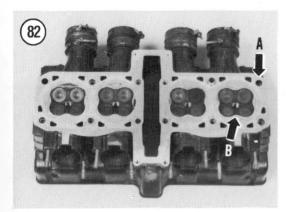

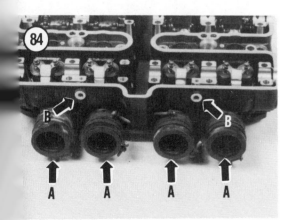

1. Feeler gauge
2. Straightedge

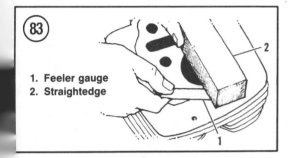

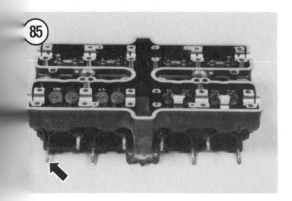

Cylinder Head Inspection

1. Remove all traces of gasket residue from head (A, **Figure 82**) and cylinder mating surfaces. Do not scratch the gasket surface.

2. Without removing valves, remove all carbon deposits from the combustion chambers (B, **Figure 82**) with a wire brush or wooden scraper. Take care not to damage the head, valves or spark plug threads.

> *CAUTION*
> *If the combustion chambers are cleaned while the valves are removed, make sure to keep the scraper or wire brush away from the valve seats to prevent damaging the seat surfaces. A damaged or even slightly scratched valve seat will cause poor valve seating.*

3. Examine the spark plug threads in the cylinder head for damage. If damage is minor or if the threads are dirty or clogged with carbon, use a spark plug thread tap to clean the threads following the manufacturer's instructions. If thread damage is severe, refer further service to a Kawasaki dealer or machine shop.

4. After all carbon is removed from combustion chambers and valve ports and the spark plug thread holes are repaired, clean the entire head in solvent.

5. Clean away all carbon on the piston crowns. Do not remove the carbon ridge at the top of the cylinder bore (B, **Figure 81**).

6. Check for cracks in the combustion chamber and exhaust ports. A cracked head must be replaced.

7. After the head has been thoroughly cleaned, place a straightedge across the gasket surface at several points (**Figure 83**). Measure warp by inserting a feeler gauge between the straightedge and cylinder head at each location. Maximum allowable warpage is listed in **Table 1**. Warpage or nicks in the cylinder head surface could cause an air leak and result in overheating. If warpage exceeds this limit, the cylinder head must be replaced.

8. Check the intake manifold boots (A, **Figure 84**) for cracks and damage that would allow unfiltered air to enter the engine. Also check the hose clamps for breakage or fatigue. Replace parts as necssary.

9. Check the exhaust pipe studs (**Figure 85**) for looseness or thread damage. Slight thread damage can be repaired with a thread file or die. If thread damage is severe, replace the damaged stud(s) as follows:

a. Screw two 6 mm nuts (thread size, not hex size) onto the end of a stud as shown in **Figure 86**.

b. With 2 wrenches, tighten the nuts against each other.

c. Unscrew the stud with a wrench on the lower nut (**Figure 87**).

d. Clean the tapped hole with solvent and check for thread damage or carbon build-up. If necessary, clean the threads with a 6×1.00 tap.

e. Remove the nuts from the old stud and install them on the end of a new stud.

f. Tighten the nuts against each other.

g. Apply Loctite 242 (blue) to the threads of the new stud.

h. Screw the stud into the cylinder head with a wrench on the upper nut. Tighten the stud securely.

i. Remove the nuts from the new stud.

10. Check the valves and valve guides as described under *Valves and Valve Components* in this chapter.

Installation

1. Clean the cylinder head (A, **Figure 82**) and cylinder mating surfaces of all gasket residue.

2. Blow out the cylinder head oil passages before installing the head. See B, **Figure 84** and **Figure 88**.

> *NOTE*
> *The cylinder head gasket is stamped with the word UP on one side (**Figure 89**). This side must face toward the right-hand side.*

3. Install a new head gasket and the 2 dowel pins (A, **Figure 81**).

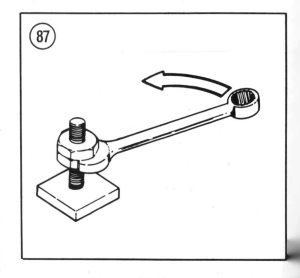

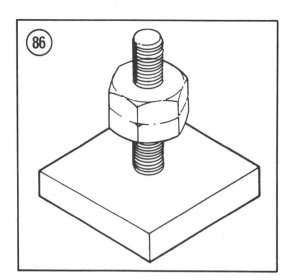

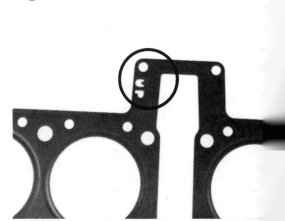

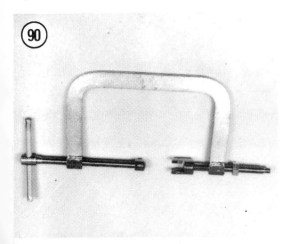

4. Install the cylinder head.
5. Install the bolts securing the cylinder head. Tighten the 10 mm bolts in 2-3 stages in a crisscross pattern (**Figure 80**) to the torque specifications listed in **Table 2**.
6. Tighten the front and rear (**Figure 79**) cylinder head bolts and nut to the torque specifications listed in **Table 2**.
7. Install the main oil pipe and banjo bolts, using new copper washers (**Figure 78**). Tighten the bolts to the specifications listed in **Table 2**.
8. Install the camshafts as described in this chapter.

VALVES AND VALVE COMPONENTS

Correct valve service requires a number of special tools. The following procedures describe how to check for valve component wear and to determine what type of service is required. In most cases, valve troubles are caused by poor valve seating, worn valve guides and burned valves. After removing the cylinder head and performing the following checks and procedures, have the valves and guides serviced by a Kawasaki dealer. A valve spring compressor (**Figure 90**) will be required to remove the valves.

Refer to **Figure 91** for this procedure.
1. Remove the cylinder head as described in this chapter.
2. Install a valve spring compressor squarely over the valve retainer with other end of tool placed against valve head.
3. Tighten valve spring compressor until the split valve keepers separate. Lift out split keepers with needlenose pliers.
4. Gradually loosen valve spring compressor and remove from head. Remove the valve spring retainer (**Figure 92**).

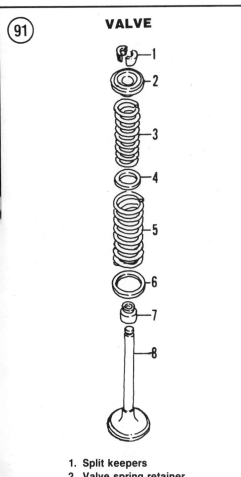

VALVE

1. Split keepers
2. Valve spring retainer
3. Inner valve spring
4. Spring seat
5. Outer valve spring
6. Spring seat
7. Oil seal
8. Valve

5. Remove the inner and outer valve springs (**Figure 93**).

6. Remove the inner valve spring seat (**Figure 94**).

7. Remove the outer valve spring seat (**Figure 95**).

> *CAUTION*
> *Remove any burrs from the valve stem grooves before removing the valve (**Figure 96**). Otherwise the valve guides will be damaged.*

8. Remove the valve.

9. Remove the oil seal (**Figure 97**).

> *CAUTION*
> *All component parts of each valve assembly (**Figure 98**) must be kept together. Do not mix with like components from other valves or excessive wear may result.*

10. Repeat Steps 2-9 and remove remaining valve(s).

Inspection

1. Clean valves in solvent. Do not gouge or damage the valve seating surface.

2. Inspect the contact surface of each valve for burning (**Figure 99**). Minor roughness and pitting can be removed by lapping the valve as described in this chapter. Excessive unevenness to the contact surface is an indication that the valve is not serviceable. The contact surface of the valve may be ground on a valve grinding machine, but it is best to replace a burned or damaged valve with a new one.

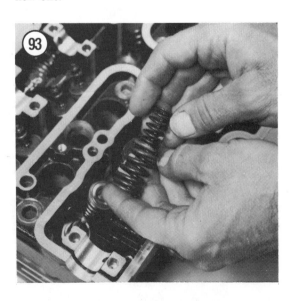

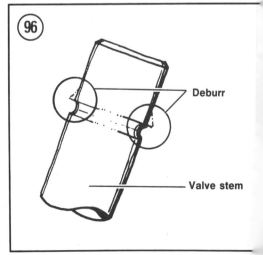

Deburr

Valve stem

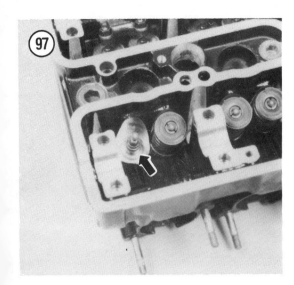

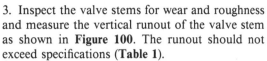

3. Inspect the valve stems for wear and roughness and measure the vertical runout of the valve stem as shown in **Figure 100**. The runout should not exceed specifications (**Table 1**).

4. Measure valve stems for wear using a micrometer (**Figure 101**). Compare with specifications in **Table 1**.

5. Remove all carbon and varnish from the valve guides with a stiff spiral wire brush before checking wear.

NOTE
Step 6 and Step 7 require special measuring equipment. If you do not have the required measuring devices, proceed to Step 8.

6. Measure each valve guide at top, center and bottom with a small hole gauge. Compare measurements with specifications in **Table 1**.

7. Subtract the measurement made in Step 4 from the measurement made in Step 6 above. The

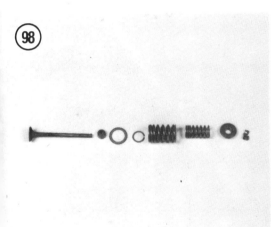

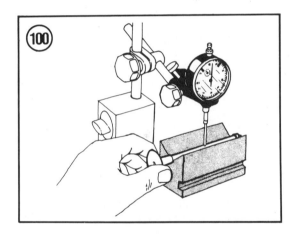

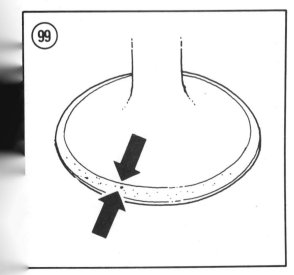

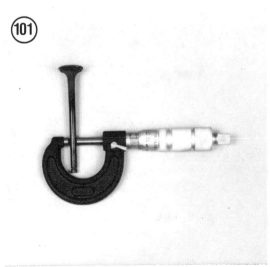

difference is the valve guide-to-valve stem clearance. See specifications in **Table 1** for correct clearance. Replace any guide or valve that is not within tolerance. Valve guide replacement is described later in this chapter.

8. If a small bore gauge is not available, measure the valve guide clearance as follows. A new intake and exhaust valve and dial indicator will be required.

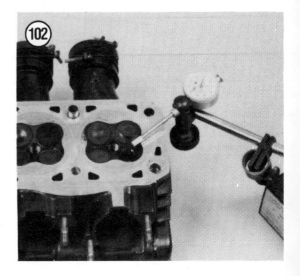

   a. Clean the valve guides as described in Step 5.

   b. Insert a *new* valve into one guide and set the plunger of a dial indicator so that it rests against the upper valve stem as shown in **Figure 102**.

   c. Move the valve back and forth and then from side to side. Record movement in both directions.

   d. Repeat for each valve guide.

   e. If the valve movement in either direction exceeds the valve guide clearance (wobble method) in **Table 1**, replace the valve guides as described in this chapter.

9. Measure the valve spring length with a vernier caliper (**Figure 103**). All should be of length specified in **Table 1** with no bends or other distortion. Replace defective springs.

10. Measure the tilt of all valve springs as shown in **Figure 104**. Replace if tilt exceeds 1.5 mm (0.059 in.).

11. Check the valve spring retainer and valve keepers. If they are in good condition, they may be reused.

12. Inspect valve seats (**Figure 105**). If worn or burned, they may be reconditioned. This should be performed by your dealer or local machine shop. Seats and valves in near-perfect condition can be reconditioned by lapping with fine carborundum paste. Lapping, however, is always inferior to precision grinding. Check as follows:

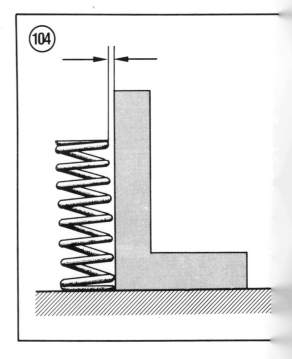

   a. Clean the valve seat and valve mating areas with contact cleaner.

   b. Coat the valve seat with machinist's blue or Dykem.

   c. Install the valve into its guide and rotate it against its seat with a valve lapping tool. See *Valve Lapping* in this chapter.

   d. Lift the valve out of the guide and measure the seat width with vernier calipers (**Figure 106**).

   e. The seat width for intake and exhaust valves should measure 0.5-1.0 mm (0.0196-0.0394 in.) all the way around the seat.

   f. If the seat is too narrow, too wide or uneven, have the valve seats reground by a Kawasaki dealer.

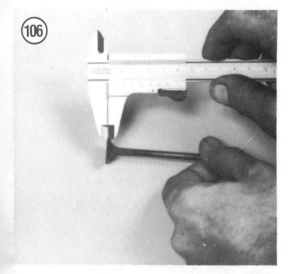

g. Remove all machinist's blue residue from the seats and valves.

Installation

1. Coat a valve stem with molybdenum disulfide paste and install it in its correct guide.

2. Carefully slide a new oil seal (**Figure 107**) over the valve and seat it onto the end of the valve guide.

> *NOTE*
> *Oil seals should be replaced whenever a valve is removed or replaced.*

3. Install the outer valve spring seat (**Figure 95**).

4. Install the inner valve spring seat (**Figure 94**).

5. Install valve springs with the narrow pitch end (end with coils closest together) facing the cylinder head. See **Figure 108**.

6. Install the valve spring retainer (**Figure 92**).

7. Push down on the upper valve seat with the valve spring compressor and install valve keepers. After releasing tension from compressor, examine valve keepers and make sure they are seated correctly (**Figure 109**).

8. Repeat Steps 1-7 for remaining valve(s).

Valve Guide Replacement

When guides are worn so that there is excessive stem-to-guide clearance or valve tipping, they must be replaced. Replace all, even if only one is worn. This job should be done only by a Kawasaki dealer or qualified specialist as special tools are required.

Valve Seat Reconditioning

This job is best left to a Kawasaki dealer. They have the special equipment and knowledge for this exacting job. You can still save considerable money by removing the cylinder head and taking just the head to the shop.

Valve Lapping

Valve lapping is a simple operation which can restore the valve seal without machining if the amount of wear or distortion is not too great.

This procedure should be performed only after determining that valve seat width and outside diameter are within specifications.

1. Smear a light coating of fine grade valve lapping compound on seating surface of valve.
2. Insert the valve into the head.
3. Wet the suction cup of the lapping stick and stick it onto the head of the valve. Lap the valve to the seat by spinning the lapping stick in both directions. Every 5 to 10 seconds, rotate the valve 180° in the valve seat. Continue this action until the mating surfaces on the valve and seat are smooth and equal in size.
4. Closely examine valve seat in cylinder head (**Figure 105**). It should be smooth and even with a smooth, polished seating "ring."
5. Thoroughly clean the valves and cylinder head in solvent to remove all grinding compound. Any compound left on the valves or the cylinder head will end up in the engine and cause excessive wear and damage.

6. After the lapping has been completed and the valve assemblies have been reinstalled into the head, the valve seal should be tested. Check the seal of each valve by pouring solvent into each of the intake and exhaust ports. There should be no leakage past the seat. If leakage occurs, combustion chamber will appear wet. If fluid leaks past any of the seats, disassemble that valve assembly and repeat the lapping procedure until there is no leakage.

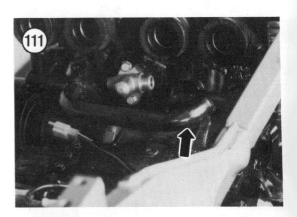

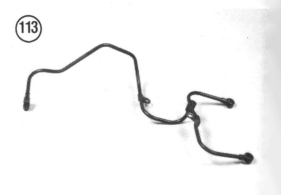

CYLINDER BLOCK

The alloy cylinder block has pressed-in cylinder sleeves, which can be bored to 0.5 mm (0.020 in.) oversize and again to 1 mm (0.040 in.) oversize.

Removal

1. Remove the cylinder head cover as described under *Cylinder Head Cover Removal/Installation* in this chapter.

2. Loosen the hose clamp (**Figure 110**) at the cylinder block water pipe and disconnect the water hose.

3. Remove the 2 screws securing the water pipe to the cylinder block. Then pull the water pipe (**Figure 111**) out of the cylinder block water port holes.

4. Remove the oil pipe mounting banjo bolt and copper washers at the cylinder head (**Figure 112**) and crankcase. Then remove the oil pipe bracket screws and remove the oil pipe. **Figure 113** shows the oil pipe. Be careful when removing the oil pipe; it is a one-piece unit and can damage easily.

5. Remove the cylinder head as described in this chapter.

6. Remove the dowel pins and head gasket.

7. Lift the front chain guide out of the cylinder housing (**Figure 114**).

8. Remove the rear cylinder acorn nuts (**Figure 115**).

9. Loosen the cylinder by tapping around the perimeter with a rubber or plastic mallet.

10. Pull the cylinder block (**Figure 116**) straight up and off the pistons and cylinder studs.

NOTE
Be sure to keep the cam chain wired up to prevent it from falling into the lower crankcase.

11. Stuff clean shop rags into the crankcase opening to prevent objects from falling into the crankcase.

12. Remove the 2 dowel pins (**Figure 117**) and base gasket.

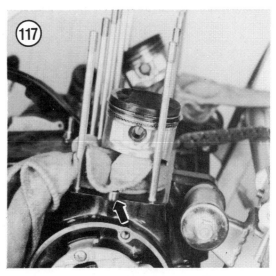

4

Inspection

1. Wash the cylinder block in solvent to remove any oil and carbon particles. The cylinder bores must be cleaned thoroughly before attempting any measurement as incorrect readings may be obtained.

2. Remove all gasket residue from the top (**Figure 118**) and bottom (A, **Figure 119**) gasket surfaces.

3. Clean the cylinder block water ports (B, **Figure 119**) of all coolant sludge build-up.

4. Measure the cylinder bores with a cylinder gauge or inside micrometer at the points shown in **Figure 120**.

5. Measure in 2 axes—in line with the piston pin and at 90° to the pin. If the taper or out-of-round is greater than specifications (**Table 1**), the cylinders must be rebored to the next oversize and new pistons and rings installed. Rebore all 4 cylinders even though only one may be worn.

> *NOTE*
> *The new pistons should be obtained first before the cylinders are bored so that the pistons can be measured. Each cylinder must be bored to match one piston only. Piston-to-cylinder clearance is specified in* ***Table 1***.

6. If the cylinder(s) are not worn past the service limits, check the bore carefully for scratches or gouges. The bore still may require boring and reconditioning.

7. If the cylinders require reboring, remove all dowel pins from the cylinders before leaving them with the dealer or machine shop.

8. After the cylinders have been serviced, wash each cylinder bore in hot soapy water. This is the only way to clean the cylinders of the fine grit material left from the bore or honing job. After washing the cylinder walls, run a clean white cloth through each wall. It shouldn't show any traces of grit or debris. If the rag is dirty, the wall is not thoroughly clean and must be rewashed. After the cylinder is cleaned, lubricate the cylinder walls with clean engine oil to prevent the cylinder liners from rusting.

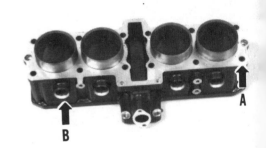

A

B

> *CAUTION*
> *A combination of soap and water is the only solution that will completely clean cylinder walls. Solvent and kerosene cannot wash fine grit out of cylinder crevices. Grit left in the cylinder will act as a grinding compound and cause premature wear to the new rings.*

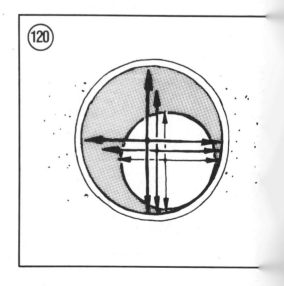

Chain Guides

The front chain guide was removed during cylinder block removal. To remove the rear chain guide, loosen and remove the chain guide Allen screws (A, **Figure 121**) and lift the chain guide (B, **Figure 121**) out of the crankcase. Reverse to install.

Inspect the chain guides (**Figure 122**). Replace them if the chain run is visibly damaged.

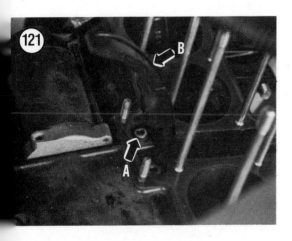

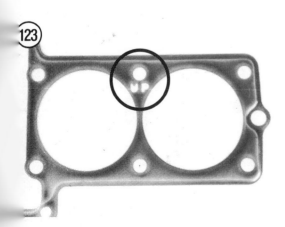

Oil Pipe

Inspect the oil pipe (**Figure 113**) for cracked or damaged joints or mounting tab brackets. Replace the pipe if necessary.

Installation

1. Install the rear chain guide if previously removed. See *Chain Guides*.
2. Check that the top and bottom cylinder surfaces are clean of all gasket residue.
3. Install the 2 dowel pins onto the crankcase (**Figure 117**).
4. Install a new cylinder base gasket so side stamped UP is installed on the right-hand side. See **Figure 123**. Make sure all holes align.
5. Install a piston holding fixture under the pistons.
6. Lubricate cylinders and pistons liberally with engine oil before installation.
7. Carefully align the cylinder with the pistons.

> *NOTE*
> *Once the cylinder is installed, run the chain and wire up through the cylinder.*

> *NOTE*
> *Make sure to align the rear chain guide with the cylinder block cam chain tunnel.*

8. Compress each ring as it enters the cylinder with your fingers or by using aircraft type hose clamps of appropriate diameter.

> *CAUTION*
> *Don't tighten the clamp any more than necessary to compress the piston rings. If the rings can't slip through easily, the clamp may gouge the rings.*

9. Remove the piston holding fixture and push the cylinder all the way down.
10. Install the cylinder block acorn nuts (**Figure 115**). Tighten the nuts to the specifications in **Table 2**.
11. Pull the cam chain straight up and insert the front cam chain guide (**Figure 114**) into the chain tunnel.
12. Install the cylinder head as described in this chapter.
13. Align the rear oil pipe with the cylinder oil gallery holes and install the banjo bolts and copper washers (**Figure 112**). Tighten the bolts to the specifications in **Table 2**.

14. Apply engine oil to the water pipe O-rings (**Figure 124**).

15. Insert the water pipe (**Figure 111**) into the cylinder block water ports. Install the water pipe mounting bolts and tighten securely.

16. Attach the hose to the water pipe inlet fitting. Tighten the hose clamp (**Figure 110**).

17. Install the cylinder head cover as described in this chapter.

PISTONS AND PISTON RINGS

Piston
Removal/Installation

1. Remove the cylinder block as described in this chapter.

2. Stuff the crankcase with clean shop rags to prevent objects from falling into the crankcase.

3. Lightly mark each piston crown with an identification number (1-4), starting with the No. 1 piston (left-hand side).

4. Remove the piston rings as described in this chapter.

5. Before removing the piston, hold the rod tightly and rock the piston. Any rocking motion (do not confuse with the normal sliding motion) indicates wear on the piston pin, rod bushing, pin bore or a combination of all three. Mark the piston and pin so that they will be reassembled into the same set.

6. Remove the circlips from the piston pin bores (**Figure 125**).

CAUTION
Discard the piston circlips. New circlips must be installed during reassembly.

7. Push the piston pin out of the piston by hand. If the pin is tight, use a homemade tool (**Figure 126**) to remove it. Do not drive the piston pin out as this action may damage the piston pin or connecting rod.

8. Lift the piston off the connecting rod.

9. Repeat Steps 4-8 for the other pistons.

10. Inspect the piston as described in this chapter.

NOTE
*New piston circlips (A, **Figure 127**) should be installed during assembly.*

11. Install one circlip in each piston on the side that faces toward the center of the engine.

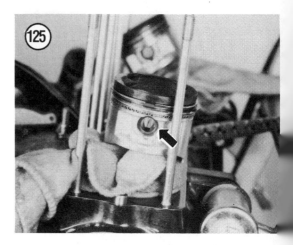

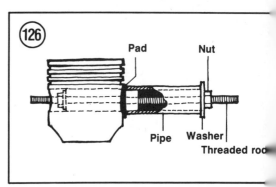

Pad   Nut

Pipe   Washer
        Threaded rod

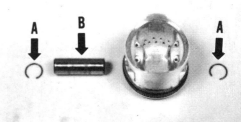

12. Coat the connecting rod bushing, piston pin and piston with assembly oil.

13. Place the piston over the connecting rod. If you are installing old parts, make sure the piston is installed on the correct rod as marked during removal. If the cylinders were bored, install the new pistons as marked by the machinist. The arrow on each piston crown must face to the front

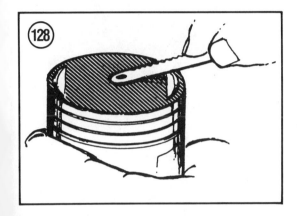

of the engine. Install the pistons in the following order:

   a. No. 2.
   b. No. 1.
   c. No. 3.
   d. No. 4.

CAUTION
When installing the piston pin (B, Figure 127) in Step 14 do not push the pin too far, or the circlip installed in Step 11 will be forced into the piston metal, destroying the circlip groove and loosening the circlip.

14. Insert the piston pin through one side of the piston until it starts to enter the connecting rod. Then it may be necessary to move the piston around until the pin enters the connecting rod. Do not force installation or damage may occur. If the pin does not slide easily, use the homemade tool (**Figure 126**) but eliminate the piece of pipe. Pull the pin in until it is centered in the piston.

15. Install the second circlip in the circlip groove.

16. Install piston ring as described in this chapter.

17. Repeat Steps 13-16 for the opposite pistons.

Piston Inspection

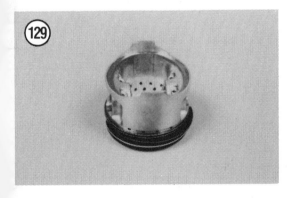

1. Carefully clean the carbon from the piston crown (**Figure 128**) with a soft scraper. Large carbon accumulations reduce piston cooling and result in detonation and piston damage. Do not remove or damage the carbon ridge around the circumference of the piston above the top ring. If the pistons, rings and cylinders are found to be dimensionally correct and can be reused, removal of the carbon ring from the top of the piston or the carbon ridges from the cylinders will promote excessive oil consumption.

CAUTION
Do not wire brush piston skirts.

2. Examine each ring groove for burrs, dented edges and wide wear. Pay particular attention to the top compression ring groove as it usually wears more than the others.

3. Check the oil control holes in the piston (**Figure 129**) for carbon or oil sludge buildup. Clean the holes with a small diameter drill bit.

4. Check the piston skirts (**Figure 130**) for cracks or other damage. If a piston(s) shows signs of partial seizure (bits of aluminum build-up on the piston skirts), the pistons should be replaced and the cylinders bored (if necessary) to reduce the possibility of engine noise and further piston seizure.

5. Measure piston-to-cylinder clearance as described under *Piston Clearance* in this chapter.

6. If damage or wear indicate piston replacement, select a new piston as described under *Piston Clearance* in this chapter.

7. Inspect the wrist pin (**Figure 131**) for chrome flaking or cracks. Replace if necessary.

Piston Clearance

1. Make sure the piston and cylinder walls are clean and dry.

2. Measure the inside diameter of the cylinder at a point 13 mm (1/2 in.) from the upper edge with a bore gauge.

3. Measure the outside diameter of the piston at a point 5 mm (3/16 in.) from the lower edge of the piston 90° to piston pin axis (**Figure 132**).

4. Subtract the piston diameter from the bore diameter; the difference is piston-to-cylinder clearance. Compare to specification in **Table 1**. If clearance is excessive, the pistons should be replaced and the cylinders rebored. Purchase the new pistons first. Then, measure their diameter and add the specified clearance to determine the proper cylinder bore diameters.

> *NOTE*
> *If one cylinder requires boring, the other cylinders must be bored also.*

Piston Ring
Removal/Installation

> *WARNING*
> *The edges of all piston rings are very sharp. Be careful when handling them to avoid cut fingers.*

1. Measure the side clearance of each ring in its groove with a flat feeler gauge (**Figure 133**) and

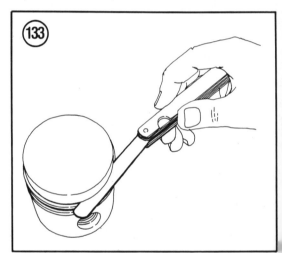

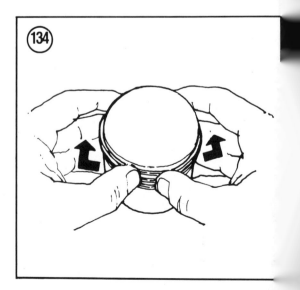

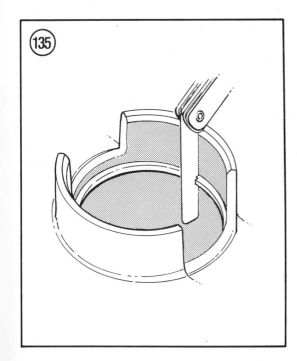
(135)

compare with the specifications in **Table 1**. If the clearance is greater than specified, the rings must be replaced. If the clearance is still excessive with the new rings, the piston must be replaced.

2. Remove the old rings with a ring expander tool or by spreading the ring ends with your thumbs and lifting the rings up evenly (**Figure 134**).

3. Using a broken piston ring, remove all carbon from the piston ring grooves.

4. Inspect grooves carefully for burrs, nicks and broken or cracked lands. Replace piston if necessary.

5. Check end gap of each ring. To check ring, insert the ring into the bottom of the cylinder bore and square it with the cylinder wall by tapping it with the piston. The ring should be pushed in about 15 mm (5/8 in.). Insert a feeler gauge as shown in **Figure 135**. Compare gap with **Table 1**. Replace ring if gap is too large. If the gap on the new ring is smaller than specified, hold a small file in a vise, grip the ends of the ring with your fingers and enlarge the gap.

6. Roll each ring around its piston groove as shown in **Figure 136** to check for binding. Minor binding may be cleaned up with a fine-cut file.

7. Install the piston rings in the order shown in **Figure 137**.

NOTE
Install all rings with the manufacturer's
markings facing up (Figure 138).

8. Install the piston rings—first the bottom, then the middle, then the top ring—by carefully spreading the ends with your thumbs and slipping the rings over the top of the piston. Remember that the piston rings must be installed with the marks on them facing up toward the top of the piston or there is the possibility of oil pumping past the rings.

   a. Install the oil ring assembly into the bottom ring groove. The assembly is composed of 2 steel rails and 1 expander. The expander is installed in the middle of the steel rails.

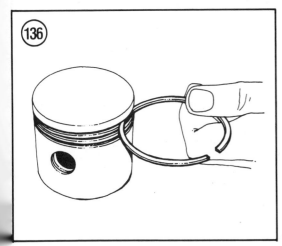
(136)

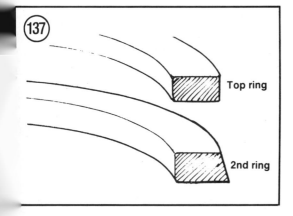
(137)

Top ring

2nd ring

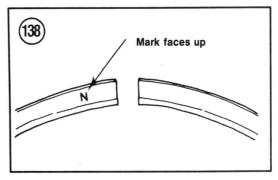
(138)

Mark faces up

N

b. The top and middle piston rings are different. The middle ring is slightly tapered and must be installed as shown in **Figure 137**. The top ring is symmetrical and must be installed as shown in **Figure 137**.

9. Make sure the rings are seated completely in their grooves all the way around the piston and that the end gaps are distributed around the piston as shown in **Figure 139**. It is important that the ring gaps are not aligned with each other when installed to prevent compression pressures from escaping past them.

10. If installing oversize compression rings, check the number to make sure the correct rings are being installed. The ring numbers should be the same as the piston oversize number.

11. If new rings are installed, the cylinders must be deglazed or honed. This will help to seat the new rings. Refer honing service to a Kawasaki dealer. After honing, measure the end clearance of each

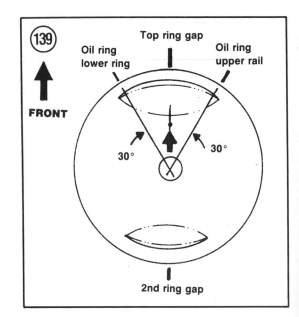

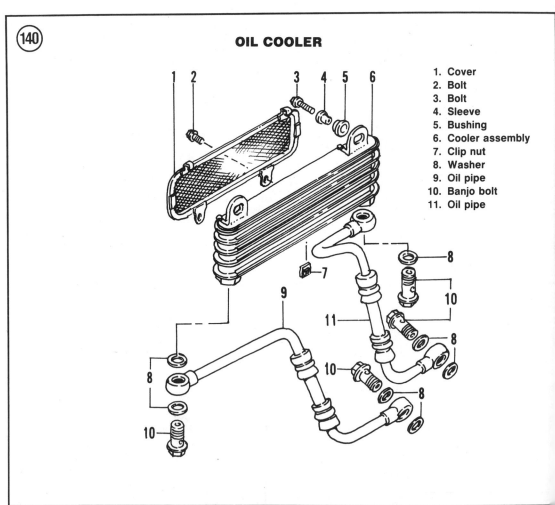

OIL COOLER

1. Cover
2. Bolt
3. Bolt
4. Sleeve
5. Bushing
6. Cooler assembly
7. Clip nut
8. Washer
9. Oil pipe
10. Banjo bolt
11. Oil pipe

ring (**Figure 135**) and compare to dimensions in **Table 1**.

> *NOTE*
> *If the cylinders were deglazed or honed, clean the cylinders as described under **Cylinder Block Inspection** in this chapter.*

OIL PUMP

The oil pan and oil pump can be removed with the engine mounted in the frame.

Service Notes

Because the lubrication system is vital to engine reliability, note the following during service and inspection:

a. Was the engine oil level correct?

b. Was the engine oil contaminated with sludge or coolant?
c. Was the oil pump properly mounted?
d. Were external oil lines damaged or their fittings loose?
e. Were banjo bolts loose or clogged?
f. Was the oil filter element clogged?
g. Was the oil pump screen clogged?
h. Was the relief valve working properly, clogged or damaged?
i. Were all O-rings properly installed or were they damaged?
j. Was the oil cooler damaged or improperly installed?
k. Were the oil passages partially restricted or clogged?

Oil Pan
Removal/Installation

1. Remove the mufflers as described under *Exhaust System Removal/Installation* in Chapter Seven.
2. Drain the engine oil and remove the oil filter as described under *Engine Oil and Filter Change* in Chapter Three.
3. Remove the bolt and washer and disconnect the electrical connector at the oil pressure switch (located next to the oil filter housing underneath the engine).
4. Remove the oil cooler pipe banjo bolts at the oil pan (**Figure 140**).
5. Keep the oil drain pan underneath the engine. Then loosen the oil pan mounting bolts all the way around the pan and allow more oil to drain into the pan.

> *NOTE*
> *The photographs used in Steps 6-8 are shown with the engine removed for clarity.*

6. Completely remove the oil pan mounting bolts and lower the pan (**Figure 141**) away from the crankcase and remove it.
7. Remove the 3 oil-passage O-rings from the bottom of the crankcase. See **Figure 142**.

8. Remove the large O-ring (**Figure 143**) from the oil pan.

9. If necessary, remove or replace the oil pressure switch or relief valve from the oil pan as described in this chapter.

10. Before cleaning the oil pan, check the inside for signs of excessive aluminum or metal debris that may indicate engine, clutch or transmission problems.

11. Installation is the reverse of these steps, noting the following:

    a. Apply clean engine oil to all O-rings.

    b. Install the large O-ring (**Figure 143**) on the oil pan.

    c. Install the 3 oil-passage O-rings (**Figure 142**) on the crankcase. These O-rings have a flat and a round surface. The flat surface must face toward the crankshaft.

    d. Remove all gasket residue from the oil pan and crankcase. Then install a new gasket. Make sure the bolt holes align properly.

    e. Install the relief valve and/or oil pressure switch if removed.

    f. Tighten the oil pan mounting bolts to the specifications in **Table 2**.

    g. Install a new oil filter and refill the engine oil as described in Chapter Three.

Oil Pump
Removal/Installation

The oil pump can be removed with the engine installed in the frame.

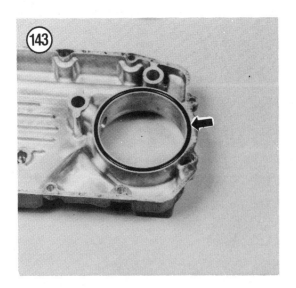

1. Remove the oil pan as described in this chapter.
2. Remove the clutch as described in Chapter Five.
3. Remove the 3 oil pump mounting screws (**Figure 144**).
4. Remove the bearing stop (**Figure 145**) and the 2 dowel pins (**Figure 146**).
5. Push the oil pump into the engine and remove it through the bottom of the crankcase (**Figure 147**).
6. Installation is the reverse of these steps. Note the following:

   a. Install the 2 dowel pins into the crankcase (**Figure 146**).

   b. To prime the oil pump, add clean engine oil into the oil pump opening while turning the pump shaft.

   c. Apply Loctite 242 (blue) to the bearing stop screws before assembly. Stake the screws with a punch (**Figure 148**) after tightening.

   d. Make sure to install the 3 crankcase O-rings. See *Oil Pan Removal/Installation* in this chapter.

Disassembly/Inspection/Assembly

Refer to **Figure 149** for this procedure.

4

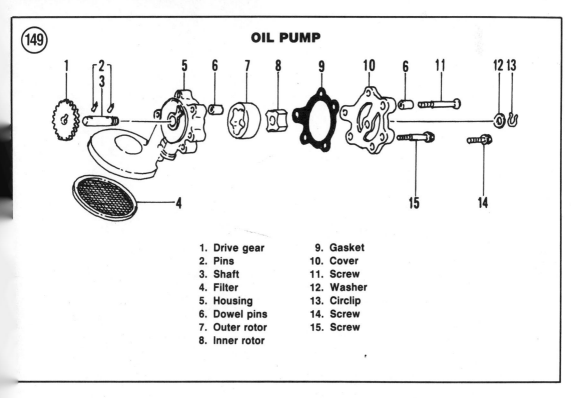

OIL PUMP

1. Drive gear	9. Gasket
2. Pins	10. Cover
3. Shaft	11. Screw
4. Filter	12. Washer
5. Housing	13. Circlip
6. Dowel pins	14. Screw
7. Outer rotor	15. Screw
8. Inner rotor	

1. Remove the oil pump as described in this chapter.

2. Remove the circlip (A, **Figure 150**) from the end of the pump shaft.

3. Slide the washer (B, **Figure 150**) off the pump shaft.

4. Remove the pump cover screws (C, **Figure 150**) and remove the cover (**Figure 151**) and gasket.

5. Remove the following:
   a. Inner rotor (**Figure 152**).
   b. Pin (**Figure 153**).
   c. Outer rotor (**Figure 154**).

6. Slide the pump shaft through the pump housing and remove the pump gear (**Figure 155**) and pin.

7. Remove the pump shaft.

8. Inspect the rotors (**Figure 156**) for wear, cracks or other damage.

9. Inspect the pump gear (**Figure 157**).

10. Inspect the oil pump housing (**Figure 158**) for cracks or bore damage.

11. Check the strainer screen (**Figure 159**) for tearing or other damage. Replace if necessary.

12. Check the pump shaft (**Figure 160**) for scoring, pin hole damage or seizure.

NOTE
Proceed with Step 13 only when the above inspection and measurement steps have been completed and all parts are known to be good.

13. Coat all parts with fresh engine oil before assembly.

14. Reverse Steps 2-7 to reassemble the oil pump.

OIL PRESSURE RELIEF VALVE

Removal/Installation

1. Remove the oil pan as described in this chapter.
2. Unscrew the relief valve (**Figure 161**) and remove it.
3. Apply Loctite 242 (blue) to the relief valve and install it. Tighten the valve to 15 N•m (11 ft.-lb.).
4. Install the oil pan as described in this chapter.

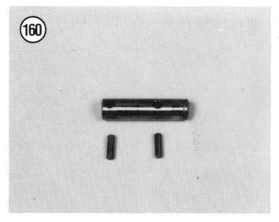

OIL PRESSURE SWITCH

Removal/Installation

1. Drain the engine oil as described under *Engine Oil and Filter Change* in Chapter Three.

2. Remove the bolt and lockwasher and disconnect the electrical connector from the oil pressure switch.

3. Unscrew the oil pressure switch (**Figure 162**).

4. Installation is the reverse of these steps. Note the following.

    a. Make sure the area around the switch mounting position is clean of all dirt and debris.

    b. Refill the engine oil as described in Chapter Three.

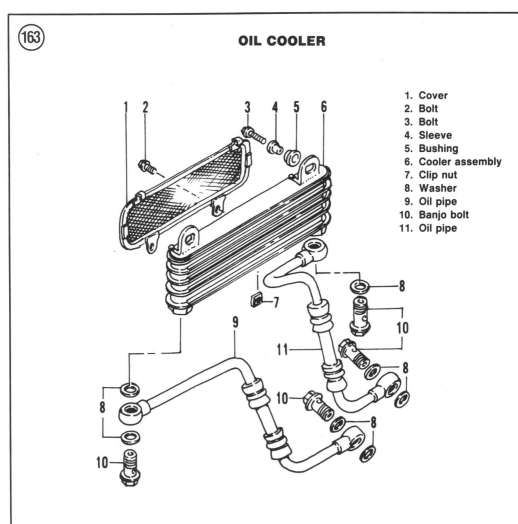

OIL COOLER

1. Cover
2. Bolt
3. Bolt
4. Sleeve
5. Bushing
6. Cooler assembly
7. Clip nut
8. Washer
9. Oil pipe
10. Banjo bolt
11. Oil pipe

OIL COOLER

Removal/Installation

Refer to **Figure 163**.
1. Remove the lower fairing assembly. See Chapter Thirteen.
2. Put the bike up on its centerstand and put an oil pan under the engine.

3. Drain the engine oil as described under *Engine Oil and Filter Change* in Chapter Three.
4. Remove the oil cooler banjo bolts and washers (**Figure 163**).
5. Remove the oil cooler mounting screws and remove the oil cooler assembly (**Figure 164**).
6. To install the cooler, reverse the removal steps. Note the following:
   a. Clean the banjo bolts in solvent and allow to dry thoroughly.
   b. Check all cooler hoses and fittings for leakage or damage.
   c. Tighten the mounting bolts securely.
   d. Make sure to install a washer on both sides of the oil hose banjo bolts (**Figure 163**).
   e. Refill engine oil as described in Chapter Three.
   f. Recheck the oil level after the engine has run a short time and add oil if necessary. See *Engine Oil Level Check* in Chapter Three.

SECONDARY SPROCKET, SHAFT AND STARTER MOTOR CLUTCH

Refer to **Figure 165** when performing procedures in this section.

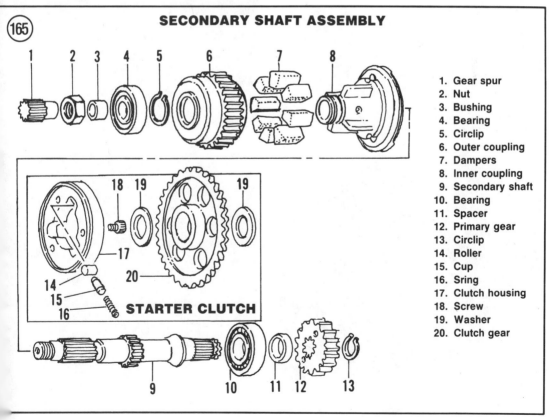

SECONDARY SHAFT ASSEMBLY

1. Gear spur
2. Nut
3. Bushing
4. Bearing
5. Circlip
6. Outer coupling
7. Dampers
8. Inner coupling
9. Secondary shaft
10. Bearing
11. Spacer
12. Primary gear
13. Circlip
14. Roller
15. Cup
16. Sring
17. Clutch housing
18. Screw
19. Washer
20. Clutch gear

STARTER CLUTCH

Removal

1. Remove the oil pan as described in this chapter.
2. Remove the oil pump as described in this chapter.
3. Remove the water pump as described in Chapter Nine.
4. Remove the clutch as described in Chapter Five.
5. Remove the alternator cover. Secure the alternator with a holder and loosen the secondary shaft nut (**Figure 166**).
6. Remove the engine and split the crankcase as described under *Crankcase Disassembly* in this chapter.
7. Remove the secondary shaft nut (**Figure 167**) and spacer (**Figure 168**).
8. Using an aluminum or brass drift and soft mallet, tap the secondary shaft (**Figure 169**) from

the left-hand side until the right-hand bearing is pushed out of the crankcase (**Figure 170**).

9. Hold the starter clutch assembly (A, **Figure 171**) and pull the secondary shaft (B, **Figure 171**) out of the crankcase together with its spacer.

10. Lift the primary chain and remove the starter clutch assembly (**Figure 172**).

Starter Motor Clutch
Disassembly/Inspection/Reassembly

1. Pull the starter clutch gear (**Figure 173**) off of the starter clutch.

2. Remove the washer (**Figure 174**).

3. Remove the roller, spring and cap (**Figure 175**) assemblies.

4. Remove the circlip (**Figure 176**) and pull the inner coupling (A, **Figure 177**) out of the secondary sprocket (B, **Figure 177**).

4

5. Remove the 8 dampers (**Figure 178**) from the secondary sprocket.

6. Inspect the starter clutch gear (A, **Figure 179**) for chipped or missing teeth. Check the bushing (B, **Figure 179**) for scoring or other damage. Replace the gear if necessary.

7. Check the rollers, springs and caps (**Figure 180**) in the starter clutch for uneven or excessive wear. Replace as a set if any are bad.

8. Inspect the dampers (**Figure 181**) for cracking, edge rounding or other abnormal wear. Replace the dampers as a set if any damper requires replacement.

9. Inspect the damper separators (**Figure 182**) in the secondary sprocket (**Figure 182**) and inner coupling (A, **Figure 183**) for cracking, splitting or other damage.

10. Check the inner coupling shaft splines (B, **Figure 183**) for excessive wear or spline damage.

11. Check the starter clutch Allen bolts (**Figure 184**) for tightness. If the bolts are loose, remove them and apply Loctite 242 (blue) to the threads.

Then install the bolts and tighten to 34 N•m (25 ft.-lb.).

12. Assembly of the starter motor clutch is the reverse of Steps 1-4. Note the following:

   a. Insert the dampers into the secondary sprocket as shown in **Figure 178**.

   b. Slide the inner coupling into the secondary sprocket (**Figure 177**) and secure the assembly with a circlip (**Figure 176**). Make sure the circlip seats completely in the inner coupling groove.

c. Install the spring, cap and roller (**Figure 175**) into each receptacle in the starter clutch.

d. Install the washer into the starter clutch (**Figure 174**).

e. Insert the starter clutch gear (**Figure 173**) into the starter clutch assembly.

13. Test the starter clutch operation as follows:

a. Turn the starter gear one way and then the other.

b. The starter gear should turn freely one way but not turn the other.

c. If the starter clutch does not operate correctly, disassemble and check for worn spring, caps, rollers or gear.

Secondary Shaft
Inspection/Disassembly/Reassembly

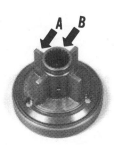

1. Clean the secondary shaft thoroughly in solvent.

2. Inspect secondary shaft gear (A, **Figure 185**) for cracks, chipped teeth or excessive wear. If necessary, replace the gear as described in Step 5.

3. Hold the secondary shaft and turn the bearing outer race (B, **Figure 185**) in both directions and check for damaged races or balls. Replace the bearing if it has excessive side or radial play. If the bearing is okay, oil the races and balls with clean engine oil. If necessary, replace the bearing as described in Step 5.

4. Inspect the secondary shaft (**Figure 185**) splines and bearing surfaces for cracks, deep scoring, excessive wear or heat discoloration. Replace the shaft if necessary.

5. Disassemble the secondary shaft and replace worn or damaged parts as follows. The following

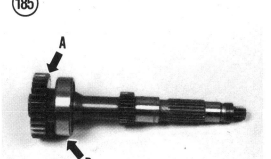

tools will be required for complete disassembly and reassembly: Universal bearing puller (**Figure 186**), Kawasaki gear pusher (part No. 57001-319, **Figure 187**) and a long hollow pipe.

   a. Remove the circlip from the end of the secondary shaft.

   b. Assemble the bearing puller onto the secondary shaft (**Figure 188**) and pull the secondary shaft gear off of the shaft.

   c. Slide the spacer off the secondary shaft.

   d. Assemble the bearing puller onto the secondary shaft and pull the bearing off the shaft.

   e. Clean the shaft bearing surfaces in solvent.

   f. Install a new bearing by driving it onto the secondary shaft as shown in **Figure 189**. Drive on the *inner* bearing race only. Drive the bearing until the inner race seats against the secondary shaft shoulder.

   g. Coat the inside of the spacer with clean engine oil and slide it onto the secondary shaft.

   h. Install the secondary shaft gear by pushing it onto the shaft with the Kawasaki gear pusher (part No. 57001-319). See **Figure 190**.

   i. Secure the gear with the circlip.

Starter Motor Idle Gear
Removal/Inspection/Installation

1. Split the crankcase as described und *Crankcase Disassembly* in this chapter.

2. Remove the crankshaft as described in th chapter.

3. Remove the lower primary chain guide (A **Figure 191**).

4. Remove the circlip and remove the idle gear (**Figure 191**).

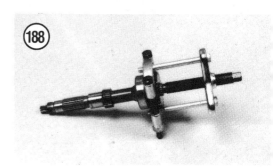

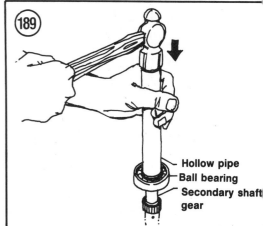

Hollow pipe
Ball bearing
Secondary shaft
gear

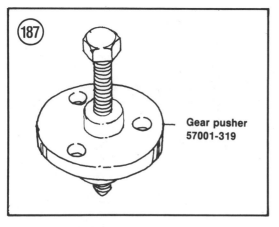

Gear pusher
57001-319

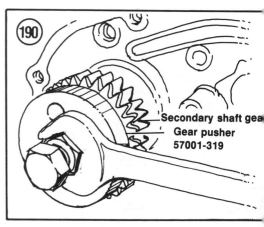

Secondary shaft gea
Gear pusher
57001-319

5. Clean the gear and shaft thoroughly in solvent. Visually check the gear and shaft for cracks, deep scoring and excessive wear. Check the gear for chipped or missing teeth. Replace the gear and shaft if necessary.

6. Installation is the reverse of these steps. Note the following:

   a. Apply engine oil to the shaft before installing the gear.

   b. Make sure the circlip seats completely in the shaft.

   c. Apply Loctite 242 (blue) to the chain tensioner Allen screws. Tighten the screws securely.

Secondary Sprocket, Shaft and Starter Motor Clutch Installation

1. Assemble the starter clutch assembly as described in this chapter.

2. Slide the washer (**Figure 192**) onto the secondary shaft.

3. Lift the primary chain and engage the secondary sprocket with the chain (**Figure 193**).

4. Insert the secondary shaft (B, **Figure 194**) into the crankcase and through the starter clutch assembly (A, **Figure 194**).

5. Tap the secondary shaft until the bearing seats into the crankcase.

6. Install the spacer (**Figure 195**) and nut (**Figure 196**).

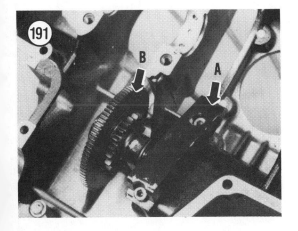

7. Assemble the crankcase and install the engine as described in this chapter.

8. Install the alternator as described in Chapter Eight.

9. Secure the alternator with a holder and tighten the secondary shaft nut to the specifications in **Table 2**.

10. Complete engine assembly as described in this chapter.

11. Install the clutch as described in Chapter Five.

CRANKCASE

Service to the lower end requires that the crankcase assembly be removed from the motorcycle frame and disassembled (split).

Disassembly

1. Remove the engine as described in this chapter. Remove all exterior assemblies from the crankcase as described in this chapter and other related chapters.

2. Remove the upper crankcase bolts (**Figure 197**).

3. Turn the engine so that the bottom end faces up.

4. Loosen the primary chain tensioner bolt (**Figure 198**) and remove the bolt, spring and pin. See **Figure 199**.

5. Remove the following parts as described in this chapter.

    a. Oil pan.

    b. Oil pump.

    c. Secondary shaft and starter clutch.

6. Loosen the lower crankcase bolts in the following order by reversing the bolt tightening sequence in **Figure 200**:

    a. 6 mm bolts.

    b. 8 mm bolts.

7. Remove the bolts.

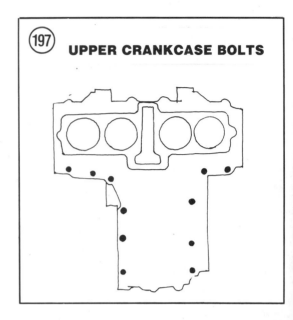

UPPER CRANKCASE BOLTS

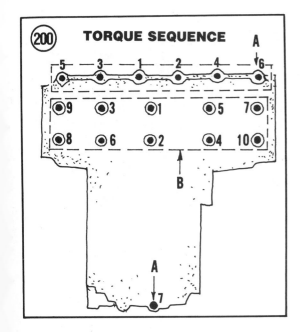

TORQUE SEQUENCE

8. Using the 4 pry points cast into the crankcase assembly, pry the lower crankcase and lift it up.

CAUTION
Do not pry the crankcase between any gasket surface. The crankcases are machined as a set and damage to one will require replacement of both.

9. After separating the crankcase halves, the transmission and crankshaft will stay in the upper crankcase half.

10. Remove the breather tube (**Figure 201**).

11. Remove the transmission, shift forks and shift drum assemblies as described in Chapter Six.

12. Remove the crankshaft and the crankshaft bearing inserts as described in this chapter.

13. Remove the 2 dowel pins. See **Figure 202**.

14. Remove the upper (A, **Figure 191**) and lower (**Figure 203**) primary chain guides.

15. Remove the starter motor idle gear as described in this chapter.

16. Remove the needle bearing set pins (A, **Figure 204**).

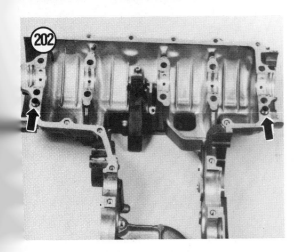

17. Remove the ball bearing set rings (B, **Figure 204**).

Inspection

1. Thoroughly clean the inside and outside of both crankcase halves with cleaning solvent. Dry with compressed air. Make sure there is no solvent residue left in the cases as it will contaminate the engine oil.
2. Make sure all oil passages are clean; blow them out with compressed air.
3. Check the crankcases for cracks or other damage. Inspect the mating surfaces of both halves. They must be free of gouges, burrs or any damage that could cause an oil leak.
4. Inspect the crankshaft bearing inserts as described in this chapter.

Crankcase Bearings
Inspection/Replacement

1. Turn the secondary shaft (A, **Figure 205**) and shift drum (B, **Figure 205**) bearings and check for damaged races, balls or rollers. Replace the bearing(s) if it has excessive side or radial side play. If bearings are okay, oil the races or rollers with clean engine oil. If necessary, replace the bearings as follows.

> *NOTE*
> *If bearing replacement is required, purchase the new bearing(s) and place them in a freezer for approximately 2 hours before installation. Chilling the bearings will reduce their overall diameter while the hot crankcase is slightly larger due to heat expansion. This will make installation much easier.*

> *WARNING*
> *When heating the crankcase as described in Step 2, first wash the crankcase thoroughly in soap and water. Make sure there are no gasoline or solvent fumes present.*

2. The bearings are installed with a slight interference fit. The crankcase must be heated to a temperature of about 212° F (100° C) in an oven.

> *CAUTION*
> *Do not heat the case with a torch (propane or acetylene)—never bring a flame into contact with the bearing or case. The direct heat may warp the case.*

> *WARNING*
> *Wear insulated gloves when handling heated parts.*

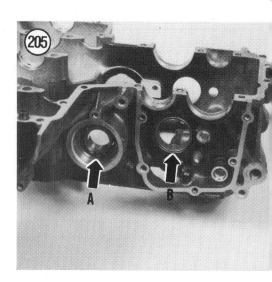

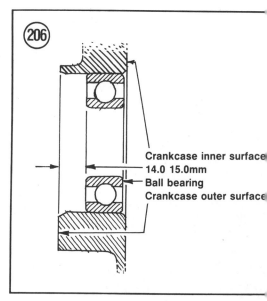

Crankcase inner surface
14.0 15.0mm
Ball bearing
Crankcase outer surface

3. Remove the case from the oven and place onto wooden blocks.

4. Tap the bearings out of the crankcase with a block of wood or a large socket and extension.

5. Reheat the crankcase in the oven.

6. Remove the crankcase and place it on wood blocks as before.

7. Press the new bearing(s) into place in the crankcase by hand until it seats completely. Do not hammer it in. If the bearing will not seat, remove it and freeze it again. Reheat the crankcase and install the bearing again. Install the secondary shaft bearing (A, **Figure 205**) to the dimensions indicated in **Figure 206**. Install the shift drum bearing so that the outside bearing surface is even with the crankcase.

Assembly

1. Before assembly, coat all parts with assembly oil or engine oil.

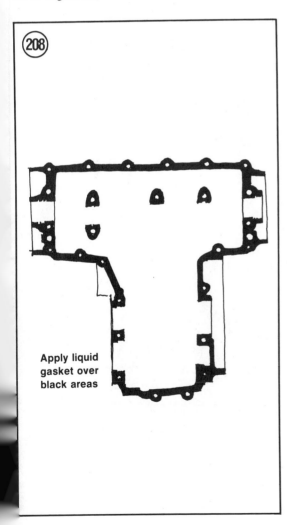

Apply liquid gasket over black areas

2. Install the crankshaft bearing inserts as described under *Crankshaft Removal/Installation* in this chapter. If reusing old bearings, make sure that they are installed in the same location. Refer to marks made during crankshaft removal. Make sure they are locked in place.

3. Install the needle bearing set pins (A, **Figure 204**).

4. Install the ball bearings set rings (B, **Figure 204**).

5. Install the starter motor idle gear as described under *Starter Motor Idle Gear Removal/Inspection/Installation* in this chapter.

6. Install the upper (A, **Figure 191**) and lower (**Figure 203**) primary chain guides. Apply Loctite 242 (blue) to the chain guide screws before installation. Tighten the screws securely.

7. Install the shift drum, shift forks and transmission assemblies as described in Chapter Six.

> *CAUTION*
> *When installing the transmission shaft assemblies, make sure the set pins (A, Figure 204) and both set rings (B, Figure 204) are in place in the upper crankcase before installing the transmission assemblies. See Chapter Six.*

8. Shift the transmission into NEUTRAL. **Figure 207** shows the neutral detent engaged with the shift drum in NEUTRAL.

9. Install the crankshaft, primary chain, and camshaft drive chains as described under *Crankshaft Removal/Installation* in this chapter.

10. Attach the breather tube to the plate nozzle (**Figure 201**). Lock the breather tube clip securely.

11. Install the starter clutch and secondary shaft as described in this chapter.

12. Make sure the case half sealing surfaces are perfectly clean and dry.

13. Install the 2 locating dowel pins. See **Figure 202**.

14. Apply a light coat of gasket sealer to the lower crankcase half sealing surface. Cover only flat surfaces, not curved bearing surfaces (**Figure 208**). Make the coating as thin as possible. Do not apply sealant close to the edge of the bearing inserts as it would restrict oil flow and cause damage.

> *NOTE*
> *Use Gasgacinch Gasket Sealer, Three Bond or equivalent. A black colored silicone sealant (RTV) works well and blends with the black crankcases.*

15. In the upper crankcase, position the shift drum into NEUTRAL. See Step 8. The shift forks should

be located in the approximate positions shown in A, **Figure 209**.

> *NOTE*
> *When assembling the crankcase halves in Step 16, make sure to insert the breather tube through the hole in the lower crankcase. See B, **Figure 209**.*

16. Position the lower crankcase onto the upper crankcase. Set the front portion down first and lower the rear while making sure the shift forks engage properly into the transmission assemblies.
17. Lower the crankcase completely.

> *CAUTION*
> *Do not install any crankcase bolts until the sealing surface around the entire crankcase perimeter has seated completely.*

18. Before installing the bolts, slowly spin the transmission shafts and shift the transmission through all 6 gears. This is done to check that the shift forks are properly engaged.
19. Apply oil to the threads of all crankcase bolts and install them finger-tight.
20. Tighten the 8 mm bolts in two stages in the torque sequence shown in **Figure 200**. Tighten to the following specifications:
    a. Stage 1: 14 N•m (10 ft.-lb.).
    b. Stage 2: 27 N•m (20 ft.-lb.).
21. Tighten the 6 mm bolts to 12 N•m (9 ft.-lb.).
22. Turn the crankcase assembly over and install all upper crankcase bolts only finger-tight (**Figure 197**). Tighten the bolts to 12 N•m (9 ft.-lb.).
23. Install the oil pump and oil pan as described in this chapter.

24. Install the primary chain tensioner bolt, spring and pin. See **Figure 199** and **Figure 198**.
25. Reverse Step 1 and install all engine assemblies that were removed.
26. Install the engine as described in this chapter

CRANKSHAFT

Removal/Installation

1. Split the crankcase as described under *Crankcase Disassembly* in this chapter.
2. Remove the secondary shaft and starter motor clutch as described in this chapter.
3. Lift the crankshaft out of the crankcase (**Figure 210**). Then slip the primary and camshaft chains off the crankshaft (**Figure 211**).
4. Remove the crankshaft oil seals. See **Figure 212** (left) and **Figure 213** (right).
5. Remove the crankcase main bearing inserts (**Figure 214**) from the upper and lower crankcase halves. Mark the backsides of the inserts with a 1, 2, 3, 4 or 5 and U (upper) or L (lower) starting from the left-hand side so they can be reinstalled into the same positions.
6. Installation is the reverse of these steps. Note the following:
    a. Install the primary and camshaft drive chains over the crankshaft (**Figure 211**).
    b. Install new crankshaft oil seals. See **Figure 212** (left) and **Figure 213** (right).

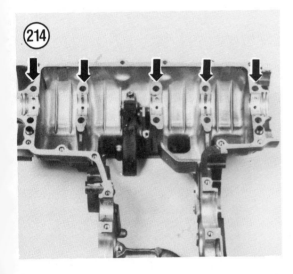

Crankshaft Inspection

1. Clean crankshaft thoroughly with solvent. Clean oil holes with rifle cleaning brushes. Flush thoroughly and dry with compressed air. Lightly oil all oil journal surfaces immediately to prevent rust.
2. Inspect each journal (A, **Figure 215**) for scratches, ridges, scoring, nicks, etc.
3. If the surface on all journals is satisfactory, measure the journals with a micrometer (**Figure 216**) and check out-of-roundness, taper and wear on the journals. Check against measurements given in **Table 1**.
4. Inspect the camshaft (B, **Figure 215**) and primary (C, **Figure 215**) chain drive sprockets. If they are worn or damaged, the crankshaft will have to be replaced.

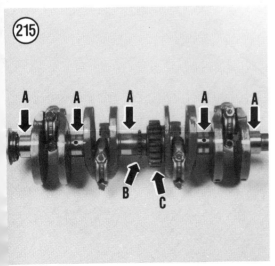

5. Inspect both drive chains. Stretch each chain tight and measure a 21-pin length (**Figure 217**). If the length from the 1st pin to the 21st pin exceeds the limit in **Table 1**, install a new chain.

6. Install the upper crankcase bearing inserts and the crankshaft. Measure the crankshaft side clearance by inserting a feeler gauge between the No. 2 crankcase main journal and the crankshaft machined web as shown in **Figure 218**. Replace the crankcase assembly if the clearance exceeds the service limit in **Table 1**.

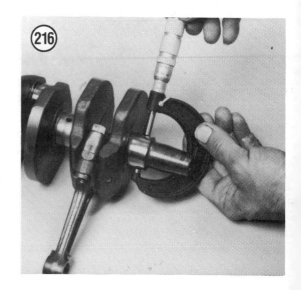

Crankshaft Main Bearing Clearance Measurement

1. Check the inside and outside surfaces of the bearing inserts for wear, bluish tint (burned), flaking-abrasion and scoring. If the bearings are good they may be reused. If any insert is questionable, replace the entire set.

2. Clean the bearing surfaces of the crankshaft and the main bearing inserts.

3. Measure the main bearing clearance by performing the following steps.

4. Set the upper crankcase upside down on the workbench on wood blocks.

5. Install the existing main bearing inserts into the upper and lower crankcase into their original positions. See **Figure 214**.

6. Install the crankshaft (**Figure 210**) into the upper crankcase.

7. Place a piece of Plastigage over each main bearing journal parallel to the crankshaft (**Figure 219**).

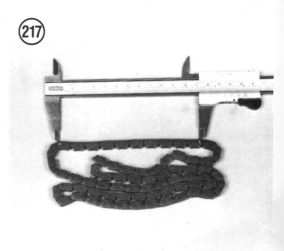

> *CAUTION*
> *Do not rotate crankshaft while Plastigage is in place.*

8. Install the lower crankcase over the upper crankcase. Install and tighten the lower crankcase 8 mm bolts as described under *Crankcase Assembly* in this chapter.

9. Remove the 8 mm bolts in the reverse order of installation.

10. Carefully remove the lower crankcase and measure width of flattened Plastigage according to the manufacturer's instructions (**Figure 220**). Measure at both ends of the strip. A difference of 0.025 mm (0.001 in.) or more indicates a tapered crankpin. Confirm with a micrometer. Remove the Plastigage strips from all bearing journals.

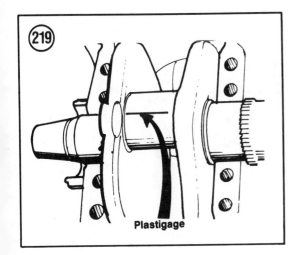

Plastigage

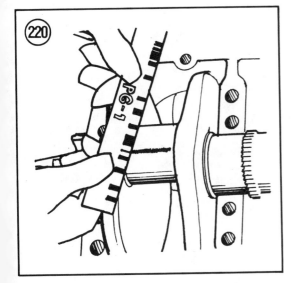

11. New bearing clearance should be 0.014-0.038 mm (0.0005-0.0015 in.) with a service limit of 0.08 mm (0.003 in.). Remove the Plastigage strips from all bearing journals.

12. If the bearing clearance is greater than specified, use the following steps for new bearing selection.

13. If the bearing clearance is between 0.038 mm (0.0015 in.) and 0.08 mm (0.003 in.), replace the bearing inserts with factory inserts painted blue and recheck the bearing clearance. Always replace all 10 inserts at the same time. The clearance may exceed 0.038 mm (0.0015 in.) slightly but it must not be less than the minimum clearance of 0.008 mm (0.0005 in.) or bearing seizure will occur.

14. If the bearing clearance exceeds the service limit, measure the crankshaft journal OD with a micrometer (**Figure 216**). See **Table 1** for specifications. If any journal exceeds the wear limit, replace the crankshaft.

15. If the crankshaft has been replaced, determine new bearing inserts as follows:
   a. Purchase a new crankshaft. Then cross-reference the main journal crankshaft diameter markings (**Figure 221**) with the upper crankcase half marks (**Figure 222**). Record these marks and cross-reference them with **Table 3** for new crankshaft main bearing insert selection.
   b. Recheck the clearance with the new inserts and crankshaft. The clearance should be less than the service limit and as close to the standard as possible, but not less than the standard.

16. Clean and oil the main bearing journals and insert faces.

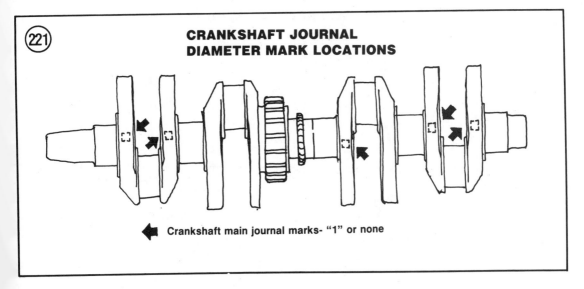

CRANKSHAFT JOURNAL DIAMETER MARK LOCATIONS

Crankshaft main journal marks- "1" or none

CONNECTING RODS

Removal/Installation

1. Remove the engine as described in this chapter.
2. Split the crankcase and remove the crankshaft as described in this chapter.
3. Measure the connecting rod big end side clearance. Insert a feeler gauge between a connecting rod big end and either crankshaft machined web (**Figure 223**). Record the clearance for each connecting rod and compare to the specifications in **Table 1**. If the clearance is excessive, replace the connecting rod(s) and recheck clearance. If clearance is still excessive, replace the crankshaft.

> *NOTE*
> *Before disassembly, mark the rods and caps with a "1", "2", "3" and "4" starting from the left-hand side.*

4. Remove the connecting rod cap nuts (**Figure 224**) and separate the rods from the crankshaft (**Figure 225**). Keep each cap with its original rod with the weight mark on the end of the cap matching the mark on the rod (**Figure 226**).

> *NOTE*
> *Some rods do not have a diameter mark at the point indicated in **Figure 226**. If there is no mark, draw a line across the big end cap and connecting rod with a crayon to indicate alignment.*

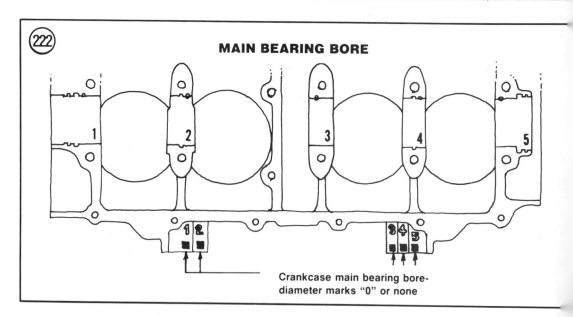

MAIN BEARING BORE

Crankcase main bearing bore-diameter marks "0" or none

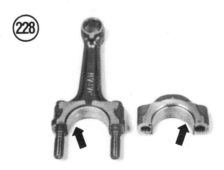

NOTE
Keep each bearing insert in its original place in the crankcase, rod or rod cap. If you are going to assemble the engine with the original inserts, they must be installed exactly as removed in order to prevent rapid wear.

5. Install by reversing these removal steps. Note the following procedures.

6. Install the bearing inserts into each connecting rod and cap. Make sure they are locked in place correctly. See **Figure 227**.

7. Apply assembly lube to the bearing inserts.

8. If new bearing inserts are going to be installed, check the bearing clearance as described in this chapter.

9. The 2 left- and 2 right-hand rods are matched (same weight) to reduce vibration. If replacing connecting rods, make sure to match weights.

10. Tighten the connecting rod nuts (**Figure 224**) to torque specifications in **Table 2**.

Connecting Rod Inspection

1. Check each rod for obvious damage such as cracks and burns.

2. Check the piston pin bushing for wear or scoring.

3. Take the rods to a machine shop and have them checked for twisting and bending.

4. Examine the bearing inserts (**Figure 228**) for wear, scoring or burning. They are reusable if in good condition. Make a note of the bearing size (if any) stamped on the back of the insert if the bearing is to be discarded. A previous owner may have used undersize bearings.

5. Remove the connecting rod bearing bolts and check them for cracks or twisting. Replace any bolts as required.

6. Check bearing clearance as described in this chapter.

**Connecting Rod Bearing
and Clearance Measurement**

> *CAUTION*
> *If the old bearings are to be reused be sure that they are installed in their exact original locations.*

1. Wipe bearing inserts and crankpins clean. Install bearing inserts in rod and cap.

2. Place a piece of Plastigage on one crankpin parallel to the crankshaft.

3. Install rod and cap. Tighten nuts to torque specifications in **Table 2**.

> *CAUTION*
> *Do not rotate crankshaft while Plastigage is in place.*

4. Remove rod cap.

5. Measure width of flattened Plastigage according to the manufacturer's instructions (**Figure 229**). Measure at both ends of the strip. A difference of 0.025 mm (0.001 in.) or more indicates a tapered crankpin. The crankshaft must be replaced. Confirm with a micrometer measurement of the journal OD.

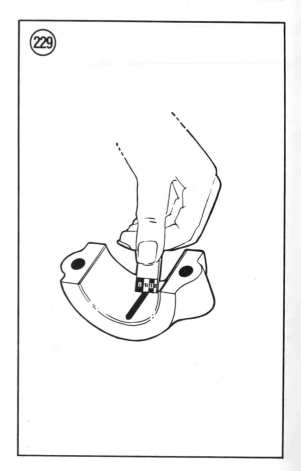

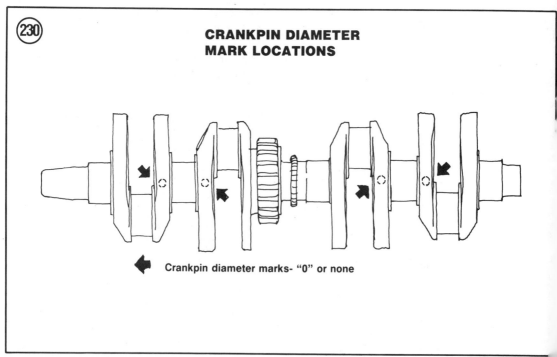

**CRANKPIN DIAMETER
MARK LOCATIONS**

Crankpin diameter marks- "0" or none

6. If the crankpin taper is within tolerance, measure the bearing clearance with the same strip of Plastigage. Correct bearing clearance is specified in **Table 1**. Remove Plastigage strips.

7. New bearing clearance should be 0.035-0.059 mm (0.0013-0.0023 in.) with a service limit of 0.10 mm (0.0.0039 in.). Remove the Plastigage strips from all bearing journals.

8. If the bearing clearance is greater than specified, use the following steps for new bearing selection.

9. If the bearing clearance is between 0.059 mm (0.0023 in.) and 0.10 mm (0.0039 in.) replace the bearing inserts with factory inserts painted blue and recheck the bearing clearance. Always replace all 8 inserts at the same time. The clearance may exceed 0.059 mm (0.0023 in.) slightly but it must not be less than the minimum clearance of 0.035 mm (0.0013 in.) or bearing seizure will occur.

10. If the bearing clearance exceeds the service limit, measure the crankshaft journal OD with a micrometer. See **Table 1** for specifications. If any journal exceeds the wear limit, replace the crankshaft.

11. If the crankshaft has been replaced, determine new bearing inserts as follows:

a. Purchase a new crankshaft. Then cross-reference the crankpin journal diameter markings (**Figure 230**) with the connecting rod mark (**Figure 226**). The connecting rod will be marked with an "0" around the weight mark or there will be no "0" around the weight mark. Refer to **Table 4** and cross-reference the crankpin diameter markings (**Figure 230**) and the connecting rod marks (**Figure 226**).

b. Recheck the clearance with the new inserts and crankshaft. The clearance should be less than the service limit and as close to the standard as possible, but not less than the standard.

12. Clean and oil the main bearing journals and insert faces.

13. After new bearings have been installed, recheck clearance with Plastigage. If the clearance is out of specifications, either the connecting rod or the crankshaft is worn beyond the service limit.

4

Tables are on the following pages.

Table 1 ENGINE SPECIFICATIONS

	Standard mm (in.)	Wear limit mm (in.)
Cam lobe height	36.150-36.299 (1.4235-1.4291)	36.06 (1.4196)
Camshaft bearing clearance	0.078-0.121 (0.003-0.0047)	0.21 (0.0082)
Camshaft journal diameter	22.900-22.922 (0.9015-0.9024)	22.87 (0.9004)
Camshaft bearing inside diameter	23.000-23.021 (0.9055-0.9063)	23.03 (0.9067)
Camshaft runout		0.1 (0.0039)
Camshaft chain (21 pins)	127.0-127.4 (5.0-5.016)	128.9 (5.075)
Rocker arm inside diameter	12.000-12.018 (0.4724-0.4731)	12.05 (0.4744)
Rocker arm shaft diameter	11.976-11.994 (0.4714-0.4722)	11.97 (0.4712)
Cylinder diameter		
ZX500	55.000-55.012 (2.1653-2.1658)	55.10 (2.1692)
ZX600	60.000-60.012 (2.3622-2.3626)	60.10 (2.3661)
Piston diameter		
ZX500	54.952-54.957 (2.1634-2.1636)	54.80 (2.1574)
ZX600	59.942-59.957 (2.3599-2.3606)	59.80 (2.3543)
Piston-to-cylinder clearance	0.043-0.070 (0.0016-0.0027)	
Piston ring groove clearance		
Top	0.03-0.07 (0.0693-0.0027)	0.17 (0.0067)
Second	0.02-0.06 (0.0007-0.0024)	0.16 (0.0063)
Piston ring groove width		
Top	1.02-1.04 (0.0401-0.0409)	1.12 (0.0441)
Second	1.21-1.23 (0.047-0.048)	1.31 (0.051)
Oil	2.51-2.53 (0.0988-0.0996)	2.6 (0.1023)
Piston ring thickness		
Top	0.97-0.99 (0.0382-0.0389)	0.9 (0.0354)
Second	1.17-1.19 (0.046-0.047)	1.1 (0.043)
Piston ring end gap		
Top	0.15-0.30 (0.006-0.011)	0.6 (0.023)
Second	0.15-0.035 (0.006-0.013)	0.065 (0.025)
Oil		
ZX500	0.2-0.7 (0.0078-0.0275)	1.0 (0.3937)
ZX600	0.3-0.9 (0.011-0.035)	2.0 (0.047)
Valve head thickness		
Intake	0.5 (0.0196)	0.3 (0.012)
Exhaust	0.8 (0.031)	0.4 (0.015)
Valve stem runout		0.05 (0.019)
Valve stem diameter		
Intake	4.975-4.990 (0.195-0.196)	4.96 (0.1953)
Exhaust	4.955-4.970 (0.1950-0.1957)	4.94 (0.9944)
Valve guide inside diameter	5.000-5.013 (0.1968-0.1973)	5.08 (0.1999)
Valve-to-valve guide clearace		
(wobble method)		
Intake	0.03-0.10 (0.0011-0.0039)	0.24 (0.0094)
Exhaust	0.08-0.15 (0.0031-0.0059)	0.29 (0.0114)
Valve spring free length		
Inner	31.0 (1.220)	30.0 (1.181)
Outer	35.0 (1.378)	33.4 (1.315)
Valve seat surface		
Outside diameter		
Intake	20.7-20.9 (0.815-0.822)	
Exhaust	18.3-18.5 (0.720-0.728)	
Width (intake and exhaust)	0.5-1.0 (0.0196-0.039)	
Connecting rod side clearance	0.09-0.20 (0.0035-0.0078)	0.40 (0.0157)
Connecting rod bearing clearance	0.035-0.059 (0.0014-0.0023)	0.10 (0.0039)
Crankpin wear limit		32.97 (1.2980)
Crankshaft runout		0.05 (0.0019)
Crankshaft journal clearance	0.014-0.038 (0.0005-0.0015)	0.08 (0.0031)
Crankshaft main journal diameter		31.96 (1.2583)
Crankshaft thrust clearance	0.05-0.20 (0.0019-0.0079)	0.40 (0.0157)

Table 2 ENGINE TIGHTENING TORQUES

	N·m	ft.-lb.
Rocker arm shaft Allen bolt	15	11
Rocker arm bearing caps	12	9
Cam cover bolts	9.8	7.2
Cam sprocket bolts	15	11
Cylinder block accorn nuts	12	9
Cylinder head		
Nuts	15	11
Bolts	12	9
Tensioner cap	25	18
Front tensioner bracket screw	15	11
Oil line bolts		
At cylinder head	12	9
At crankcase	25	18
At oil cooler	25	18
Oil drain plug	20	14.5
Oil pan bolts	12	9
Oil filter bolt	20	14.5
Bypass valve	15	11
Oil pressure switch	15	11
Neutral switch	15	11
Connecting rod nuts	36	27
Secondary shaft nut	59	54
Crankcase bolts		
Upper crankcase	12	9
Lower crankcase	27	20

4

Table 3 CRANKSHAFT MAIN BEARING SELECTION

Crankcase bore mark	Crankshaft main journal diameter mark	Insert color	Journal No.
	1	Brown	2, 4
	None	Black	1, 3, 5
None	1	Black	2, 4
None	None	Blue	2, 4
None	None	Blue	1, 3, 5

Table 4 CONNECTING ROD BEARING SELECTION

Connecting rod mark	Crankpin diameter mark	Insert color
	None	Blue
	0	Black
one	None	Black
one	0	Brown

CHAPTER FIVE

CLUTCH

This chapter provides complete service procedures for the clutch and clutch release mechanism.

The clutch is a wet-multi-plate type which operates immersed in engine oil. It is mounted on the right-hand side of the transmission mainshaft. The clutch can be serviced with the engine in the frame.

Table 1 (end of chapter) lists clutch specifications.

CLUTCH

Clutch Cover
Removal/Installation

1. Remove the lower fairing. See Chapter Thirteen.
2. Drain the engine oil as described under *Engine Oil and Filter Change* in Chapter Three.
3. Loosen the handlebar clutch cable adjust nut and loosen the adjuster (**Figure 1**).
4. Loosen the clutch cable locknuts at the engine adjuster (**Figure 2**) and disconnect the cable from the clutch release mechanism.
5. Remove the bolts securing the clutch cover in place and remove it. See **Figure 3**.

> *NOTE*
> *The lower cover bolts use tabs to clamp the pick-up coil wire. Mark these so that they can be reinstalled in the same position.*

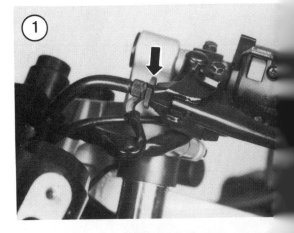

6. Remove the dowel pins (A, **Figure 4**) and gasket (B, **Figure 4**).

7. Installation is the reverse of these steps. Note the following:

    a. Replace the clutch cover gasket if damaged.

    b. Remove all gasket residue from the clutch cover and crankcase mating surfaces.

    c. Turn the clutch release mechanism shaft in the clutch cover so that the notch in the shaft aligns with the notch cast into the cover. See **Figure 5**.

    d. Align the clutch mechanism notch (**Figure 5**) with the clutch pushrod (**Figure 6**) and assemble the clutch cover. When the clutch cover is correctly assembled, the clutch mechanism adjuster arm (A, **Figure 7**) will face toward the clutch cable arm (C, **Figure 7**).

5

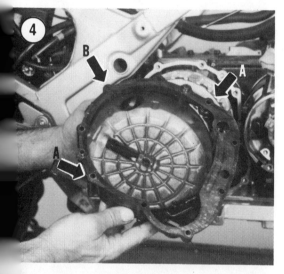

NOTE
When installing the cover screws, check that each one sticks up the same amount before you screw them all in. If not, you've got a short screw in a long hole or vice versa.

e. Refill the engine oil as described in Chapter Three.

**Clutch Cover Oil Seal
and Bearing Replacement**

A needle bearing installed in the clutch cover supports the clutch mechanism shaft and an oil seal (**Figure 8**) prevents oil leakage and bearing contamination. Replace the seal by carefully prying it out of the cover with a screwdriver. Install a new seal by driving it into the cover with a small socket. Bearing replacement requires the use of a bearing puller and installer. Follow the manufacturer's instructions when replacing the bearing.

CLUTCH RELEASE MECHANISM

Routine clutch cable free play and adjustment are described under *Clutch Lever Adjustment* in Chapter Three.

The clutch release mechanism is mounted inside the clutch cover. The release mechanism consists of a release shaft that rides on a bearing inside the clutch housing. The clutch cable is attached to the shaft. When pulled, it rotates the shaft, which moves toward the clutch and pushes against the clutch pushrod, which releases the clutch pressure plate from the friction and steel plates.

Removal/Installation

1. Remove the clutch cover as described in this chapter.
2. Remove the screw in the clutch cover (B, **Figure 7**) and pull the release mechanism shaft (A, **Figure 7**) out of the cover.
3. Clean the release mechanism shaft in solvent.
4. Check the shaft (**Figure 9**) surfaces and both notches for cracks, deep scoring and excessive wear. Replace the shaft if necessary.
5. The end of the shaft screw is machined to locate in the top shaft groove during installation. Check the end of the screw for excessive wear or damage. Replace the screw if necessary. Make sure to use the correct type screw.
6. Apply oil to the shaft and insert into the clutch cover. Install the screw and tighten securely.

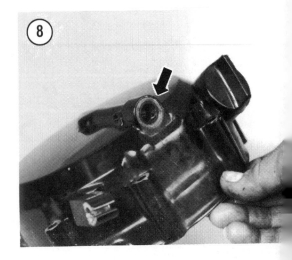

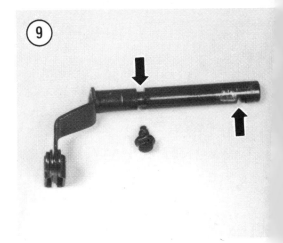

CLUTCH

Refer to **Figure 10**.

Removal

1. Remove the clutch cover as described in chapter.
2. Loosen the 5 pressure plate screws (**Figure** in a crisscross pattern. Remove the screws springs (**Figure 12**).
3. Remove the pressure plate (A, **Figure 13**) pushrod (B, **Figure 13**).
4. Remove a friction disc (**Figure 14**) and a c plate (**Figure 15**). Continue until all plate removed. Stack plates in order.

NOTE
To keep the clutch housing from turning when removing the clutch hub nut in Step 5, use the "Grabbit" special tool available from motorcycle dealers.

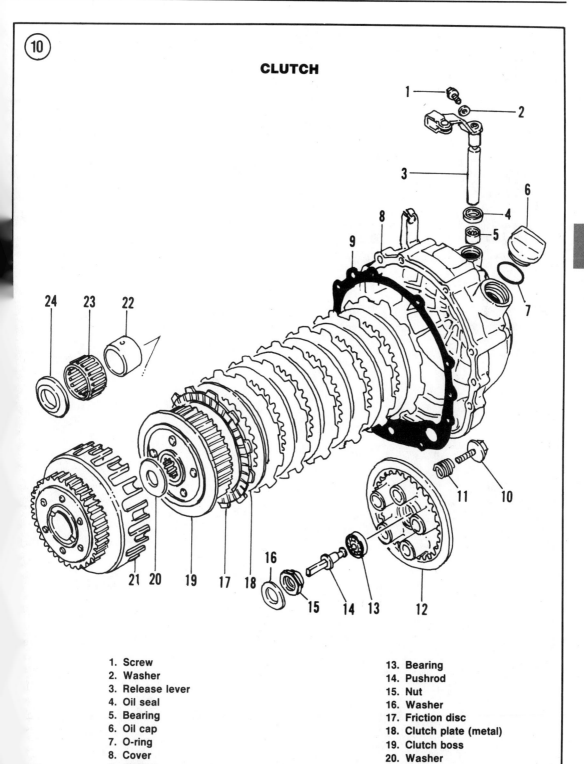

CLUTCH

1. Screw
2. Washer
3. Release lever
4. Oil seal
5. Bearing
6. Oil cap
7. O-ring
8. Cover
9. Gasket
10. Screw
11. Spring
12. Pressure plate
13. Bearing
14. Pushrod
15. Nut
16. Washer
17. Friction disc
18. Clutch plate (metal)
19. Clutch boss
20. Washer
21. Clutch housing
22. Spacer
23. Bearing
24. Washer

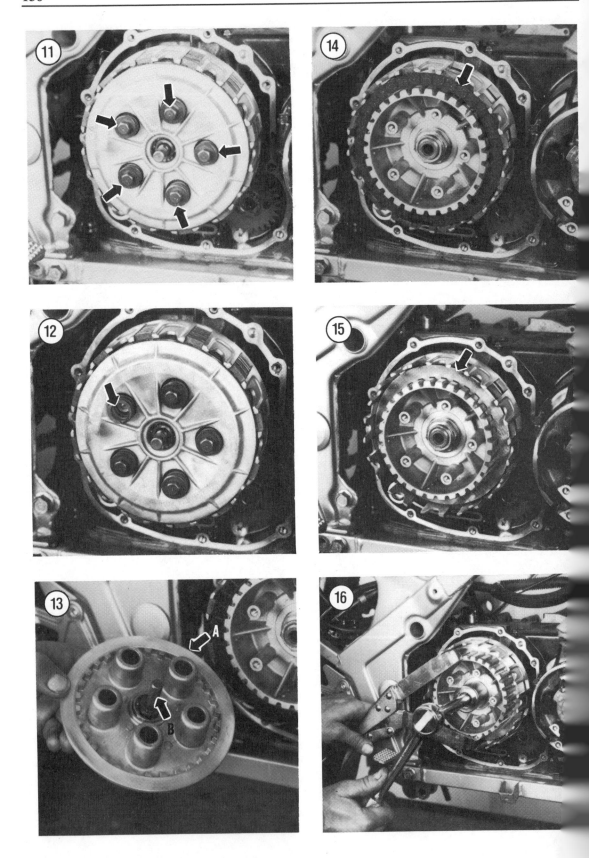

5. Straighten out the locking tab on the clutch nut and remove the clutch nut (**Figure 16**).
6. Remove the washer (**Figure 17**).
7. Remove the clutch boss (**Figure 18**).
8. Remove the washer (**Figure 19**).
9. Remove the clutch housing (**Figure 20**).
10. Remove the clutch bearing (**Figure 21**) and bearing sleeve (**Figure 22**).
11. Remove the spacer (**Figure 23**).

Inspection

1. Clean all clutch parts in a petroleum-based solvent such as kerosene, and dry thoroughly with compressed air.

5

2. Measure the free length of each clutch spring as shown in **Figure 24**. Replace any springs that are too short (**Table 1**).

3. Measure the thickness of each friction disc at several places around the disc as shown in **Figure 25**. See **Table 1** for specifications. Replace all friction discs if any one is found too thin. Do not replace only 1 or 2 discs.

4. Check the clutch metal plates for warpage as shown in **Figure 26**. If any plate is warped more than specified (**Table 1**), replace the entire set of plates. Do not replace only 1 or 2 plates.

5. Inspect the clutch boss assembly for cracks or galling in the grooves (A, **Figure 27**) where the clutch plate teeth slide. They must be smooth for chatter-free clutch operation.

6. Inspect the shaft splines (B, **Figure 27**) in the clutch boss assembly. If damage is only a slight amount, remove any small burrs with a fine-cut file. If damage is severe, replace the assembly.

7. Inspect the clutch release bearing in the pressure plate (**Figure 28**). Rotate the bearing race and check for excessive play or roughness. Replace the bearing by pulling it out of the pressure plate.

8. Inspect the pressure plate for signs of damage or warpage (A, **Figure 29**). Check the release bearing ring (B, **Figure 29**) for cracks or damage. Check the spring towers (C, **Figure 29**) for cracks or damage. Replace the pressure plate if necessary.

9. Inspect the clutch housing for cracks or galling in the grooves (A, **Figure 30**) where the clutch friction disc tabs slide. They must be smooth for chatter-free clutch operation.

10. Check clutch housing bearing bore (B, **Figure 30**) for cracks, deep scoring, excessive wear or heat discoloration. If the bearing bore is damaged, also check the clutch bearing and bearing sleeve (**Figure 31**) for damage. Replace worn or damaged parts.

11. Check the clutch housing drive gear (**Figure 32**) for tooth wear, damage or cracks. Replace the clutch housing if necessary.

12. Check the ends of the pushrod (**Figure 33**) for wear or damage. Replace if necessary.

Installation

Refer to **Figure 10**.

1. Install the spacer with the tapered side facing out (**Figure 23**).

2. Install the bearing sleeve (**Figure 22**) and clutch bearing (**Figure 21**).

3. Install the clutch housing (**Figure 20**) and washer (**Figure 19**).

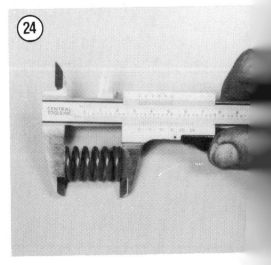

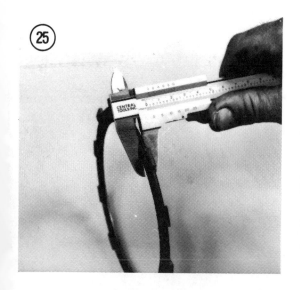

5

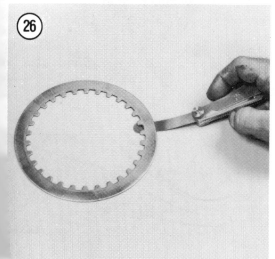

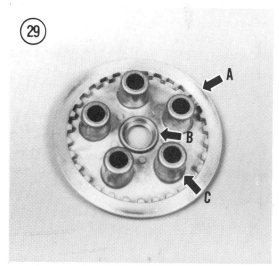

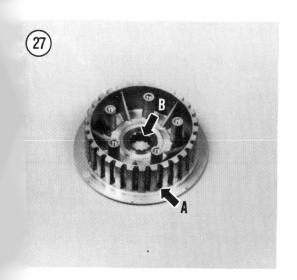

4. Install the clutch boss (**Figure 18**) and washer (**Figure 17**).

NOTE
Use the same tool as during removal to prevent the clutch boss from turning when tightening the clutch nut.

5. Use a new clutch locknut. Install the clutch locknut and tighten to 135 N•m (100 ft.-lb.). See **Figure 16**.

NOTE
If you are installing new dry plates, first wet them with oil to prevent clutch plate seizure.

6. Install the clutch plates. The sequence is friction (**Figure 14**) and then metal (**Figure 15**) plates, ending with a friction plate. Take care to align the plate tabs carefully with the clutch housing and clutch boss splines.

7. Install the release bearing into the pressure plate, if removed. See **Figure 28**.

8. Insert the pushrod into the release bearing as shown in B, **Figure 13**.

9. Install the pressure plate (A, **Figure 13**), aligning its splines with the clutch boss splines. Also insert the pushrod into the transmission mainshaft when installing the pressure plate.

10. Install the clutch springs and bolts (**Figure 11**). Tighten the bolts gradually in a crisscross pattern.

11. Install the clutch cover as described in this chapter.

Table 1 CLUTCH SPECIFICATIONS

	Standard mm (in.)	Wear limits mm (in.)
Clutch spring free length	32.6 (1.283)	31.7 (1.248)
Friction plate thickness	2.9-3.1 (0.114-0.122)	2.8 0.110)
Friction and clutch plate warpage		0.3 (0.011)

CHAPTER SIX

TRANSMISSION

6

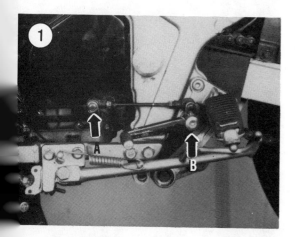

This chapter covers all the parts that transmit power from the clutch to the drive chain: engine sprocket, transmission gears, shift drum, shift forks and shift linkage. **Table 1** (end of chapter) lists transmission specifications.

SPROCKET COVER

Removal/Installation

1. Remove the shift linkage (**Figure 1**). Remove the pinch screw (A) and the pivot screw (B) securing the shift linkage and pull the shift linkage off. If the pivot boss is tight on the shaft, spread the slot open with a screwdriver.
2. Remove the screws securing the engine sprocket cover and remove the cover (**Figure 2**).
3. To install the sprocket cover, reverse the removal steps.

NEUTRAL SWITCH

Removal/Installation

The neutral light is activated by a switch mounted in the shift linkage cover (**Figure 3**) under the sprocket cover. The switch is turned on when the shift drum end plate is at its NEUTRAL positon.

1. Disconnect the electrical connector at the neutral switch.
2. Using a socket, unscrew the neutral switch and remove it.
3. Reverse to install.

ENGINE SPROCKET

The engine sprocket is on the left-hand end of the transmission countershaft, behind the sprocket cover. The drive chain is endless—it has no master link. To remove the drive chain, remove the engine sprocket from the countershaft and remove the swing arm. See *Rear Swing Arm Removal/Installation* in Chapter Eleven.

Removal/Installation

1. Remove the engine sprocket cover as described in this chapter.
2. Remove the 2 sprocket retainer screws (**Figure 4**) and remove the retainer (**Figure 5**).

> *NOTE*
> *You may have to loosen the drive chain to allow sprocket removal in Step 3. See* **Drive Chain Adjustment** *in Chapter Three.*

3. Slide the sprocket and chain off the countershaft (**Figure 6**).
4. Installation is the reverse of these steps. Note the following:
   a. Position the drive chain on the sprocket, then slide the sprocket onto the countershaft (**Figure 6**).
   b. Slide the sprocket retainer on the countershaft. Then turn the retainer and align its mounting holes with the sprocket screw holes. See **Figure 4**.
   c. Install the 2 screws and tighten to 9.8 N•m (87 in.-lb.).
   d. Adjust the drive chain. See *Drive Chain Adjustment* in Chapter Three.

Inspection

1. Inspect the engine sprocket for wear. If the teeth are undercut as shown in **Figure 7**, install a new sprocket.
2. Check the teeth on the sprocket retainer for wear, cracks, or damage (A, **Figure 8**). Replace the retainer if necessary.
3. Inspect the sprocket screws (B, **Figure 8**) for thread damage or other wear. Replace the screws if necessary.

EXTERNAL SHIFT MECHANISM

Refer to **Figure 9**. The external shift mechanism can be serviced with the engine in the frame.

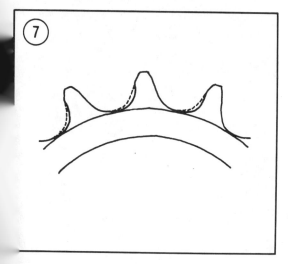

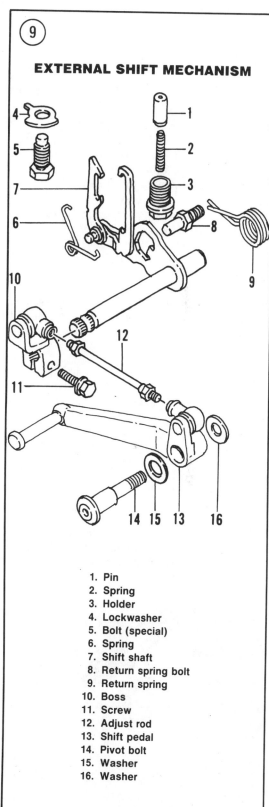

EXTERNAL SHIFT MECHANISM

1. Pin
2. Spring
3. Holder
4. Lockwasher
5. Bolt (special)
6. Spring
7. Shift shaft
8. Return spring bolt
9. Return spring
10. Boss
11. Screw
12. Adjust rod
13. Shift pedal
14. Pivot bolt
15. Washer
16. Washer

6

Removal/Installation

1. Remove the engine sprocket as described in this chapter.

2. Drain the engine oil as described under *Engine Oil and Filter Change* in Chapter Three.

3. Disconnect the electrical connector at the neutral switch (**Figure 3**).

4. Remove the screws, then remove the shift linkage cover (**Figure 10**) and gasket. Tap the cover loose with a soft mallet, if necessary. Use care. The cover is positioned with dowel pins.

5. Remove the 2 dowel pins (**Figure 11**).

> *CAUTION*
> *Do not pull the shift fork rod (C, **Figure 12**) out. If it is pulled out, the shift forks within the crankcase will fall off the rod. This would require removal and disassembly of the engine to reposition the forks.*

6. Move the shift linkage arms out of engagement with the shift drum (A, **Figure 12**) and pull the shift linkage (B, **Figure 12**) out of the crankcase.

Inspection

1. Inspect the seals in the shift linkage cover (**Figure 13**). Replace any damaged seals. Heat the cover in an oven to about 212° F and tap the old seals out. Install new seals flush with the surface of the cover, with their numbered sides out.

2. If the transmission fails to shift gears, check for a weak pawl spring (A, **Figure 14**); bent, worn or binding pawls (B, **Figure 14**); a broken return spring (**Figure 15**); a broken return spring pin; or worn shift drum pins.

3. If the transmission undershifts or overshifts, check for a binding, bent or worn detent; a weak detent spring; bent or worn pawls; worn shift drum pins; a loose return spring pin; or a bent or weak return spring.

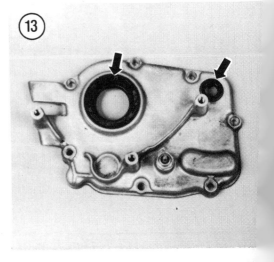

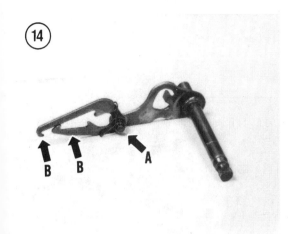

4. If the transmission jumps out of gear, check for a binding, bent or worn detent or a weak detent spring. See *Shift Detent* in this chapter.

5. Replace any other broken, bent, binding or worn parts, including shift drum pins.

Installation

1. Connect the pawl spring to the shift linkage as shown in **Figure 16**.

2. Attach the return spring to the pawl carrier as shown in **Figure 15**.

3. Spread the shift linkage pawls as you install the linkage in the crankcase, mating the pawls to the shift drum. See A, **Figure 12**.

4. Make sure the return spring is centered on the return spring pin as shown in **Figure 12**.

5. Install the 2 linkage cover dowel pins (**Figure 11**).

6. Install the cover and a new gasket (**Figure 10**). Install the screws and tighten securely.

7. Attach the connector to the neutral switch (**Figure 3**).

8. Install the engine sprocket as described in this chapter.

9. Install the engine sprocket cover as described in this chapter.

10. Refill the engine oil as described in Chapter Three.

6

SHIFT DETENT

The shift drum has a cam pinned on the external shift linkage end. A spring-loaded detent is mounted inside the oil pan, riding on the face of the shift drum cam (**Figure 17**). The detent locks the shift drum in position after a shift has been made, to help keep the transmission from jumping out of gear.

Remove and inspect the detent assembly whenever the transmission will not stay in gear or if it is very hard to shift.

Removal/Installation

1. Remove the oil pan as described under *Oil Pan Removal/Installation* in Chapter Four.
2. Pry the lockwasher tab away from the bolt (**Figure 18**).
3. Remove the shift drum detent bolt (**Figure 18**), spring and pin.
4. Remove the lockwasher (**Figure 19**).
5. Check that the plunger slides freely inside the bolt (**Figure 20**).
6. Check the spring for cracks or fatigue.
7. Check the end of the plunger for cracks, deep scoring or excessive wear.
8. Replace any part in Steps 5-7 as required.
9. Installation is the reverse of these steps. Note the following:
   a. Replace the lockwasher if the metal lock appears fatigued or excessively worn.
   b. Install the lockwasher so that the small angled tip fits into the crankcase hole. This locates the lockwasher and prevents it from turning.
   c. Apply Loctite 242 (blue) to the bolt and tighten to 25 N•m (18 ft.-lb.).
   d. Bend one end of the lockwasher against the bolt to lock it.

TRANSMISSION GEARS

Removal/Installation

Refer to **Figure 21** for this procedure.
1. Remove the engine and split the crankcase as described under *Crankcase Disassembly* in Chapter Four.

> *NOTE*
> *It is not necessary to remove crankshaft, primary chain or starter clutch when removing the transmission shafts.*

2. Before removing the transmission shafts, check gear backlash as follows:
   a. Mount a dial indicator onto a magnetic stand or some other support and place the plunger against one gear. See **Figure 22**.
   b. Rotate the gear with the plunger while holding the mating gear and note the dial indicator reading.
   c. The difference between the highest and lowest readings recorded in Step b is gear backlash. Replace both gears if the backlash exceeds the service limit specified in **Table 1**.
   d. Repeat for each set of mating gears.

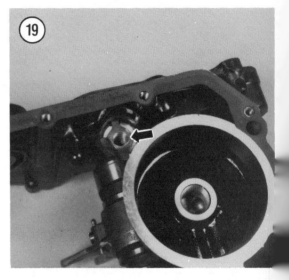

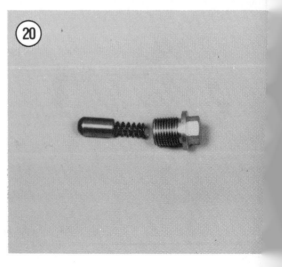

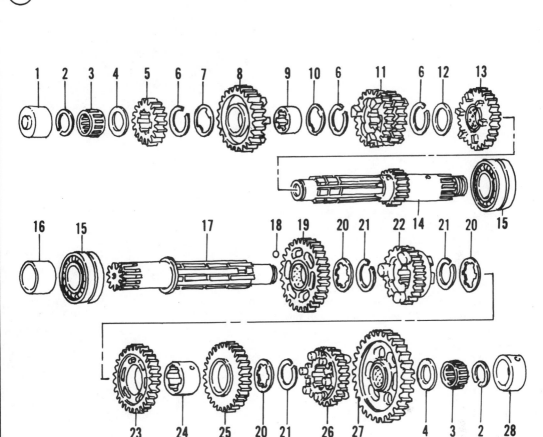

1. Bushing
2. Circlip (20 mm)
3. Bearing
4. Spacer (20.3×30×2 mm)
5. Mainshaft 2nd gear
6. Circlip (24 mm)
7. Spacer (25.5×32×1 mm)
8. Mainshaft 6th gear
9. Spacer
10. Spacer (25.3×32×1 mm)
11. Mainshaft 3rd/4th gear combination
12. Spacer (25.3×30×1)
13. Mainshaft 5th gear
14. Mainshaft/1st gear

15. Bearing
16. Spacer
17. Countershaft
18. Balls (5/32 in.)
19. Countershaft 2nd gear
20. Spacer (28.3×33.5×1)
21. Circlip (25.9 mm)
22. Countershaft 6th gear
23. Countershaft 4th gear
24. Spacer
25. Countershaft 3rd gear
26. Countershaft 5th gear
27. Countershaft 1st gear
28. Bushing

TRANSMISSION

6

3. See **Figure 23**. Carefully lift the mainshaft (A) and then the countershaft (B) out of the upper crankcase.

4. Install by reversing these steps. Note the following:

   a. Before installing any components, coat all bearing surfaces with assembly oil.

   b. When installing the transmission shaft assemblies, make sure the set pins (A, **Figure 24**) and both set rings (B, **Figure 24**) are in place in the upper crankcase before installing the transmission assemblies.

> *CAUTION*
> *If the mainshaft and countershaft bearings do not engage the set pins and set rings correctly, there will be no clearance between the crankcase and the outer bearing races.*

   c. Align the pin hole in the bearing race (A, **Figure 25**) and the circlip groove in the ball bearing (B, **Figure 25**) with the pins (A, **Figure 24**) and set rings (B, **Figure 25**) and install the transmission assemblies in the upper crankcase. See **Figure 23**.

   d. Assemble and install the engine as described in Chapter Four.

Transmission Service Notes

1. A divided container such as an egg carton can be used to help maintain correct alignment and positioning of the parts as they are removed from the transmission shafts.

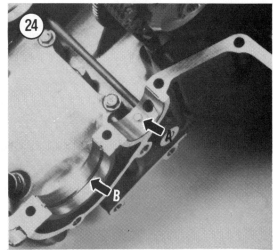

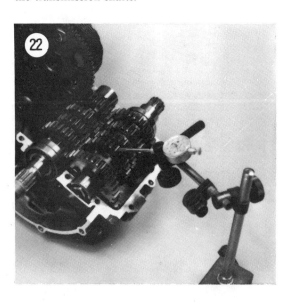

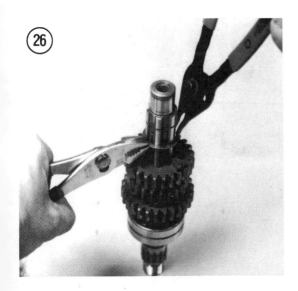

2. The circlips are a tight fit on the transmission shafts. They should all be replaced during reassembly.

3. Circlips will turn and fold over, making removal and installation difficult. To ease replacement, open the circlip with a pair of circlip pliers while at the same time holding the back of the circlip with a pair of pliers and remove it. See **Figure 26**. Repeat for installation.

Mainshaft
Disassembly/Assembly

Refer to **Figure 21**.
1. Remove the bearing race (**Figure 27**).
2. Remove the circlip (**Figure 28**) and slide off the needle bearing (**Figure 29**).
3. Remove the washer (**Figure 30**).

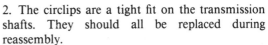

6

4. Slide off second gear (**Figure 31**).

5. Remove the circlip and washer (**Figure 32**).

6. Slide off sixth gear (**Figure 33**).

7. Remove the spacer (**Figure 34**).

8. Remove the washer and circlip (**Figure 35**).

9. Slide off the third/fourth combination gear (**Figure 36**).

10. Remove the circlip and washer (**Figure 37**).

11. Slide off fifth gear (**Figure 38**).

12. If necessary, remove the mainshaft bearing (**Figure 39**) with a bearing puller. Install a new bearing with a press; refer service to a machine shop.

13. Inspect the mainshaft assembly as described in this chapter.

14. Assemble by reversing these disassembly steps. Note the following:

   a. When installing circlips on splined shafts, position them so that their openings fall on top of a spline groove and do not align with a splined washer tooth (**Figure 40**).

   b. Align the sixth gear bushing oil hole with the hole in the mainshaft (**Figure 34**).

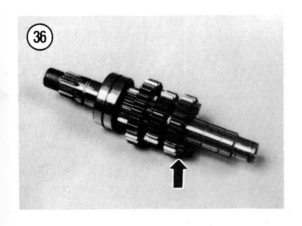

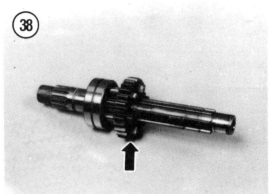

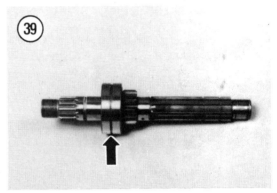

6

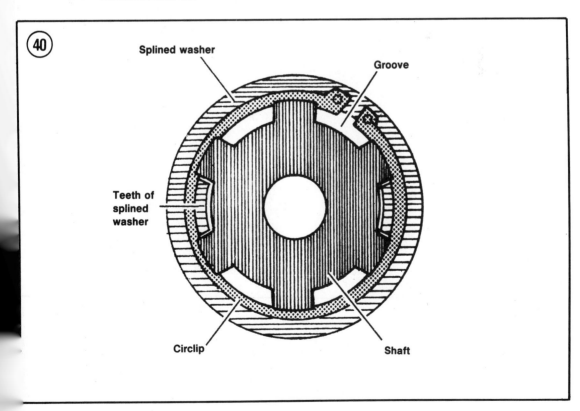

Splined washer

Groove

Teeth of
splined
washer

Circlip

Shaft

c. Refer to **Figure 41** for correct placement of the gears.

d. Make sure each gear engages properly to the adjoining gear where applicable.

Countershaft
Disassembly/Assembly

Refer to **Figure 21**.

1. Remove the bearing race (**Figure 42**).
2. Remove the circlip (**Figure 43**) and remove the bearing (**Figure 44**).
3. Remove the washer (**Figure 45**).
4. Slide off first gear (**Figure 46**).
5. Remove fifth gear (**Figure 47**) as follows. Fifth gear (**Figure 47**) has 3 steel balls located between the gear and the shaft. These are used for neutral location when shifting from first gear. To remove the gear, spin the shaft in a vertical position while holding onto third gear. Pull fifth gear up and off the shaft.
6. Remove the circlip and washer (**Figure 48**).
7. Slide off third gear (**Figure 49**).
8. Slide off fourth gear (**Figure 50**).
9. Remove the spacer (**Figure 51**).

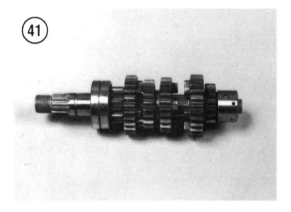

(41)

(42)

(43)

(44)

(45)

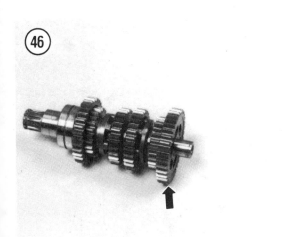

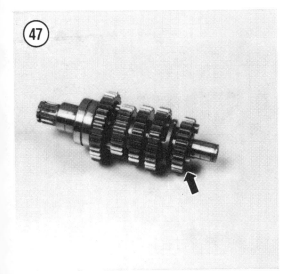

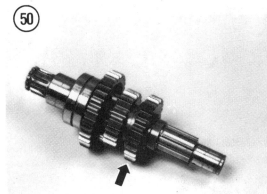

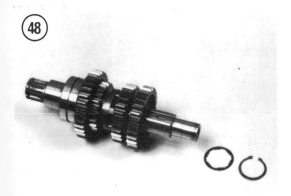

6

10. Remove the washer and circlip (**Figure 52**).

11. Slide off sixth gear (**Figure 53**).

12. Remove the circlip and washer (**Figure 54**).

13. Slide off second gear (A, **Figure 55**).

14. If necessary, remove the bearing (B, **Figure 55**) with a bearing puller. Install the new bearing with a press. Refer service to a machine shop.

15. Inspect the countershaft assembly as described in this chapter.

16. Assemble by reversing these disassembly steps. Note the following:

    a. When installing circlips on splined shafts, position them so that their openings fall on top of a spline groove and do not align with a splined washer tooth (**Figure 40**).

    b. Align the fourth gear bushing oil hole with the hole in the countershaft (**Figure 56**).

    c. When installing the 3 balls into fifth gear (**Figure 47**), *do not use grease* to hold them in place. The balls must be able to move freely during normal transmission operation.

    d. Refer to **Figure 57** for correct placement of the gears.

    e. Make sure each gear engages properly to the adjoining gear where applicable.

Inspection

1. Clean all parts in cleaning solvent and dry thoroughly.

2. Inspect the gears visually for cracks, chips, broken teeth and burned teeth. Check the gear dogs (**Figure 58**) to make sure they are not rounded off. If dogs are rounded off, check the shift forks as

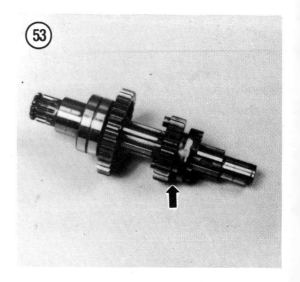

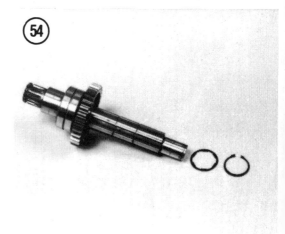

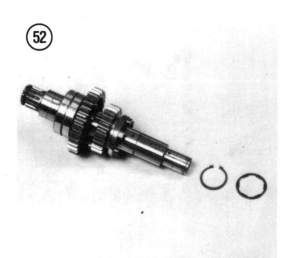

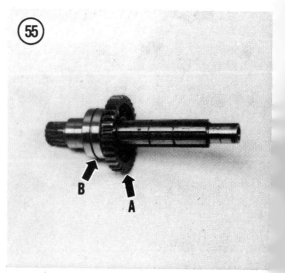

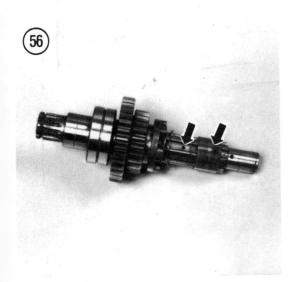

(56)

(57)

(58)

described later in this chapter. More than likely, one or more of the shift forks is bent.

NOTE
Defective gears should be replaced. It is a good idea to replace the mating gear even though it may not show as much wear or damage. Remember that accelerated wear to new parts is normally caused by contact from worn parts.

3. Inspect all freewheeling gear bearing surfaces (**Figure 59**) for wear, discoloration and galling. Inspect the mating shaft bearing surface also. If there is any metal flaking or visual damage, replace both parts.

4. Inspect the mainshaft and countershaft shaft splines for wear or discoloration. Check the mating gear internal splines also. If no visual damage is apparent, install each sliding gear on its respective shaft and work the gear back and forth to make sure gear operates smoothly.

5. Replace any washers that show wear.

6. Discard the circlips and replace them during assembly.

7. Inspect the needle bearings and their housings for wear or damage. Replace if necessary.

8. Check the countershaft slot (**Figure 60**) where the fifth gear ball bearings engage. If the slot is

6

(59)

(60)

worn or damaged, the countershaft must be replaced.

Shift Drum and Forks
Removal/Installation

Refer to **Figure 61**.

1. Remove the mainshaft and countershaft as described in this chapter.

2. Remove the shift fork shaft and remove the 2 shift forks from the lower crankcase. See **Figure 62**.

3. Pry the lockwasher tab away from the shift drum detent bolt (**Figure 63**).

4. Remove the shift drum detent bolt (**Figure 63**), spring and pin.

5. Remove the shift drum as follows:

  a. Remove the circlip (**Figure 64**).

  b. Remove the cam (**Figure 65**) and pin (**Figure 66**) from the end of the shift drum.

  c. Remove the cotter pin (**Figure 67**) and pin (**Figure 68**) from the shift drum/shift fork assembly.

  d. Pull the shift drum out partway (A, **Figure 69**) and remove the fifth/sixth gear shift fork (B, **Figure 69**).

e. Remove the shift drum (**Figure 70**).

NOTE
Label the shift forks so that they can be reinstalled in their original positions.

6. Inspect the shift drum and fork assembly as described in this chapter.

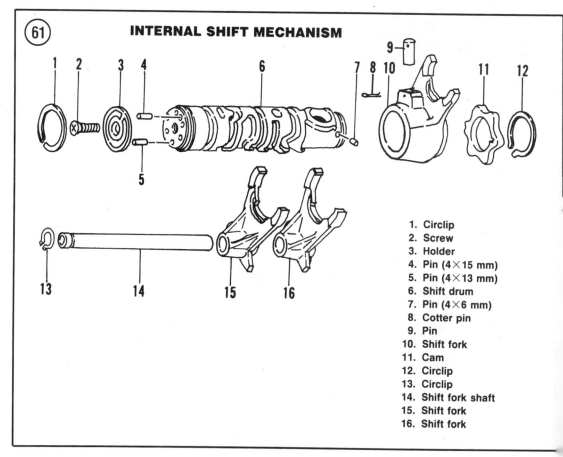

INTERNAL SHIFT MECHANISM

1. Circlip
2. Screw
3. Holder
4. Pin (4×15 mm)
5. Pin (4×13 mm)
6. Shift drum
7. Pin (4×6 mm)
8. Cotter pin
9. Pin
10. Shift fork
11. Cam
12. Circlip
13. Circlip
14. Shift fork shaft
15. Shift fork
16. Shift fork

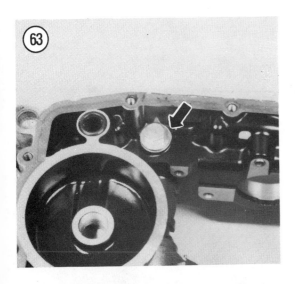

6

7. Install the shift drum as follows:
   a. Insert the shift drum partway into the crankcase (**Figure 70**).
   b. Install the fifth/sixth gear shift fork onto the shift drum so that the long end faces as shown in B, **Figure 69**.
   c. Push the shift drum (A, **Figure 69**) in all the way.
   d. Align the pin hole in the shift fork (A, **Figure 71**) with the center shift drum groove (B, **Figure 71**). Then insert the pin through the shift fork pin hole and into the shift drum groove (**Figure 68**).
   e. Install a *new* circlip through the shift fork and pin (**Figure 67**). Bend the end of the cotter pin over to lock it (**Figure 72**).
   f. Install the pin (**Figure 66**) into the end of the shift drum.
   g. Align the slot in the cam with the pin and install the cam (**Figure 65**).
   h. Secure the cam with the circlip (**Figure 64**).

8. Install the shift detent as follows:
   a. Assemble the shift detent assembly (**Figure 73**) and install into the crankcase.
   b. Replace the detent bolt lockwasher if the metal lock appears fatigued or excessively worn.
   c. Install the lockwasher so that small angled tip fits in into the crankcase hole. This locates the lockwasher and prevents it from turning.
   d. Apply Loctite 242 (blue) to the bolt (**Figure 63**) and tighten to 25 N•m (18 ft.-lb.).
   e. Bend one end of the lockwasher against the bolt to lock it.

9. Install the 2 independent shift forks as follows:
   a. Make sure the circlip is installed on the end of the shift fork shaft (**Figure 74**).

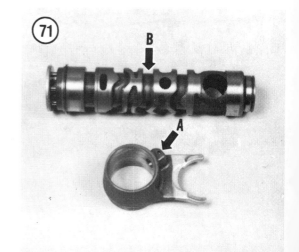

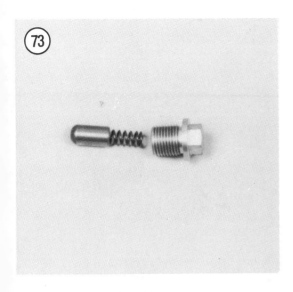

b. Install the shift fork shaft partway through the crankcase (**Figure 75**).

c. Install the shift forks onto the shift fork shaft (**Figure 76**). Engage the pins on the shift forks with the shift drum grooves as shown in **Figure 76**. Insert the shift fork shaft all the way.

10. Install the transmission shafts as described in this chapter.

Shift Drum Disassembly

1. Remove the screw (**Figure 77**) from the end of the shift drum. Then remove the following parts:

   a. Pin plate.

   b. Pins.

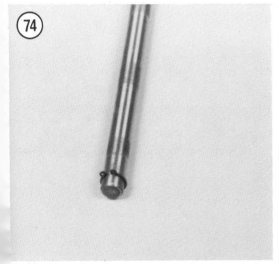

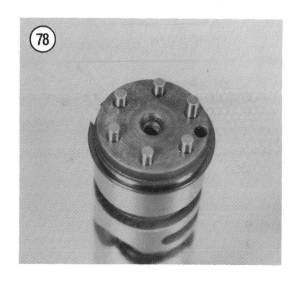

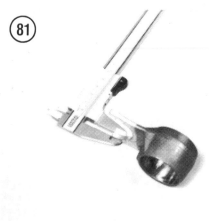

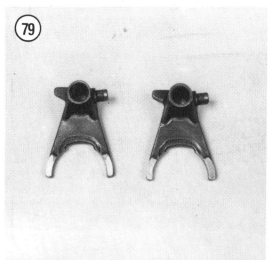

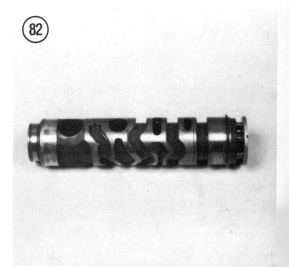

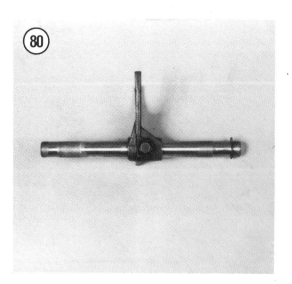

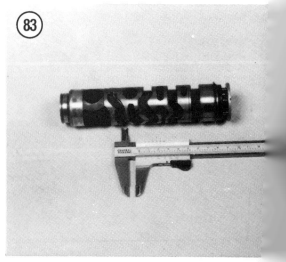

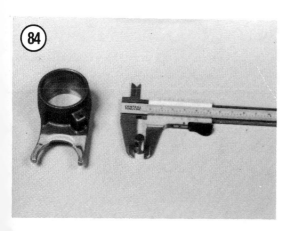

2. Inspect the shift drum as described in this section.

3. Install the long pin (which times the neutral indicator light) as shown in relation to the hole on the end of the drum (**Figure 78**).

NOTE
If the neutral holder is installed incorrectly, the neutral indicator light will not light when the transmission is in NEUTRAL.

4. Apply Loctite 242 (blue) to the screw and install it into the shift drum. Tighten the screw securely.

Inspection

1. Inspect each shift fork for signs of wear or cracking. See **Figure 79**. Examine the shift forks at the points where they contact the slider gear. This surface should be smooth with no signs of wear or damage. Make sure the forks slide smoothly on the shaft (**Figure 80**) or shift drum. Make sure the shaft is not bent. This can be checked by removing the shift forks from the shaft and rolling the shaft on a piece of glass. Any clicking noise detected indicates a bent shaft.

2. Measure the tips of each shift fork (**Figure 81**) and compare to the specificatons in **Table 1**. Replace a shift fork if the tips are is too thin.

3. Check grooves in the shift drum (**Figure 82**) for wear or roughness. Measure the groove's width with a vernier caliper (**Figure 83**). Replace the shift drum if any groove is too wide (**Table 1**).

4. Measure the shift fork guide pin diameter (**Figure 84**). Replace the shift fork(s) if the guide pin diameter is too small (**Table 1**).

6

Table 1 TRANSMISSION SPECIFICATIONS

	Standard mm (in.)	Wear limit mm (in.)
ear backlash	0-0.17 (0-0.0067)	0.25 (0.0098)
ear shift fork groove width	5.05-5.15 (0.199-0.203)	5.3 (0.209)
hift fork guide pin diameter	7.9-8.0 (0.311-0.315)	7.8 (0.307)
hift fork ear thickness	4.9-5.0 (0.193-0.197)	4.8 (0.189)
ift drum groove width	8.05-8.20 (0.317-0.323)	8.3 (0.327)

NOTE: If you own a 1988 or later model, first check the Supplement at the back of this book for any new service information.

CHAPTER SEVEN

FUEL, EMISSION CONTROL AND EXHAUST SYSTEMS

This chapter describes complete procedures for servicing the fuel, emission control and exhaust systems. Carburetor specifications are listed in **Table 1** (end of chapter).

CARBURETOR

Removal/Installation

Remove all 4 carburetors as an assembled unit.

1. Park the motorcycle on the centerstand.

2. Remove the top fairing assembly and the side rails. See Chapter Thirteen.

3. Remove the fuel tank as described in this chapter.

4. Remove the battery as described under *Battery Removal/Installation and Electrolyte Level Check* in Chapter Three.

5. Pull the vacuum switch air hose out of the air filter housing (A, **Figure 1**).

6. Remove the carburetor-to-air cleaner housing hose springs. Then disconnect the hoses at the rear of the carburetor.

7. Remove the air cleaner housing screws and lift the housing (B, **Figure 1**) out of the frame.

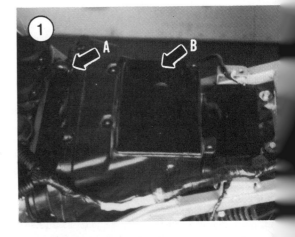

NOTE
Label the throttle cables before disconnecting them in Step 8 and Step 9.

8. Remove the screws securing the throttle housing (**Figure 2**) and separate the housing. Then pull the throttle cables out of the twist grip.

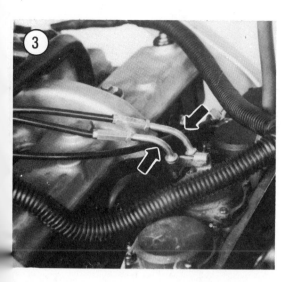

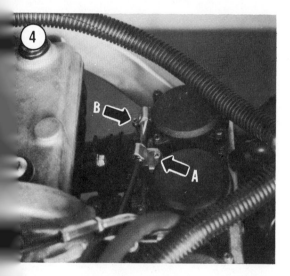

9. Disconnect the throttle cables at the carburetor (**Figure 3**).

10. Loosen the choke cable bracket screw (A, **Figure 4**) and disconnect the cable at the carburetor (B, **Figure 4**).

11. Remove the carburetor-to-intake manifold boot clamps (**Figure 5**).

12. Grasp the carburetors on both ends and work them up and down and remove from the intake manifold boots (**Figure 6**).

13. Stuff clean shop rags into the intake manifold to prevent dirt from entering the engine.

14. Installation is the reverse of these steps. Note the following:

   a. Make sure the carburetors are fully seated forward in the rubber carburetor holders. You should feel a solid "bottoming out" when they're correctly installed. Tighten the boot clamps securely.

> *CAUTION*
> *Make sure the carburetor boots are airtight. Air leaks can cause severe engine damage because of a lean mixture or the intake of dirt.*

   b. Tighten the air cleaner housing mounting screws after the carburetors have been installed.

   c. Check throttle cable routing after installation. The cables must not be twisted, kinked or pinched.

   d. Adjust the throttle cables as described under *Throttle Cable Adjustment* in Chapter Three.

   e. Adjust the choke cable as described under *Choke Cable Adjustment* in Chapter Three.

   f. Check carburetor adjustment as described under *Carburetor* in Chapter Three. Adjust if necessary.

7

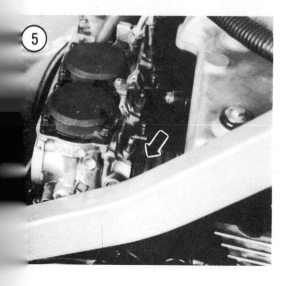

⑦

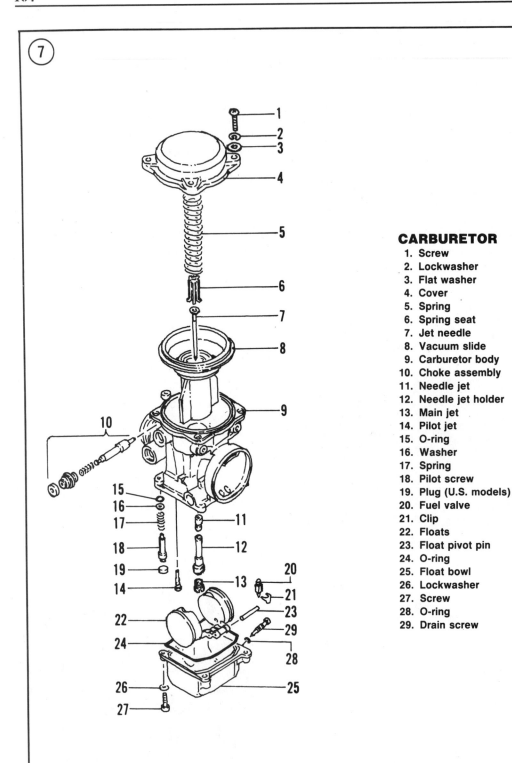

CARBURETOR
1. Screw
2. Lockwasher
3. Flat washer
4. Cover
5. Spring
6. Spring seat
7. Jet needle
8. Vacuum slide
9. Carburetor body
10. Choke assembly
11. Needle jet
12. Needle jet holder
13. Main jet
14. Pilot jet
15. O-ring
16. Washer
17. Spring
18. Pilot screw
19. Plug (U.S. models)
20. Fuel valve
21. Clip
22. Floats
23. Float pivot pin
24. O-ring
25. Float bowl
26. Lockwasher
27. Screw
28. O-ring
29. Drain screw

Disassembly/Reassembly

Refer to **Figure 7**. Disassemble and reassemble only one carburetor at a time to prevent accidental interchange of parts.

1. Remove the upper chamber cover (**Figure 8**).
2. Remove the spring and spring seat (**Figure 9**).
3. Remove the jet needle (**Figure 10**).
4. Lift the diaphragm out of the carburetor (**Figure 11**).
5. Remove the float bowl (**Figure 12**).

NOTE
*When removing the No. 1 and No. 2 float bowls, it will be necessary to disconnect the idle adjusting screw holder (**Figure 13**).*

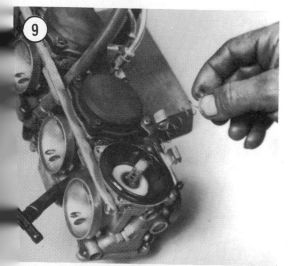

7

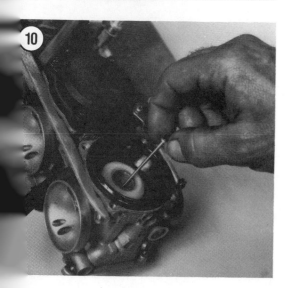

6. Remove the float pin (**Figure 14**) and float (**Figure 15**).

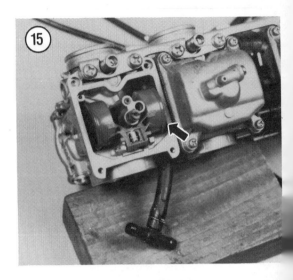

NOTE
*Be sure to remove the float valve needle and its hanger clip from the float (**Figure 16**).*

7. Remove the main jet (**Figure 17**).
8. Remove the needle jet (**Figure 18**).
9. Remove the pilot jet (**Figure 19**).
10A. *All models except U.S.:* Carefully screw in the mixture screw until it seats *lightly*. Count and record the number of turns so it can be installed in the same position during assembly. Then remove

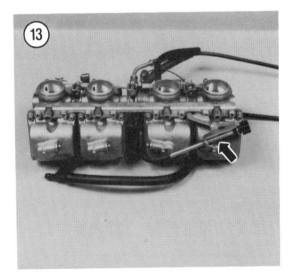

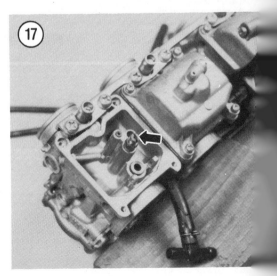

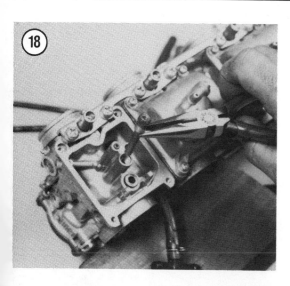

the idle mixture screw (**Figure 20**), spring, washer and O-ring.

10B. *U.S. models:* The idle mixture screw is sealed at the factory. If necessary, remove it as described under *Idle Mixture Screw Removal/Installation (U.S. Models)* in this chapter.

11. Repeat for the opposite carburetors.

12. Separation of the carburetors is not required for cleaning.

13. Clean and inspect the carburetors as described in this chapter.

14. Installation is the reverse of these steps. Note the following.

15. Assemble the spring and spring seat as shown in **Figure 21**.

16. Replace the float bowl O-ring (**Figure 22**) if deformed, cracked or if the bowl leaked.

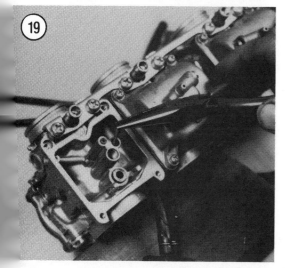

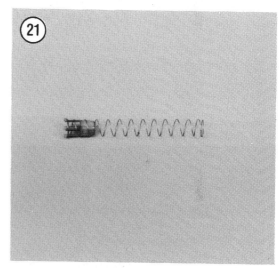

7

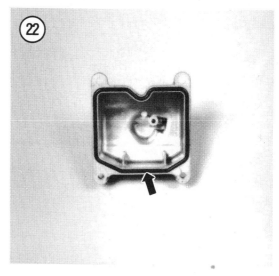

17. Install the needle jet through the center hole in the vacuum piston (A, **Figure 23**). See **Figure 10**. Turn the needle seat so that it does not block the off-center hole at the bottom of the vacuum piston (B, **Figure 23**).

18. When installing the upper chamber cover, push up on the piston just enough so that there is no crease on the diaphragm lip. Install the upper chamber cover and screws.

19. Check the fuel level. See *Fuel Level Inspection/Adjustment* in this chapter.

Idle Mixture Screw Removal/Installation (U.S. Models)

The idle mixture screws are sealed at the factory with a plug bonded to the top of the pilot screw bore (**Figure 24**). When disassembling the carburetors for overhaul, the bonding agent and cover must be removed for access to the plug, O-ring and screw.

1. Carefully scrape out the bonding agent from the recess in the carburetor body.

2. Punch and pry out the plug with a small screwdriver or awl.

3. Carefully screw in the idle mixture screw (**Figure 20**) until it seats *lightly*. Count and record the number of turns so it can be installed in the *same* position during assembly.

4. Remove the mixture screw, O-ring and spring from the carburetor body.

5. Repeat for the other carburetors. Make sure to keep each carburetor's parts separate.

6. Inspect the O-ring and the end of the mixture screw. Replace if damaged or worn.

7. Install the mixture screws in the same position as noted during removal (Step 3).

8. Install new plugs. Secure the plugs with a small amount of non-hardening bonding agent.

> *CAUTION*
> *Apply only a small amount of bonding agent. Too much may close off the air passage.*

Cleaning and Inspection

1. Thoroughly clean and dry all parts. If a special carburetor cleaning solution is used, all non-metal parts must be removed (gaskets, O-rings, etc.).

> *NOTE*
> *If a carburetor cleaning solution is used, rinse the parts in clean water and allow to dry before assembly.*

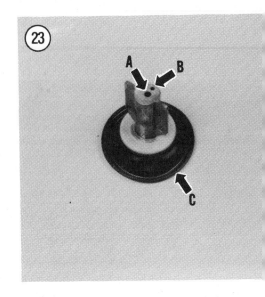

(23)

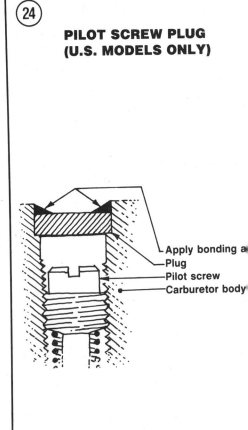

(24)

PILOT SCREW PLUG (U.S. MODELS ONLY)

Apply bonding a
Plug
Pilot screw
Carburetor body

2. Blow out all the passages and jets with compressed air. Don't use wire to clean any of the orifices. Wire will enlarge or gouge them and offset the air/fuel ratio.

3. Check the cone of the float needle (**Figure 25**) and replace it if it is scored or pitted.

4. Examine the end of the air mixture screw for grooves or roughness. Replace it if damaged. Replace a worn O-ring.

5. Inspect the throttle slide for scoring and wear. Replace if necessary.

6. Inspect the diaphragm (C, **Figure 23**) for tears, cracks or other damage. Replace the throttle slide assembly if the diaphragm is damaged.

Separation

See **Figure 26**. The carburetors are joined by upper and lower mounting plates on the front side (**Figure 27**) and an upper plate on the rear side (**Figure 28**). Almost all carburetor parts can be replaced without separating the carburetors. If the carburetors must be cleaned internally in a carburetor cleaning solution or if the pipe fittings (**Figure 26**) must be replaced, the carburetors must be separated.

Remove the idle adjusting screw holder (**Figure ?**).

NOTE
An impact driver with a Phillips bit (see Chapter One) will be necessary to loosen the screws securing the holding plates onto the carburetor housings. Attempting to loose the screws with a Phillips screwdriver may ruin the screw heads.

2. Remove the 3 carburetor mounting plates. See **Figure 26**.

3. Carefully separate the carburetors. Note the position of any springs and cable brackets.

4. Assemble the carburetors by reversing these steps. Note the following:
   a. Replace all fuel pipe O-rings.
   b. Assemble the fuel pipe O-rings as shown in **Figure 29**.
   c. The carburetor bores (**Figure 27**) must be parallel. If not, place the assembly on a flat surface and align the carburetors (**Figure 30**).
   d. Apply Loctite 242 (blue) to all carburetor mounting plate screws before installation. Tighten the screws securely.

FUEL LEVEL

The fuel level in the carburetor float bowls is critical to proper performance. The fuel flow rate from the bowl up to the carburetor bore depends not only on the vacuum in the throttle bore and the size of the jets, but also on the fuel level. Kawasaki gives a specification of actual fuel level, measured from the top edge of the float bowl with the carburetor held level (**Figure 31**).

This measurement is more useful than a simple float height measurement because the actual fuel level can vary from bike to bike, even when their floats are set at the same height. Fuel level inspection requires a special fuel level gauge (Kawasaki part No. 57001-1017). See **Figure 31**.

The fuel level is adjusted by bending the float arm tang.

Inspection/Adjustment

Carburetors leave the factory with float levels properly adjusted. Rough riding, a worn needle valve or bent float tang can cause the float level to

7

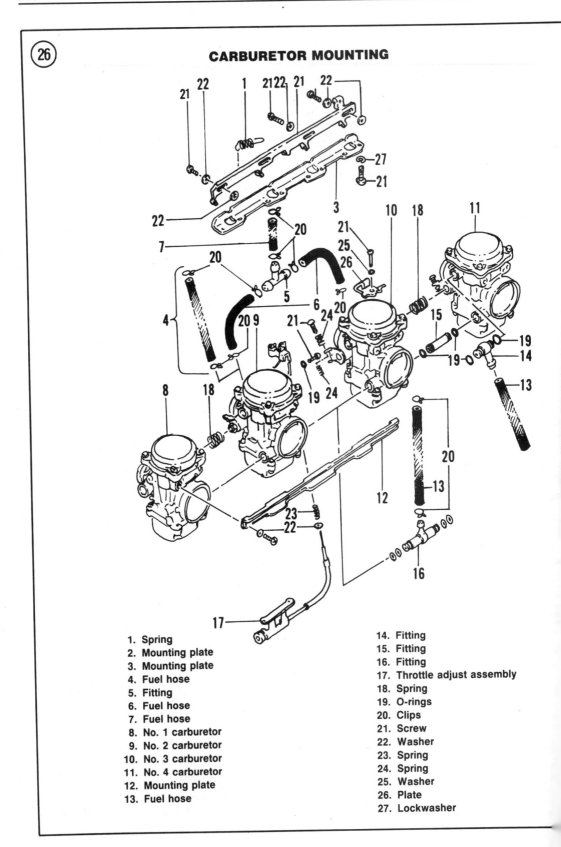

CARBURETOR MOUNTING

1. Spring
2. Mounting plate
3. Mounting plate
4. Fuel hose
5. Fitting
6. Fuel hose
7. Fuel hose
8. No. 1 carburetor
9. No. 2 carburetor
10. No. 3 carburetor
11. No. 4 carburetor
12. Mounting plate
13. Fuel hose
14. Fitting
15. Fitting
16. Fitting
17. Throttle adjust assembly
18. Spring
19. O-rings
20. Clips
21. Screw
22. Washer
23. Spring
24. Spring
25. Washer
26. Plate
27. Lockwasher

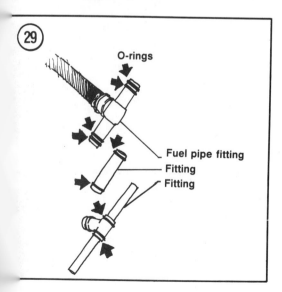

change. To adjust the float level on these carburetors, perform the following.

WARNING
Some gasoline will drain from the carburetors during this procedure. Work in a well-ventilated area, at least 50 feet from any open flame. Do not smoke. Wipe up spills immediately.

1. Remove the carburetors as described in this chapter.

2. Mount the carburetors on a fabricated wooden stand or blocks so that they are in a perfectly vertical position.

3. Remove the fuel tank and place it on wooden blocks higher than the carburetors. Then connect a length of fuel hose (6 mm in diameter and approximately 300 mm long) to the fuel tank and carburetor.

4. Connect a length of hose to the float bowl as shown in **Figure 31**. Connect a fuel level gauge (Kawasaki part No. 57001-1017) to the opposite end of the hose. Hold the fuel level gauge against the carburetor so that the "0" line on the gauge is several millimeters higher than the bottom edge of the carburetor housing (**Figure 31**).

5. Turn the fuel valve to PRI. Then turn the carburetor drain plug a few turns.

6. Wait until the fuel in the gauge settles. Then slowly lower the gauge until the "0" line is even with the bottom edge of the carburetor body (**Figure 31**). The fuel level should be 0.5 ±-1 mm above the edge of the carburetor body.

7. Turn the fuel valve to ON.

8. If the fuel level is incorrect, adjust the float height. Remove the float bowl from the carburetor

7

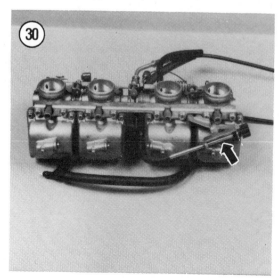

and remove the float. Bend the float tang (**Figure 32**) as required to get the right float level. Install the float bowl and recheck the fuel level.

9. Repeat for each carburetor.

10. Install the carburetors as described in this chapter.

FUEL TANK

WARNING
Some fuel may spill in the following procedure. Work in a well-ventilated area at least 50 feet from any sparks or flames, including gas appliance pilot lights. Do not smoke in the area. Keep a BC rated fire extinguisher handy.

Removal/Installation

1. Check that the ignition switch is off.
2. Place the bike on its centerstand.
3. Remove the seat and both side covers.
4. Remove the battery cover and disconnect the negative battery terminal (**Figure 33**).
5. Disconnect the fuel level sensor connector (**Figure 34**).
6. Turn the fuel tap to ON and disconnect the fuel and vacuum lines at the fuel tap.
7. Label and disconnect the hose(s) at the rear of the fuel tank.

WARNING
Plug the hoses disconnected in Step 7.

8. Remove the bolts from the rear of the fuel tank.
9. Pull the tank up and to the rear and remove it.

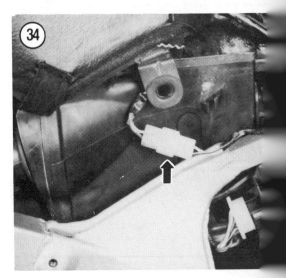

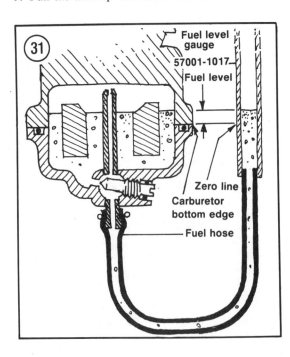

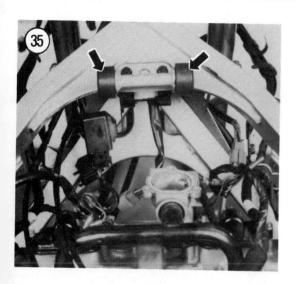

10. Pour the fuel in a container approved for gasoline storage.

11. Inspect the fuel tank dampers (**Figure 35**) for damage and replace if necessary. Check the damper mount (**Figure 35**) for looseness. Tighten the mounting bolts if necessary.

12. To install the fuel tank, reverse the removal steps. Note the following:

    a. Don't pinch any wires or control cables during installation.

    b. Reconnect all hoses and connectors.

FUEL VALVE

The vacuum-operated fuel valve (**Figure 36**) has no OFF position. The valve should pass no fuel in

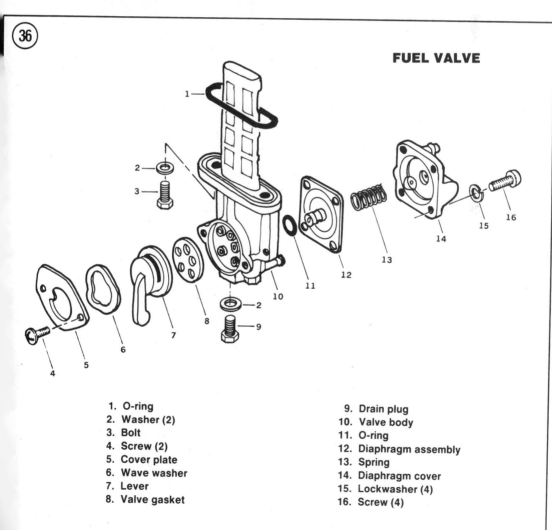

FUEL VALVE

1. O-ring
2. Washer (2)
3. Bolt
4. Screw (2)
5. Cover plate
6. Wave washer
7. Lever
8. Valve gasket
9. Drain plug
10. Valve body
11. O-ring
12. Diaphragm assembly
13. Spring
14. Diaphragm cover
15. Lockwasher (4)
16. Screw (4)

ON or RES until a running engine provides the vacuum required to operate the diaphragm valve. In PRI (prime) the valve will pass fuel whether the engine is running or not.

Removal/Installation

> *WARNING*
> *Some fuel may spill in the following procedure. Work in a well-ventilated area at least 50 feet from any sparks or flames, including gas appliance pilot lights. Do not smoke in the area. Keep a BC rated fire extinguisher handy.*

1. Remove the fuel tank as described in this chapter.
2. Turn the fuel valve to PRI (prime) and drain the fuel into a container approved for gasoline storage.
3. Remove the 2 fuel valve mounting bolts, the valve and O-ring.
4. Inspect the fuel valve mounting O-ring and clean the feed tube screen whenever the valve is removed (**Figure 37**).
5. Install the fuel valve by reversing these steps. Note the following:
    a. Make sure that fuel does not flow in the ON position when the engine is *not* running.
    b. Pour a small amount of gasoline into the tank after installing the fuel valve and check for leaks.

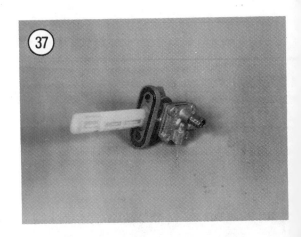

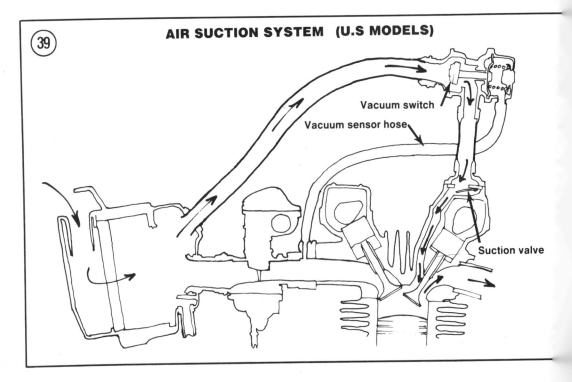

AIR SUCTION SYSTEM (U.S MODELS)

Vacuum switch

Vacuum sensor hose

Suction valve

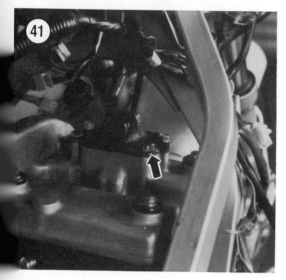

AIR SUCTION SYSTEM (U.S. MODELS)

The air suction system (**Figure 39**) consists of a vacuum switch, 2 air suction valves (reed valves) and air and vacuum hoses. This system does not pressurize air, but uses the momentary pressure differentials generated by the exhaust gas pulses to introduce fresh air into the exhaust ports.

The vacuum switch normally allows fresh air pulses into the exhaust ports but shuts off air flow during engine braking. This helps prevent backfiring in the exhaust system due to the greater amount of unburned fuel in the exhaust gas during deceleration.

The air suction valves, on top of the valve cover, are basically check valves. They allow the fresh air to enter the exhaust port and prevent any air or exhaust from reversing back into the system.

Suction Valve Removal/Installation

If the engine idle is not smooth, if engine power decreases seriously or if there are any abnormal engine noises, remove the air suction valves and inspect them.

WARNING
Some fuel may spill in the following procedure. Work in a well-ventilated area at least 50 feet from any sparks or flames, including gas appliance pilot lights. Do not smoke in the area. Keep a BC rated fire extinguisher handy.

1. Check that the ignition switch is off.
2. Remove the fuel tank as described in this chapter.
3. Remove the ignition coils as described in Chapter Eight.
4. Loosen the baffle plate screws and move the plate forward (**Figure 40**).
5. Slide up the lower hose clamps and pull the hoses off the air suction valve covers.

NOTE
*The air suction valves (**Figure 41**) can be removed with the cylinder head cover installed on the engine. The following steps show the cylinder head cover removed for clarity.*

Inspection

See **Figure 36**. Disassemble the valve and check that the O-ring (**Figure 38**) and diaphragm are clean and undamaged. Look for pin holes in the diaphragm. Any bit of debris on the valve O-ring will prevent the valve from closing.

Make sure the diaphragm spring is in place. Install the diaphragm cover as shown in **Figure 36**.

FUEL LEVEL SENSOR

A fuel level sensor is mounted in the bottom of fuel tank. When installing a sensor, make sure gasket is in good condition.

6. Remove the bolts securing the air suction valve covers and remove the covers (**Figure 42**) and gaskets.

7. Pull the air suction valves (**Figure 43**) out of the cylinder head cover.

8. Check the suction valves for cracks, folds, warpage or any other damage (**Figure 44**).

9. Check the sealing lip around the perimeter of the suction valve. It must be free of grooves, scratches or signs of damage.

NOTE
The valve assembly cannot be repaired.
If damaged, it must be replaced.

10. Wash off any carbon deposits between the reed and the reed contact area with solvent.

CAUTION
Do not scrape deposits off the suction
valve or the assembly will be damaged.

11. Carefully remove any carbon deposits from the valve cover port (**Figure 45**).

12. Install by reversing these steps.

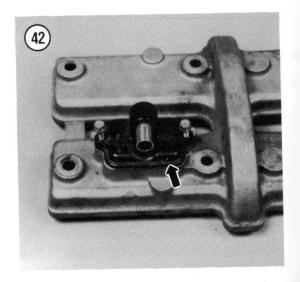

Vacuum Switch
Removal/Installation

1. Check that the ignition switch is off.

2. Remove the fuel tank as described in this chapter.

3. Remove the ignition coils as described in Chapter Eight.

4. Slide up the lower hose clamps and pull the hoses off the air suction valve covers.

5. Disconnect the small vacuum line at the switch (A, **Figure 46**).

6. Disconnct the hose (B, **Figure 46**) at the air cleaner housing.

7. Remove the vacuum switch (C, **Figure 46**).

8. Check all hoses for cuts, damage or soft spots.

9. Install by reversing these steps.

Vacuum Switch Test

Inspect the vacuum switch if there is backfiring during deceleration or other abnormal engine noise. A vacuum gauge and small syringe are required for this test.

1. Remove the vacuum switch as described in this chapter.

2. Attach the vacuum gauge and syringe to the vacuum hoses as shown in **Figure 47**.

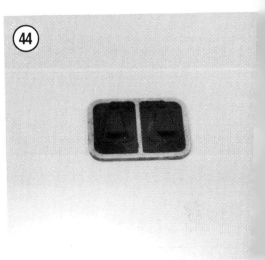

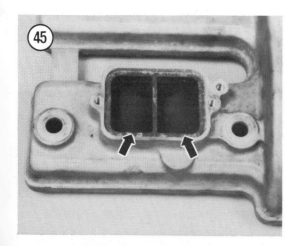

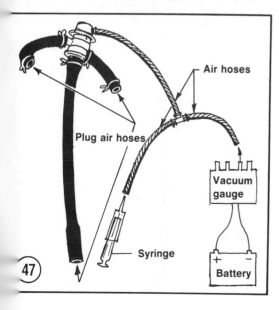

3. Raise the vacuum with the vacuum gauge and check valve operation by pumping air into the vacuum hose. When the vacuum is low, the vacuum switch should allow air to flow. When the vacuum rises to 54-68 kPa (510-10 mm Hg), the vacuum switch should stop the flow of air from the syringe.

4. If the vacuum switch failed to operate as described in Step 3, replace it.

EMISSION CONTROL

All 1985-on models sold in California are equipped with an evaporative emission control system to meet the California (CARB) regulations in effect at the time of the model's manufacture. When the engine is running, fuel vapors are routed into the engine for burning. When the engine is stopped, fuel vapors are routed into a canister.

Inspection/Replacement

Maintenance to the evaporative emission control system consists of periodic inspection of the hoses for proper routing and a check of the canister mounting brackets.

When removal or replacement of an emission part is required, refer to **Figure 48**.

> *WARNING*
> *Because the evaporative emission control system stores fuel vapors, make sure the work area is free of all flame or sparks before working on the emission system.*

1. Whenever servicing the evaporative system, make sure the ignition switch is turned off.

2. Make sure all hoses are attached as indicated in **Figure 48** and that they are not damaged or pinched.

3. When removing the separator it is important not to turn the separator upside down or sideways. Doing so will allow gasoline to flow into the canister.

4. Replace any worn or damaged parts immediately.

5. The canister is capable of working through the motorcycle's life without maintenance, provided that it is not damaged or contaminated.

EXHAUST SYSTEM

Removal/Installation

1. Remove the lower fairing as described in Chapter Thirteen.

2. Remove the oil cooler as described under *Oil Cooler Removal/Installation* in Chapter Four.

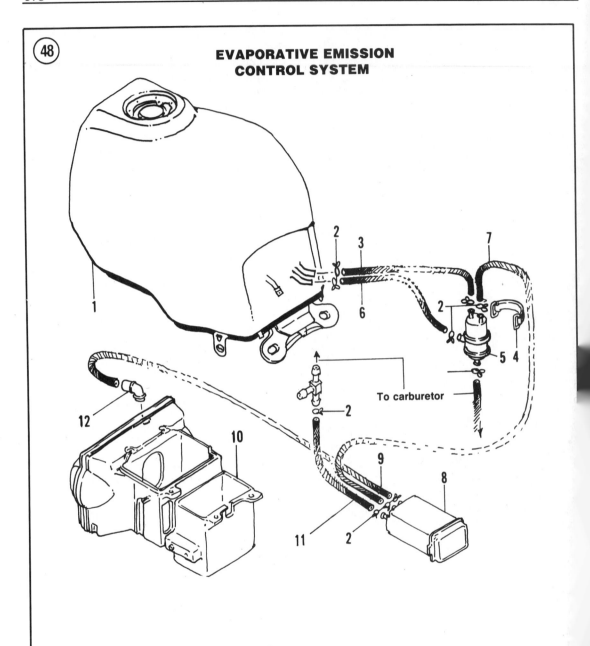

**EVAPORATIVE EMISSION
CONTROL SYSTEM**

48

To carburetor

1. Fuel tank
2. Hose clips
3. Breather hose (blue)
4. Clamp
5. Vapor separator
6. Fuel return hose (red)
7. Breather hose (blue)
8. Canister
9. Purge hose (green)
10. Air filter housing
11. Breather hose (yellow)
12. Elbow

3. Remove the fairing bracket (A, **Figure 49**).
4. Remove the exhaust pipe holder nuts and work the holders free from the studs (B, **Figure 49**).
5. Remove the rear exhaust pipe mounting nuts and bolts.
6. Pull the exhaust pipe and muffler assemblies out of the cylinder head and remove the split collars.
7. Remove the exhaust pipe assembly.

8. To install, reverse the removal steps. Note the following:
   a. Use new gaskets in the cylinder head exhaust ports.
   b. Tighten the exhaust pipe holder nuts at the cylinder head first, gradually and evenly. Then tighten the rear bolts and nuts.
   c. Start the engine and check for leakage. Tighten the clamps again after the engine has cooled down.

Maintenance

The exhaust system is a vital key to the motorcycle's operation and performance. You should periodically inspect, clean and polish (if required) the exhaust system. Special chemical cleaners and preservatives compounded for exhaust systems are available at most motorcyle shops.

Severe dents which cause flow restrictions require replacement of the damaged part.

To prevent internal rust buildup, remove the pipes and turn them to drain any trapped moisture.

7

Table 1 CARBURETOR SPECIFICATIONS

	ZX500 (European)	ZX600 (49-state)	ZX600 (California)
Make	Keihin	Keihin	Keihin
Size	CVK30	CVK32	CVK32
Main jet			
Cylinders			
1 and 4	105	105	108
2 and 3	108	108	108
Main air jet	100	100	100
Jet needle	N27P	N27L	N27L
Pilot jet	35	38	38
Pilot air jet	140	145	145
Pilot screw	2	2	—
Starter jet	52	45	42
Fuel level	0.5	0.5	0.5
Float height	17	17	17

NOTE: If you own a 1988 or later model, first check the Supplement at the back of this book for any new service information.

CHAPTER EIGHT

ELECTRICAL SYSTEM

This chapter describes service procedures for the electrical system. **Tables 1-4** are at the end of the chapter.

ALTERNATOR

Troubleshooting

Refer to *Charging System* in Chapter Two.

Rotor
Removal/Installation

A rotor puller (Kawasaki part No. 57001-1216 or equivalent, **Figure 1**) and a rotor holding tool (**Figure 2**) are required for this procedure.

1. Park the bike on its centerstand.
2. Remove the lower fairing. See Chapter Thirteen.
3. Remove the alternator cover (**Figure 3**).
4. Secure the rotor with a holding tool and remove the rotor bolt. See **Figure 4**.
5. Screw in a rotor puller (**Figure 5**) until it stops. Use a wrench on the puller and hold the rotor to keep it from turning. Gradually tighten the puller until the rotor disengages from the crankshaft (**Figure 6**).

> NOTE
> *If the rotor is difficult to remove, strike the end of the puller with a hammer a few times. This will usually break it loose. Do **not** hit the rotor.*

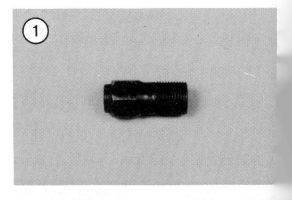

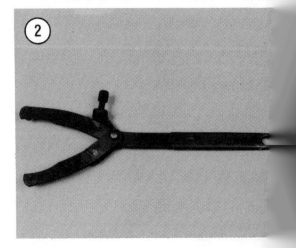

If normal rotor removal attempts fail, do not force the puller as the threads may be stripped out of the rotor causing expensive damage. Take it to a dealer and have them remove it.

6. Remove the puller and rotor. Unscrew the puller from the rotor.

7. Install by reversing these removal steps. Note the following:

    a. Check the rotor magnets (**Figure 7**) for any metal trash that may have collected while the rotor was removed.

    b. Clean the rotor and crankshaft tapers with contact cleaner.

    c. Slide the rotor onto the crankshaft. Hold the rotor with the same tool used during removal. Install the rotor bolt and tighten to 145 N•m (110 ft.-lb.).

8

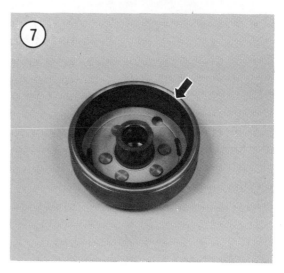

d. Install the alternator cover so that the notch in the gasket surface faces to the bottom (**Figure 8**).

Stator
Removal/Installation

1. Drain the coolant as described in Chapter Three.
2. Remove the rotor as described in this chapter.
3. Remove the engine sprocket cover as described under *Sprocket Cover* in Chapter Six.
4. Disconnect the alternator connector (**Figure 9**).
5. Pull the neutral switch connector off of the switch (**Figure 10**).
6. Remove the water pump holding bolt (**Figure 11**) and pull the water pump (**Figure 12**) slightly out of the crankcase.
7. Pull the alternator connector and neutral switch wire out from behind the water pump hose. Guide the wire harness carefully to prevent damage.
8. Pull the wire harness rubber plug (**Figure 13**) out of the crankcase.
9. Remove the 3 stator Allen bolts (A, **Figure 14**) and pull the stator (B, **Figure 14**) away from the crankcase.
10. Install by reversing these steps. Note the following:
    a. Apply Loctite 242 (blue) to the stator Allen bolts and tighten to 12 N•m (9 ft.-lb.).
    b. Fit the wire harness rubber plug into the crankcase notch (**Figure 13**).
    c. Slide the water pump (**Figure 12**) into the crankcase and tighten the holding bolt (**Figure 11**) securely.
    d. Refill the engine coolant as described in Chapter Three.

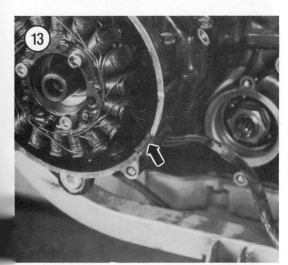

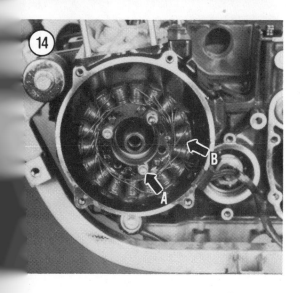

TRANSISTORIZED IGNITION

Troubleshooting

Refer to *Ignition System* in Chapter Two.

Pickup Coil
Removal/Installation

The pickup coil is located on the right-hand side behind the pickup coil cover.

1. Remove the lower fairing as described in Chapter Thirteen.
2. Remove the right-hand side cover.
3. Remove the pickup coil cover (**Figure 15**).
4. Disconnect the pickup coil connector (**Figure 16**).

8

5. Pull the pickup coil wire harness away from the clips on the clutch cover (**Figure 17**).

6. Pull the wire harness away from the frame and engine. Note the path of the wire harness as it must be routed the same during installation.

7. Pull the rubber harness wire plug (**Figure 18**) out of the crankcase.

8. Remove the 3 pickup coil screws (**Figure 19**) and remove the pickup coil assembly.

9. Remove the bolt (A, **Figure 20**) and remove the timing plate (B, **Figure 20**) from the end of the crankshaft.

10. Install by reversing these steps. Note the following:

   a. Align the hole in the back of the timing plate with the pin in the crankshaft and install the timing plate. Apply Loctite 242 (blue) onto the timing plate bolt and tighten to 25 N•m (18 ft.-lb.).

   b. Apply Loctite 242 (blue) to the pickup coil screws and tighten to 12 N•m (9 ft.-lb.).

   c. Fit the wire harness rubber plug into the crankcase notch (**Figure 18**).

   d. Install the pickup coil cover with its notch facing down.

Ignition Coil
Removal/Installation

1. Remove the side covers.
2. Remove the seat.
3. Remove the fuel tank as described in Chapter Seven.

NOTE
Label all wires and cables disconnected in Steps 4 and 5.

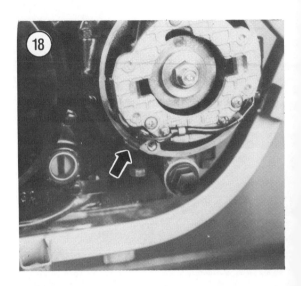

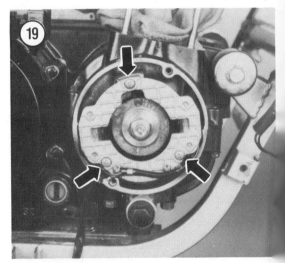

4. Disconnect the spark plug leads by grasping the spark plug leads as near to the plug as possible and pulling them off the plugs.

5. Disconnect the primary leads to the ignition coil.

6. Remove the coil mounting bolts (**Figure 21**) and the coils (**Figure 22**) and brackets. Note any ground leads at the bracket bolts.

7. Install by reversing these steps.

IC Igniter
Removal/Installation

1. Remove the right-hand side cover.

2. Unplug the connector (A, **Figure 23**) and pull the igniter (B, **Figure 23**) out of its mounting bracket.

3. Installation is the reverse of these steps. Note the following:

    a. Check the rubber igniter mount for cracks or damage. Replace the mount if necessary.

    b. Clean the connector with electrical contact cleaner before assembly.

Rectifier/Regulator
Removal/Installation

1. Remove the left-hand side cover.

2. Unplug the connector (A, **Figure 24**).

3. Remove the rectifier/regulator mounting screws and remove the unit (B, **Figure 24**).

4. Installation is the reverse of these steps. Clean the connector with electrical contact cleaner before assembly.

8

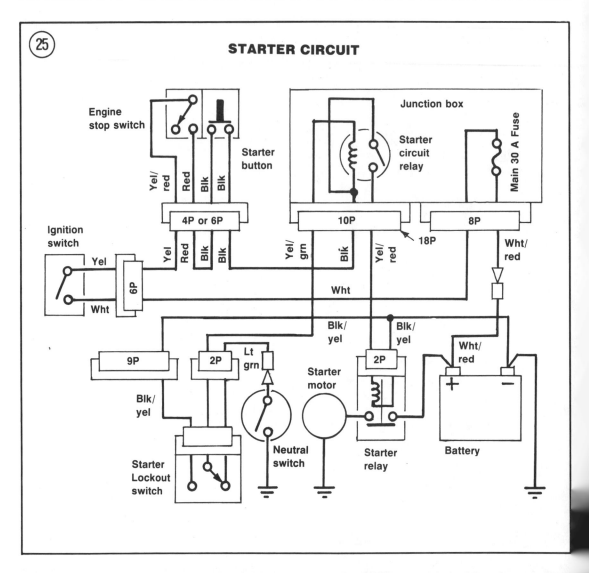

㉕ **STARTER CIRCUIT**

Engine
stop switch

Starter
button

Ignition
switch

Junction box

Starter
circuit
relay

Main 30 A Fuse

Yel/
red   Red   Blk   Blk

4P or 6P

10P

8P

Yel   Red   Blk   Blk

Yel   Red

6P

Yel

Yel/
grn   Blk   Yel/
red

18P

Wht/
red

Wht

Wht

Blk/
yel   Blk/
yel

9P

2P   Lt
grn

Starter
motor

2P

Wht/
red

Blk/
yel

+   −

Starter
Lockout
switch

Neutral
switch

Starter
relay

Battery

㉖

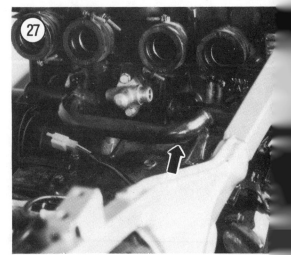

㉗

ELECTRIC STARTER

The starter circuit includes the starter button, starter relay, battery and starter motor. **Figure 25** illustrates the starter circuit.

Removal/Installation

1. Remove the lower fairing as described in Chapter Thirteen.
2. Drain the engine oil as described under *Engine Oil and Filter Change* in Chapter Three.
3. Drain the cooling system as described under *Coolant Change* in Chapter Three.
4. Remove the fuel tank as described in Chapter Seven.
5. Remove the left-hand fairing side rail as described in Chapter Thirteen.
6. Loosen the hose clamp at the water pump hose at the engine and disconnect the hose (**Figure 26**).
7. Remove the water pipe holding bolts and pull the pipe out of the cylinder (**Figure 27**).
8. Remove the water pump holding bolt (**Figure 28**) and slide the water pump out of the crankcase.
9. Remove the oil pipe banjo bolts and washers and remove the pipe to provide access to the starter.
10. Disconnect the cable at the starter.
11. Remove the starter mounting bolts and pull the starter (**Figure 29**) away from the crankcase.
12. Install by reversing these removal steps. Note the following:

   a. Clean the starter motor lugs at the starter case and crankcase with contact cleaner. The starter is grounded at these points and the surfaces must be clean of all dirt and oil residue.

   b. Apply engine oil to the starter O-ring (**Figure 30**) before assembly.

   c. Apply engine oil to the water pipe O-rings (**Figure 31**) before assembly.

8

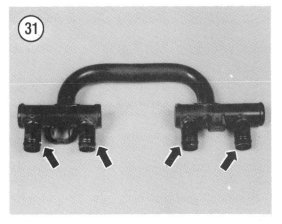

d. Refill the cooling system as described in Chapter Three.

e. Refill the engine oil as described in Chapter Three.

Disassembly/Reassembly

Starter motor repair is generally a job for electrical shops or a Kawasaki dealer. The following procedure describes how to check overall starter condition. Refer to **Figure 32**.

1. Remove both starter end covers.

2. Slide the armature out of the housing.

3. Measure the length of each brush with a vernier caliper (**Figure 33**). If the length is less than specified in **Table 1**, it must be replaced. Replace the brushes as a set even though only one may be worn to this dimension.

4. Inspect the condition of the commutator. The mica in a good commutator is below the surface of the copper bars. On a worn commutator, the mica and copper bars may be worn to the same level. See **Figure 34**. If necessary, have the commutator serviced by a dealer or electrical repair shop.

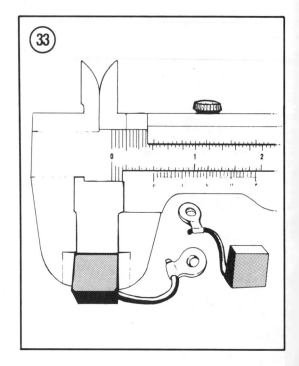

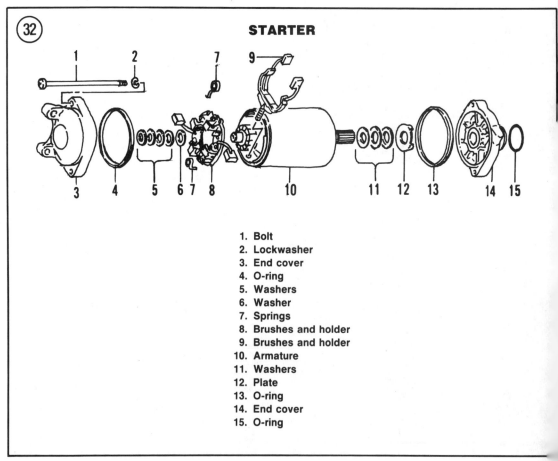

STARTER

1. Bolt
2. Lockwasher
3. End cover
4. O-ring
5. Washers
6. Washer
7. Springs
8. Brushes and holder
9. Brushes and holder
10. Armature
11. Washers
12. Plate
13. O-ring
14. End cover
15. O-ring

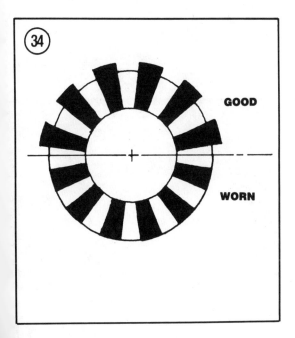

GOOD

WORN

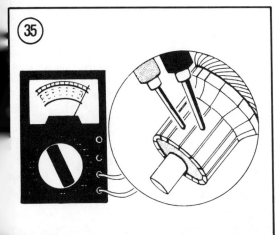

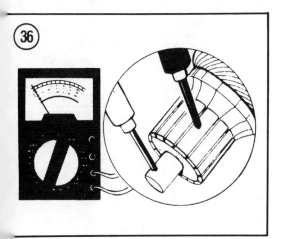

5. Use an ohmmeter and check for continuity between the commutator bars (**Figure 35**). There should be continuity between pairs of bars. Also check continuity between the commutator bars and the shaft (**Figure 36**). There should be no continuity. If the unit fails either of these tests the armature is faulty and must be replaced.

6. Use an ohmmeter and inspect the field coil by checking continuity between the starter cable terminal and the starter case. There should be no continuity. Also check continuity between the starter cable terminal and each brush wire terminal. There should be continuity. If the unit fails either of these tests, the case/field coil assembly must be replaced.

7. Connect one probe of an ohmmeter to the brush holder plate and the other probe to each of the positive (insulated) brush holders. There should be no continuity. If the unit fails at either brush holder, the brush holder assembly should be replaced.

8. Assemble the starter as follows:

   a. Remove the brush springs from the brush plate.

   b. Slide the armature into the housing.

   c. Align the brush plate with the housing and fit the brush leads into the plate notches. Then align the tab on the brush plate with the notch in the armature and insert the plate into the housing.

   d. Hold the housing so that the brush plate faces up.

   e. Place a brush spring over one of the spring posts on the brush plate (**Figure 37**). Then turn the spring half a turn clockwise and engage the end of the spring with the notch in the back of the brush. Repeat for each spring.

8

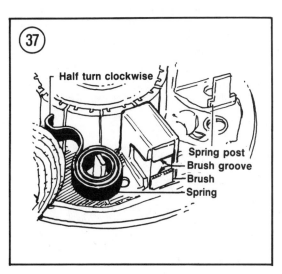

Half turn clockwise

Spring post
Brush groove
Brush
Spring

f. Install the end covers and secure with the through-bolts. Tighten the bolts securely.

Starter Relay
Removal/Installation

The starter relay (**Figure 38**) is installed on the left-hand side of the bike.

1. Remove the left-hand side cover.
2. Make sure the ignition switch is turned to OFF.
3. Label and disconnect the wires at the starter relay (**Figure 38**) and pull it out of its holder.
4. Install by reversing these steps.

Starter Relay
Testing

1. Remove the left-hand side cover.

> *CAUTION*
> *Because the battery positive lead at the starter relay is connected directly to the battery, even when the ignition switch is in the OFF position, do not allow the end of the lead to touch any part of the bike during the following procedure.*

2. Disconnect the starter motor lead and the battery positive cable from the starter relay terminal (**Figure 38**).
3. Connect an ohmmeter across the relay terminals (**Figure 38**).
4. Press the starter button. The relay should click and the ohmmeter should indicate zero resistance. If the relay clicks but the meter indicates any value greater than zero, replace the relay.
5. If the relay does not click, replace it.

LIGHTING SYSTEM

The lighting system consists of the headlight, taillight/brakelight combination, directional signals, warning lights and speedometer and tachometer illumination lights. In the event of trouble with any light the first thing to check is the affected bulb itself. If the bulb is good, check all wiring and connections with a test light.

Headlight Replacement

> *CAUTION*
> *All models are equipped with quartz-hologen bulbs (**Figure 39**). Do not touch the bulb glass with your fingers because traces of oil on the bulb will drastically reduce the life of the bulb. Clean any traces of oil from the bulb with a cloth moistened in alcohol or lacquer thinner.*

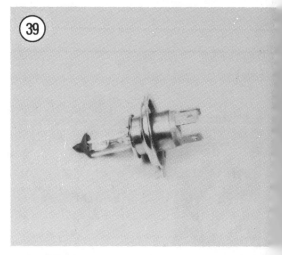

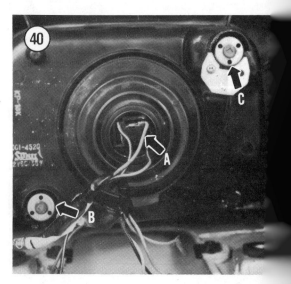

WARNING
*If the headlight has just burned out or turned off it will be **hot**. Don't touch the bulb until it cools off.*

1. Disconnect the connector at the bulb (**A, Figure 40**).

2. Lift the rubber dust cover away from the fairing mount. Then remove it from around the bulb. See **A, Figure 41**.

3. Lift the hook spring up and pivot it away from the bulb (**Figure 42**).

4. Lift the bulb (**Figure 43**) out of the headlight assembly.

5. Install by reversing these steps. Note the following:

  a. Align the tabs on the bulb with the notches in the bulb socket when installing the bulb.

  b. Make sure to lock the hook spring into the bulb socket.

  c. Install the dust cover so that the end labeled TOP faces up (B, **Figure 41**).

Headlight Adjustment

Adjust the headlight horizontally and vertically according to the Department of Motor Vehicles regulations in your area.

1. There are 2 adjustments; horizontal (B, **Figure 40**) and vertical (C, **Figure 40**).

2. When performing this procedure, make sure the tire pressure is correct and that the fuel tank is approximately 1/2 full to full. Have an assistant sit on the seat.

3. *Horizontal adjustment:* Perform the following:

  a. Remove the right inner fairing. See *Upper Fairing Removal/Installation* in Chapter Thirteen.

  b. Insert a screwdriver into the horizontal adjuster guide (B, **Figure 40**).

  c. Turn the adjuster clockwise or counterclockwise until the headlight beam points straight ahead.

4. *Vertical adjustment:* Perform the following:

  a. Insert a screwdriver into the vertical adjuster guide (C, **Figure 40**).

  c. Turn the adjuster clockwise or counterclockwise to adjust the headlight beam vertically.

5. Install the right inner fairing.

Taillight Replacement

1. Remove the seat.

2. Pull the socket assembly out of the taillight housing.

3. Replace the bulb.

8

Directional Signal Light Replacement

Remove the two screws securing the lens (**Figure 44**) and remove it. Wash out the inside and outside of it with a mild detergent. Replace the bulb. Install the lens. Do not overtighten the screws as that will crack the lens.

Speedometer and Tachometer Illumination Bulb Replacement

1. Remove the upper fairing assembly as described in Chapter Thirteen.
2. Remove the socket from the meter assembly and remove the bulb. See **Figure 45**, typical.
3. Install a new bulb and push the socket into the meter.
4. Installation is the reverse of these steps.

SWITCHES

Switches can be tested for continuity with an ohmmeter (see Chapter One) or a test light at the switch connector plug by operating the switch in each of its operating positions and comparing results with the switch operation. For example, **Figure 46** shows a continuity diagram for a typical horn button. It shows which terminals should show continuity when the horn button is in a given position.

When the horn button is pushed there should be continuity between terminals Blk/Wht and Blk/Yel. This is indicated by the line on the continuity diagram. An ohmmeter connected between these 2 teminals should indicate little or no resistance and a test lamp should light. When the horn button is free, there should be no continuity between the same terminals.

If the switch or button doesn't perform properly, replace it. Refer to the following figures when testing the switches:

   a. **Figure 47**: All models.
   b. **Figure 48**: U.S. and Canada models only.
   c. **Figure 49**: All models other than U.S and Canada.

When testing switches, note the following:

   a. First check the fuses as described under *Fuses* in this chapter.
   b. Check the battery as described under *Battery* in Chapter Three. Bring the battery to the correct state of charge, if required.

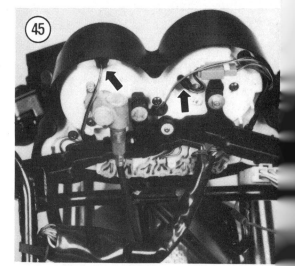

HORN BUTTON

	Blk/wht	Blk/yel
Free		
Push on	o———————o

SWITCHES (ALL MODELS)

Ignition switch

	Brn	Wht	Yel	Blu	Red	Wht/blk	Org/grn
Off, lock							
On	O———O———O			O———O		O———O	
P (park)		O———————————O				O———O	
						U.S., Canada	

Starter lockout switch

	Blk/yel	Yel/grn	Lt grn
Cluch lever is pulled in	O———O		
Clutch lever is released		O———O	

Side stand switch

	Brn	Blk/yel	Grn/wht
Side stand is up	O———O		
Side stand is down		O———O	

Engine stop switch

	Red	Yel/red
Off		
Run	O———O	

Starter button

	Blk	Blk
Free		
Push on	O———O	

Turn signal switch

	Gry	Org	Grn
R	O———O		
N			
L		O———O	

Hazard switch

	Gry	Org	Grn
Off ⊓			
On ⊏	O———O———O		

Front brake light switch

	Brn	Blu
Brake lever pulled in	O—O	

Rear brake light switch

	Brn	Blu
Brake pedal pushed in	O—O	

Neutral switch

	Lt grn	Ground
Transmission is in neutral	O———O	
Transmission is not in neutral		

Oil pressure switch

	Sw. term	Ground
Engine is stopped	O———O	
Engine is running		

8

48

SWITCHES (U.S AND CANADIAN MODELS)

Dimmer switch

	Blu/yel	Blu/orn	Red/yel	Red/blk
HI	O————————————————————O	O————O		
LO	O	O————O		O

c. Disconnect the negative cable from the battery if the switch connectors are not disconnected in the circuit.

CAUTION
Do not attempt to start the engine with the battery negative cable disconnected or you will damage the wiring.

d. When separating 2 connectors, pull on the connector housings and not the wires.

e. After locating a defective circuit, check the connectors to make sure they are clean and properly connected. Check all wires going into a connector housing to make sure each wire is properly positioned and that the wire end is not loose.

f. To properly connect connectors, push them together until they click into place.

g. When replacing handlebar switch assemblies, make sure the cables are routed correctly so that they are not crimped when the handlebar is turned from side to side.

Ignition Switch Replacement

1. Remove the upper fairing assembly as described in Chapter Thirteen.
2. Disconnect the ignition switch electrical connector.
3. Remove the bolts securing the ignition switch to the steering stem and remove the switch (**Figure 50**).
4. Installation is the reverse of these steps.

 49

SWITCHES (ALL MODELS EXCEPT U.S AND CANADA)

Headlight switch

	Red/wht	Red/blu	Red	Blu/yel
Off				
■ On	O————O		O————O	

Dimmer switch

	Red/blk	Blu/yel	Red/yel
HI	O————O		
LO		O————O	

Passing button

	Brn	Red/blk
Free		
Push on	O————O	

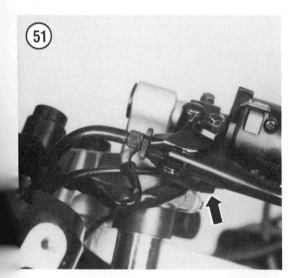

Neutral Switch Replacement

Refer to *Neutral Switch Removal/Installation* in Chapter Six.

Oil Pressure Switch Replacement

Refer to *Oil Pressure Switch Removal/ Installation* in Chapter Four.

Starter Lockout Switch Replacement

The starter lockout switch is mounted onto the clutch handlebar lever assembly (**Figure 51**). Disconnect the connector and remove the switch screws. Reverse to install.

Front Brake Light Switch Replacement

The front brake switch is mounted underneath the front brake master cylinder (**Figure 52**). Disconnect the connector and remove the switch screw. Reverse to install. Check switch operation. The rear brake light should come on when applying the front brake lever.

Rear Brake Light Switch Replacement

The rear brake switch is mounted on the right-hand side next to the rear brake pedal mount (**Figure 53**).
1. Disconnect the electrical connector at the switch.
2. Disconnect the spring at the switch.
3. Unscrew the switch and remove it.
4. Screw a new switch into the switch mount. Attach the spring, then plug in the connector.

8

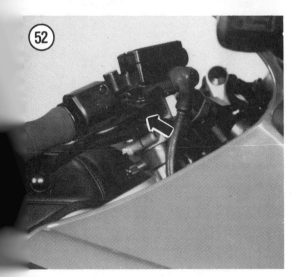

5. Adjust the rear brake switch as described under *Rear Brake Light Switch Adjustment* in Chapter Three.

Side Stand Switch
Replacement

The side stand switch is mounted on the side stand (**Figure 54**).

1. Place the bike on its centerstand.
2. Pull the side stand down to gain access to the switch.
3. Disconnect the connector and remove the switch screws.
4. Install by reversing these steps.

Left Handlebar Switch
Replacement

1A. *U.S. and Canada:* The left handlebar switch housing is equipped with the following switches:
    a. Horn.
    b. Hazard.
    c. Turn signal.
    d. Dimmer.
    e. Starter lockout.

1B. *All models except U.S. and Canada:* The left-hand handlebar switch housing is equipped with the following switches:
    a. Horn.
    b. Hazard.
    c. Turn signal.
    d. Dimmer.
    e. Passing.
    f. Starter lockout.

2. Remove the upper fairing as described in Chapter Thirteen.
3. Disconnect the switch connector(s).
4. Remove the switch housing screws and separate the housings. Pull the choke cable at the lower housing.
5. Remove the switch housing and wiring harness. See **Figure 55**.
6. Installation is the reverse of these steps. Adjust the choke cable as described under *Choke Cable Adjustment* in Chapter Three.

Right Handlebar Switch
Replacement

1A. *U.S. and Canada:* The right-hand handlebar switch housing is equipped with the following switches:
    a. Engine stop.
    b. Starter.

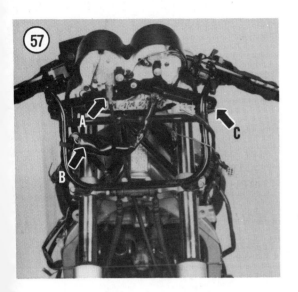

1B. *All models except U.S. and Canada:* The right-hand handlebar switch housing is equipped with the following switches:

  a. Engine stop.
  b. Starter.
  c. Headlight.

2. Remove the upper fairing as described in Chapter Thirteen.
3. Disconnect the switch connector(s).
4. Remove the switch housing screws and separate the housings. Pull the throttle grip out of the housings.
5. Remove the switch housing and wiring harness. See **Figure 56**.
6. Installation is the reverse of these steps. Adjust the throttle cables as described under *Throttle Cable Adjustment* in Chapter Three.

WIRING AND CONNECTORS

Many electrical troubles can be traced to damaged wiring or connectors that are contaminated with dirt and oil. Connectors can be serviced by disconnecting them and cleaning with electrical contact cleaner. Multiple pin connectors should be packed with a dielectric silicone grease (available at most automotive supply stores).

Wiring Check

Inspect all wiring for fraying, burning, etc. Connectors can be serviced by disconnecting them and cleaning with electrical contact cleaner. Multiple pin connectors should be packed with a electric silicone grease.

3. Check wiring continuity of individual circuits as follows:

  a. Disconnect the negative cable from the battery.

> *NOTE*
> *When making a continuity test, it is best not to disconnect a connector. Instead, insert the test leads into the back of the connectors and check both sides. Because corrosion between the connector contacts may be causing an open circuit, your trouble may be at the connector instead of with the wiring.*

  b. Zero the ohmmeter according to the manufacturer's instructions. Switch the meter to the $R \times 1$ scale.
  c. Attach the test leads to the circuit you want to check.
  d. There should be continuity (indicated low resistance). If there is no continuity, there is an open (break or bad connection) in the circuit.

INSTRUMENT CLUSTER

> *CAUTION*
> *Whenever the instrument cluster is removed from the bike, it must be placed so that the gauges face up. If the meter is left in any other position it will become damaged.*

Removal/Installation

1. Remove the upper fairing assembly as described in Chapter Thirteen.
2. Disconnect the speedometer cable (A, **Figure 57**).
3. Disconnect the instrument cluster wiring harness connectors (B, **Figure 57**).
4. Remove the screws securing the instrument cluster bracket and remove the instrument cluster (C, **Figure 57**).

> *CAUTION*
> *Do not turn or store the instrument cluster on its side or back as this would damage the instruments.*

5. Install by reversing these steps.

Tachometer/Voltmeter
Testing

The tachometer/voltmeter circuit is shown in **Figure 58**.

1. Check that rubber dampers are installed at all mounting brackets. Replace missing dampers or dampers that have become cracked or hardened.

2. Referring to **Figure 58**, perform the *Wiring Check* as described in this chapter. Interpret results as follows:

    a. If there is no continuity, there is an open in the circuit.

    b. If the tachometer/voltmeter still is not operating correctly after the wiring is repaired, replace the tachometer/voltmeter.

Fuel Gauge Testing

The fuel gauge circuit is shown in **Figure 59**. Perform the *Wiring Check* to test it.

Water Temperature Gauge
Testing

The water temperature gauge circuit is shown in **Figure 60**. Perform the *Wiring Check* to test it.

THERMOSTATIC FAN SWITCH

Testing

The fan switch controls the radiator fan according to engine coolant temperature.

1. Remove the fan switch as described under *Thermostatic Fan Switch and Water Temperature Sensor Removal/Installation* in Chapter Nine.

2. Fill a beaker or pan with water and place on a stove.

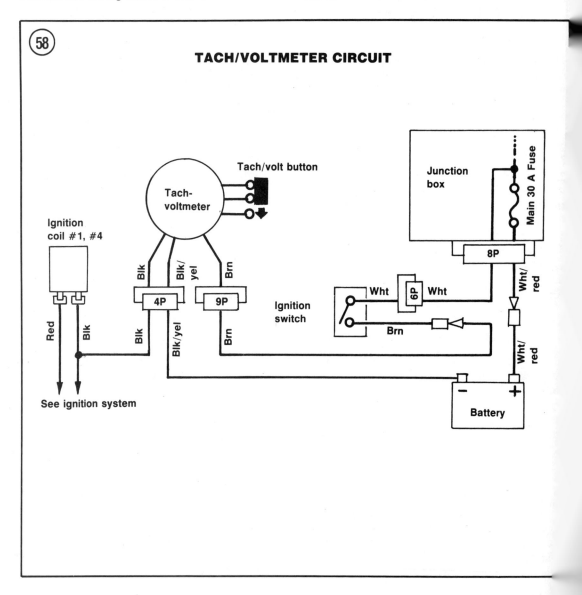

TACH/VOLTMETER CIRCUIT

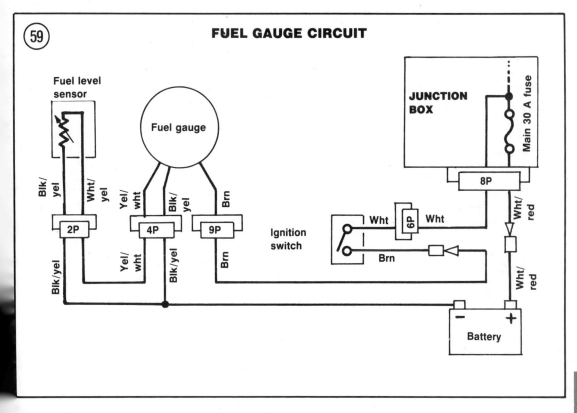

FUEL GAUGE CIRCUIT

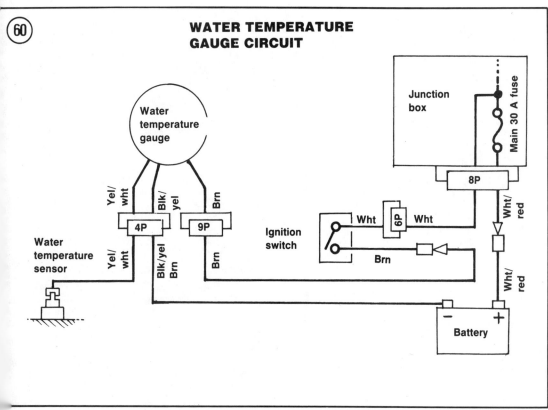

WATER TEMPERATURE GAUGE CIRCUIT

8

3. Mount the fan switch so that the temperature sensing tip and the threaded portion of the body are submerged as shown in **Figure 61**.

4. Place a thermometer in the pan of water (use a cooking or candy thermometer that is rated higher than the test temperature).

5. Attach one ohmmeter lead to the fan switch terminal and the other lead to the body as shown in **Figure 61**. Check resistance as follows:

a. Gradually heat the water.

b. When the temperature rises from 201-212° F (94-100° C), the resistance reading should be 0.5 ohms or less.

c. Gradually reduce the heat.

d. When the temperature falls to approximately 194° F (90° C), the ohmmeter should read 1 ohm or higher.

6. Replace the fan switch if it failed to operate as described in Step 5.

WATER TEMPERATURE SENSOR

Testing

1. Remove the water temperature sensor as described under *Thermostatic Fan Switch and Water Temperature Sensor Removal/Installation* in Chapter Nine.

2. Fill a beaker or pan with water and place on a stove.

3. Mount the water temperature sensor so that the temperature sensing tip and the threaded portion of the body are submerged as shown in **Figure 62**.

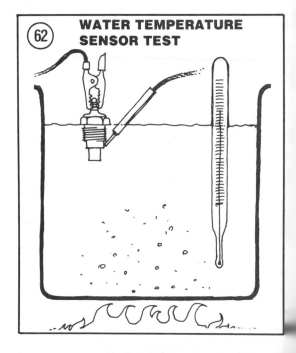

⑥② WATER TEMPERATURE SENSOR TEST

⑥③

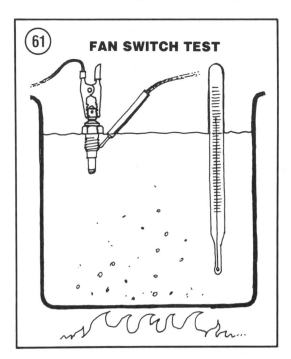

⑥① FAN SWITCH TEST

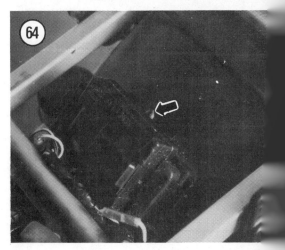

⑥④

4. Place a thermometer in the pan of water (use a cooking or candy thermometer that is rated higher than the test temperature).

5. Attach one ohmmeter lead to the water temperature terminal and the other lead to the body as shown in **Figure 62**. Check resistance as follows:

  a. Gradually heat the water.

  b. When the temperature reaches 176° F (80° C), the resistance reading should be approximately 57 ohms.

  c. Continue to heat the water. When the temperature reaches 212° F (100° C), the resistance reading should be approximately 27 ohms.

6. Replace the water temperature sensor if it failed to operate as described in Step 5.

HORN

Removal/Installation

1. Remove the oil cooler as described under *Oil Cooler Removal/Installation* in Chapter Four.

2. Remove the exhaust pipes as described in Chapter Seven.

3. Disconnect the horn electrical connector.

4. Remove the bolts securing the horn bracket and remove the horn assembly (**Figure 63**).

5. Installation is the reverse of these steps.

Testing

1. Disconnect horn wires from harness.

2. Connect horn wires to 12-volt battery. If it is good, it will sound.

JUNCTION BOX AND FUSES

The junction box is mounted underneath the seat (**Figure 64**) and houses the fuses, diodes and relays. The junction box circuit is shown in **Figure 65**. The diodes and relays are an integral part of the junction box and cannot be removed. If they fail, the junction box must be replaced.

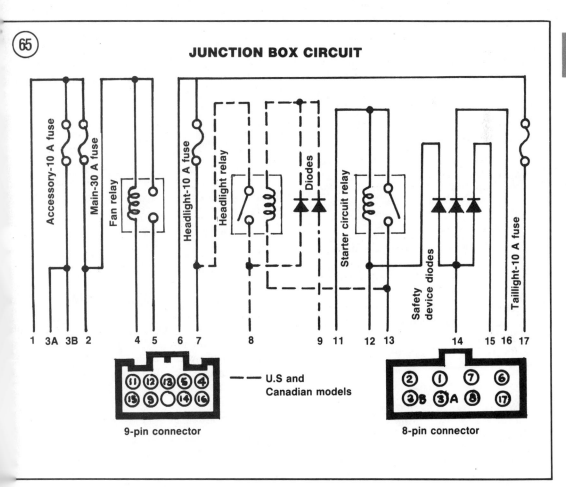

8

Junction Box
Removal/Installation

To remove the junction box, disconnect the electrical connectors and remove the fastening screws. Reverse to install.

Fuses Replacement

There are 4 fuses located in the junction box mounted underneath the seat. The fuse functions are:
  a. Taillight (10 amp).
  b. Headlight relay (10 amp).
  c. Accessory (10 amp).
  d. Main fuse (30 amp).
If a fuse blows, remove the seat and remove the fuse cover (**Figure 66**). Remove the fuse by pulling it out of the junction box with needlenose pliers. Install a new fuse with the same amperage rating.

NOTE
The junction box is equipped with one 10-amp and one 30-amp replacement fuse. Always carry extra fuses.

Whenever a fuse blows, find out the reason for the failure before replacing the fuse. Usually, the trouble is a short circuit in the wiring. Check by testing the circuit that the fuse protects. A blown fuse may be caused by worn-through insulation or a disconnected wire shorting to ground.

CAUTION
Never substitute tinfoil or wire for a fuse. Never use a higher amperage fuse than specified. An overload could result in fire and complete loss of the bike.

Junction Box Inspection

This test describes checks for the fuse and relay (fan, starter circuit and headlight) circuits.
1. Remove the junction box as described in this chapter.
2. Check that the connector terminals are clean and straight. If necessary, carefully straighten any bent terminal.
3. Perform all tests in Steps 4-6 with an ohmmeter set on R×1.

NOTE
*Refer to **Figure 65** for pin connector locations when performing Steps 4-6.*

4. Check continuity between the fuse circuit terminals listed in **Table 2**. Record readings and compare to those given in **Table 2**.

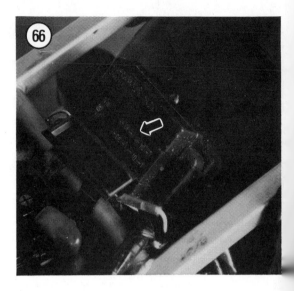

5. Check continuity between the relay circuit terminals listed in **Table 3**. Record readings and compare to those given in **Table 3**.
6. Check the relay circuit (with battery connected) as follows:
  a. Connect a battery and ohmmeter to the junction box terminals as specified in **Table 4**.
  b. The correct reading for each test is 0 ohms.
7. Replace the juction box if it failed any of the tests in Steps 4-6.

Diode Circuit Test

Test the diode circuit as follows.
1. With an ohmmeter set on R×1, check continuity between each of the following terminal (**Figure 65**):
  a. 13 and 8.
  b. 13 and 9.
  c. 12 and 4.
  d. 15 and 14.
  e. 16 and 14.
2. Switch the ohmmeter leads and recheck the continuity as described in Step 1.
3. For the diode circuit to be normal, the reading should be low in one direction and more than ten times higher with the ohmmeter leads reversed.
4. Replace the junction box if the diode circuit does not test as described in Step 3.

WIRING DIAGRAMS

Full color wiring diagrams are located at the end of this book.

Table 1 ELECTRICAL SPECIFICATIONS

Starter motor	
Brush length	12 mm (0.472 in.)
Wear limit	6 mm (0.236 in.)
Commutator diameter	28 mm (1.102 in.)
Wear limit	27 mm (1.063 in.)

Table 2 JUNCTION BOX: FUSE INSPECTION

Meter connection	Meter reading
1 and 2	0 ohms
1 and 3	0 ohms
6 and 7	0 ohms
6 and 17	0 ohms
1 and 7	Infinity
3A and 8	Infinity
8 and 17	Infinity

Table 3 JUNCTION BOX: RELAY CIRCUIT INSPECTION (BATTERY DISCONNECTED)

Meter connection	Meter reading
2 and 5	Infinity
4 and 5	Infinity
7 and 8	Infinity
7 and 13	Infinity
11 and 13	Infinity
12 and 13	Infinity

Table 4 JUNCTION BOX: RELAY CIRCUIT INSPECTION (BATTERY CONNECTED)

Meter connection	Battery connection (+)	Meter reading (−)	
and 5	2	4	0 ohms
and 8 *	9	13	0 ohms
1-13	11	12	0 ohms

U.S. and Canadian models only

NOTE: If you own a 1988 or later model, first check the Supplement at the back of this book for any new service information.

CHAPTER NINE

COOLING SYSTEM

The pressurized cooling system consists of the radiator, water pump, radiator cap, thermostat, electric cooling fan and a coolant reservoir tank.

It is important to keep the coolant level to the FULL mark on the coolant reservoir tank (**Figure 1**). Always add coolant to the reservoir tank, not to the radiator.

> *CAUTION*
> *Drain and flush the cooling system at least every 2 years. Refill with a mixture of ethylene glycol antifreeze (formulated for aluminum engines) and distilled water. Do not reuse the old coolant as it deteriorates with use. Do not operate the cooling system with only distilled water even in climates where antifreeze protection is not required. This is important because the engine is all aluminum; it will not rust but it will oxidize internally and have to be replaced. Refer to **Coolant Change** in Chapter Three.*

This chapter describes repair and replacement of cooling system components. **Table 1** at the end of the chapter lists all of the cooling system specifications. For routine maintenance of the system, refer to *Cooling System Inspection* in Chapter Three.

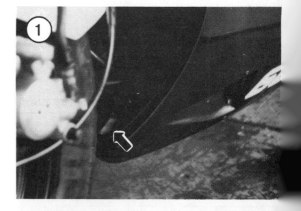

WARNING
Do not remove the radiator cap when the engine is hot. The coolant is very hot and is under pressure. Severe scalding could result if the coolant comes in contact with your skin.

WARNING
The radiator fan and fan switch are connected to the battery. Whenever the engine is warm or hot, the fan may start even with the ignition switch in the OFF position. Never work around the fan or touch the fan until the engine is completely cool.

The cooling system must be cooled before removing any component of the system.

COOLING SYSTEM INSPECTION

1. If a substantial coolant loss is noted, the head gasket may be blown. In extreme cases sufficient

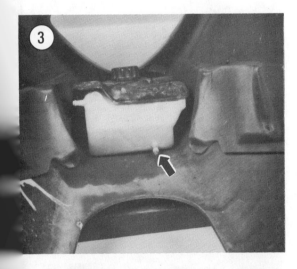

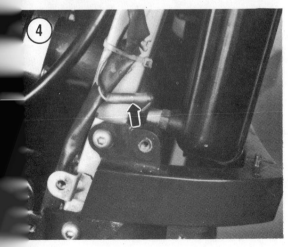

coolant will leak into a cylinder(s) when the bike is left standing for several hours so the engine cannot be turned over with the starter. White smoke (steam) might also be observed at the muffler(s) when the engine is running. Coolant may also find its way into the oil. To check, observe the oil level window on the clutch cover (**Figure 2**). If the oil looks like a "green chocolate malt" or is white and foamy, there is coolant in the oil system. If so, correct the problem immediately.

CAUTION
*After the problem is corrected, drain and thoroughly flush out the engine oil system to eliminate all coolant residue. Refill with fresh engine oil. Refer to **Engine Oil and Filter Change** in Chapter Three.*

2. Check the radiator for clogged or damaged fins. If more than 15 percent of the radiator fin area is damaged, repair or replace the radiator.
3. Check all coolant hoses for cracks or damage. Replace all questionable parts. Make sure the hose clamps are tight, but not so tight that they cut the hoses.
4. Pressure test the cooling system as described under *Cooling System Inspection* in Chapter Three.

COOLANT RESERVOIR

The coolant reservoir tank is located inside the lower fairing (**Figure 3**). To remove the reservoir tank, remove the lower fairing as described in Chapter Thirteen. Replace the reservoir tank if cracked or otherwise damaged.

RADIATOR AND FAN

WARNING
The radiator fan and fan switch are connected to the battery. Whenever the engine is warm or hot, the fan may start with the ignition switch in the OFF position. Never work around the fan or touch the fan until the engine is completely cool.

Removal/Installation

The radiator and fan are removed as an assembly.
1. Place the bike on the centerstand.
2. Remove the upper and lower fairings as described in Chapter Thirteen.
3. Drain the cooling system as described under *Coolant Change* in Chapter Three.
4. Disconnect the fan switch lead (**Figure 4**) and the fan motor connector (A, **Figure 5**).

9

5. Remove the baffle plate bolts and remove the baffle plate (**Figure 6**).

6. Loosen the clamping screws on the upper (B, **Figure 5**) and lower radiator hose bands. Move the bands back onto the hoses and off of the necks of the radiator.

> *NOTE*
> *It is not necessary to drain the engine oil when loosening the oil cooler in Step 7.*

7. Remove the oil cooler mounting bracket bolts and remove the bracket (A, **Figure 7**). Then remove the oil cooler mounting bolts and allow the cooler to hang from the bracket (B, **Figure 7**).

8. Remove the upper radiator mounting bolts (C, **Figure 5**).

9. Remove the front fairing bracket bolts (A, **Figure 8**) and remove the radiator (B, **Figure 8**), fairing bracket and fan as an assembly.

10. Remove the fairing bracket from the radiator.

11. Remove the radiator screen (**Figure 9**), if necessary.

12. Replace the radiator hoses if deterioration or damage is noted.

13. Installation is the reverse of these steps. Note the following:
   a. Make sure the fan switch ground lead is attached as shown in **Figure 10**.
   b. Refill the coolant as described under *Coolant Change* in Chapter Three.

Inspection

> *CAUTION*
> *When flushing the radiator fins with a hose, always point the hose perpendicular to the radiator and at a distance of 20 in. Never point a water or air hose at an angle to the radiator fins.*

1. Flush off the exterior of the radiator with a garden hose on low pressure. Spray both the front and the back to remove all road dirt and bugs. Carefully use a whisk broom or stiff paint brush to remove any stubborn dirt.

> *CAUTION*
> *Do not press too hard or the cooling fins and tubes may be damaged, causing a leak.*

2. Carefully straighten out any bent cooling fins (**Figure 9**) with a broad-tipped screwdriver.

3. Check for cracks or leakage (usually a moss-green colored residue) at the filler neck, the

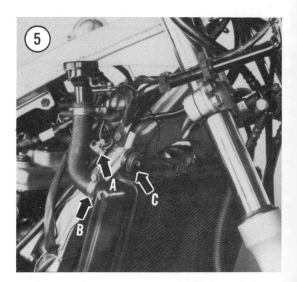

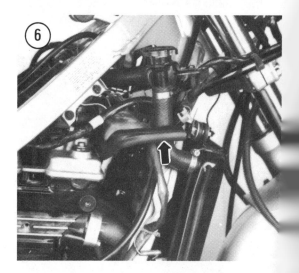

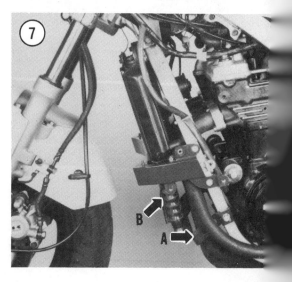

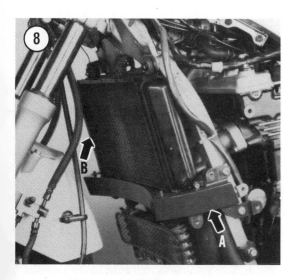

inlet and outlet hose fittings and the upper and lower tank seams.

4. Refer to **Figure 11**. Inspect the radiator cap top (A) and bottom (B) seals for deterioration or damage. Check the spring for damage. Pressure test the radiator cap as described under *Cooling System Inspection* in Chapter Three. Replace the radiator cap if necessary.

Cooling Fan
Removal/Installation

1. Remove the radiator as described in this chapter.
2. Remove the bolts securing the fan shroud and fan (**Figure 12**) assembly and remove the assembly.

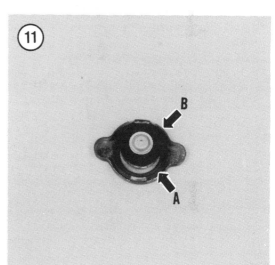

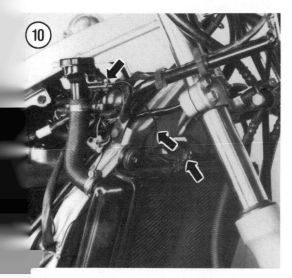

3. Installation is the reverse of these steps. Apply Loctite 242 (blue) to the fan mounting bolts and tighten securely.

THERMOSTAT

Removal/Installation

1. Remove the seat and both side covers.
2. Remove the fuel tank as described in Chapter Seven.
3. Drain the cooling system as described under *Coolant Change* in Chapter Three.
4. Remove the thermostat cover bolts and lift the cover off the housing. See A, **Figure 13**.
5. Lift the thermostat (**Figure 14**) out of the housing.
6. Test the thermostat as described in this chapter.
7. Install by reversing these steps. Note the following:
   a. Replace the cover O-ring, if necessary.
   b. Refill the cooling system with the recommended type and quantity of coolant as described under *Coolant Change* in Chapter Three.

Thermostat Housing
Removal/Installation

1. Remove the seat and both side covers.
2. Remove the fuel tank as described in Chapter Seven.
3. Drain the cooling system as described under *Coolant Change* in Chapter Three.
4. Disconnect the water temperature sensor connector at the thermostat housing.
5. Disconnect the radiator hose at the thermostat housing (B, **Figure 13**).
6. Remove the water pipe (C, **Figure 13**) screws.
7. Pull the air hose (A, **Figure 15**) out of the air cleaner housing and disconnect the vacuum hose (B, **Figure 15**) at the vacuum switch valve.
8. Remove the thermostat housing with the water pipe attached.
9. Pull water pipe out of the thermostat.
10. Install by reversing these steps. Note the following:
   a. Oil the water pipe O-ring before installation.
   b. Refill the cooling system with the recommended type and quantity of coolant as described under *Coolant Change* in Chapter Three.

Inspection

Test the thermostat to ensure proper operation. The thermostat should be replaced it it remains open at normal room temperature or stays closed after the specified temperature has been reached during the test procedure.

Place the thermostat on a small piece of wood in a pan of water (**Figure 16**). Place a thermometer in the pan of water (use a cooking or candy thermometer that is rated higher than the test temperature). Gradually heat the water and continue to gently stir the water until it reaches 157-162 F (69.5-72.5 C). At this temperature the thermostat should open.

NOTE
Valve operation is sometimes sluggish.
It usually takes 3-5 minutes for the
valve to operate properly.

If the valve fails to open, the thermostat should be replaced (it cannot be serviced). Be sure to replace it with one of the same temperature rating.

WATER PUMP

Removal/Installation

1. Drain the engine oil as described under *Engine Oil and Filter Change* in Chapter Three.
2. Drain the cooling system as described under *Coolant Change* in Chapter Three.
3. Loosen the hose clamps at the water pump cover radiator hose (**Figure 17**). Then twist the hose and slide it off the cover neck.
4. Remove the water pump mounting bolt (**Figure 18**).

9

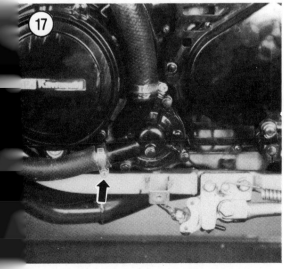

5. Pull the water pump (**Figure 19**) out of the housing and remove it.

6. Remove the water pump housing screws and remove the housing (**Figure 20**).

7. Installation is the reverse of these steps. Note the following:

   a. Tighten the water pump mounting bolt securely.

   b. Refill the cooling system with the recommended type and quantity of coolant as described under *Coolant Change* in Chapter Three.

Disassembly/Inspection/Reassembly

> *NOTE*
> *The water pump is sold as a complete unit only. If any component is damaged, the entire water pump must be replaced. The 2 O-rings, however, can be replaced separately.*

1. If the coolant level has been dropping, check the water pump body drainage outlet passage (A, **Figure 21**) for leakage. If coolant leaks from the outlet passage, an internal seal is damaged. Replace the water pump unit. If there is no indication of coolant leakage from the outlet passage, reinstall the water pump and pressure test the cooling system as described under *Cooling System Inspection* in Chapter Three.

2. Check the O-ring (B, **Figure 21**) for flat spots or damage. Replace if necessary.

3. Remove the water pump cover bolts and separate the pump assembly (C, **Figure 21**).

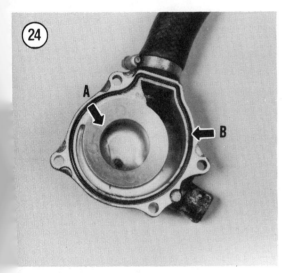

HOSES

Hoses deteriorate with age and should be replaced periodically or whenever they show signs of cracking or leakage. To be safe, replace the hoses every 2 years. The spray of hot coolant from a cracked hose can injure the rider and passenger. Loss of coolant can also cause the engine to overheat, causing damage.

Whenever any component of the cooling system is removed, inspect the hoses(s) and determine if replacement is necessary.

Inspection

1. With the engine cool, check the cooling hoses for brittleness or hardness. A hose in this condition will usually show cracks and must be replaced.
2. With the engine hot, examine the hoses for swelling along the entire hose length. Eventually a hose will rupture at this point.
3. Check area around hose clamps. Signs of rust around clamps indicate possible hose leakage.

Replacement

Hose replacement should be performed when the engine is cool.
1. Drain the cooling system as described under *Coolant Change* in Chapter Three.
2. Loosen the hose clamps on the hose to be replaced. Slide the clamps along the hose and out of the way.
3. Twist the hose end to break the seal and remove from the connecting joint. If the hose has been on for some time it may have become fused to the joint. If so, cut the hose parallel to the joint connections with a knife or razor. The hose then can be carefully pried loose with a screwdriver.

CAUTION
Excessive force applied to the hose during removal could damage the connecting joint.

4. Examine the connecting joint for cracks or other damage. Repair or replace parts as required. If the joint is okay, clean it of any rust with sandpaper.
5. Inspect hose clamps and replace as necessary.
6. Slide hose clamps over outside of hose and install hose to inlet and outlet connecting joint.

9

. Check the impeller blades (**Figure 22**) for orrosion or damage. If corrosion is minor, clean he blades. If corrosion is severe or if the blades are racked or broken, replace the water pump unit.

. Turn the impeller shaft (**Figure 23**) and check he bearing for excessive noise or roughness. If the earing operation is rough, replace the water pump nit.

. Inspect the water pump coolant passage (A, **igure 24**) for corrosion or sludge buildup. If orrosion is minor, clean the passage. If corrosion severe or if the water passage is pitted, replace e water pump unit.

Replace the water pump O-ring (B, **Figure 24**) if eformed or cracked or if there are indications of oolant leakage.

Reverse Step 3 to assemble the water pump sembly. Tighten the bolts securely.

Make sure hose clears all obstructions and is routed properly.

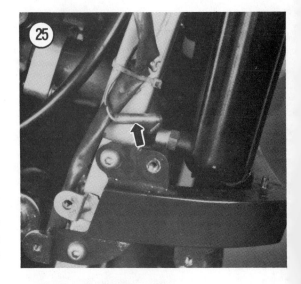

> *NOTE*
> *If it is difficult to install a hose on a joint, soak the end of the hose in hot water for approximately 2 minutes. This will soften the hose and ease installation.*

7. With the hose positioned correctly on joint, position clamps back away from end of hose slightly. Tighten clamps securely, but not so much that hose is damaged.

8. Refill cooling system as described under *Coolant Change* in Chapter Three. Start the engine and check for leaks. Retighten hose clamps as necessary.

THERMOSTATIC FAN SWITCH AND WATER TEMPERATURE SENSOR

Removal/Installation

1. Drain the cooling system as described under *Coolant Change* in Chapter Three.

2. Remove the upper and lower fairings as described in Chapter Thirteen.

3. *Thermostatic fan switch:* Perform the following:
   a. Disconnect the connector at the switch (**Figure 25**).

   b. Unscrew the switch (**Figure 26**) from the bottom of the radiator and remove it.
   c. Apply a liquid gasket sealer to the fan switch threads before installation.
   d. Install the switch and tighten to 7.4 N•m (65 in.-lb.).

4. *Water temperature sensor:* Perform the following:
   a. Remove the thermostat as described in this chapter.
   b. Unscrew the sensor (**Figure 27**) from the thermostat housing.
   c. Apply a liquid gasket to the sensor threads before installation.
   d. Tighten the sensor to 7.8 N•m (69 in.-lb.).
   e. Install the thermostat as described in this chapter.

5. Refill the cooling system with the recommended type and quantity of coolant as described under *Coolant Change* in Chapter Three.

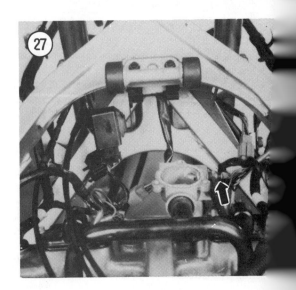

Testing

Refer to *Thermostatic Fan Switch Testing* or *Water Temperature Sensor Testing* Chapter Eight.

Table 1 COOLING SYSTEM SPECIFICATIONS

Capacity	2.0 L (2.1 qts.)
Coolant ratio	57 percent water/43 percent coolant
Radiator cap	14-18 psi (0.95-1.25 kg/cm²)
Thermostat	
Opening temperature	157.1-163.0° F (69.5-72.5° C)
Valve opening lift	Not less than 8 mm (5/16 in.)
	@ 195° F (85° C)

9

CHAPTER TEN

FRONT SUSPENSION AND STEERING

This chapter discusses service operations on suspension components, steering, wheels and related items. **Table 1** lists service specifications. **Table 1** and **Table 2** are at the end of the chapter.

FRONT WHEEL

Removal/Installation

1. Support the motorcycle with a jack so that the front wheel is clear of the ground.
2. Loosen the speedometer cable nut (**Figure 1**) and pull the cable out of the speedometer drive unit.
3. Remove one brake caliper's mounting bolts (**Figure 2**) and lift the caliper off of the brake disc. Support the caliper with a bunji cord (**Figure 3**) to prevent stress buildup on the brake hose.
4. Loosen the right-hand axle clamp bolt (A, **Figure 4**). Then loosen the axle on the right-hand side (B, **Figure 4**).
5. Remove the axle from the right-hand side.
6. Pull the wheel forward to disengage the attached caliper from the brake disc. See **Figure 5**.
7. Remove the speedometer drive gear (**Figure 6**) from the left-hand side.
8. Remove the spacer (**Figure 7**) from the right-hand side.
9. If necessary, loosen the left-hand axle clamp bolt (A, **Figure 8**) and remove the axle nut (B, **Figure 8**).

> *CAUTION*
> *Do not set the wheel down on the disc surface as it may be scratched or warped. Either lean the wheel against a wall or place it on a couple of wooden blocks.*

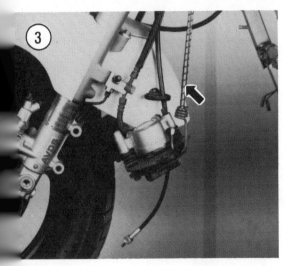

10

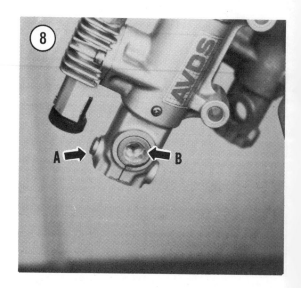

NOTE
Insert a piece of wood in the calipers in place of the disc. That way, if the brake lever is inadvertently squeezed, the piston will not be forced out of the cylinder. If this does happen, the calipers might have to be disassembled to reseat the piston and the system will have to be bled. By using the wood, bleeding the brake is not necessary when installing the wheel.

10. When servicing the wheel assembly, install the spacer, speedometer drive gear, washer and nut on the axle to prevent their loss. See **Figure 9**.

11. Installation is the reverse of these steps. Note the following:

   a. To prevent axle seizure, coat the axle with an anti-seize compound such as Bostik Never-seez Lubricating & Anti-seize Compound (part No. 49501).

   b. Tighten the axle nut to specifications in **Table 2**.

   c. Align the 2 tabs in the speedometer gear housing (**Figure 10**) with the 2 speedometer drive slots (**Figure 11**) in the front wheel and install the gear housing. See A, **Figure 12**.

   d. When installing the front wheel, align the tab on the speedometer gear housing (B, **Figure 12**) with the slot in the back of the left-hand fork tube (**Figure 13**). This procedure locates the speedometer drive gear and prevents it from rotating when the wheel turns.

   e. Make sure that the speedometer gear housing does not move as the axle nut is tightened.

   f. Remove the brake caliper from the bunji cord and carefully align it with the brake disc and install it. Install the 2 caliper bolts and tighten to 32 N•m (24 ft.-lb.).

   g. Apply the front brake and compress the front forks several times to make sure the axle is installed correctly without binding the forks. Then tighten the axle pinch bolts to specifications (**Table 2**).

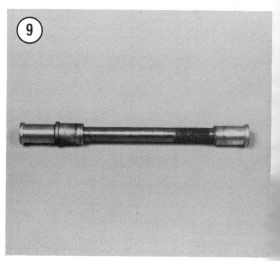

Inspection

1. Remove any corrosion on the front axle with a piece of fine emery cloth.

2. Check axle runout. Place the axle on V-blocks that are set 100 mm (4 in.) apart (**Figure 14**). Place the tip of a dial indicator in the middle of the axle. Rotate the axle and check runout. If the runout exceeds 0.2 mm (0.008 in.) but does not exceed 0.7 mm (0.027 in.), have it straightened by a dealer or machine shop to read less than 0.2 mm (0.008 in.)

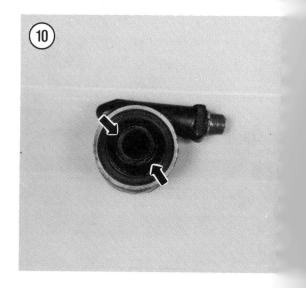

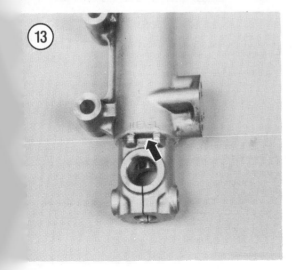

runout. If the runout exceeds 0.7 mm (0.027 in.), replace the axle. Do not attempt to straighten it.

3. Check rim runout as follows:

    a. Remove the tire from the rim as described in this chapter.

    b. Measure the radial (up and down) runout of the wheel rim with a dial indicator. If runout exceeds 0.8 mm (0.03 in.), check the wheel bearings.

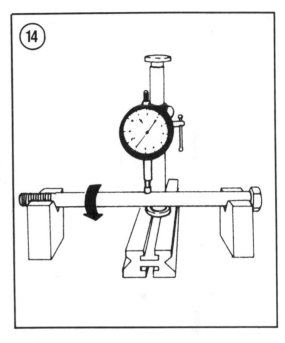

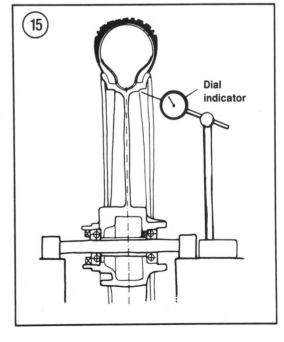

Dial indicator

10

c. Measure the axial (side to side) runout of the wheel rim with a dial indicator as shown in **Figure 15**. If runout exceeds 0.5 mm (0.01 in.), check the wheel bearings.

d. If the wheel bearings are okay, the wheel cannot be serviced, but must be replaced.

e. Replace the front wheel bearings as described under *Front Hub* in this chapter.

4. Inspect the wheel rim for dents, bending or cracks. Check the rim and rim sealing surface for cracks or scratches that are deeper than 0.5 mm (0.020 in.). If any of these conditions are present, replace the wheel.

Speedometer Gear Lubrication

The speedometer gear should be lubricated with high-temperature grease according to the maintenance schedule (**Table 1**) in Chapter Three.

1. Remove the front wheel from the motorcycle.

2. Clean all old grease from the gear housing (**Figure 10**) and gear. Pack the gear with high-temperature grease.

3. Install the front wheel as described in this chapter.

FRONT HUB

Disassembly/Inspection/Reassembly

Refer to **Figure 16**.

1. Check the wheel bearings by rotating the inner race. Check for bearing roughness, excessive noise or damage. If necessary, replace the bearings as follows. Always replace bearings in a set.

2. Remove the circlip and lift the speedometer gear drive out of the wheel (**Figure 17**).

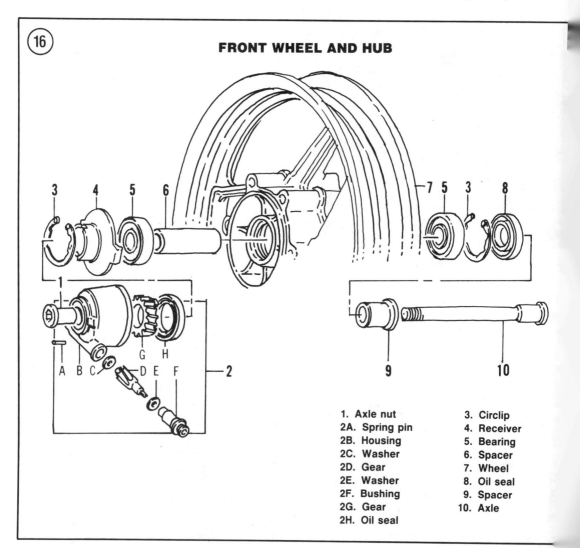

FRONT WHEEL AND HUB

1. Axle nut	3. Circlip
2A. Spring pin	4. Receiver
2B. Housing	5. Bearing
2C. Washer	6. Spacer
2D. Gear	7. Wheel
2E. Washer	8. Oil seal
2F. Bushing	9. Spacer
2G. Gear	10. Axle
2H. Oil seal	

3. Using a long drift or screwdriver, pry the oil seal from the right-hand side. See **Figure 18**.

4. Remove the circlip from the right-hand side (**Figure 16**).

5. Using a long drift and hammer, tilt the center spacer away from one side of the left-hand bearing (**Figure 19**). Then drive the left-hand bearing out of the hub. See **Figure 19**.

6. Remove the center spacer and remove the right-hand bearing.

7. Clean the axle spacer and hub thoroughly in solvent.

8. Tap the right-hand bearing into place carefully using a suitable size socket placed on the outer bearing race (**Figure 20**).

9. Install the right-hand circlip. Make sure it seats in its groove.

10. Install the center spacer and install the left-hand bearing as described in Step 8.

11. Install the speedometer drive and circlip on the left-hand side. Make sure the circlip seats in its groove. See **Figure 17**.

12. Install a new right-hand grease seal. Drive the seal in squarely with a large diameter socket on the outer portion of the seal. Drive the seal until it seats against the circlip.

WHEEL BALANCE

An unbalanced wheel results in unsafe riding conditions. Depnding on the degree of unbalance and the speed of the motorcycle, the rider may experience anything from a mild vibration to a violent shimmy and loss of control.

10

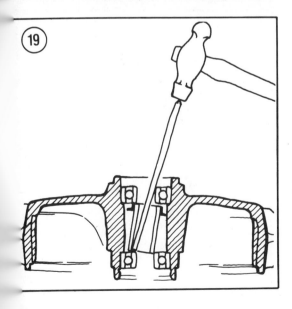

Weights are attached to the rim (**Figure 21**). Weight kits are available from motorcycle dealers. These kits (**Figure 21**) contain test weights and strips of adhesive-backed weights that can be cut to the desired length and attached directly to the rim. Kawasaki offers weights that can be crimped on the aluminum rims (**Figure 22**).

NOTE
Be sure to balance the wheel with the brake disc(s) attached as it also affects the balance.

Before attempting to balance the wheels, check to be sure that the wheel bearings are in good condition and properly lubricated. The wheel must rotate freely.
1. Remove the wheel as described in this chapter or in Chapter Eleven.
2. Mount the wheel on a fixture such as the one in **Figure 23** so it can rotate freely.
3. Give the wheel a spin and let it coast to a stop. Mark the tire at the lowest point.
4. Spin the wheel several more times. If the wheel keeps coming to rest at the same point, it is out of balance.
5. Tape a test weight to the upper (or light) side of the wheel.
6. Experiment with different weights until the wheel, when spun, comes to rest at a different position each time.
7. Remove the test weight and install the correct size weight.

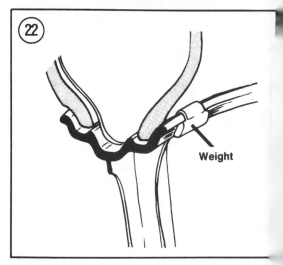

Weight

NOTE
*When installing crimp-type weights to aluminum rims, it may be necessary to let some air out of the tire. After installing the weight, refill the tire to the correct air pressure. See **Tire Pressure** in Chapter Three.*

TUBELESS TIRES

WARNING
Do not install an inner tube inside a tubeless tire. The tube will cause an abnormal heat buildup in the tire.

Tubeless tires have the word TUBELESS molded in the tire sidewall (**Figure 24**) and the rims have TUBELESS cast on them (**Figure 25**).
When a tubeless tire is flat, it best to take it to a motorcycle dealer for repair. Punctured tubeless tires should be removed from the rim to inspect the inside of the tire and to apply a combination

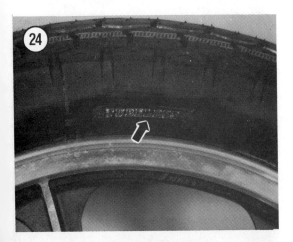

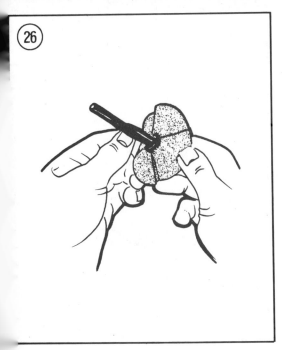

plug/patch from the inside. Don't rely on a plug or cord repair applied from outside the tire. They might be okay on a car, but they're too dangerous on a motorcycle.

After repairing a tubeless tire, don't exceed 50 mph (80 kph) for the first 24 hours. Never race on a repaired tubeless tire. The patch could work loose from tire flexing and heat.

Repair

Do not rely on a plug or cord patch applied from outside the tire. Use a combination plug/patch applied from inside the tire (**Figure 26**).
1. Remove the tire from the rim as described in this chapter.
2. Inspect the rim inner flange. Smooth any scratches on the sealing surface with emery cloth. If a scratch is deeper than 0.5 mm (0.020 in.) the wheel should be replaced.
3. Inspect the tire inside and out. Replace a tire if any of the following is found:
    a. A puncture larger than 1/8 in. (3 mm) diameter.
    b. A punctured or damaged sidewall.
    c. More than 2 punctures in the tire.
4. Apply the plug/patch, following the instructions supplied with the patch.

TUBELESS TIRE CHANGING

10

The wheels can easily be damaged during tire removal. Special care must be taken with tire irons when changing a tire to avoid scratches and gouges to the outer rim surface. Insert scraps of leather between the tire iron and the rim to protect the rim from damage.

The stock cast wheels are designed for use with tubeless tires.

Tire repair is different and is covered under *Tubeless Tires* in this chapter.

When removing a tubeless tire, take care not to damage the tire beads, inner liner of the tire or the wheel rim flange. Use tire levers or flat-handled tire irons with rounded ends.

Removal

NOTE
While removing a tire, support the wheel on 2 blocks of wood so the brake disc doesn't contact the floor.

1. Mark the valve stem location on the tire, so the tire can be installed in the same position for easier balancing. See **Figure 27**.

2. Remove the valve core to deflate the tire.

> *NOTE*
> *Removal of tubeless tires from their rims can be very difficult because of the exceptionally tight bead/rim seal. Breaking the bead seal may require the use of a special tool (**Figure 28**). If you have trouble breaking the seal take the tire to a motorcycle dealer.*

> *CAUTION*
> *The inner rim and tire bead area are sealing surfaces on a tubeless tire. Do not scratch the inside of the rim or damage the tire bead.*

3. Press the entire bead on both sides of the tire into the center of the rim.

4. Lubricate the beads with soapy water.

> *CAUTION*
> *Use rim protectors (**Figure 29**) or insert scraps of leather between the tire irons and the rim to protect the rim from damage.*

5. Insert the tire iron under the bead next to the valve (**Figure 30**). Force the bead on the opposite side of the tire into the center of the rim and pry the bead over the rim with the tire iron.

6. Insert a second tire iron next to the first to hold the bead over the rim. Then work around the tire with the first tool prying the bead over the rim (**Figure 31**).

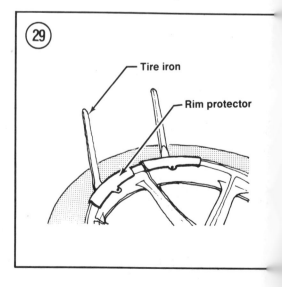

> *NOTE*
> *Step 7 is required only if it is necessary to completely remove the tire from the rim.*

7. Turn the wheel over. Insert a tire tool between the second bead and the same side of the rim that the first bead was pried over (**Figure 32**). Force the bead on the opposite side from the tool into the center of the rim. Pry the second bead off the rim, working around the wheel with 2 tire irons as with the first.

8. Inspect the valve stem seal. Because rubber deteriorates with age, it is advisable to replace the valve stem when replacing a tire. See **Figure 33**.

Installation

1. Carefully inspect the tire for any damage, especially inside.

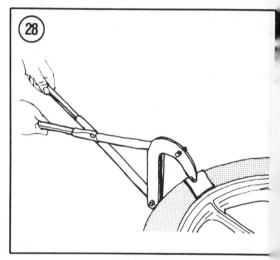

Tire iron

Rim protector

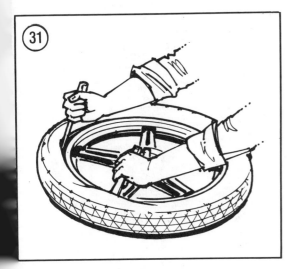

2. A new tire may have balancing rubbers inside. These are not patches and should not be disturbed. A colored spot near the bead indicates a lighter point on the tire. This spot should be placed next to the valve stem (**Figure 27**). In addition, most tires have directional arrows labeled on the side of the tire that indicate in which direction the tire should rotate (**Figure 34**). Make sure to install the tire accordingly.

3. Lubricate both beads of the tire with soapy water.

4. Place the backside of the tire into the center of the rim. The lower bead should go into the center

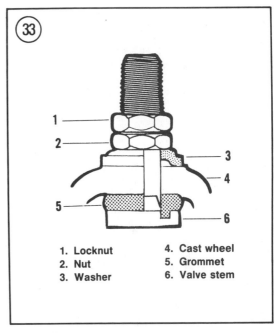

1. Locknut   4. Cast wheel
2. Nut   5. Grommet
3. Washer   6. Valve stem

10

of the rim and the upper bead outside. Work around the tire in both directions (**Figure 35**). Use a tire iron for the last few inches of bead (**Figure 36**).

5. Press the upper bead into the rim opposite the valve (**Figure 37**). Pry the bead into the rim on both sides of the initial point with a tire tool, working around the rim to the valve.

6. Check the bead on both sides of the tire for an even fit around the rim.

7. Place an inflatable band around the circumference of the tire. Slowly inflate the band until the tire beads are pressed against the rim. Inflate the tire enough to seat it, deflate the band and remove it.

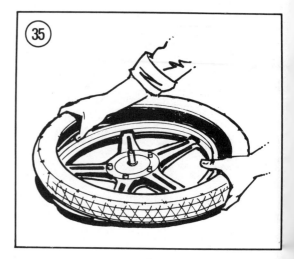

> *WARNING*
> *In the next step never exceed 56 psi (4.0 k/cm²) inflation pressure as the tire could burst causing severe injury. Never stand directly over the tire while inflating it.*

8. After inflating the tire, check to see that the beads are fully seated and that the tire rim lines (**Figure 38**) are the same distance from the rim all the way around the tire. If the beads won't seat, deflate the tire and relubricate the rim and beads with soapy water.

9. Reinflate the tire to the required pressure. See *Tire Pressure* in Chapter Three. Screw on the valve stem cap.

10. Balance the wheel assembly as described in this chapter.

HANDLEBARS

Removal/Installation

The Ninja uses separate handlebar assemblies (**Figure 39**) that slip over the top of the fork tubes and are bolted directly to the upper steering stem.

The handlebars can be removed individually by removing the 2 Allen bolts (**Figure 40**) and lifting the handlebar (**Figure 39**) off of the upper steering stem. Allow the handlebar(s) to hang by their control cables while performing service procedures.

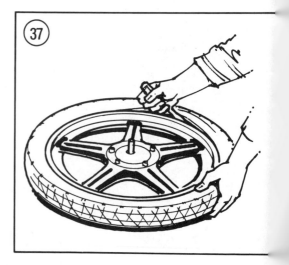

If it is necessary to replace a handlebar, remove the handlebar switches as described under *Switches* in Chapter Eight. Remove the master cylinder as described in Chapter Twelve.

Tighten the handlebar Allen bolts to the specifications in **Table 2**.

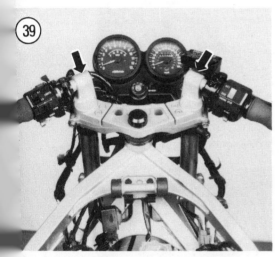

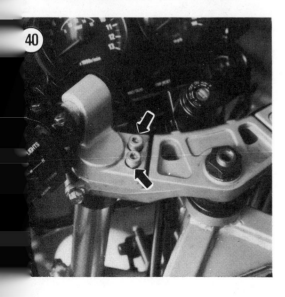

Inspection

Check the handlebars at their bolt holes and along the entire mounting area for cracks or damage. Replace a bent or damaged handlebar immediately. If the bike is involved in a crash, examine the handlebars, steering stem and front forks carefully.

STEERING HEAD

Disassembly

Refer to **Figure 41**.

1. Support the bike on the centerstand.

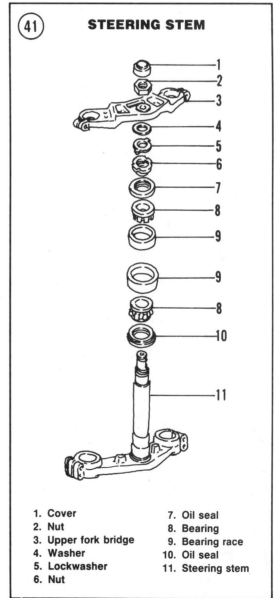

STEERING STEM

1. Cover	7. Oil seal
2. Nut	8. Bearing
3. Upper fork bridge	9. Bearing race
4. Washer	10. Oil seal
5. Lockwasher	11. Steering stem
6. Nut	

10

2. Remove the upper and lower fairings as described in Chapter Thirteen.

3. Remove the front wheel as described in this chapter.

4. Remove the fuel tank as described in Chapter Seven.

5. Remove the ignition switch bolts and separate the switch (**Figure 42**) from the upper steering stem.

6. Remove the instrument cluster as described in Chapter Eight.

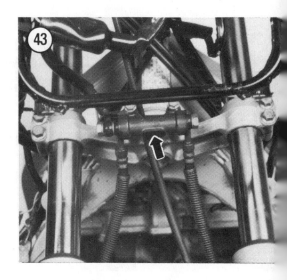

> *NOTE*
> *It is not necessary to disconnect the brake lines when performing Step 7.*

7. Remove the bolts securing the brake hose joint to the steering stem (**Figure 43**) pull it away from the stem.

8. Remove the front fairing bracket (**Figure 44**) and allow the bracket to hang down.

9. Remove the handlebars as described in this chapter.

10. Remove the front forks as described in this chapter.

11. Remove the steering nut (A, **Figure 45**) and flat washer.

12. Lift the upper steering stem head (B, **Figure 45**) off the steering stem shaft.

13. Remove the lockwasher and remove the steering adjust nut (**Figure 46**) with a spanner wrench.

14. Remove the bearing cap and pull the steering stem out of the frame (**Figure 47**).

15. Lift the upper bearing from the frame tube.

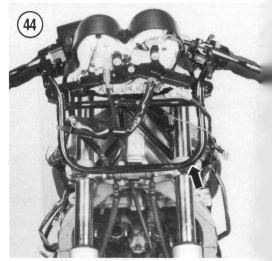

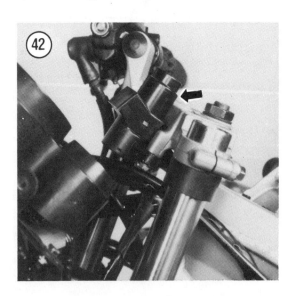

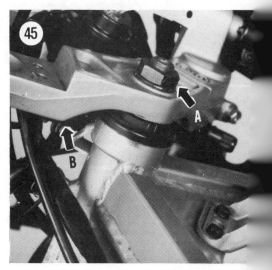

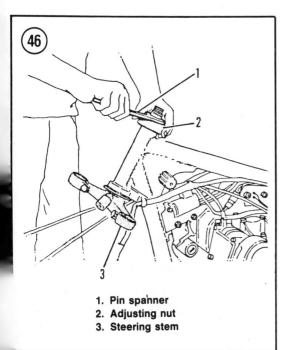

1. Pin spanner
2. Adjusting nut
3. Steering stem

16. Remove the lower bearing (**Figure 48**) as follows:
   a. Install a bearing puller (**Figure 49**) onto the steering stem and bearing.
   b. Pull the bearing off of the steering stem.
   c. Slide the seal (**Figure 48**) off the steering stem.

Installation

Refer to **Figure 41**.

1. If the lower bearing was removed from the steering stem, install a new bearing as follows:
   a. Clean the steering stem thoroughly in solvent.
   b. Slide a new seal (**Figure 48**) onto the steering stem.
   c. Slide the new bearing onto the steering stem until it stops.
   d. Align the bearing with the machined portion of the shaft and slide a long hollow pipe over the steering stem (**Figure 50**). Drive the bearing until it rests against the seal.

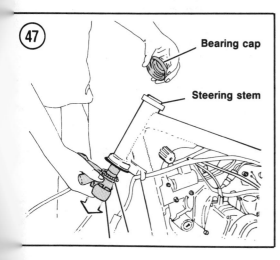

Bearing cap

Steering stem

Steering stem
Bearing
Seal

10

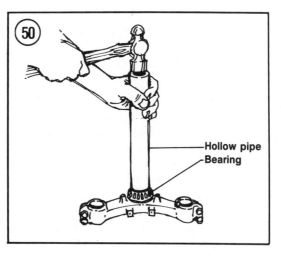

Hollow pipe
Bearing

2. Apply a coat of wheel bearing grease to both bearings.

3. Apply a coat of wheel bearing grease to both bearing races.

4. Carefully slide the steering stem up through the frame neck.

5. Install the upper bearing and the bearing cap (**Figure 47**).

6. Install the steering adjust nut and tighten to 39 N•m (29 ft.-lb.).

7. Turn the steering stem by hand to make sure it turns freely and does not bind. Repeat Step 6 if necessary.

8. Install the lockwasher (5, **Figure 41**).

9. Install the upper steering stem head (B, **Figure 45**).

10. Install the washer and steering nut (A, **Figure 45**). Tighten the steering nut to 39 N•m (29 ft.-lb.).

11. Turn the steering stem again by hand to make sure it turns freely and does not bind. If the steering stem is too tight, the bearings can be damaged. If the steering stem is too loose, the steering will become unstable. Repeat Steps 6-10 if necessary.

12. Reverse *Disassembly* Steps 1-10 to complete installation.

13. Recheck the steering adjustment. Repeat if necessary.

14. If a brake line was disconnected, bleed the brake system as described under *Bleeding the System* in Chapter Twelve.

Inspection

1. Clean the bearing races in the steering head and both bearings with solvent.

2. Check for broken welds on the frame around the steering stem. If any are found, have them repaired by a competent frame shop or welding service familar with motorcycle frame repair.

3. Check the bearings for pitting, scratches, or discoloration indicating wear or corrosion. Replace them in sets if any are bad.

4. Check the upper and lower races in the steering head for pitting, galling and corrosion. If any of these conditions exist, replace them as described under *Bearing Race Replacement* in this chapter.

5. Check steering stem for cracks and check its race for damage or wear. Replace if necessary.

Bearing Race Replacement

The headset and steering stem bearing races are pressed into place. Because they are easily bent, do not remove them unless they are worn and require replacement.

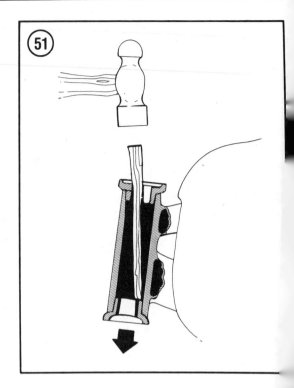

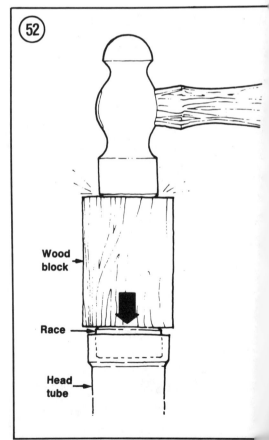

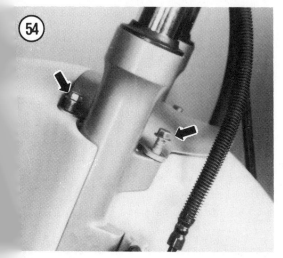

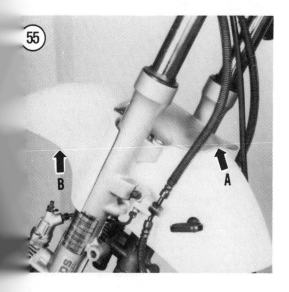

To remove a headset race, insert a hardwood stick into the head tube and carefully tap the race out from the inside (**Figure 51**). Tap all around the race so that neither the race nor the head tube is bent. To install a race, fit it into the end of the head tube. Tap it slowly and squarely with a block of wood (**Figure 52**).

FRONT FORK

Removal/Installation

1. Place the motorcycle on the centerstand.
2. Remove the front wheel as described in this chapter.
3. Remove the brake caliper(s) as described under *Front Caliper Removal/Installation* in Chapter Twelve.

NOTE
Insert a piece of wood in the calipers in place of the disc. That way, if the brake lever is inadvertently squeezed, the piston will not be forced out of the calipers. If it does happen, the calipers might have to be disassembled to reseat the piston. By using the wood, bleeding the brake is not necessary when installing the wheel.

4. Remove the air valve cap and depress the valve (**Figure 53**) to release fork air pressure.
5. Remove the front fender bolts (**Figure 54**). Then remove the fender brace (A, **Figure 55**) and the front fender (B, **Figure 55**).

NOTE
Step 6 describes how to loosen the fork caps while the forks are held in the steering stems.

WARNING
The fork caps are held under spring pressure. Take precautions to prevent the caps from flying into your face during removal. Furthermore, if the fork tubes are bent, the fork caps will be under considerable pressure. Have them removed by a Kawasaki dealer.

6. If the front fork will be disassembled, remove the handlebars as described in this chapter. Then

10

loosen the fork caps (but do not remove) with the drive end of a 1/2 in. ratchet (**Figure 56**).

NOTE
Do not disconnect any hydraulic line
when performing Step 7 and Step 8.

7. Remove the Allen bolts securing the brake plunger (**Figure 57**) to the anti-dive housing and pull the brake plunger away from the fork tube.

8. Remove the junction block bolts (**Figure 58**) and pull the junction block (**Figure 59**) away from the fork tube. Secure the brake caliper with a bunji cord to prevent brake line damage.

9. Loosen the upper (**Figure 60**) and lower (**Figure 61**) fork tube pinch bolts.

10. Twist the fork tube and pull it down until the fork tube circlip (**Figure 62**) is accessible. Tighten the lower fork tube pinch bolt (**Figure 61**).

11. Using a small-tipped screwdriver, pry the circlip out of its groove and slide it off of the fork tube (**Figure 63**).

12. Loosen the lower fork tube pinch bolt (**Figure 61**) and slide the fork tube out of the lower steering stem.

13. Repeat for the opposite side.

14. Install by reversing these removal steps. Note the following:

   a. Apply a coat of light machine oil to the fork cap threads before installation.

   b. After installing the fork tube through the lower steering stem, slide the circlip over the top of the fork tube (**Figure 63**) and seat it in the fork tube groove (**Figure 62**).

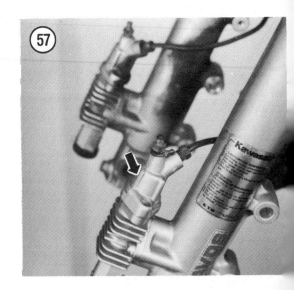

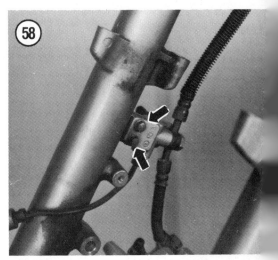

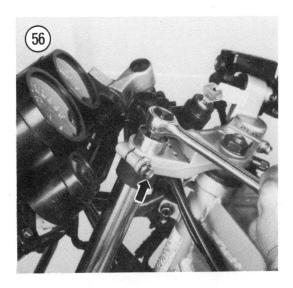

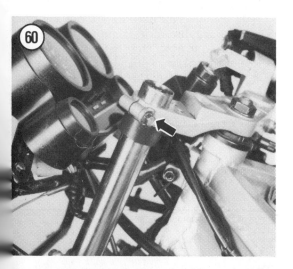

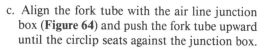

c. Align the fork tube with the air line junction box (**Figure 64**) and push the fork tube upward until the circlip seats against the junction box.

d. Tighten the upper and lower fork tube pinch bolts to the specifications in **Table 2**.

e. Tighten the junction block and brake plunger bolts securely.

f. Apply Loctite 242 (blue) to the front fender bolts and tighten securely.

g. After installing the front wheel, squeeze the front brake lever. If the brake lever feels spongy, bleed the brake(s) as described under *Bleeding the System* in Chapter Twelve.

h. Refill the front fork air pressure as described under *Suspension Adjustment* in Chapter Three.

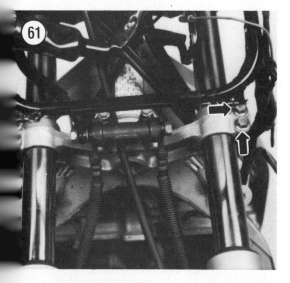

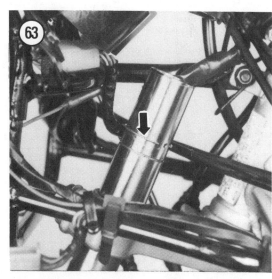

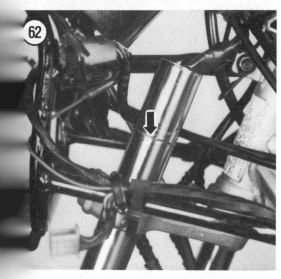

10

Disassembly

Refer to **Figure 65**.

1. Secure the fork tube in a vise with soft jaws.

2. The fork cap was loosened during removal. Remove the fork cap (**Figure 66**).

3. Remove the fork spring (**Figure 67**).

4. Remove the fork from the vise. Turn the fork slightly so that the travel control valve (**Figure 68**) slides out.

5. Hold the fork tube over a drain pan and pour the oil out and discard it. Pump the fork several times by hand to expel most of the remaining oil.

6. Remove the Allen bolt and gasket (**Figure 69**) from the bottom of the outer tube. Prevent the cylinder from turning with Kawasaki tools 57001-183 and 57001-1057 (**Figure 70**).

NOTE
The Allen bolt may be removed without holding the cylinder if an air impact driver is used.

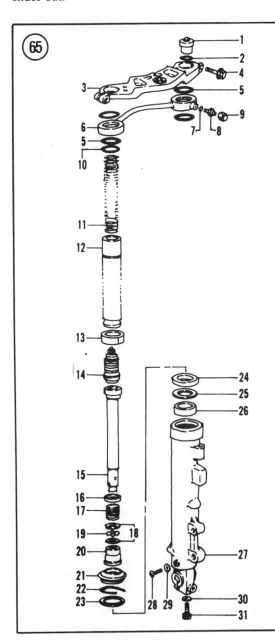

FRONT FORK
1. Fork cap
2. O-ring
3. Upper fork crown
4. Bolt
5. O-ring
6. Air pipe
7. O-ring
8. Air valve
9. Cap
10. Snap ring
11. Fork spring
12. Upper fork tube
13. Inner bushing
14. Fork valve assembly
15. Damper rod
16. Piston ring
17. Spring
18. Washers
19. Spring washers
20. Oil lock piece
21. Fork seal
22. Clip
23. Washer
24. Oil seal
25. Washer
26. Bushing
27. Slider
28. Drain screw
29. Washer
30. Washer
31. Allen bolt

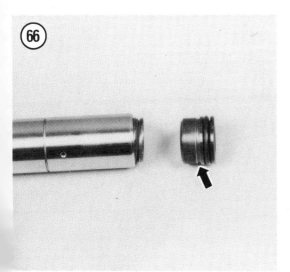

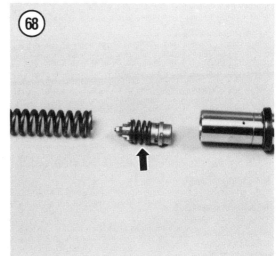

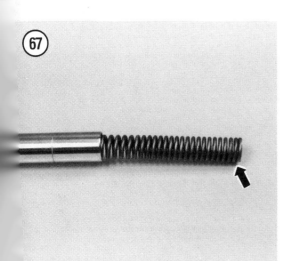

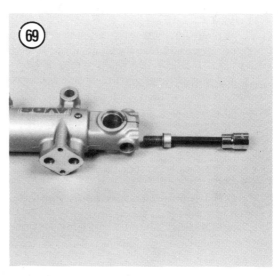

10

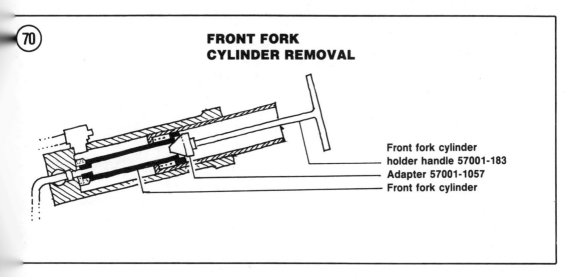

**FRONT FORK
CYLINDER REMOVAL**

Front fork cylinder
holder handle 57001-183
Adapter 57001-1057
Front fork cylinder

7. Pull the rubber boot (**Figure 71**) out of the notch in the lower fork tube and slide it off of the upper fork tube.

8. Pry the circlip (**Figure 72**) out of the lower fork tube and remove the washer (**Figure 73**).

9. Grasp the upper fork tube in one hand and the lower fork tube in the other. Work the lower fork tube back and forth and separate the fork tube assemblies.

10. Remove the oil seal and washer from the upper fork tube.

11. Remove the oil lock piece (**Figure 74**) and the 3 washers (**Figure 75**) from the damper rod and slide the damper rod and spring (**Figure 76**) out of the upper fork tube.

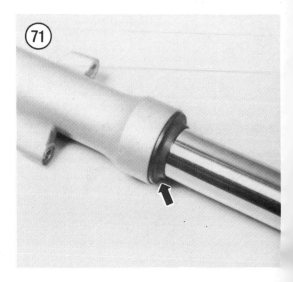

Inspection

1. Thoroughly clean all parts in solvent and blow dry them.

2. Check both fork tubes for wear or scratches. Check the upper fork tube for straightness. If bent, refer service to a Kawasaki dealer.

3. Check the upper fork tube for chrome flaking or creasing. This condition will damage oil seals. Replace the fork tube if necessary.

4. Check the lower fork tube oil seal area (**Figure 77**) for dents or other damage that would allow oil leakage. Replace the fork tube if necessary.

5. Check the damper rod for straightness (A, **Figure 78**).

6. Check the damper rod piston ring (B, **Figure 78**) for tearing, cracks or damage.

7. Check the guide bushings (**Figure 79**) for scoring, nicks or damage. Replace if necessary by pulling off the fork tube.

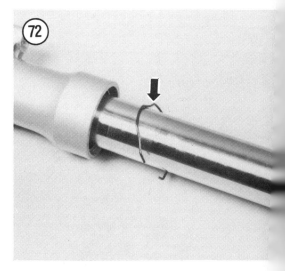

> *NOTE*
> *Do not disassemble the travel control valve in Step 8. If the valve is damaged, it must be replaced.*

8. Check the travel control valve (**Figure 80**) for any signs of damage.

9. Measure the uncompressed length of the fork springs (**Figure 81**) with a tape measure and compare to specifications in **Table 1**. Replace the fork spring(s) if too short.

> *WARNING*
> *If one fork spring is replaced, compare the measurement of the new and the remaining old spring. If the length difference is great between a new spring and the old usable spring, it is best to replace both springs to keep the forks balanced for steering stability.*

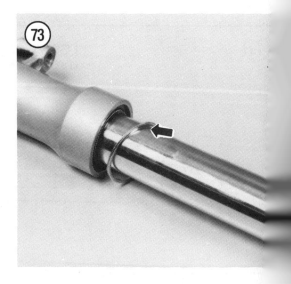

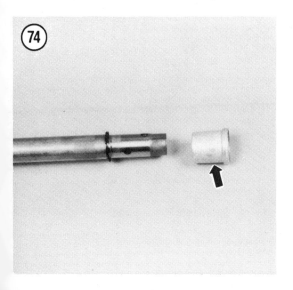

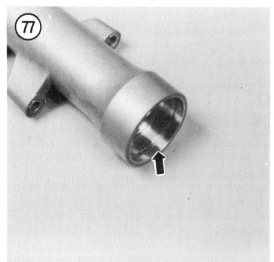

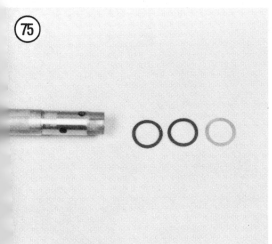

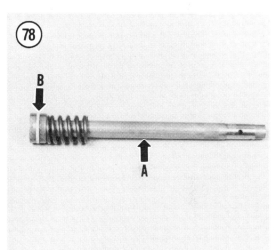

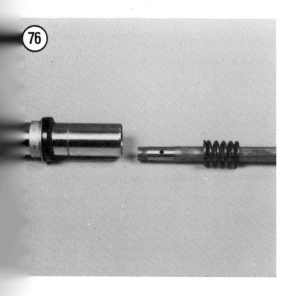

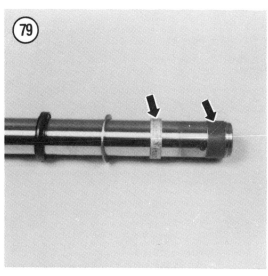

10

10. Replace the fork cap O-ring (**Figure 82**) if deformed or damaged.

11. Check the rubber boot (**Figure 83**) for weather deterioration, cracks or other damage. Replace if necessary.

Assembly

1. Slide the spring onto the damper rod and insert the damper rod and spring into the upper fork tube (**Figure 76**).

2. Install 2 spring washers and 1 flat washer (**Figure 75**) onto the damper rod.

3. Slide the oil lock piece (**Figure 74**) onto the damper rod.

4. Insert the damper rod/upper fork tube into the lower fork tube (**Figure 84**).

> *NOTE*
> *If the guide bushings are difficult to install into the lower fork tube, install an old outer tube guide bushing and drive the bushings into the lower fork tube with Kawasaki special driver (part No. 57001-1104). A piece of galvanized pipe can also work as a tool. If both ends of the pipe are threaded, wrap one end with duct tape (**Figure 85**) to prevent the threads from damaging the interior of the slider.*

5. Apply Loctite 242 (blue) onto the fork tube Allen bolt (**Figure 69**). Install the Allen bolt and tighten to specifications in **Table 2**. Use the same tool to prevent the damper rod (**Figure 70**) from turning as during disassembly.

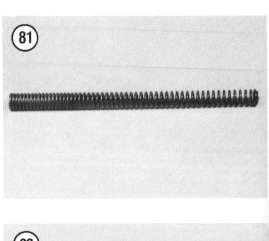

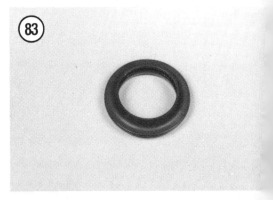

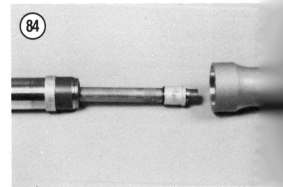

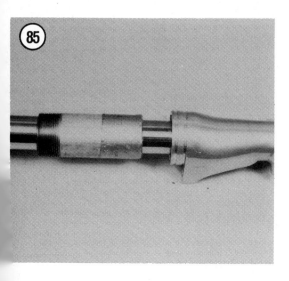

6. Slide the washer (**Figure 86**) down the upper fork tube and rest it on the lower fork tube.

7. Position the oil seal with the marking facing upward and slide down onto the fork tube (**Figure 87**). Drive the seal into the lower fork tube with Kawasaki special tool (part No. 57001-1104). Refer to **Figure 88**. Drive the oil seal in until the groove in the slider can be seen above the top surface of the oil seal.

NOTE
The oil seal can be driven in with a homemade tool as described in the NOTE following Step 4.

8. Slide the washer down the inner fork tube until it rests against the oil seal (**Figure 73**). Make sure the groove in the lower fork tube can be seen above the top surface of the washer. If not, the oil seal will have to pushed farther into the lower fork tube. See Step 7.

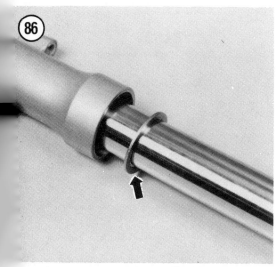

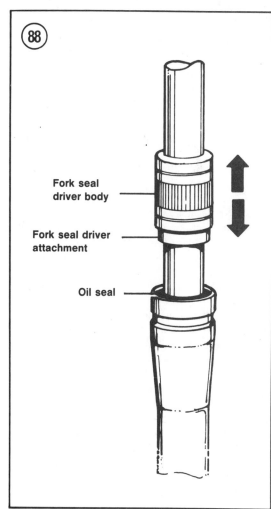

Fork seal driver body

Fork seal driver attachment

Oil seal

10

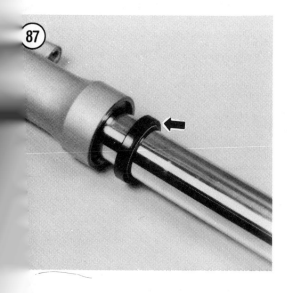

9. Slide the circlip (**Figure 72**) down the inner fork tube and seat it in the lower fork tube groove. Make sure the circlip is completely seated in the groove.

10. Slide the dust seal down the inner fork tube (**Figure 89**) and seat it in the lower fork tube (**Figure 71**).

11. Fill the fork tube with the correct quantity of 10W-20 fork oil as specified in **Table 1**. Check the oil level as described under *Front Fork Oil Change* in Chapter Three.

12. Install the travel control valve through the inner fork tube so that the nuts face to the top of the fork. See **Figure 68**.

13. Install the fork spring with the closer wound coils toward the top of the fork (**Figure 67**).

14. Pull the upper and lower fork tubes far apart as possible. Apply a light coat of oil to the fork cap and install it by slightly compressing the fork spring. Once the fork cap is installed, it can be tightened after installing the fork tube onto the motorcycle. See *Front Fork Removal/Installation* in this chapter.

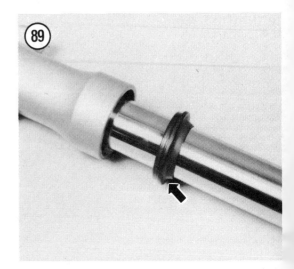

Automatic Variable Damping System Troubleshooting

If the front fork does not operate correctly, perform the following:

1. No damping during the fork compression stroke:

   a. Disassemble the front fork as described in this chapter.

   b. Check the damper rod piston ring (B, **Figure 78**) for damage. Replace if necessary.

   c. If the damper rod piston ring is okay, the travel control valve may be damaged. Check the valve (**Figure 80**) for damage. No adjustment is provided for the valve. Replace the valve if necessary.

2. No damping force during fork extension:

   a. Check the front fork oil level as described under *Front Fork Oil Change* in Chapter Three and recheck fork operation.

   b. Disassemble the front fork as described in this chapter.

   c. Check the damper rod orifices for contamination. Clean in solvent if necessary.

   d. Check the damper rod piston ring (B, **Figure 78**) for damage. Replace if necessary.

   e. If the above checks do not solve the damping problem, the travel control valve is damaged. Replace the valve.

3. Reassemble the front forks as described in this chapter.

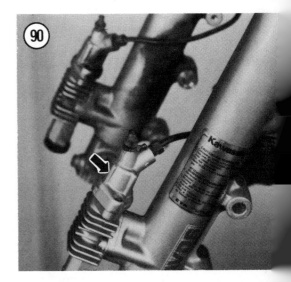

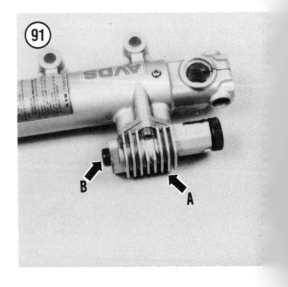

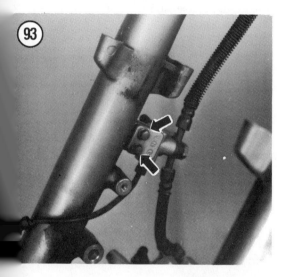

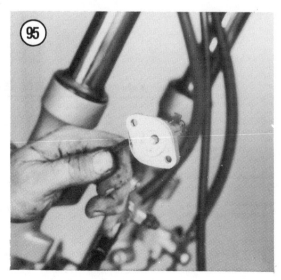

BRAKE PLUNGER AND ANTI-DIVE

Removal/Installation

The anti-dive assembly can be removed with the front forks installed on the bike.

1. Drain the fork oil as described under *Front Fork Oil Change* in Chapter Three.

2. Remove the Allen bolts securing the brake plunger (**Figure 90**) to the anti-dive housing and pull the brake plunger away from the fork tube. Disconnect the brake line at the brake plunger and remove it.

3. Remove the Allen bolts securing the anti-dive housing (A, **Figure 91**) to the lower fork tube and remove it.

4. Check the anti-dive O-rings (**Figure 92**) for flat spots or damage. Replace if necessary.

5. The anti-dive unit cannot be disassembled. If damaged, replace the unit.

6. Install by reversing these steps.

7. Bleed the front brake as described under *Bleeding the System* in Chapter Twelve.

Brake Plunger Test

1. Remove the brake plunger from the anti-dive unit but do not disconnect the brake line.

2. Remove the junction block screws (**Figure 93**) and pull the junction block away from the fork tube (**Figure 94**). This will prevent oil pipe damage when performing this procedure.

3. Lightly apply the front brake lever and check that the brake plunger (**Figure 95**) extends 2 mm (3/32 in.). Release the brake lever and push the brake plunger back in with your finger. If the plunger did not extend correctly or if it is tight,

10

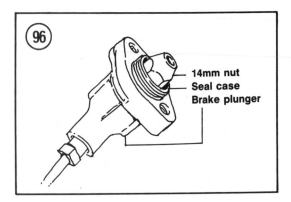

14mm nut
Seal case
Brake plunger

1. Remove the brake plunger as described in this chapter.

2. Insert a 14 mm nut into the end of the brake plunger and unscrew the seal case (**Figure 96**).

3. Replace the rubber parts.

4. Reverse to install.

Anti-Dive Assembly Test

Anti-dive operation can be checked as follows.

1. Remove the front fork, fork cap and spring as described in this chapter.

2. Hold the front fork upright.

3. Compress the upper fork leg a few times. Then compress the upper fork leg while holding the anti-dive rod (B, **Figure 91**) in with your finger.

4. Interpret results as follows:

    a. The fork compression stroke should be light and smooth when the valve is not pushed in.

    b. A noticeable difference in damping should occur when the anti-dive rod is held in.

5. If the anti-dive unit did not operate as described in Step 4, replace it as described in this chapter.

replace the brake plunger assembly as described in this chapter.

Brake Plunger
Seal Replacement

At the service intervals specified in Chapter Three (**Table 1**), the brake plunger rubber cap, O-ring and seal ring should be replaced.

Table 1 FRONT SUSPENSION SPECIFICATIONS

Front fork spring free length	
New	478 mm (18.818 in.)
Wear limit	468 mm (18.425 in.)
Front fork oil capacity	
Change	273 cc (9.230 oz.)
Rebuild	317-325 cc (10.72-11.0 oz.)

Table 2 FRONT SUSPENSION TIGHTENING TORQUES

	N•m	ft.-lb.
Front axle nut	88	66
Front axle pinch bolt	20	14.5
Fork caps	23	16.5
Upper triple clamp pinch bolts	21	15
Steering stem pinch bolts	21	15
Anti-dive bolts	7	61 in.-lb.
Damper rod Allen bolt	29	22
Handlebar Allen bolts	23	16.5
Steering stem nut	39	29
Steering adjust nut	4.9	43 in.-lb.

NOTE: If you own a 1988 or later model, first check the Supplement at the back of this book for any new service information.

CHAPTER ELEVEN

REAR SUSPENSION

This chapter includes repair and replacement procedures for the rear wheel, drive chain and rear suspension components.

Table 1 (end of chapter) lists rear suspension tightening torques.

REAR WHEEL

Removal/Installation

1. Support the bike so that the rear wheel clears the ground.

2. Loosen the torque link nut (**Figure 1**).
3. Loosen the drive chain adjusting locknuts and adjuster bolts (**Figure 2**).
4. Remove the cotter pin and remove the rear axle nut (**Figure 3**) from the right-hand side.
5. Slide the axle (**Figure 4**) out of the wheel and allow the wheel to drop to the ground.
6. Lift the drive chain off the sprocket and pull the wheel away from the swing arm (**Figure 5**).
7. Remove the right- (**Figure 6**) and left-hand (**Figure 7**) axle spacers.

11

CAUTION
Do not set the wheel down on the disc surface as it may be scratched or warped. Either lean the wheel against a wall or place it on a couple of wooden blocks.

NOTE
Insert a piece of wood in the caliper in place of the disc. That way, if the brake lever is inadvertently squeezed, the piston will not be forced out of the cylinder. If this does happen, the caliper might have to be disassembled to reseat the piston and the system will have to be bled. By using the wood, bleeding the brake is not necessary when installing the wheel.

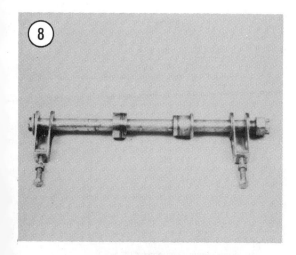

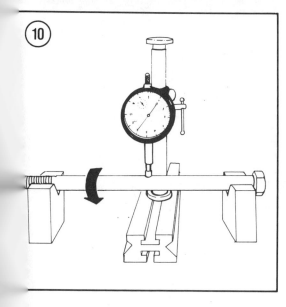

8. If the wheel is going to be off for any length of time or if it is to be taken to a shop for repair, install the chain adjusters and axle spacers on the axle along with the axle nut to prevent losing any parts (**Figure 8**).

9. If necessary, service the rear sprocket as described under *Rear Sprocket and Coupling* in this chapter.

10. Installation is the reverse of these steps. Note the following:

   a. To prevent axle seizure, coat the axle with an anti-seize compound such as Bostik Never-Seez Lubricating & Anti-seize Compound (part No. 49501).

   b. Insert the rear sprocket/coupling assembly into the rear hub if removed. See **Figure 9**.

   c. Adjust the drive chain as described under drive chain adjustment in Chapter Three.

   d. Tighten the torque link nut securely.

   e. Tighten the axle nut to specifications in **Table 1**. Secure the nut with a new cotter pin.

   f. Adjust the rear brake as described under *Rear Brake Pedal Height Adjustment* and *Rear Brake Light Switch Adjustment* in Chapter Three.

   g. Spin the wheel several times to make sure it rotates freely and that the brake works properly.

Inspection

1. Remove any corrosion on the rear axle with a piece of fine emery cloth.

2. Check axle runout. Place the axle on V-blocks that are set 100 mm (4 in.) apart (**Figure 10**). Place the tip of a dial indicator in the middle of the axle. Rotate the axle and check runout. If the runout exceeds 0.2 mm (0.008 in.) but does not exceed 0.7 mm (0.027 in.), have it straightened by a dealer or machine shop to read less than 0.2 mm (0.008 in.) runout. If the runout exceeds 0.7 mm (0.027 in.), replace the axle. Do not attempt to straighten it.

3. Check rim runout as follows:

   a. Remove the tire from the wheel as described under *Tubless Tire Changing* in Chapter Ten.

   b. Measure the radial (up and down) runout of the wheel rim with a dial indicator. If runout exceeds 0.8 mm (0.03 in.), check the wheel bearings as described under *Rear Hub* in this chapter.

   c. Measure the axial (side to side) runout of the wheel rim with a dial indicator as shown in **Figure 10**. If runout exceeds 0.5 mm (0.020 in.), check the wheel bearings as described under *Rear Hub* in this chapter.

11

d. If the wheel bearings are okay, the wheel cannot be serviced, but must be replaced.

e. Replace the rear wheel bearings as described under *Rear Hub* in this chapter.

4. Inspect the wheel rim for dents, bending or cracks. Check the rim and rim sealing surface for scratches that are deeper than 0.5 mm (0.020 in.). If any of these conditions are present, replace the wheel.

REAR HUB

Disassembly/Inspection/Reassembly

Refer to **Figure 12**.

1. Check the wheel bearings (**Figure 13**) by rotating the inner race. Check for bearing roughness, excessive noise or damage. If necessary, replace the bearings as follows. Always replace bearings in a set.

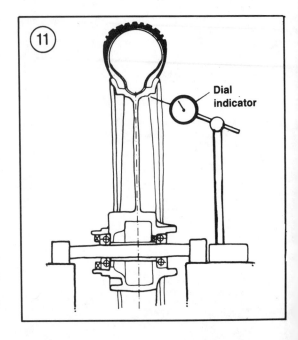

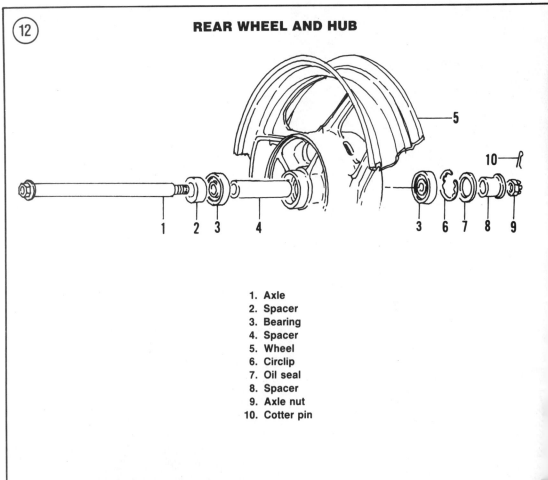

REAR WHEEL AND HUB

1. Axle
2. Spacer
3. Bearing
4. Spacer
5. Wheel
6. Circlip
7. Oil seal
8. Spacer
9. Axle nut
10. Cotter pin

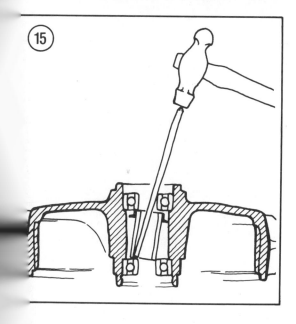

2. Lift the rear sprocket/coupling assembly (**Figure 9**) out of the rear hub.

3. Using a long drift or screwdriver, pry the oil seal from the right-hand side. See **Figure 14**.

4. Remove the circlip from the right-hand side (**Figure 12**).

5. Using a long drift and hammer, tilt the center spacer away from one side of the left-hand bearing (**Figure 15**). Then drive the left-hand bearing out of the hub. See **Figure 15**.

6. Remove the center spacer and remove the right-hand bearing.

7. Clean the center spacer and hub thoroughly in solvent.

8. Tap the right-hand bearing into place carefully using a suitable size socket placed on the outer bearing race (**Figure 16**).

9. Install the right-hand circlip. Make sure it seats in its groove.

10. Install the center spacer and install the left-hand bearing as described in Step 8.

11. Install a new right-hand grease seal. Drive the seal in squarely with a large diameter socket on the outer portion of the seal. Drive the seal until it seats against the circlip.

REAR SPROCKET AND COUPLING

The rear wheel coupling (**Figure 17**) connects the rear sprocket to the rear wheel. The coupling housing is equipped with an oil seal, ball bearing and spacer. Rubber shock dampers installed in the coupling absorb some of the shock that results from torque changes during acceleration or braking.

11

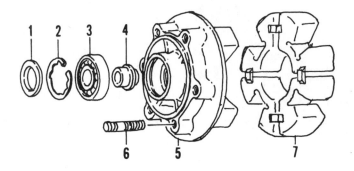

REAR WHEEL COUPLING ASSEMBLY

1. Oil seal
2. Circlip
3. Bearing
4. Spacer
5. Housing assembly
6. Sprocket studs
7. Dampers

Removal/Installation

1. Remove the rear wheel as described in this chapter.

2. Pull the rear wheel coupling assembly (**Figure 9**) up and out of the wheel hub.

3. Pull the dampers (**Figure 18**) out of the housing.

4. Remove the spacer (**Figure 19**).

5. To remove the sprocket loosen and remove the nuts and lift the sprocket (A, **Figure 20**) off of the housing.

6. Perform *Inspection/Disassembly/Reassembly* as described in this chapter.

7. Install by reversing these steps. Note the following:

   a. Install the sprocket so that the chamfered side faces toward the housing.

b. Apply Loctite 242 (blue) to the sprocket nuts and tighten them to the specifications in **Table 1**.

Inspection/Disassembly/Reassembly

1. Visually inspect the rubber dampers (**Figure 21**) for damage or deterioration. Replace, if necessary, as a complete set.

2. Inspect the flange assembly housing and damper separators for cracks or damage. Replace the coupling housing if necessary.

3. If necessary, replace the coupling housing bearing as follows:

a. Pry the seal from the housing (B, **Figure 20**).

b. Remove the bearing circlip.

c. Using a large diameter socket or drift on the bearing, drive it out of the housing (from the inside out).

d. Discard the bearing.

e. Clean the housing thoroughly in solvent and check for cracks or damage in the bearing area.

f. Blow any dirt or foreign matter out of the housing before installing the bearings.

g. Pack non-sealed bearings with grease before installation. Sealed bearings do not require packing.

h. Tap the bearing into position with a socket placed on the outer bearing race.

i. Install the circlip. Make sure it seats in the housing groove.

j. Install a new seal (B, **Figure 20**) by driving it in squarely with a socket and hammer.

Sprocket Inspection

Inspect the teeth of the sprocket. If the teeth are visibly worn, replace both sprockets and the drive chain. Never replace any one sprocket or chain as a separate item. Worn parts will cause rapid wear of the new component. If necessary, replace the front sprocket as described under *Engine Sprocket* in Chapter Six.

DRIVE CHAIN

Because the drive chain is endless (has no master link), the swing arm must be removed to remove the drive chain.

> *WARNING*
> *Kawasaki uses an endless chain on this model for strength and reliability. Do not cut the chain with a chain cutter or install chain with a master link. The chain may fail and rear wheel lockup could result in an accident.*

11

Removal/Installation

1. Remove the rear wheel as described in this chapter.

2. Remove the shift linkage (**Figure 22**). Remove the pinch screw (A) and the pivot screw (B) securing the shift linkage and pull the shift linkage off. If the pivot boss is tight on the shaft, spread the slot open with a screwdriver.

3. Remove the screws securing the engine sprocket cover and remove the cover (**Figure 23**).

4. Remove the chain guard (**Figure 24**).

5. Remove the swing arm pivot shaft covers (**Figure 25**).

6. Loosen and remove the swing arm pivot shaft nut (**Figure 26**).

7. Remove the following:
   a. Lower shock absorber shaft (A, **Figure 27**).
   b. Lower tie rod shaft (B, **Figure 27**).

8. Remove the swing arm pivot shaft and pull the swing arm toward the rear.

9. Slip the drive chain off of the swing arm.

10. Install by reversing the removal steps. Note the following:
   a. Make sure the bearing caps are installed on the swing arm.
   b. Tighten the lower shock absorber shaft and the Uni-trak nuts to the specifications in **Table 1**.
   c. Tighten the pivot shaft to specifications (**Table 1**).
   d. Adjust the drive chain as described under *Drive Chain Adjustment* in Chapter Three.
   e. Tighten the axle nut to the torque values in **Table 1**.
   f. Rotate the wheel several times to make sure it rotates smoothly. Apply the brake several times to make sure it operates correctly.

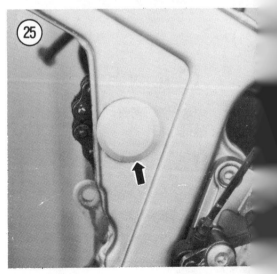

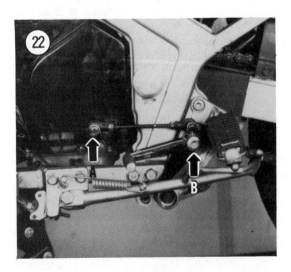

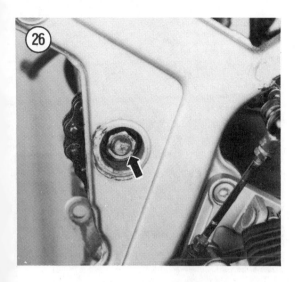

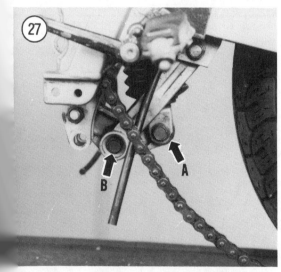

g. Adjust the rear brake as described under *Rear Brake Pedal Height Adjustment* and *Rear Brake Light Switch Adjustment* in Chapter Three.

Cleaning

CAUTION
The factory drive chain is equipped with O-rings between the side plates that seal lubricant between the pins and bushings. To prevent damaging these O-rings use only kerosene or diesel oil for cleaning. Do not use gasoline or other solvents that will cause the O-rings to swell or deteriorate.

Occasionally, the drive chain should be removed from the bike for a thorough cleaning and soak lubrication. Perform the following:
a. Brush off excess dirt and grit.
b. Remove the drive chain as described in this chapter.
c. Soak the chain in kerosene or diesel oil for about half an hour and clean it thoroughly. Then hang the chain from a piece of wire and allow it to dry.
d. Install the chain on the motorcycle as described in this chapter.

Lubrication

For lubrication of the drive chain, refer to *Drive Chain Lubrication* in Chapter Three.

WHEEL BALANCING

For complete information refer to *Wheel Balance* in Chapter Ten.

TIRE CHANGING AND REPAIR

Refer to *Tubeless Tires* and *Tubeless Tire Changing* in Chapter Ten.

REAR SHOCK ABSORBER

Removal/Installation

1. Park the bike on its centerstand.
2. Remove the side covers.
3. Remove the air valve mounting nut and pull the air valve (**Figure 28**) out of the frame mounting ring.

11

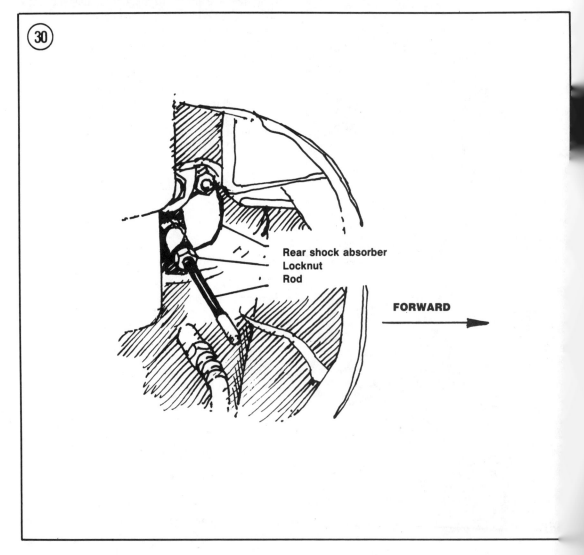

Rear shock absorber
Locknut
Rod

FORWARD

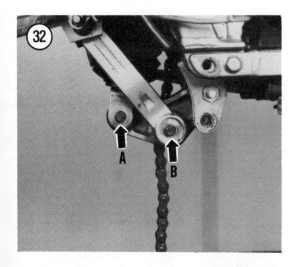

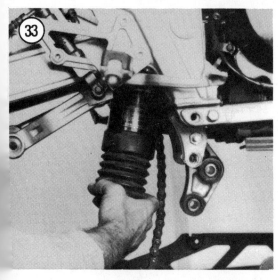

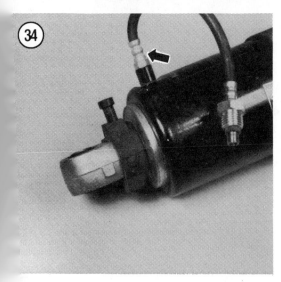

4. Disconnect the igniter connector and remove the igniter (**Figure 29**). Then remove the igniter bracket.

5. Loosen the adjust rod locknut at the shock absorber and unscrew the rod (**Figure 30**).

6. Remove the upper (**Figure 31**) and lower (A, **Figure 32**) shock absorber nuts and pivot bolts.

7. Remove the tie-rod nut and bolt (B, **Figure 32**).

8. Lower the shock absorber and remove it from underneath the swing arm. See **Figure 33**.

> *WARNING*
> *The shock absorber contains highly compressed nitrogen gas. Do not tamper with or attempt to open the cylinder or air valve fitting (**Figure 34**). Do not place it near an open flame or other extreme heat. Do not weld on the frame near it. Do not dispose of the shock absorber yourself. Take it to a Kawasaki dealer where it can be deactivited and disposed of properly.*

9. Inspect the shock absorber boot (**Figure 35**) for tears, deterioration or damage. Repace the boot if necessary.

10. Install by reversing these steps. Note the following:

   a. Tighten the shock absorber and tie-rod pivot bolts to the specifications in **Table 1**.

   b. Check the shock absorber air pressure as described under *Suspension Adjustment* in Chapter Three.

REAR SWING ARM

Removal/Installation

Refer to **Figure 36**.

1. Park the motorcycle on its centerstand.

11

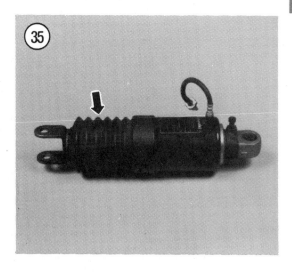

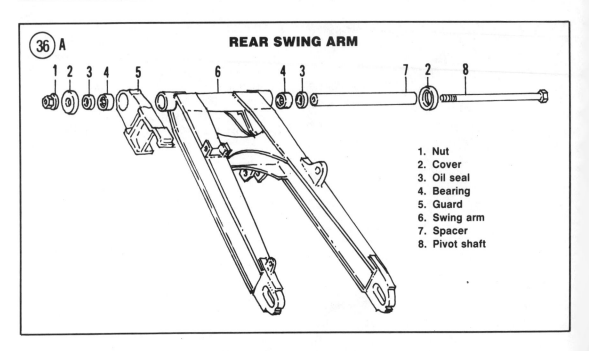

REAR SWING ARM

1. Nut
2. Cover
3. Oil seal
4. Bearing
5. Guard
6. Swing arm
7. Spacer
8. Pivot shaft

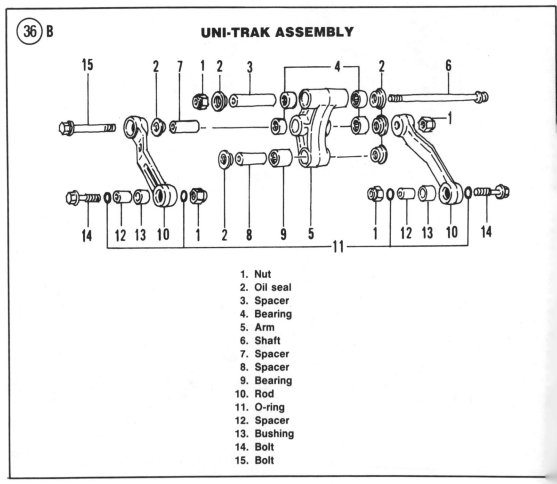

UNI-TRAK ASSEMBLY

1. Nut
2. Oil seal
3. Spacer
4. Bearing
5. Arm
6. Shaft
7. Spacer
8. Spacer
9. Bearing
10. Rod
11. O-ring
12. Spacer
13. Bushing
14. Bolt
15. Bolt

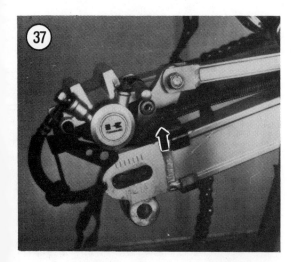

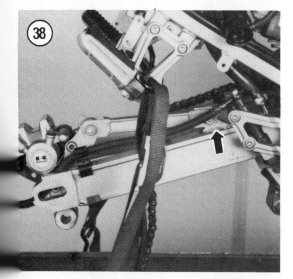

2. Remove the mufflers.

3. Remove the rear wheel as described in this chapter.

4. Pull the rear brake hose out of the swing arm hose clamp (**Figure 37**).

NOTE
It is not necessary to disconnect any brake hose when performing Step 5.

5. Remove the torque arm nut and bolt (**Figure 38**) at the swing arm and pull the rear brake caliper away from the swing arm. Secure the caliper with a bunji cord.

6. Remove the chain guard (**Figure 24**).

7. Remove the following:
   a. Lower shock absorber shaft (A, **Figure 32**).
   b. Lower tie-rod shaft (B, **Figure 32**).

8. Before removing the swing arm, grasp the swing arm as shown in **Figure 39** and move the swing arm from side to side and up and down. If you feel any more than a very slight movement of the swing arm and the pivot bolt is correctly tightened, remove the swing arm and check the bearings as described in this chapter.

9. Remove the swing arm pivot shaft covers (**Figure 25**).

10. Loosen and remove the swing arm pivot shaft nut (**Figure 26**).

11. Remove the swing arm pivot shaft (**Figure 40**) and pull the swing arm toward the rear.

12. Pull the swing arm (**Figure 41**) away from the motorcycle.

13. Remove the bearing caps (**Figure 42**) from the swing arm.

14. Remove the drive chain, if necessary.

11

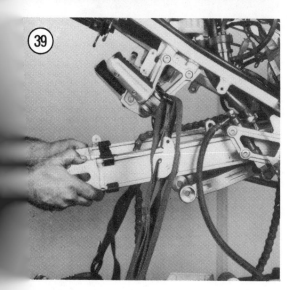

15. Remove the tie-rod and rocker arm as described in this chapter.

16. Installation is the reverse of these steps. Note the following:

   a. Replace the swing arm chain pad (**Figure 43**) if it is worn severely or damaged.

   b. Tighten the swing arm pivot shaft nut to specifications (**Table 1**).

   c. Tighten the lower shock absorber and tie-rod pivot shafts to the specifications in **Table 1**.

   d. Tighten the brake torque link nut securely.

   e. Adjust the drive chain as described under *Drive Chain Adjustment* in Chapter Three.

Inspection and Bearing Replacement

Refer to **Figure 36**.

1. Check the swing arm (**Figure 44**) for cracks, twisting, weld breakage or other damage. Refer repair to a competent welding shop.

2. Pry the bearing seals (**Figure 43**) out of the swing arm.

3. The roller bearings (**Figure 45**) wear very slowly and the wear is difficlt to measure. Turn the bearings by hand. Make sure they rotate smoothly. Check the rollers for evidence of wear, pitting, or color change indicating heat from lack of lubrication. In severe instances, the needles will fall out of the bearing cage.

4. Replace the bearings as follows:

   a. Using a long metal rod or drift punch, tap one of the bearings out of the swing arm (**Figure 46**).

   b. Remove the center sleeve and remove the opposite bearing.

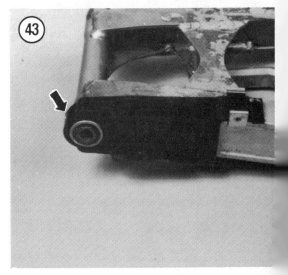

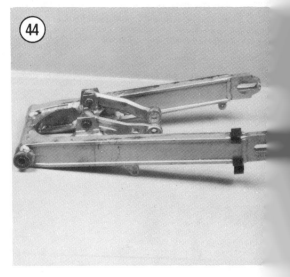

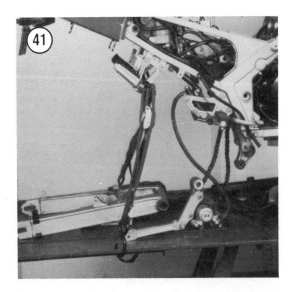

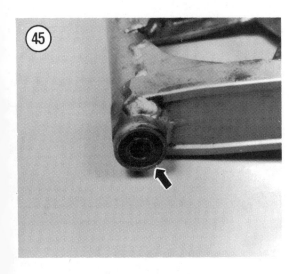

c. Clean the swing arm bearing bore with solvent and allow to dry.

d. Lubricate the bearings with oil before installation.

e. Install the new bearings with a hydraulic press. Make sure to install the center sleeve after installing the first bearing. If a press is not available, a bearing installer can be fabricated with a piece of pipe and a long threaded rod.

> *WARNING*
> *Never reinstall a needle bearing that has been removed. During removal it is damaged and no longer true to alignment. If installed it will damage the sleeve and create an unsafe riding condition.*

f. Apply a coat of molybdenum disulfide grease to the inner needle bearing surfaces.

Tie-Rod
Removal/Installation

The tie-rods can be removed without having to remove the swing arm.

1. Place the motorcycle on its centerstand.

2. Remove the tie-rod nut and pivot bolt (A, **Figure 47**) at the connecting rod.

3. Remove the nut and bolt (A, **Figure 48**) at the swing arm and remove the tie-rods (B, **Figure 48**).

4. Install by reversing these steps. Tighten the tie-rod nuts and bolts to the torque specifications in **Table 1**.

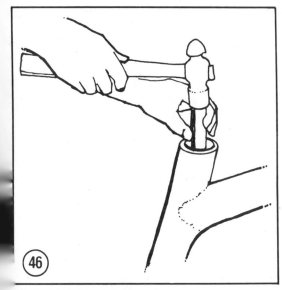

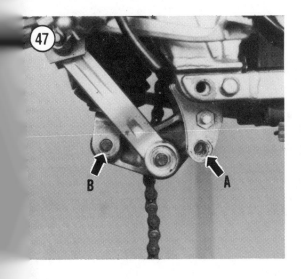

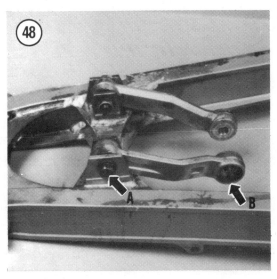

11

Connecting Rod
Removal/Installation

The connecting rod can be removed without having to remove the swing arm.

1. Place the motorcycle on its centerstand.
2. Remove the tie-rod (A, **Figure 47**) and lower shock absorber (B, **Figure 47**) pivot bolts at the connecting rod.
3. Remove the connecting rod pivot bolt (A, **Figure 49**) and remove the connecting rod (B, **Figure 49**).
4. Install by reversing these steps. Tighten all Uni-trak nuts to the specifications in **Table 1**.

Connecting Rod
Bearing Replacement

The connecting rod is equipped with needle bearings. The bearings (**Figure 36**) wear very slowly and the wear is difficult to measure. Turn the bearings by hand. Make sure they rotate smoothly.

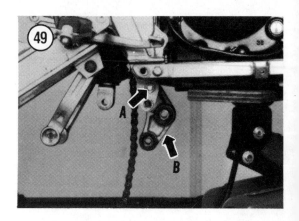

Check the rollers for evidence of wear, pitting, or color change indicating heat from lack of lubrication. In severe instances, the needles will fall out of the bearing cage. If necessary, have the bearings replaced by a machine shop or dealer as a press is required.

Table 1 REAR SUSPENSION TIGHTENING TORQUES

	N·m	ft.-lb.
Rear axle nut	110	80
Front sprocket bolt	9.8	87 in.-lb.
Rear sprocket nuts	88	64
Shock absorber bolts and nuts	49	39
Pivot shaft nut	88	65
Uni-Trak nuts	49	39
Brake stay arm nuts	34	25

NOTE: If you own a 1988 or later model, first check the Supplement at the back of this book for any new service information.

CHAPTER TWELVE

BRAKES

All models are equipped with front and rear disc brakes. This chapter describes repair and replacement procedures for all brake components.

Refer to **Tables 1** for brake specifications. **Table** and **Table 2** are found at the end of the chapter.

DISC BRAKES

The disc brake units are actuated by hydraulic fluid controlled by the hand lever (front brake) or brake pedal (rear brake). As the front brake pads wear, the brake fluid level drops in the master cylinder reservoir and automatically adjusts for pad wear. Rear disc brake pad wear must be compensated for by periodic rear brake pedal adjustment. See *Rear Brake Pedal Height Adjustment* and *Rear Brake Light Switch Adjustment* in Chapter Three.

When working on a hydraulic brake system, it is necessary that the work area and all tools be absolutely clean. Any tiny particles of foreign matter or grit on the caliper assembly or the master cylinder can damage the components. Also, sharp tools must not be used inside a caliper or on a caliper piston. If there is any doubt about your ability to correctly and safely carry out major service on the brake components, take the job to a Kawasaki dealer or brake specialist.

When adding brake fluid use only a type clearly marked DOT 3 and use it from a sealed container. Brake fluid will draw moisture which greatly reduces its ability to perform correctly, so it is a good idea to purchase brake fluid in small containers.

Whenever *any* component has been removed from the brake system the system is considered "opened" and must be bled to remove air bubbles. Also, if the brake feels "spongy," this usually means there are air bubbles in the system and it must be bled. For safe brake operation, refer to *Bleeding the System* in this chapter for complete details.

CAUTION
Disc brake components rarely require disassembly, so do not disassemble unless necessary. Do not use solvents of any kind on the brake system's internal components. Solvents will cause the seals to swell and distort. When disassembling and cleaning brake components (except brake pads) use new brake fluid.

BRAKE PAD REPLACEMENT

There is no recommended mileage interval for changing the friction pads on the disc brakes. Pad

12

wear depends greatly on riding habits and conditions. The pads should be checked for wear at specified intervals. See Chapter Three (**Table 1**).

Service Notes

Observe the following service notes before replacing brake pads.

1. Brake pads should be replaced only as a set.
2. Disconnecting the hydraulic brake hose is not required for brake pad replacement. Disconnect the hose only if caliper removal is required.

WARNING
Use brake fluid clearly marked DOT 3 from a sealed container. Other types may vaporize and cause brake failure. Always use the same brand name. Do not intermix brake fluids. Many brands are not compatible.

WARNING
*Do not ride the motorcycle until you are sure the brake is operating correctly. If necessary, bleed the brake as described under **Bleeding the System** in this chapter.*

**Front and Rear
Pad Replacement**

Brake pad replacement is the same for the front and rear calipers. Refer to **Figure 1** (front) or **Figure 2** (rear) for this procedure.

1A. *Front brake:* Remove the 2 caliper bolts and lift the caliper off the front fork (**Figure 3**).
1B. *Rear brake:* Pull the rear brake hose out of the swing arm clip (A, **Figure 4**). Then remove the 2 caliper bolts (B, **Figure 4**) and lift the caliper off of the swing arm.

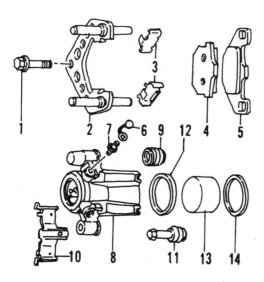

① FRONT BRAKE CALIPER

1. Bolt
2. Holder
3. Spring pad stopper
4. Brake pad
5. Brake pad
6. Cap
7. Bleed valve
8. Housing
9. Boot
10. Pad spring
11. Boot
12. Piston seal
13. Piston
14. Piston seal

REAR BRAKE CALIPER

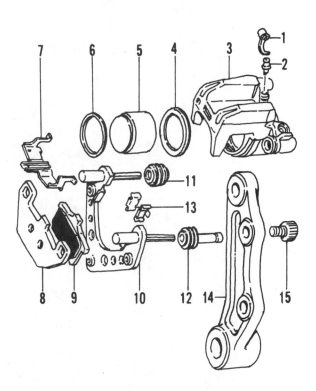

1. Cap
2. Bleed valve
3. Housing
4. Piston seal
5. Piston
6. Piston seal
7. Pad spring
8. Brake pad
9. Brake pad
10. Holder
11. Boot
12. Boot
13. Spring pad stopper
14. Holder
15. Bolts

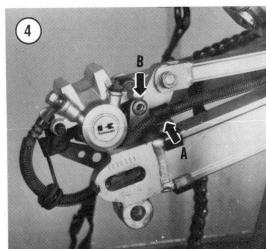

12

2. Lift the inner brake pad (**Figure 5**) out of the caliper.

3. Push the caliper holder (A, **Figure 6**) toward the piston and remove the outer brake pad (B, **Figure 6**).

4. Lift the anti-rattle spring (**Figure 7**) out of the caliper.

5. Check the caliper holder (A, **Figure 8**) to make sure the clips (B, **Figure 8**) are installed. **Figure 9** shows the caliper holder (A) and clips (B) with the holder removed for clarity.

6. Remove the cap and diaphragm from the master cylinder. See **Figure 10** (front) or **Figure 11** (rear). Slowly push the piston (**Figure 12**) into the caliper while checking the reservoir to make sure it doesn't overflow. The piston should move freely. You may need to use a C-clamp to push the piston back into the caliper. If the piston sticks, remove the caliper and rebuild it as described in this chapter.

7. Install a new anti-rattle spring into the caliper (**Figure 7**).

8. Align the holes in the outer brake pad plate and install it onto the caliper holder (**Figure 6**).

9. Drop the inner brake pad (**Figure 5**) into the caliper.

NOTE
The friction material on both brake pads must face inward.

10. Carefully align the brake pads with the brake disc and install the caliper. Install the caliper bolts and tighten to the specifications in **Table 2**.

11. Support the motorcycle with either the front or rear wheel off the ground. Spin the wheel and pump the brake until the pads are seated against the disc.

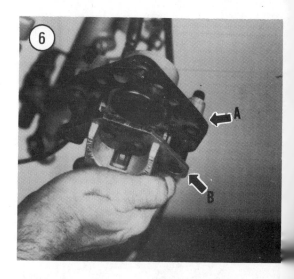

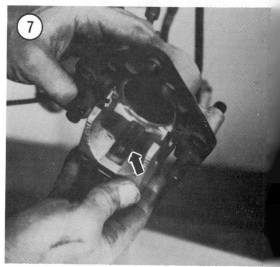

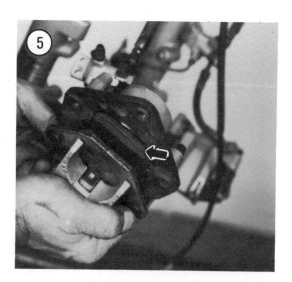

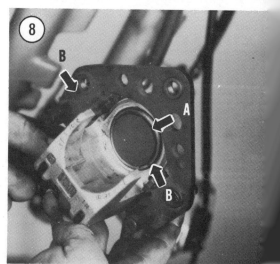

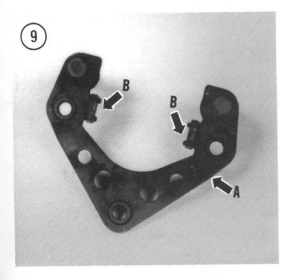

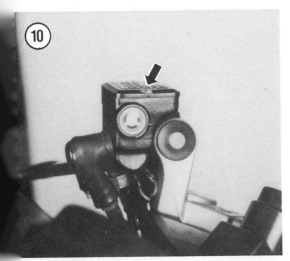

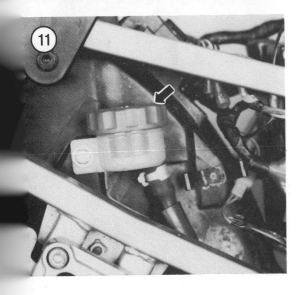

12. Refill the master cylinder reservoir, if necessary, to maintain the correct fluid level. Install the diaphragm and top cap.

> *WARNING*
> *Use brake fluid clearly marked DOT 3 from a sealed container. Other types may vaporize and cause brake failure. Always use the same brand name. Do not intermix brake fluids. Many brands are not compatible.*

> *WARNING*
> *Do not ride the motorcycle until you are sure the brakes are working correctly.*

BRAKE CALIPERS

Front Caliper
Removal/Installation

Refer to **Figure 1**.

1. Drain the master cylinder as follows:
   a. Attach a hose to the brake caliper bleed screw (**Figure 13**).

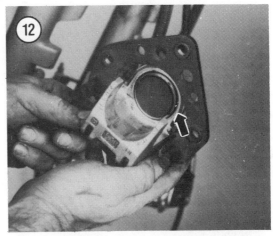

12

b. Place the end of the hose in a clean container (**Figure 14**).

c. Open the bleed screw (**Figure 13**) and operate the brake lever to drain all brake fluid from the master cylinder reservoir.

d. Close the bleed screw and disconnect the hose.

e. Discard the brake fluid.

2. Remove the bolt and copper sealing washers attaching the brake hose to the caliper. To prevent the loss of brake fluid, cap the end of the brake hose and tie it up to the fender. Be sure to cap or tape the ends to prevent the entry of moisture and dirt.

3. Remove the brake pads as described under *Brake Pad Replacement* in this chapter.

4. Installation is the reverse of these steps. Note the following:

a. Torque the caliper attaching bolts to specifications in **Table 2**.

b. Install the brake hose using new copper washers.

c. Tighten the brake hose banjo bolt to specifications in **Table 2**.

d. Bleed the brakes as described under *Bleeding the System* in this chapter.

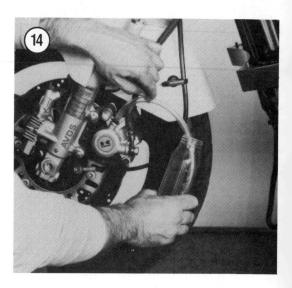

> *WARNING*
> *Do not ride the motorcycle until you are sure that the brakes are operating properly.*

Rear Caliper
Removal/Installation

Refer to **Figure 2**.

1. Drain the master cylinder as follows:

a. Attach a hose to the brake caliper bleed screw (**Figure 15**).

b. Place the end of the hose in a clean container (**Figure 15**).

c. Open the bleed screw (**Figure 15**) and operate the brake pedal to drain all brake fluid from the master cylinder reservoir.

d. Close the bleed screw and disconnect the hose.

e. Discard the brake fluid.

2. Remove the bolt and copper sealing washers attaching the brake hose to the caliper (**Figure 16**). To prevent the loss of brake fluid, cap the end of the brake hose and tie it up to the fender. Be sure to cap or tape the ends to prevent the entry of moisture and dirt.

3. Remove the brake pads as described under *Brake Pad Replacement* in this chapter.

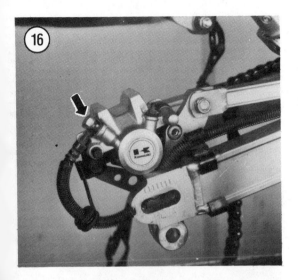

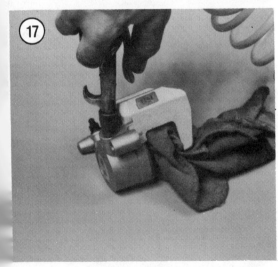

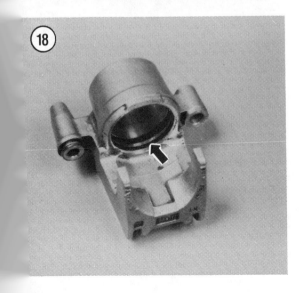

4. Installation is the reverse of these steps. Note the following:

a. Torque the caliper attaching bolts to specifications in **Table 2**.

b. Install the brake hose using new copper washers.

c. Tighten the brake hose banjo bolt to specifications in **Table 2**.

d. Bleed the brakes as described under *Bleeding the System* in this chapter.

> *WARNING*
> *Do not ride the motorcycle until you are sure that the brakes are operating properly.*

Caliper Rebuilding

Refer to **Figure 1** (front) or **Figure 2** (rear).

1. Remove the brake caliper as described in this chapter.

2. Pull the caliper holder out of the housing.

> *NOTE*
> *Compressed air will be required to remove the piston.*

> *WARNING*
> *Keep your fingers and hand out of the caliper bore area when removing the piston in Step 3. The piston will fly out of the bore with considerable force and could crush your fingers or hand.*

3. Pad the piston with shop rags or wooden blocks as shown in **Figure 17**. Then apply compressed air through one of the caliper ports and blow the piston out of the caliper (**Figure 17**).

4. Remove the dust seal (**Figure 18**) and piston seal (**Figure 19**) from the caliper bore.

5. Clean all caliper parts (except brake pads) in new DOT 3 brake fluid. Place the cleaned parts on a lint-free cloth while performing the following inspection procedures.

6. Check the caliper bore (**Figure 20**) for cracks, deep scoring or excessive wear.

7. Check the caliper piston (**Figure 21**) for deep scoring, excessive wear or rust.

8. Replace the caliper housing or piston if necessary.

9. The piston seal (**Figure 19**) maintains correct brake pad-to-disc clearance. If the seal is worn or damaged, the brake pads will drag and cause excessive pad wear and brake fluid temperatures. Replace the piston and dust seals (**Figure 22**) if the following conditions exist:

   a. Brake fluid leaks around the inner brake pad.
   b. The piston seal (**Figure 19**) is stuck in the caliper groove.
   c. There is a large difference in inner and outer brake pad wear (**Figure 23**).

10. Measure the brake pad friction material with a ruler or caliper (**Figure 24**) and compare to wear limits in **Table 1**. Replace both brake pads if any one pad is too thin.

11. Check the caliper holder (**Figure 25**) for cracks or other damage. Replace the support if necessary.

FRONT MASTER CYLINDER

Removal/Installation

> *CAUTION*
> *Cover the fuel tank, front fender and instrument cluster with a heavy cloth or plastic tarp to protect them from accidental spilling of brake fluid. Wash any spilled brake fluid off any painted or plated surfaces immediately as it will destroy the finish. Use soapy water and rinse completely.*

1. Drain the master cylinder as follows:
   a. Attach a hose to the brake caliper bleed screw (**Figure 13**).
   b. Place the end of the hose in a clean container (**Figure 14**).
   c. Open the bleed screw (**Figure 13**) and operate the brake lever to drain all brake fluid from the master cylinder reservoir.
   d. Close the bleed screw and disconnect the hose.
   e. Discard the brake fluid.

2. Disconnect the brake switch wires at the master cylinder.

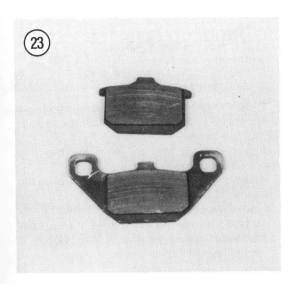

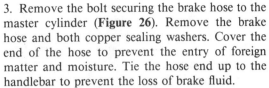

3. Remove the bolt securing the brake hose to the master cylinder (**Figure 26**). Remove the brake hose and both copper sealing washers. Cover the end of the hose to prevent the entry of foreign matter and moisture. Tie the hose end up to the handlebar to prevent the loss of brake fluid.

4. Remove the 2 clamping bolts (A, **Figure 27**) and clamp securing the master cylinder to the handlebar and remove the master cylinder (B, **Figure 27**).

5. Install by reversing these removal steps. Note the following:

    a. Install the master cylinder clamp with the arrow facing upward.

    b. Tighten the upper clamp bolt first, then the lower bolt to specifications in **Table 2**. There should be a gap at the lower part of the clamp after tightening.

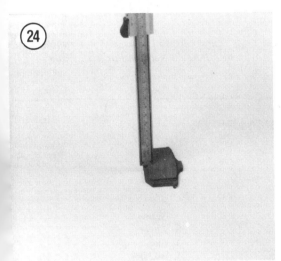

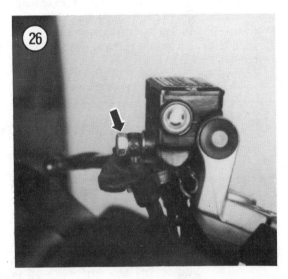

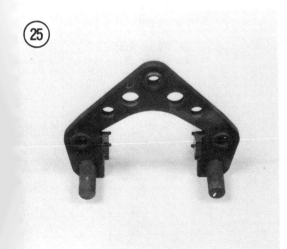

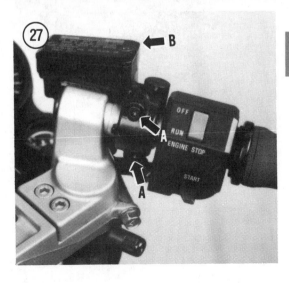

12

c. Install the brake hose onto the master cylinder. Be sure to place a copper sealing washer on each side of the hose fitting and install the banjo bolt. Tighten the banjo bolt to the specifications in **Table 2**.

d. Bleed the brake system as described under *Bleeding the System* in this chapter.

> *WARNING*
> *Do not ride the motorcycle until the front brake is operating correctly.*

Disassembly/Reassembly

Refer to **Figure 28**.

1. Remove the master cylinder as described in this chapter.

2. Remove the screws securing the reservoir cap and diaphragm. Pour out the remaining brake fluid and discard it. *Never* reuse brake fluid.

3. Remove the rubber boot from the area where the hand lever actuates the internal piston.

4. Remove the brake lever.

5. Remove the dust cover.

> *CAUTION*
> *Do not remove the secondary cup from the piston when removing the piston assembly in Step 6. Removing the secondary cup from the piston will damage the cup.*

6. Remove the piston assembly and spring as shown in **Figure 28**. Remove the primary cup from the piston assembly.

7. Inspect the master cylinder assembly as described in this chapter.

8. Assembly is the reverse of these steps. Note the following:

a. Soak the new caps in fresh brake fluid for at least 15 minutes to make them pliable. Coat the inside of the cylinder with fresh brake fluid before assembling the parts.

> *CAUTION*
> *When installing the piston assembly, do not allow the cups to turn inside out as they will be damaged and allow brake fluid to leak within the cylinder bore.*

 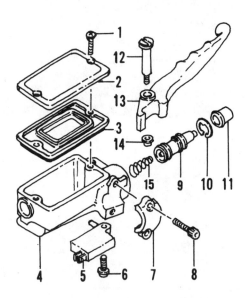

FRONT MASTER CYLINDER

1. Screw
2. Cover
3. Diaphragm
4. Housing
5. Front brake switch
6. Screw
7. Holder
8. Screw
9. Piston assembly
10. Circlip
11. Cover
12. Pivot bolt
13. Lever
14. Nut
15. Spring

b. Install the master cylinder piston assembly in the order shown in **Figure 28**. Make sure the dust cover is firmly seated in the groove in the cylinder.

Inspection

1. Clean all parts in fresh DOT 3 brake fluid. Place the master cylinder components on a clean lint-free cloth when performing the following inspection procedures.
2. Inspect the cylinder bore and piston contact surfaces for signs of wear or damage. If either part is less than perfect, replace it.
3. Check the end of the piston for wear caused by the hand lever. Replace the entire piston assembly if any portion of it requires replacement. If the

piston assembly is replaced, also replace the primary cup.
4. Check the secondary cup (on the piston) for damage, softness or for swollen conditions. Replace the piston assembly if necessary.
5. Check the primary cup for the same conditions in Step 3. Replace the primary cup if necessary.
6. Inspect the pivot hole in the hand lever. If worn, it must be replaced.
7. Make sure the passages in the bottom of the brake fluid reservoir are clear. Check the reservoir cap and diaphragm for damage and deterioration. Replace if necessary.
8. Inspect the condition of the threads in the master cylinder body where the brake hose banjo bolt screws in. If the threads are damaged or partially stripped, replace the master cylinder body.

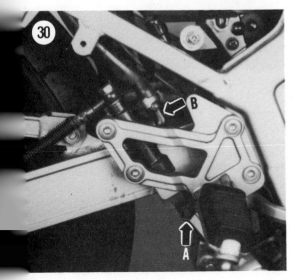

REAR MASTER CYLINDER

Removal/Installation

CAUTION
Wash any spilled brake fluid off any painted or plated surfaces immediately as it will destroy the finish. Use soapy water and rinse completely.

1. Drain the master cylinder as follows:
   a. Attach a hose to the brake caliper bleed screw (**Figure 15**).
   b. Place the end of the hose in a clean container (**Figure 15**).
   c. Open the bleed screw (**Figure 15**) and operate the brake pedal to drain all brake fluid from the master cylinder reservoir.
   d. Close the bleed screw and disconnect the hose.
   e. Discard the brake fluid.
2. Remove the bolt securing the brake hose to the master cylinder (**Figure 29**). Remove the brake hose and both copper sealing washers. Cover the end of the hose to prevent the entry of foreign matter and moisture. Tie the hose end up to prevent the loss of brake fluid.
3. Disconnect the rear brake light switch connector.
4. Disconnect cotter pin (A, **Figure 30**) and disconnect the brake pedal rod at the master cylinder pushrod.

12

5. See **Figure 31**. Loosen the master cylinder (A) and footpeg (B) bracket bolts. Then remove the footpeg bracket bolts (B) and pull the bracket assembly away from the frame.
6. Disconnect the reservoir hose (B, **Figure 30**) at the master cylinder.
7. Remove the master cylinder bolts (A, **Figure 31**) and remove the master cylinder assembly.
8. Install by reversing these removal steps. Note the following:
   a. Install the brake hose into the U-shaped notch in the master cylinder. Be sure to place a copper sealing washer on each side of the hose fitting and install the banjo bolt. Tighten the banjo bolt to the specifications in **Table 2**.
   b. Insert the reservoir hose into the master cylinder and secure it.
   c. Tighten the master cylinder mounting bolts (A, **Figure 31**) after installing the footpeg bracket bolts (B, **Figure 31**). Tighten the bolts to the specifications in **Table 2**.
   d. Bleed the brake system as described under *Bleeding the System* in this chapter.
   e. Adjust the rear brake pedal as described in Chapter Three. Refer to *Rear Brake Pedal Height Adjustment* and *Rear Brake Light Switch Adjustment*.

WARNING
Do not ride the motorcycle until the front brake is operating correctly.

Reservoir
Removal/Installation

The master cylinder reservoir can be removed by first draining the master cylinder as described under *Master Cylinder Removal/Installation*. Disconnect the hose at the reservoir (A, **Figure 32**) and remove the reservoir (B, **Figure 32**). Reverse to install. Bleed the brake as described under *Bleeding the System* in this chapter.

Disassembly/Reassembly

Refer to **Figure 33**.
1. Remove the master cylinder as described in this chapter.
2. Remove the circlip and remove the piston stop and pushrod as an assembly.

CAUTION
Do not remove the secondary cup from the piston when removing the piston assembly in Step 3. Removing the secondary cup from the piston will damage the cup.

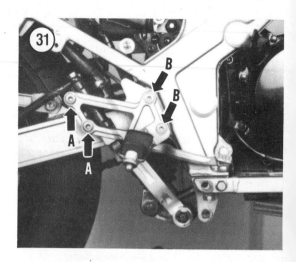

3. Remove the piston assembly and spring as shown in **Figure 33**. Remove the primary cup from the piston assembly.
4. Inspect the master cylinder assembly as described in this chapter.
5. Assembly is the reverse of these steps. Note the following:
   a. Soak the new cups in fresh brake fluid for at least 15 minutes to make them pliable. Coat the inside of the cylinder with fresh brake fluid before assembling the parts.

CAUTION
When installing the piston assembly, do not allow the cups to turn inside out as they will be damaged and allow brake fluid to leak within the cylinder bore.

REAR MASTER CYLINDER

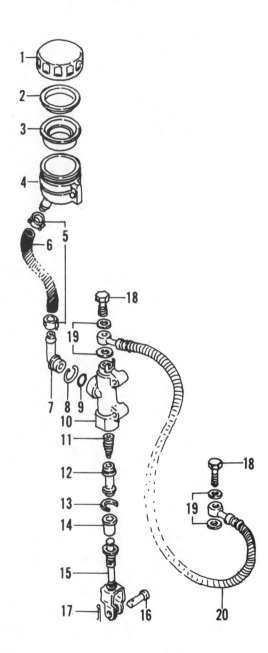

1. Cap
2. Diaphragm plate
3. Diaphragm
4. Reservoir
5. Hose clamp
6. Hose
7. Pipe joint
8. Circlip
9. O-ring
10. Housing
11. Spring
12. Piston assembly
13. Clip
14. Cover seal
15. Brake rod
16. Pin
17. Cotter pin
18. Banjo bolt
19. Washer
20. Fluid hose

12

b. Install the master cylinder piston assembly in the order shown in **Figure 33**. Make sure the dust cover is firmly seated against the master cylinder.

Inspection

1. Clean all parts in fresh DOT 3 brake fluid. Place the master cylinder components on a clean lint-free cloth when performing the following inspection procedures.
2. Inspect the cylinder bore and piston contact surfaces for signs of wear or damage. If either part is less than perfect, replace it.
3. Check the end of the piston for wear caused by the piston stop. Replace the entire piston assembly if any portion of it requires replacement. If the piston assembly is replaced, also replace the primary cup.
4. Check the secondary cup (on the piston) for damage, softness or for swelling. Replace the piston assembly if any of these conditions are found.
5. Check the primary cup for the same conditions in Step 3. Replace the primary cup if necessary.
6. Inspect the piston stop and pushrod assembly for damage or bending. Replace if necessary.
7. Make sure the passages in the bottom of the brake fluid reservoir are clear. Check the reservoir cap and diaphragm for damage and deterioration. Replace if necessary.
8. Inspect the condition of the threads in the master cylinder body where the brake hose banjo bolt screws in. If the threads are damaged or partially stripped, replace the master cylinder body.

BRAKE HOSE REPLACEMENT

A brake hose should replaced whenever it shows cracks, bulges or other damage. The deterioration of rubber by ozone and other atmospheric elements may require hose replacement every 4 years.

CAUTION
Cover components with a heavy cloth or plastic tarp to protect them from the accidental spilling of brake fluid. Wash any spilled brake fluid off of any painted or plated surface immediately, as it will destroy the finish. Use soapy water and rinse completely.

1. Before replacing a brake hose, inspect the routing of the old hose carefully, noting any guides and grommets the hose may go through.

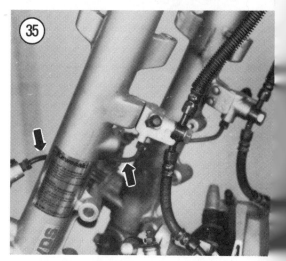

2. Drain the master cylinder as described under *Front Master Cylinder Removal/Installation* or *Rear Master Cylinder Removal/Installation* in this chapter.

3. Disconnect the banjo bolts securing the hose at either end and remove the hose with its banjo bolts and 2 washers at both ends.

4. To remove the front brake banjo joint (**Figure 34**), disconnect the hoses at the joint. Then remove the attaching bolts and remove the joint.

5. To remove the anti-dive brake pipe (**Figure 35**), loosen the 2 pipe nuts and remove the pipe.

6. Install new brake hoses, copper sealing washers and bolts in the reverse order of removal. Be sure to install the new sealing washers in their correct positions. Tighten all banjo bolts to specifications in **Table 2**.

7. Refill the master cylinder(s) with fresh brake fluid clearly marked DOT 3. Bleed the brake as described under *Bleeding the System* in this chapter.

> *WARNING*
> *Do not ride the motorcycle until you are sure that the brakes are operating properly.*

BRAKE DISC

Inspection

It is not necessary to remove the disc from the wheel to inspect it. Small marks on the disc are not important, but deep radial scratches, deep enough to snag a fingernail, reduce braking effectiveness and increase brake pad wear. If these grooves are found, the disc should be resurfaced or replaced.

1. Measure the thickness around the disc at several locations with vernier calipers or a micrometer (**Figure 36**). The disc must be replaced if the thickness at any point is less than the minimum specified in **Table 1**.

2. Make sure the disc bolts are tight prior to performing this check. Check the disc runout with a dial indicator as shown in **Figure 37**. Slowly rotate the wheel and watch the dial indicator. If the runout is 0.3 mm (0.012 in.) or greater, the disc must be replaced.

3. Clean the disc of any rust or corrosion and wipe clean with lacquer thinner. Never use an oil-based solvent that may leave an oil residue on the disc.

Removal/Installation

1. Remove the front or rear wheel as described in Chapter Ten or Chapter Eleven.

12

> *NOTE*
> *Place a piece of wood in the calipers in place of the disc. This way, if the brake lever is inadvertently squeezed, the piston will not be forced out of the cylinder. If this does happen, the caliper might have to be disassembled to reseat the piston and the system will have to be bled. By using the wood, bleeding the system is not necessary when installing the wheel.*

2. Remove the bolts securing the disc to the wheel and remove the disc (**Figure 38**).

3. Install by reversing these removal steps. Note the following:
   a. Apply Loctite 242 (blue) to the bolts before installation.
   b. Tighten the disc bolts to the specifications in **Table 2**.

BLEEDING THE SYSTEM

This procedure is necessary when the brakes feel spongy, there is a leak in the hydraulic system, a component has been replaced or the brake fluid has been replaced.

All models are equipped with an anti-dive unit and junction block mounted onto the front forks. It is necessary to bleed the anti-dive mechanism and junction block as well as the brake caliper. When bleeding the front brake calipers, bleed the following components in order:
   a. Caliper air bleed valve (A, **Figure 39**).
   b. Anti-dive bleed valve (B, **Figure 39**).
   c. Junction block bleed valve (C, **Figure 39**).
1. Flip off the dust cap from the brake bleeder valve.
2. Connect a length of clear tubing to the bleeder valve on the caliper. Place the other end of the tube into a clean container. Fill the container with enough fresh brake fluid to keep the end submerged. The tube should be long enough so that a loop can be made higher than the bleeder valve to prevent air from being drawn into the caliper during bleeding. See **Figure 40**.

> *CAUTION*
> *Cover parts with a heavy cloth or plastic tarp to protect them from the accidental spilling of brake fluid. Wash any spilled brake fluid off of any painted or plated surface immediately, as it will destroy the finish. Use soapy water and rinse completely.*

3. Clean the top of the master cylinder of all dirt and foreign matter. Remove the cap and diaphragm. Fill the reservoir to about 10 mm (3/8 in.) from the top. Install the diaphragm to prevent the entry of dirt and moisture.

> *WARNING*
> *Use brake fluid clearly marked DOT 3 only. Others may vaporize and cause brake failure. Always use the same brand name. Do not intermix the brake fluids as many brands are not compatible.*

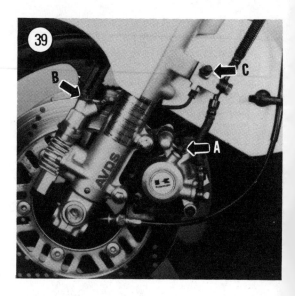

4. Slowly apply the brake lever (front) or pedal (rear) several times. Hold the lever in the applied position and open the bleeder valve about 1/2 turn. Allow the lever to travel to its limit. When this limit is reached, tighten the bleeder screw. As the brake fluid enters the system, the level will drop in the master cylinder reservoir. Maintain the level at about 10 mm (3/8 in.) from the top of the reservoir to prevent air from being drawn into the system.
5. Continue to pump the lever or pedal and fill the reservoir until the fluid emerging from the hose is completely free of air bubbles.

> *NOTE*
> *If bleeding is difficult, it may be necessary to allow the fluid to stabilize for a few hours. Repeat the bleeding procedure when the tiny bubbles in the system settle out.*

6. Hold the lever or pedal in the applied position and tighten the bleeder valve. Remove the bleeder tube and install the bleeder valve dust cap.
7. If necessary, add fluid to correct the level in the master cylinder reservoir. It must be above the LOWER level line.
8. Install the cap and tighten the screws.

> *NOTE*
> *If bleeding the front brake caliper(s), also bleed the anti-dive bleed valve (B, **Figure 39**) and the junction block bleed valve (C, **Figure 39**) in order.*

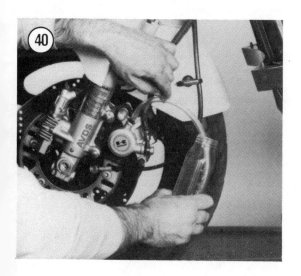

9. Test the feel of the brake lever or pedal. It should feel firm and should offer the same resistance each time it's operated. If it feels spongy, it is likely that air is still in the system and it must be bled again. When all air has been bled from the system, and the brake fluid level is correct in the reservoir, double-check for leaks and tighten all fittings and connections.

WARNING
Before riding the motorcycle, make certain that the brakes are operating correctly by operating the lever several times. Then make the test ride a slow one at first to make sure the brake is operating correctly.

Table 1 BRAKE SPECIFICATIONS

	Standard mm (in.)	Wear limit mm (in.)
Pad lining thickness		
Front and rear	5.0 (0.1968)	1.0 (0.039)
Disc thickness		
Front	4.8-5.1 (0.189-0.200)	4.5 (0.177)
Rear	5.8-6.1 (0.228-0.240)	5.5 (0.216)
Disc runout		0.3 (0.012)

Table 2 BRAKE TIGHTENING TORQUES

	N•m	ft.-lb.
Brake disc bolts	23	16.5
Front brake caliper bolts	32	24
Rear brake caliper bolts	18	13
Brake hose union (banjo) bolts	29	22
Brake hose joint bolts		
Front	7.8	69 in.-lb.
Rear	32	24
Anti-dive hydraulic line	18	13
Rear master cylinder reservoir bolt	5.9	52 in.-lb.

12

NOTE: If you own a 1988 or later model, first check the Supplement at the back of this book for any new service information.

CHAPTER THIRTEEN

FAIRING

This chapter contains removal and installation procedures for the fairing assembly (**Figure 1**).

When removing a fairing component, it is best to reinstall all mounting hardware onto the removed part or store it in plastic bags taped to the inside of the fairing. After removal, fairing components should be placed away from the service area to prevent accidental damage.

Upper Fairing
Removal/Installation

1. Park the motorcycle on its centerstand.
2. Remove the inner fairing screws and remove the left- and right-hand inner fairings. See **Figure 2**.
3. Disconnect the headlight connector inside the fairing. **Figure 3** shows the connector with the fairing removed for clarity.
4. Remove the upper fairing mounting screws and bolts (**Figure 1**).
5. Lift the fairing slightly and move it forward. Then disconnect the headlight wiring connector from the headlight.
6. Remove the upper fairing assembly (**Figure 4**).
7. Remove the rubber boarder strip (**Figure 5**).

8. Install by reversing these steps. Note the following.
9. Disconnect the headlight wire connector before installing the upper fairing all the way on.

Lower Fairing
Removal/Installation

1. Park the motorcycle on its centerstand.
2. Remove the lower fairing mounting screws and lower the fairing (**Figure 6**) slightly.
3. Disconnect the reservoir-to-radiator hose at the reservoir (**Figure 7**).
4. Remove the lower fairing (**Figure 6**) and store so that the reservoir tank cannot drain.
5. Install by reversing these steps.
6. Refill the reservoir tank with antifreeze. See *Coolant Change* in Chapter Three.

Lower Fairing Stay
Removal/Installation

1. Remove the upper and lower fairings described in this chapter.

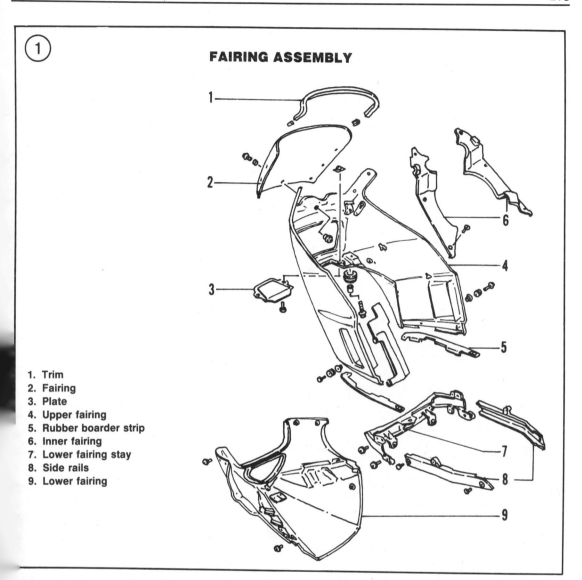

① **FAIRING ASSEMBLY**

1. Trim
2. Fairing
3. Plate
4. Upper fairing
5. Rubber boarder strip
6. Inner fairing
7. Lower fairing stay
8. Side rails
9. Lower fairing

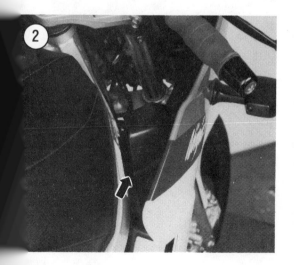

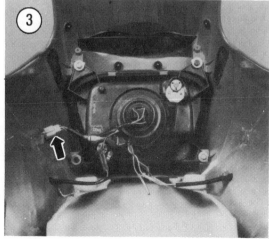

13

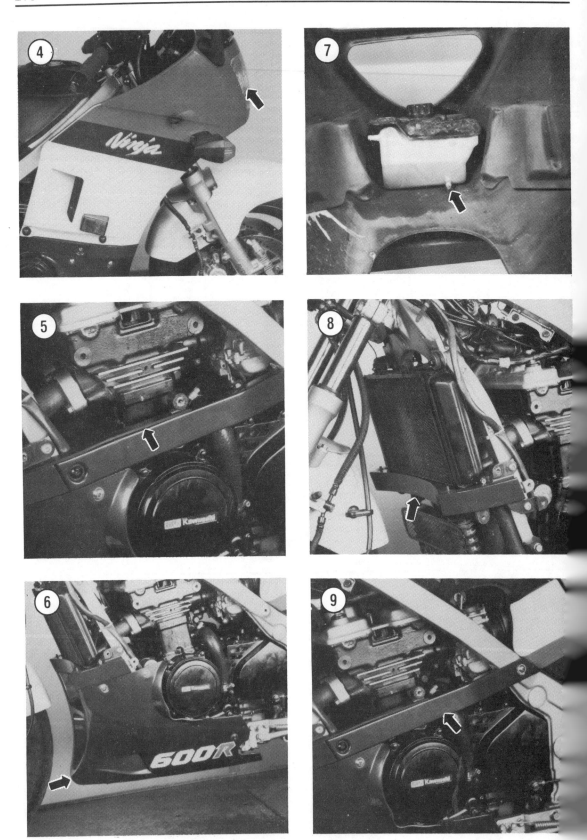

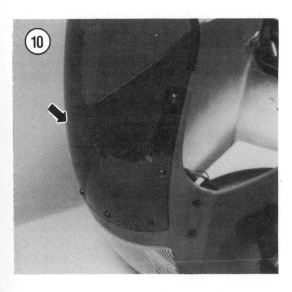

2. Remove the lower fairing stay screws and remove the fairing stay (**Figure 8**).

3. Install by reversing these steps.

Side Rail
Removal/Installation

Remove the side rail screws and remove the side rails (**Figure 9**). Reverse to install.

Windshield

The windshield (**Figure 10**) can be replaced by removing the mounting screws. Reverse to install.

Windshield Cleaning

Be very careful when cleaning the windshield (**Figure 10**) as it can be scratched or damaged. Do not use a cleaner with an abrasive, a combination cleaner and wax or any solvent that contains ethyl or methyl alcohol. Never use gasoline or cleaning solvent. These products scratch or destroy the surface of the windshield.

To remove oil, grease or road tar use isopropyl alcohol. Then wash the windshield with a solution of mild soap and water. Dry *gently* with a soft cloth or chamois.

NOTE
When removing road tar, make sure there are no small stones or sand imbedded in it. Carefully remove any abrasive particles before performing any rubbing action with a cleaner. This will help minimize scratching.

Many commercial windshield cleaners are available. If using a cleaner make sure it is safe for use on plastic and test it on a small area first.

13

SUPPLEMENT

1988 AND LATER SERVICE INFORMATION

The following supplement provides procedures unique to the 1988 and later ZX500 and ZX600 models. All other service procedures are identical to earlier models.

The chapter headings in this supplement correspond to those in the main body of this book. If a procedure is not included in the supplement, use the information given for the prior years in the main body of this book.

Tables 1-4 are located within this supplement.

CHAPTER THREE

LUBRICATION, MAINTENANCE AND TUNE-UP

PERIODIC LUBRICATION

Front Fork Oil Change

Front fork oil change is identical to prior years with the exception of the fork oil quantity and fork oil level for each leg. These forks are not symmetrical internally and require different oil quantities and levels. Be sure to add the correct amount of fork oil to the correct fork leg and maintain the correct oil level.

NOTE
The fork oil level is taken with the fork springs removed and with the fork leg fully compressed.

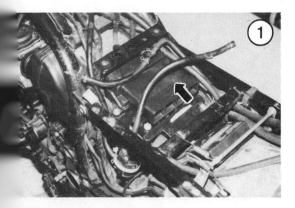

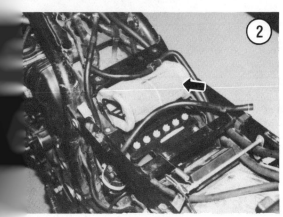

Refer to **Table 1** for the specified fork oil quantity and oil level.

The recommended front fork air pressure is 0 kg/cm^2 (0 psi).

PERIODIC MAINTENANCE

Drive Chain Adjustment

Drive chain adjustment is identical to prior years except that the nuts at each end of the rear brake caliper torque link must both be loosened in order to adjust the drive chain correctly.

After the drive chain is adjusted, tighten the torque link nuts to 34 N•m (25 ft.-lb.).

Air Cleaner
Removal/Installation

A clogged air cleaner element can decrease the efficiency and life of the engine. Never run the engine without the air cleaner element installed. Even minute particles of dust can cause severe internal engine wear.

The service specifications in **Table 1** in Chapter Three in the main body of this book, should be followed with general use. However, the air cleaner should be serviced more often if the bike is ridden in dusty areas.

1. Remove the rider's seat.
2. Remove the air cleaner cover screws and remove the cover (**Figure 1**).
3. Remove the air cleaner element (**Figure 2**).
4. Separate the air cleaner element from the element frame (**Figure 3**).
5. Gently clean the element in cleaning solvent until all dirt is removed. Thoroughly dry with a clean shop cloth until all solvent residue is removed. Let it dry for about one hour.
6. Inspect the element; if it is torn or broken in any area, it should be replaced. Do not run a bike with a

14

damaged element as it may allow dirt to enter the engine.

7. Pour a small amount of SAE 30 engine oil or foam air cleaner oil onto the element and work it into the porous material. Do not oversaturate the element as too much oil will restrict the air flow. The element will be discolored by the oil and should have an even color indicating that the oil is distributed evenly.

8. If foam air cleaner oil is used, let the element dry for another hour prior to installation. If installed too soon, the chemical carrier in the oil will be drawn into the engine and may cause damage.

9. Install the air cleaner element onto the element frame.

10. Install the air cleaner element and frame assembly into the air box. Correctly fit both locating tabs (A, **Figure 4**) of the element frame into the grooves (B, **Figure 4**) in the air box. This is necessary to avoid an unfiltered air leak.

SUSPENSION ADJUSTMENT

Front Fork Air Pressure

The factory recommended front fork air pressure for these models is 0 kg/cm^2 (0 psi).

Rear Shock Absorber Adjustment

Air pressure adjustment

Rear shock absorber air pressure adjustment procedure is identical to prior years with the exception of the maximum allowable air pressure. Do *not* exceed 2.0 kg/cm^2 (28 psi) or the internal oil seal will be damaged. Refer to **Table 2** for the recommended rear shock absorber air pressure.

TUNE-UP

Compression Test

The compression test procedure is identical to prior years with the exception of the specified pressure. The specified pressure is as follows:

    a. ZX500R B1 and later: 9.5-14.5 kg/cm^2 (135-206 psi).

    b. ZX600R C1 and later: 9.8-15.0 kg/cm^2 (139-213 psi).

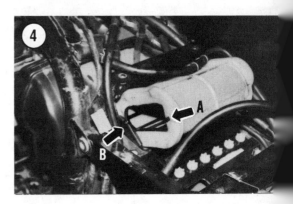

Table 1 FRONT FORK OIL CAPACITY

Fork leg	Change	Rebuild	Oil level
Right-hand	305 cc (10.31 oz.)	352-360 cc (11.90-12.17 oz.)	152-156 mm (5.9-6.1 in.)
Left-hand	265 cc (8.96 oz.)	307-315 cc (10.38-10.65 oz.)	180-184 mm (7.0-7.2 in.)
1994-on Non-U.S. models			
Both fork legs	300 cc (10.14 oz.)	345-353 cc (11.66-11.93 oz.)	124-128 mm (4.8-5.0 in.)

Table 2 REAR SHOCK ABSORBER AIR PRESSURE

Road/load conditions	kg/cm^2	psi
Good/light	0	0
Bad/hard	2.0	28

CHAPTER FOUR

ENGINE

ENGINE

Removal/Installation

1. Place the motorcycle on its centerstand.

2. Remove the fairing assembly. See Chapter Thirteen in this supplement.

3. Disconnect the negative battery terminal.

4. Remove the fuel tank and seat.

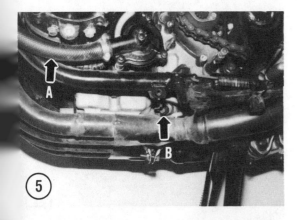

5. Drain the engine oil as described under *Engine Oil and Filter Change* in Chapter Three in the main body of this book.

6. Drain the cooling system as described in Chapter Three in the main body of this book.

7. Disconnect the spark plug wires. Then disconnect the ignition coil electrical connectors and remove the coils.

8. *U.S. models:* Disconnect the hoses and remove the air suction valve and the vacuum switch valve.

9. Remove the following as described in the Chapter Nine section of this supplement:

    a. Radiator.

    b. Thermostat housing.

10. Remove the exhaust system as described in Chapter Seven in the main body of this book.

11. Remove the carburetors as described in Chapter Seven in the main body of this book.

12. Remove the baffle plate from the cylinder head cover.

13. Remove the radiator lower hose (A, **Figure 5**) from the water pump.

14. Loosen the clutch cable at the hand grip. Then disconnect the clutch cable at the crankcase.

15. Disconnect the crankcase breather tube.

16. Disconnect the water pipe fitting from the cylinder head.

17. Remove the engine sprocket as described under *Engine Sprocket Removal/Installation* in Chapter Six in the main body of this book.

18. Disconnect the following wiring connectors:

    a. Oil pressure switch (B, **Figure 5**).

    b. Pickup coil lead.

    c. Starter motor (A, **Figure 6**).

    d. Sidestand switch (B, **Figure 6**).

    e. Alternator and neutral switch (C, **Figure 6**).

19. Remove the electrical harness clamps (D, **Figure 6**).

14

20. Remove the sidestand switch bolts or nuts and remove the switch (**Figure 7**).

21. Remove the heat guard screws and remove the heat guard (**Figure 8**).

22. *Engine disassembly:* If the engine requires disassembly, it will be easier to remove many of the large sub-assemblies while the engine is in the frame. Remove the following as described in Chapter Four in the main body of this book unless otherwise noted:

    a. Cylinder head (this section of this supplement).

    b. Cylinder block.

    c. Pistons.

    d. Alternator and pickup (Chapter Eight in the main body of this book).

    e. Starter (Chapter Eight in the main body of this book).

    f. Clutch (Chapter Five in the main body of this book).

    g. External shift mechanism (Chapter Six in the main body of this book).

23. Place a small jack under the engine with a piece of wood to protect the crankcase and apply a small amount of jack pressure to take the weight off the mounting bolts.

24. Remove the rear mounting bolts, the bracket bolts and the brackets (A, **Figure 9**).

25. Remove the front mounting bolts, the bracket bolts and the brackets (B, **Figure 9**).

26. Carefully remove the engine out through the right-hand side of the frame.

27. While the engine is removed for service, check all of the frame engine mounts for cracks or other damage. If any cracks are detected, take the chassis assembly to a Kawasaki dealer for further examination.

28. Install by reversing these removal steps. Note the following.

29. Tighten the engine mounting bolts and nuts as follows:

    a. Front mounting bolts: 23 N•m (16.5 ft.-lb.).

    b. Front bracket mounting bolts: 19 N•m (13.5 ft.-lb.).

    c. Rear mounting bolts: 23 N•m (16.5 ft.-lb.).

    d. Rear bracket mounting bolts: 42 N•m (31 ft.-lb.).

30. Fill the crankcase with the recommended type and quantity of engine oil. Refer to *Engine Oil and Filter Change* in Chapter Three in the main body of this book.

31. Refill the cooling system. See *Coolant Change* in Chapter Three in the main body of this book.

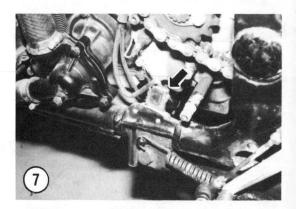

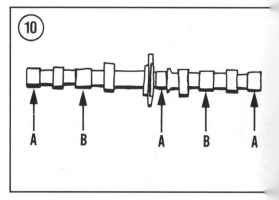

32. Adjust the following as described in Chapter Three in the main body of this book:
   a. Clutch.
   b. Drive chain.
   c. Rear brake.
   d. Throttle cables.
   e. Choke cable.

33. Start the engine and check for leaks.
34. Install the fairing assembly. See Chapter Thirteen in this supplement.

CYLINDER HEAD COVER AND CAMSHAFTS

Camshaft Bearing Clearance Measurement

Camshaft bearing clearance procedures are identical to prior years with one exception. The specified clearance is taken at two different locations as shown in **Figure 10**. The specified clearance is listed in **Table 3**.

CYLINDER HEAD

Removal

Cylinder head removal is identical to prior years except for the layout of the external oil line connected to the backside of the cylinder head.

Remove the cylinder head oil line banjo bolts and copper washers. Refer to **Figure 11** and **Figure 12**.

OIL COOLER

Removal/Installation (ZX600R C1 and Later)

The engine on these models is no longer equipped with an oil cooler.

Table 3 CAMSHAFT OIL CLEARANCE

Journal	Standard	Wear
A	0.028-0.071 mm (0.0011-0.0028 in.)	0.16 mm (0.0063 in.)
B	0.078-0.121 mm (0.0030-0.0047 in.)	0.21 mm (0.0083 in.)

CHAPTER FIVE

CLUTCH

CLUTCH RELEASE MECHANISM

The clutch release mechanism is identical to prior models except that an additional needle bearing is used in the cover to support the release lever as shown in **Figure 13**.

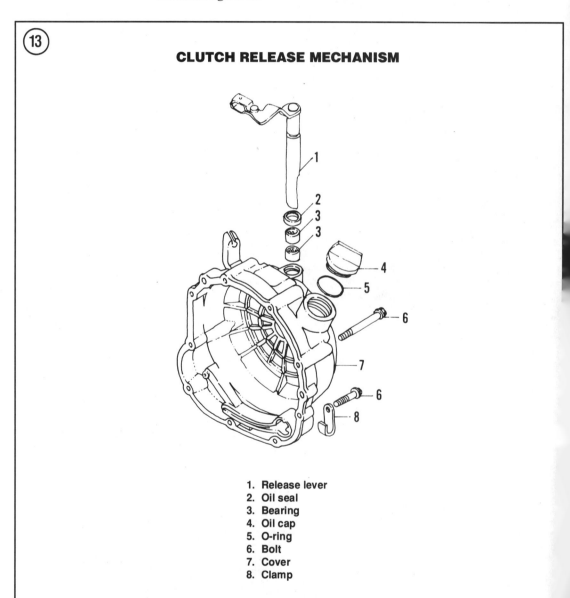

13

CLUTCH RELEASE MECHANISM

1. Release lever
2. Oil seal
3. Bearing
4. Oil cap
5. O-ring
6. Bolt
7. Cover
8. Clamp

CHAPTER SIX

TRANSMISSION

ENGINE SPROCKET (1995-ON GERMAN MODELS)

The sprocket is held in place with a nut and lockwasher.

Install a new lockwasher, tighten the nut to 98 N•m (72 ft.-lb.) and bend the lockwasher over the nut.

EXTERNAL SHIFT MECHANISM

Removal/Installation

1. Remove the engine sprocket cover (**Figure 14**) as described in Chapter Six in the main body of this book.
2. Drain the engine oil as described under *Engine Oil and Filter Change* in Chapter Three in the main body of this book.
3. Remove the sidestand switch bolts.
4. Disconnect the sidestand switch electrical connector (A, **Figure 15**) and remove the sidestand switch (B, **Figure 15**) from the frame.
5. Disconnect the neutral switch electrical connector (C, **Figure 15**).
6. Remove the engine sprocket as described in Chapter Six in the main body of this book.
7. Remove the screws, then remove the shift linkage cover (**Figure 16**) and gasket. Tap the cover loose

14

with a soft mallet, if necessary. Use care as the cover is positioned on dowel pins.

8. Remove the 2 dowel pins (**Figure 17**).

CAUTION
Do not pull the shift fork rod (C, Figure 18) out. If it is pulled out, the shift forks within the crankcase will fall off the rod. This would require removal and disassembly of the engine to reposition the forks.

9. Move the shift arms out of engagement with the shift drum (A, **Figure 18**) and pull the shift linkage (B, **Figure 18**) out of the crankcase.

Inspection and Installation

The inspection and installation procedures are the same as on previous models as described in Chapter Six in the main body of this book. Be sure to install the sidestand switch and reconnect the electrical connector.

TRANSMISSION GEARS

Mainshaft
Disassembly/Assembly

The disassembly and assembly procedures of the mainshaft are the same as on previous models with the exception of one of the spacers.

On prior years, the spacer between the 24 mm circlip and the 5th gear is identified as a spacer (28.3 × 33.5 × 1) and is a free rotating type with no inner teeth.

On these models, this washer has been replaced with one with inner teeth, or splines, that fit into the grooves on the transmission shaft (**Figure 19**).

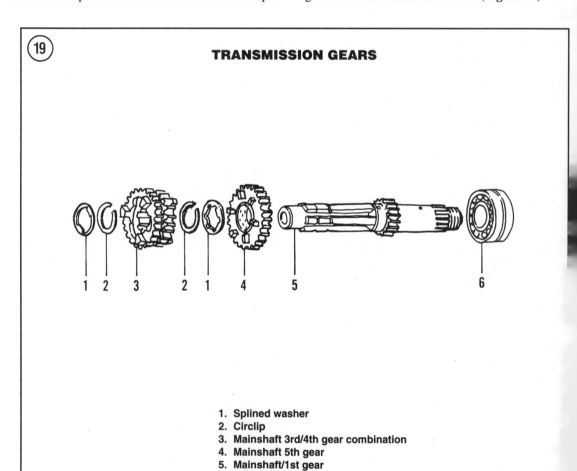

(19) TRANSMISSION GEARS

1. Splined washer
2. Circlip
3. Mainshaft 3rd/4th gear combination
4. Mainshaft 5th gear
5. Mainshaft/1st gear
6. Bearing

CHAPTER SEVEN

FUEL, EMISSION CONTROL AND EXHAUST

Carburetor specifications for these models are listed in **Table 4**.

FUEL TANK

Removal/Installation

WARNING
Some fuel may spill in the following procedure. Work in a well-ventilated

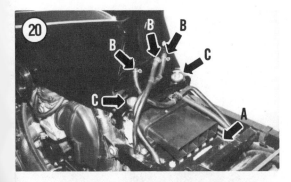

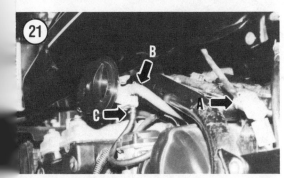

area at least 50 feet from any sparks or flames, including gas appliance pilot lights. Do not smoke in the area. Keep a B:C rated fire extinguisher handy.

1. Check that the ignition switch is off.
2. Place the bike on the centerstand.
3. Remove the seat and both side covers.
4. Disconnect the negative battery terminal (A, **Figure 20**).
5. Disconnect the fuel level sensor connector (A, **Figure 21**).
6. Turn the fuel valve to the OFF position and disconnect the fuel line (B, **Figure 21**) and vacuum line (C, **Figure 21**) from the fuel valve.
7. Label and disconnect the hose(s) (B, **Figure 20**) at the rear of the fuel tank.

WARNING
Plug the hoses disconnected in Step 7.

8. Remove the bolts (C, **Figure 20**) at the rear of the tank.
9. On California models, raise the rear of the tank and disconnect the emission control hose (**Figure 22**) from the fuel tank fitting.
10. Pull the tank toward the rear and remove it.
11. Pour the fuel in a container approved for gasoline storage.
12. Inspect the fuel tank dampers (**Figure 23**) for damage and replace if necessary.
13. To install the fuel tank, reverse the removal steps. Note the following:
    a. Don't pinch any wires or control cables during installation.

14

b. Reconnect all hoses and connectors to the correct fittings.

FUEL VALVE

Removal/Installation

The removal and installation procedures of the fuel valve are the same as on previous models with the exception of some of the internal components. If the fuel valve requires disassembly, refer to **Figure 24**.

AIR SUCTION SYSTEM

Suction Valve
Removal/Installation

If the engine idle is not smooth, if engine power decreases seriously or if there are any abnormal engine noises, remove the air suction valves and inspect them.

1. Check that the ignition switch is OFF.

2. Remove the fuel tank as described in this supplement.

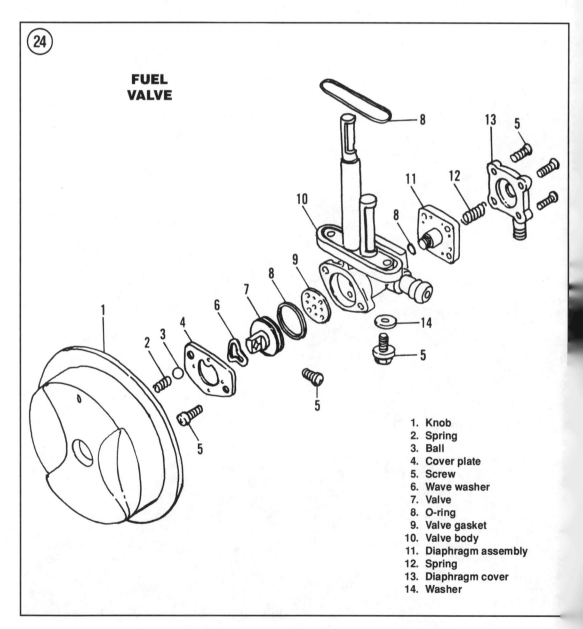

FUEL VALVE

1. Knob
2. Spring
3. Ball
4. Cover plate
5. Screw
6. Wave washer
7. Valve
8. O-ring
9. Valve gasket
10. Valve body
11. Diaphragm assembly
12. Spring
13. Diaphragm cover
14. Washer

3. Disconnect the electrical connectors and remove the harness bracket.

4. Slide the hose clamps off the vacuum switch valve.

5. Slide the hose clamps off the air suction valve. Refer to A, **Figure 25** and A, **Figure 26**.

6. Remove the bolts securing the air suction valve covers and remove the covers and gaskets. Refer to B, **Figure 25** and B, **Figure 26**.

7. Pull the suction valves out of the cylinder head cover.

8. Check the suction valves for cracks, folds, warpage or any other damage (**Figure 27**).

9. Check the sealing surface around the perimeter of the suction valve. It must be free of grooves, scratches or signs of damage.

NOTE
The valve assembly cannot be repaired. If damaged, it must be replaced.

10. Wash off any carbon deposits between the reed and the reed contact area with solvent.

CAUTION
Do not scrape deposits off the suction valve or the assembly will be damaged.

NOTE
The air suction valves can be removed with the cylinder head cover installed on the engine. It is shown removed in the following step for clarity.

11. Carefully remove any carbon deposits from the cylinder head cover port (**Figure 28**).
12. Install by reversing these steps.

Table 4 CARBURETOR SPECIFICATIONS

	ZX500 (European)	ZX600 (49-state and European)	ZX600 (California)	
Make	Keihin	Keihin	Keihin	
Size	CVK30	CVK32	CVK32	(continued)

14

Table 4 CARBURETOR SPECIFICATIONS (continued)

	ZX500 (European)	ZX600 (49-state and European)	ZX600 (California)
Main jet			
Cylinders			
1 and 4	105	105	105
2 and 3	105	105	105
Main air jet	100	100	100
Jet needle	N52P	N52Q	N52T
Pilot jet	35	35	35
Pilot air jet	160	150	160
Pilot screw	2 turns out	2 turns out	—
Starter jet	52	52	48
Fuel level	0.4-0.6 mm (0.016-0.024 in.)	0.4-0.6 mm (0.016-0.024 in.)	0.4-0.6 mm (0.016-0.024 in.)
Float height	17 mm (43/64 in.)	17 mm (43/64 in.)	17 mm (43/64 in.)

CHAPTER EIGHT

ELECTRICAL SYSTEM

WATER TEMPERATURE SENSOR (1989 AND LATER MODELS)

Testing

1. Remove the water temperature sensor as described under *Thermostatic Fan Switch and Water Temperature Sensor Removal/Installation* in Chapter Nine in the main body of this book.
2. Fill a beaker or pan with water and place on a stove.
3. Attach the ohmmeter test leads to the water temperature sensor terminals as shown in **Figure 29**.
4. Mount the water temperature sensor so that the temperature sensing tip and the threaded portion of the body are submerged as shown in **Figure 29**.
5. Place a thermometer in the pan of water (use a cooking or candy thermometer that is rated higher than the test temperature).
6. Check the resistance as follows:
   a. Gradually heat the water.
   b. When the temperature rises and reaches 196-203° F (91-95° C), the resistance reading should be approximately 1 M ohm.
   c. Continue to heat the water. When the temperature rises and reaches 205-212° F (96-100° C), the resistance reading should be approximately 0.5 ohms.
7. Replace the water temperature sensor if it failed to operate as described in Step 6.

JUNCTION BOX AND FUSES (1989 AND LATER MODELS)

The fan relay has been removed from the junction box.

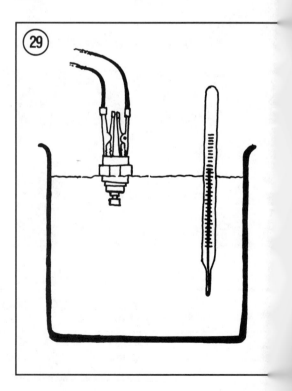

CHAPTER NINE

COOLING SYSTEM

RADIATOR AND FAN

WARNING
The radiator fan and fan switch are connected directly to the battery. Whenever the engine is warm or hot, the fan may start with the ignition switch in the OFF position. Never work around the fan or touch the fan until the engine is completely cool.

Removal/Installation

The radiator and fan are removed as an assembly.
1. Place the bike on the centerstand.
2. Remove the fuel tank as described in this supplement.
3. Remove the front fairing as described in the Chapter Thirteen section of this supplement.

4. Drain the cooling system as described under *Coolant Change* in Chapter Three in the main body of this book.
5. Disconnect the fan motor lead (A, **Figure 30**) and the fan switch lead (B, **Figure 30**).
6. Remove the baffle plate bolts and remove the baffle plate from the top of the cylinder head cover.
7. Loosen the clamping screws on the upper (A, **Figure 31**) and lower radiator hose bands. Move hose bands onto the hoses and off the necks of the radiator.
8. Disconnect the horn electrical connectors and pull the horn leads out of the guide on the radiator.
9. Disconnect the front fork ESCS electrical connector and pull the ESCS lead out of the guide on the radiator (B, **Figure 31**).
10. Remove the mounting bolt (C, **Figure 31**) on each side securing the radiator at the top and carefully remove the radiator and fan assembly from the frame.
11. Replace the radiator hoses if they are deteriorated or damaged.
12. Inspect the radiator as described in Chapter Nine in the main body of this book.
13. Install by reversing these removal steps. Refill the cooling system as described under *Coolant Change* in Chapter Three in the main body of this book.

THERMOSTAT

Removal/Installation

1. Place the bike on the centerstand.
2. Remove the fuel tank as described in this supplement.
3. Drain the cooling system as described under *Coolant Change* in Chapter Three in the main body of this book.
4. Disconnect the electrical connectors and remove the harness bracket (**Figure 32**).
5. Remove the thermostat cover bolts (A, **Figure 33**).
6. Remove the thermostat housing mounting bolts (B, **Figure 33**).
7. Lift the cover (C, **Figure 33**) off the housing.
8. Lift the thermostat out of the housing.

14

9. Test the thermostat as described under *Thermostat Inspection* in Chapter Nine in the main body of this book.

10. Install by reversing these removal steps. Note the following:

    a. Replace the cover O-ring, if necessary.

    b. Refill the cooling system with the recommended type and quantity of coolant as described under *Coolant Change* in Chapter Three in the main body of this book.

Thermostat Housing
Removal/Installation

1. Place the bike on the centerstand.

2. Remove the fuel tank as described in Chapter Seven in this supplement.

3. Drain the cooling system as described under *Coolant Change* in Chapter Three in the main body of this book.

4. Remove the front fairing as described in Chapter Thirteen in this supplement.

5. Disconnect the electrical connectors and remove the harness bracket (**Figure 32**).

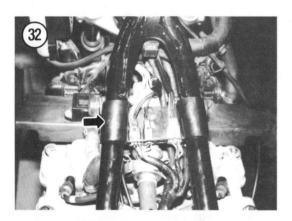

6. Disconnect the water temperature sensor electrical connector (A, **Figure 34**) from the thermostat housing.

7. Loosen the clamping screw (**Figure 35**) on the thermostat housing outlet port. Move the hose band onto the hose and off the neck on the outlet port.

8. Loosen the clamping screws on the cylinder head cover water pipe inlet on each side of the cylinder head cover. Move the hose bands onto the hoses (A, **Figure 36**) and off the neck on the water pipe inlets.

9. *U.S. models:* Remove the mounting bolts on the right-hand air suction valve cap (B, **Figure 36**) and move it out of the way.

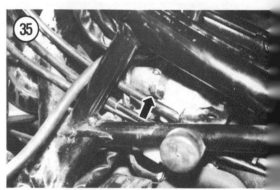

10. Remove the thermostat housing mounting bolts (B, **Figure 34**).

11. Carefully remove the thermostat housing and hose assembly out through the right-hand side of the frame.

12. Replace the thermostat housing hoses if they are deteriorated or damaged.

13. Install by reversing these removal steps. Refill the cooling system as described under *Coolant Change* in Chapter Three in the main body of this book.

CHAPTER TEN

FRONT SUSPENSION AND STEERING

FRONT WHEEL

Removal/Installation

1. Support the bike with a jack or wood blocks so that the front wheel is off the ground.

2. Unscrew the speedometer cable retainer (A, **Figure 37**) and remove the cable from the speedometer drive unit.

NOTE
It is only necessary to remove one of the brake caliper assemblies. Either one can be removed while the other caliper is left in place.

3. Remove the mounting bolts (B, **Figure 37**) on one of the brake calipers and lift the caliper off of the brake disc. Support the caliper with a Bungee cord or piece of wire to prevent stress on the brake hose.

4. Loosen the right-hand axle clamp bolt and nut (**Figure 38**).

5. Remove the axle nut (**Figure 39**) on the left-hand side.

14

6. Withdraw the axle (**Figure 40**) from the right-hand side.

7. Pull the wheel forward to disengage the attached caliper from the brake disc and remove the wheel.

8. Remove the speedometer drive gear from the left-hand side.

9. Remove the spacer from the right-hand side.

CAUTION
Do not set the wheel down on the disc surface as it may get scratched or warped. Either lean the wheel against a wall or place it on a couple of wood blocks.

NOTE
Insert a piece of wood in each caliper in place of the disc. That way, if the brake lever is inadvertently squeezed, the pistons will not be forced out of the cylinders. If this does happen, the calipers may have to be disassembled to reseat the pistons and the system will have to be bled. By using the piece of wood, bleeding the system is not necessary when installing the wheel.

10. When servicing the wheel assembly, install the spacer, speedometer drive gear and the nut on the axle to avoid misplacing them.

11. Inspect the front wheel as described under *Front Wheel Inspection* in Chapter Ten in the main body of this book.

12. Installation is the reverse of these steps. Note the following:

    a. To prevent axle seizure, coat the axle with an anti-seize compound such as Bostik Never-seez Lubricating and Anti-seize Compound, or equivalent.

    b. Align the 2 tabs (A, **Figure 41**) in the speedometer gear housing with the 2 speedometer

drive slots (B, **Figure 41**) in the front wheel and install the gear housing.

    c. When installing the front wheel, align the tab (A, **Figure 42**) on the speedometer gear housing with the slot (B, **Figure 42**) on the back of the left-hand fork tube. This procedure locates the speedometer drive gear and prevents it from rotating when the wheel turns.

    d. Make sure that the speedometer gear housing does not move as the axle nut is tightened.

    e. Tighten the axle nut to 88 N•m (65 ft.-lb.).

    f. Remove the caliper from the Bungee cord or wire and carefully align it with the brake disc and install it. Install the caliper mounting bolts and tighten to 33 N•m (25 ft.-lb.).

    g. Apply the front brake and compress front forks several times to make sure the axle is installed correctly without binding the forks. Tighten the axle pinch bolt to 20.5 N•m (14.9 ft.-lb.).

FRONT FORKS

Removal/Installation

1. Place the bike on the centerstand.

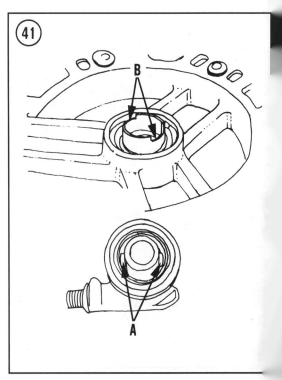

2. Remove the front fairing as described in this supplement.

3. Remove the brake caliper mounting bolts (**Figure 43**) on both caliper assemblies. Lift both calipers off of the brake discs. Support both calipers with a Bungee cord or piece of wire to prevent stress on the brake hose.

4. Remove the front wheel as described in this supplement.

5. Remove the front fender and brace mounting bolts. Then remove the fender brace.

6. Disengage the brake hose guides from each side of the fender and remove the front fender.

7. If the right-hand fork leg is to be removed, disconnect the ESCS electrical connector.

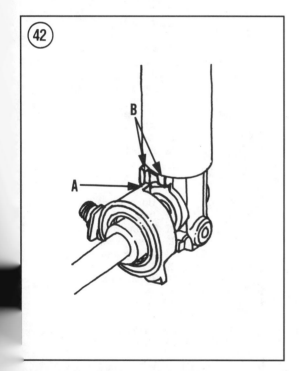

NOTE
Step 8 describes how to loosen the fork caps while the forks are held in place. If the forks are not going to be disassembled, proceed to Step 10.

WARNING
The fork cap bolts are under spring pressure. Take precautions to prevent the caps from flying into your face during removal. Furthermore, if the fork tubes are bent, the fork caps will be under considerable pressure. Have them removed by a Kawasaki dealer.

8. If the front forks will be disassembled, remove the handlebars as described in Chapter Ten in the main body of this book.

9. Loosen the upper fork tube pinch bolt. Then loosen the fork caps (but do not remove) with the drive end of a 1/2 in. ratchet.

10. Loosen all tie wraps securing either hoses or electrical wires to the fork tube.

11. Loosen the upper and lower fork tube pinch bolts and slide the fork tube from the upper and lower fork bridges. It may be necessary to rotate the fork tube slightly while pulling it down and out.

12. Repeat for the other side if necessary.

13. Install by reversing these removal steps. Note the following:

   a. Install the fork tubes through the lower and upper fork bridges. Push the fork tube so the top projects 16.0-17.5 mm (0.63-0.69 in.) above the top surface of the upper fork bridge as shown in Dimension "A" in **Figure 44**.

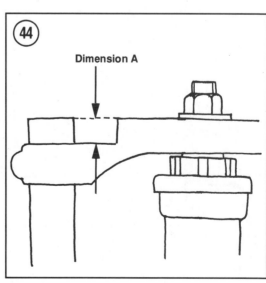

14

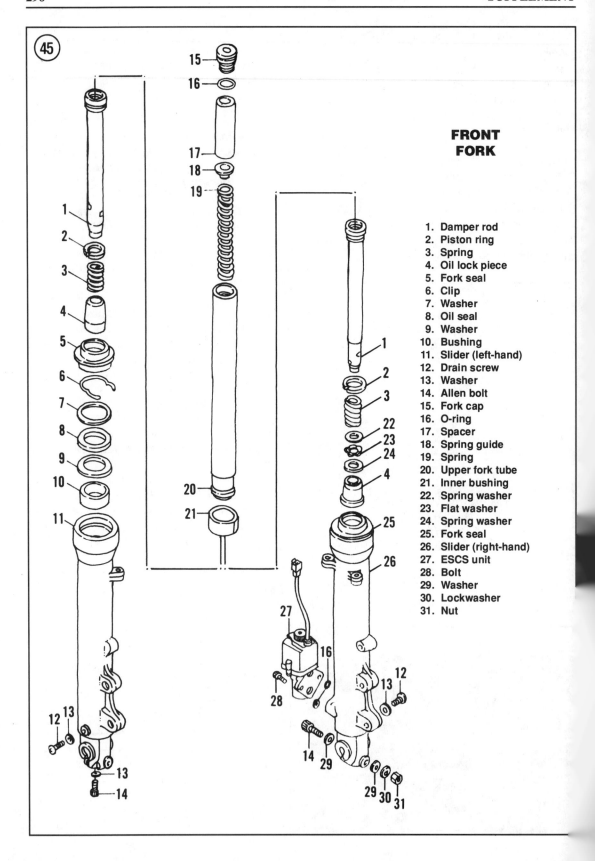

㊺

FRONT FORK

1. Damper rod
2. Piston ring
3. Spring
4. Oil lock piece
5. Fork seal
6. Clip
7. Washer
8. Oil seal
9. Washer
10. Bushing
11. Slider (left-hand)
12. Drain screw
13. Washer
14. Allen bolt
15. Fork cap
16. O-ring
17. Spacer
18. Spring guide
19. Spring
20. Upper fork tube
21. Inner bushing
22. Spring washer
23. Flat washer
24. Spring washer
25. Fork seal
26. Slider (right-hand)
27. ESCS unit
28. Bolt
29. Washer
30. Lockwasher
31. Nut

b. If loosened, tighten fork caps to 22.5 N•m (16.4 ft.-lb.).

c. Tighten the upper and lower fork bridge pinch bolts to 20.5 N•m (15 ft.-lb.).

d. Apply Loctite 242 (blue) to the front fender and brace bolts and tighten securely.

Disassembly/Inspection

Refer to **Figure 45** for this procedure.

1. Secure the fork tube vertical and clamp it in a vise with soft jaws and loosen the fork cap (if it was not loosened during the fork removal sequence).

WARNING
Be careful when removing the fork cap as the spring is under pressure. Protect your eyes accordingly.

2. Remove the fork cap (**Figure 46**), spacer and spring seat from the fork tube.

3. Remove the fork spring (**Figure 47**).

4. Turn the fork assembly upside down over a drain pan and pour the oil out and discard it. Pump the fork several times to expel most of the remaining oil.

NOTE
The Allen bolt has been secured with a locking agent and is often very difficult to remove because the damper rod will turn inside the slider. It sometimes can be removed with an air impact driver. If you are unable to remove it, take the fork tubes to a dealer and have the bolts removed.

5. Loosen the Allen bolt on the bottom of the slider. Prevent the damper rod from turning with Kawasaki tools 57001-183 and 57001-1057 (**Figure 48**).

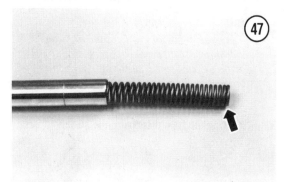

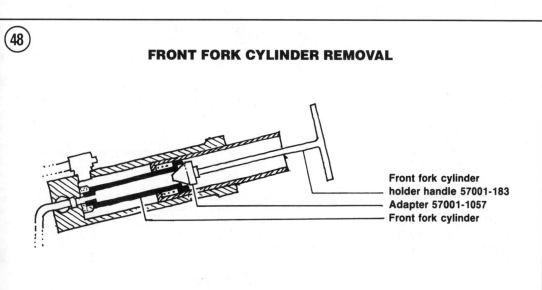

FRONT FORK CYLINDER REMOVAL

Front fork cylinder holder handle 57001-183
Adapter 57001-1057
Front fork cylinder

14

6. Remove the Allen bolt and gasket from the slider.

7. Carefully pry the dust seal out of the notch in the fork slider. Slide the dust seal up on the fork slider.

8. Pry the snap ring out of the fork slider.

> *NOTE*
> *On this type of fork, force is needed to remove the fork tube from the slider.*

9. Install the fork tube in a vise with soft jaws.

> *CAUTION*
> *In the next step, do not allow the fork tube to bottom out in the slider as the oil lock piece will be damaged.*

10. There is an interference fit between the guide bushing in the fork slider and the guide bushing on the fork tube. In order to remove the fork tube from the slider, pull hard on the fork tube using quick in-and-out strokes. Doing so will withdraw the guide bushing, washers and oil seal from the slider.

> *NOTE*
> *It may be necessary to heat the area on the slider around the oil seal slightly prior to removal. Use a rag soaked in hot water; do not apply a flame directly to the fork slider.*

11. Withdraw the fork tube from the slider.

> *NOTE*
> *Do not remove the fork tube guide bushing unless it is going to be replaced. Inspect it as described in this chapter.*

12. Refer to **Figure 49** and slide the following parts off of the fork tube:

    a. Dust seal (A).
    b. Snap ring (B).
    c. Upper washer (C).
    d. Oil seal (D).
    e. Lower washer (E).
    f. Bushing (F).

13. Withdraw the fork tube from the slider.

> *NOTE*
> *Do not remove the fork tube guide bushing unless it is going to be replaced. Inspect it as described under Front Fork Inspection in Chapter Ten in the main body of this book.*

14A. On the right-hand fork leg, remove the oil lock piece from the damper rod (**Figure 50**).

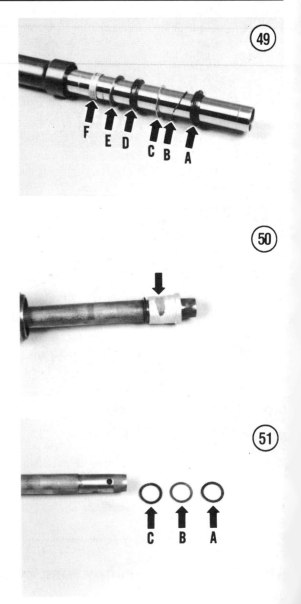

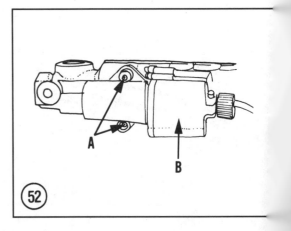

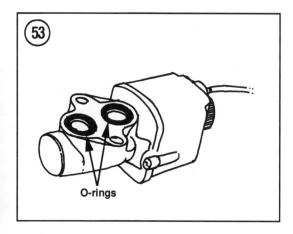

O-rings

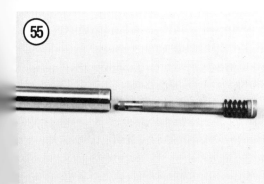

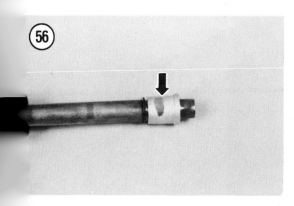

14B. On the left-hand fork leg, remove the oil lock piece from the damper rod. Then refer to **Figure 51** and slide the following parts off of the damper rod:
   a. Spring washer (A).
   b. Flat washer (B).
   c. Spring washer (C).

15. Remove the damper rod and rebound spring from the slider.

16. If necessary, remove the bolts (A, **Figure 52**) securing the ESCS unit to the right-hand fork leg and remove the unit (B, **Figure 52**). Don't lose the O-ring seals.

17. Inspect the components as described under *Front Fork Inspection* in Chapter Ten in the main body of this book. The standard new fork spring length is 481.2 mm (18.944 in.) and the wear limit is 472 mm (18.58 in.). If replacement is necessary, always replace both springs as a set to keep both fork legs balanced.

Assembly

Refer to **Figure 45** for the assembly procedure.

1. Coat all parts with fresh SAE 10W fork oil prior to installation.

2. If the ESCS unit was removed, inspect the O-ring seals (**Figure 53**) for wear or deterioration and replace if necessary. Apply a light coat of fork oil to the O-ring seals and install the ESCS unit onto the right-hand fork leg. Apply Loctite 242 (blue) to the mounting bolts and tighten to 6.9 N•m (61 in.-lb.).

3. Replace the O-ring seal (**Figure 54**) on the fork cap.

4. Install the rebound spring onto the damper rod and insert this assembly into the fork tube (**Figure 55**).

5A. On the right-hand fork leg, install the oil lock piece onto the damper rod (**Figure 56**).

5B. On the left-hand fork leg, refer to **Figure 51** and install the spring washer (C), the flat washer (B) and other spring washer (A).

6. Install the upper fork assembly into the slider (**Figure 57**).

7. Make sure the washer is on the Allen bolt.

8. Apply Loctite 242 (blue) to the threads of the Allen bolt prior to installation. Install it in the fork slider (**Figure 58**) and use the same tool set-up used during disassembly to keep the damper rod from turning while tightening the Allen bolt. On 1988-1992 models, tighten the bolt to 39 N•m (29 ft.-lb.); on 1993-on models, tighten to 29 N•m (22 ft.-lb.)

14

NOTE
The guide bushing can be installed with a piece of galvanized pipe or other piece of tubing that fits snugly over the fork tube. If both ends of the pipe are

*threaded, wrap one end with duct tape (**Figure 59**) to prevent the threads from damaging the interior of the slider. The bottom of this homemade driver must be flat so it installs the parts squarely.*

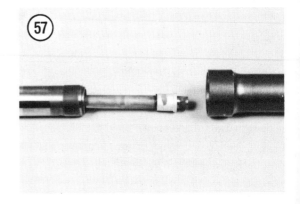

9. Slide the fork slider guide bushing over the fork tube. Turn the bushing (**Figure 60**) so that the split faces to the left or right side of the slider. Tap the guide bushing into the slider until it bottoms.

10. Slide the washer (**Figure 61**) down the fork tube and rest it on top of the guide bushing.

11. Position the new oil seal with the markings facing upward and slide it down the fork tube (**Figure 62**). Slide the upper washer down the fork tube and rest it on top of the seal. Drive the seal and upper washer into the slider using the same tool used in Step 9. Drive the oil seal in until the circlip groove in the slider can be seen above the top surface of the upper washer.

12. Install the circlip and make sure it is completely seated in the groove in the fork slider (**Figure 63**).

13. Install the dust seal into the slider (**Figure 64**).

14. Fill the fork tube with the correct quantity of fork oil as described under *Front Fork Oil Change* in this supplement.

15. Install the fork spring and the spring seat.

16. Apply fork oil to the threads and O-ring seal of the fork cap. Install the fork cap while pushing down on the spring. Start the bolt slowly, don't cross-thread it.

17. Place the slider in a vise with soft jaws and tighten the fork cap to 22.5 N•m (16.4 ft.-lb.).

18. Repeat for the other fork assembly.

19. Install the fork assemblies as described in this supplement.

ELECTRIC SUSPENSION CONTROL SYSTEM (ESCS)

Removal/Installation

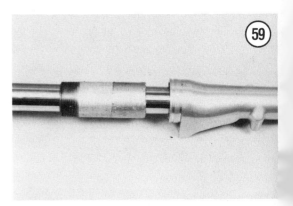

NOTE
On 1994-on non-U.S. models, the ESCS system is no longer installed on the right hand fork leg.

The ESCS unit can be removed from the right-hand fork leg with the forks installed on the bike. The ESCS unit cannot be disassembled or serviced; if faulty, the unit must be replaced.

1. Remove the front fairing as described in this supplement.

2. Drain the right-hand fork oil as described in this supplement and in Chapter Three in the main body of this book.

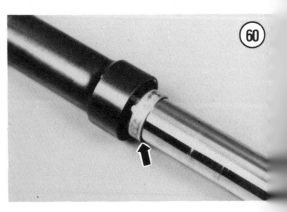

3. Disconnect the ESCS electrical connector adjacent to the coolant inlet hose to the thermostat housing on the right-hand side. Carefully pull the electrical wire and connector out through the hose and wiring guide at the top of the radiator.

NOTE
Step 4 and Step 5 are shown with the fork leg removed from the bike for clarity.

4. Remove the bolts (A, **Figure 52**) securing the ESCS unit to the right-hand fork leg and remove the unit (B, **Figure 52**).

5. Inspect the O-ring seals (**Figure 53**) for wear or deterioration and replace if necessary.

6. Make sure the O-ring seals are in place and install the ESCS unit onto the right-hand fork leg. Apply Loctite 242 (blue) to the mounting bolts and tighten to 6.9 N•m (61 in.-lb.).

7. Reroute the ESCS wire and reconnect the ESCS electrical connector.

8. Refill the right-hand fork leg as described in this supplement and in Chapter Three in the main body of this book.

9. Install the front fairing as described in this supplement.

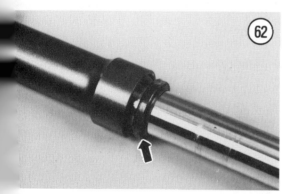

CHAPTER ELEVEN

REAR SUSPENSION

REAR SHOCK ABSORBER

Removal/Installation

Place the bike on the centerstand.
Remove the side covers.

3. Loosen the adjuster locknut and unscrew the adjuster rod.

4. Remove the air valve bracket mounting bolt.

5. Remove the shock absorber upper mounting nut (**Figure 65**).

14

CAUTION
*Slightly lift up on the rear wheel to take
the strain off the rear shock prior to
removing both mounting bolts. This will
help eliminate thread damage when the
bolts are withdrawn.*

6. Remove the shock absorber lower mounting bolt and nut (A, **Figure 66**).

7. Remove the rear suspension tie rod bolt and nut (B, **Figure 66**) and let the rocker arm pivot down out of the way.

8. Remove the shock absorber upper mounting bolt.

9. Carefully lower the shock absorber and air hose out of the frame.

10. Install by reversing these removal steps. Note the following:

   a. Install the shock absorber and the tie rod mounting bolts in from the left-hand side.

   b. Tighten all bolts and nuts to 49 N•m (36 ft.-lb.).

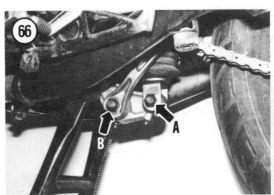

CHAPTER TWELVE

BRAKES

BRAKE PAD REPLACEMENT

Front and Rear
Pad Replacement

Front and rear brake pad replacement is identical to prior years with the exception of the removal of the caliper assemblies, and those procedures are covered in this supplement.

The caliper assemblies are equipped with 2 pistons instead of the single piston used on prior years. With the 2-piston calipers, the brake pad is wider and the standard thickness for both front and rear is 4.35 mm (0.171 in.) and the service limit thickness is 1 mm (0.039 in.).

Refer to **Figure 67** for the front brake caliper and to **Figure 68** for the rear brake caliper.

BRAKE CALIPERS

Front Caliper
Removal/Installation

Refer to **Figure 67** for this procedure.

1. Drain the master cylinder as follows:

   a. Attach a hose to the bleed screw on the brake caliper being removed.

   b. Place the end of the hose in a clean container

   c. Open the bleed screw and operate the brake lever to drain the brake fluid from the master cylinder reservoir and brake line.

   d. Close the bleed screw and disconnect the hose.

   e. Discard the brake fluid.

2. Remove the banjo bolt and sealing washers (A **Figure 69**) attaching the brake hose to the caliper

Be sure to cap or tape the ends to prevent the entry of moisture and dirt.

3. Remove the caliper mounting bolts (B, **Figure 69**) and carefully pull the caliper assembly off the brake disc.

4. Repeat for the other caliper if necessary.

5. Installation is the reverse of these steps. Note the following:

a. Tighten the caliper mounting bolts to 33 N•m (25 ft.-lb.).

b. Install the brake hose with new sealing washers on each side of the fitting.

c. Tighten the brake hose banjo bolt to 25 N•m (18 ft.-lb.).

d. Bleed the brakes as described in this supplement and under *Bleeding the System* in Chapter Twelve in the main body of this book.

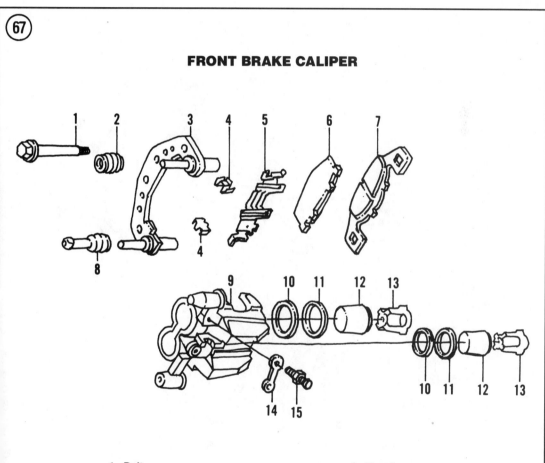

⑥⑦

FRONT BRAKE CALIPER

1. Bolt	9. Housing
2. Boot	10. Piston seal
3. Holder	11. Dust seal
4. Spring pad stopper	12. Piston
5. Anti-rattle spring	13. Piston
6. Brake pad	14. Cap
7. Brake pad	15. Bleed valve
8. Boot	

14

Rear Caliper
Removal/Installation

Refer to **Figure 68** for this procedure.

1. Drain the master cylinder as follows:

   a. Attach a hose to one of the brake caliper bleed screws.

   b. Place the end of the hose in a clean container.

   c. Open the bleed screw and operate the brake pedal to drain the brake fluid from the master cylinder reservoir and brake line.

   d. Close the bleed screw and disconnect the hose.

   e. Discard the brake fluid.

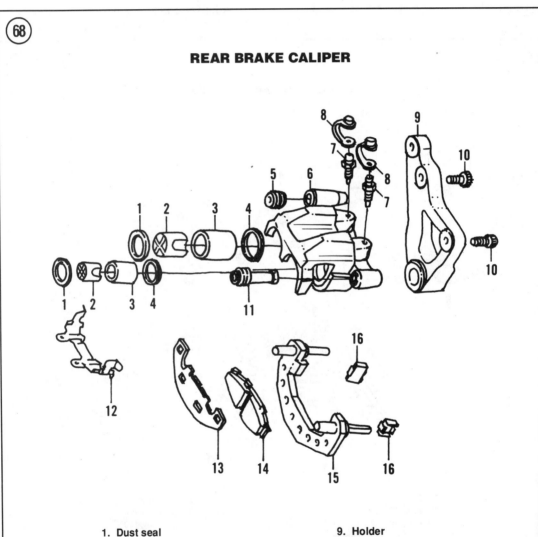

(68)

REAR BRAKE CALIPER

1. Dust seal
2. Piston seat
3. Piston
4. Piston seal
5. Boot
6. Housing
7. Bleed valve
8. Cap
9. Holder
10. Bolt
11. Boot
12. Anti-rattle spring
13. Brake pad
14. Brake pad
15. Holder
16. Spring pad stopper

2. Remove the banjo bolt and sealing washers (A, **Figure 70**) attaching the brake hose to the caliper. Be sure to cap or tape the ends to prevent the entry of moisture and dirt.

NOTE
To gain more access room to remove the caliper mounting bolts, you may want to remove the muffler.

3. Remove the caliper mounting bolts (B, **Figure 70**) and carefully pull the caliper assembly off the brake disc.

4. Installation is the reverse of these steps. Note the following:

   a. Tighten the caliper mounting bolts to 33 N•m (25 ft.-lb.).

   b. Install the brake hose with new sealing washers on each side of the fitting.

   c. Tighten the brake hose banjo bolt to 25 N•m (18 ft.-lb.).

   d. Bleed the brakes as described in this supplement and under *Bleeding the System* in Chapter Twelve in the main body of this book.

Caliper Rebuilding

Front and rear brake caliper rebuilding is identical to prior years except that the caliper assemblies are equipped with 2 pistons instead of the single piston that was previously used. Upon assembly, install the anti-rattle spring as shown in **Figure 71**.

Refer to **Figure 67** for the front brake caliper and to **Figure 68** for the rear brake caliper.

BLEEDING THE SYSTEM

Bleeding the system is identical to prior years except that the brake fluid-controlled front fork anti-dive units and the system's junction block have been eliminated.

This rear caliper is equipped with two bleed valves, one for each piston/cylinder, and both must be bled separately to remove air from each cylinder.

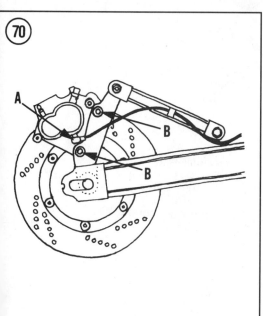

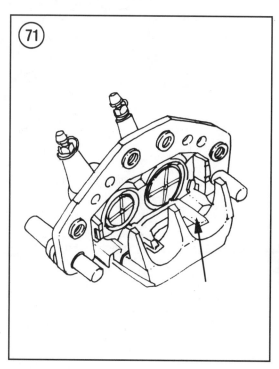

14

FAIRING ASSEMBLY

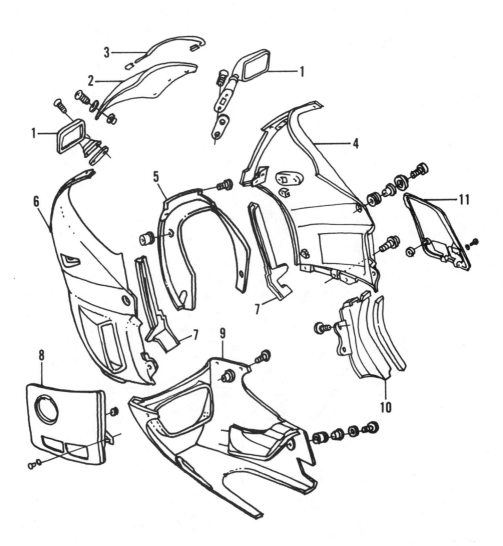

1. Rear view mirror
2. Windshield
3. Trim
4. Upper fairing (right-hand side)
5. Headlight lower cover
6. Upper fairing (left-hand side)
7. Trim panel
8. Knee grip cover
9. Lower fairing
10. Trim panel
11. Knee grip cover

CHAPTER THIRTEEN

FAIRING

FRONT FAIRING

When removing the fairing components, it is best to reinstall all mounting hardware onto the removed part or store it in plastic bags taped to the inside of the fairing. After removal, fairing components should be placed away from the service area to prevent accidental damage.

Lower Fairing
Removal/Installation

Refer to **Figure 72** for this procedure.

1. Place the bike on the centerstand.

2. Remove the 2 screws (A, **Figure 73**) and lower Allen bolt (B, **Figure 73**) securing the lower fairing to the frame.

3. Carefully lower the fairing (C, **Figure 73**) and remove it from the frame. Don't lose any of the mounting components.

4. Install by reversing these removal steps.

Upper Fairing
Removal/Installation

Refer to **Figure 72** for this procedure.

1. Remove the lower faring as described in this supplement.

2. Remove the seat and the knee grip covers.

3. Slide the rubber boot (A, **Figure 74**) up on the rear view mirror and remove the screws (B, **Figure 74**) securing the rear view mirror. Remove both mirrors.

4. Remove the lower screw (**Figure 75**) on each side.

5. Remove the upper Allen bolt (A, **Figure 76**) on each side.

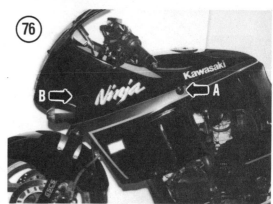

14

6. Carefully pull the upper fairing (B, **Figure 76**) assembly forward and disconnect the headlight and turn signal multi-pin electrical connector (**Figure 77**). **Figure 77** is shown with the faring removed for clarity.

7. Remove the upper fairing from the frame. Don't lose any of the mounting components.

8. Install by reversing these removal steps.

Upper Fairing Stay
Removal/Installation

Refer to **Figure 78** for this procedure.

1. Remove the lower and upper fairing as described in this supplement.

2. Disconnect the meter unit electrical connectors.

3. Disconnect the speedometer cable from the back-side of the meter unit.

4. Open the electrical cable clamps holding the cables to the backside of the meter unit.

5. Remove the bolt on each side securing the meter unit to the fairing stay and carefully remove the meter unit.

6. Remove the tie-wraps securing the coolant hose and electrical cables to the fairing stay.

7. Remove the bolts securing the coolant reservoir tank and remove the reservoir tank.

8. Remove the bolts securing the radiator filler cap mounting bracket to the fairing stay and move the filler cap assembly out of the way.

9. Remove the bolts on each side securing the fairing stay to the frame.

10. Make sure all electrical cables and hoses are disconnected from the fairing stay and carefully remove it from the frame.

11. Install by reversing these removal steps.

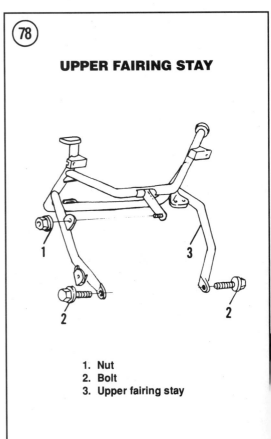

UPPER FAIRING STAY

1. Nut
2. Bolt
3. Upper fairing stay

INDEX

15

15

WIRING DIAGRAMS

ZX600 A1, A2, A3 (U.S. AND CANADA)

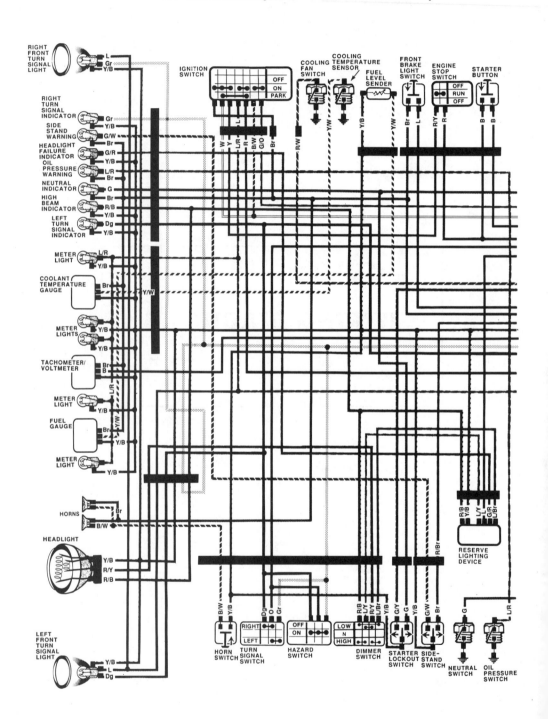

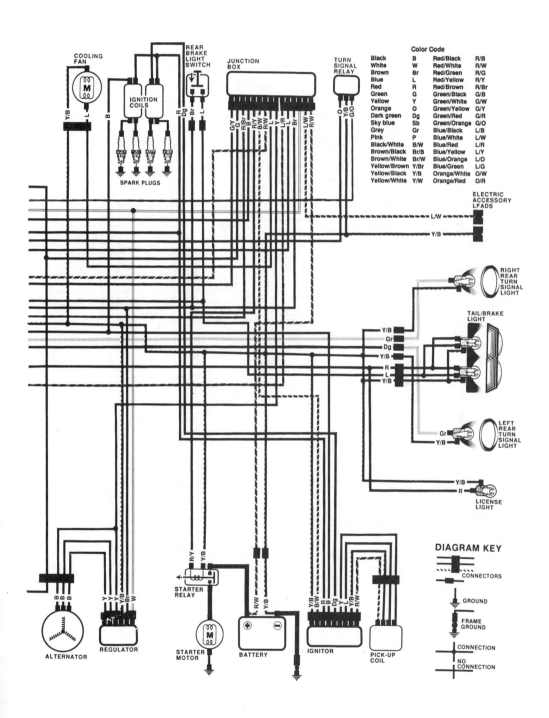

16

ZX600 C1 (U.S. AND CANADA)

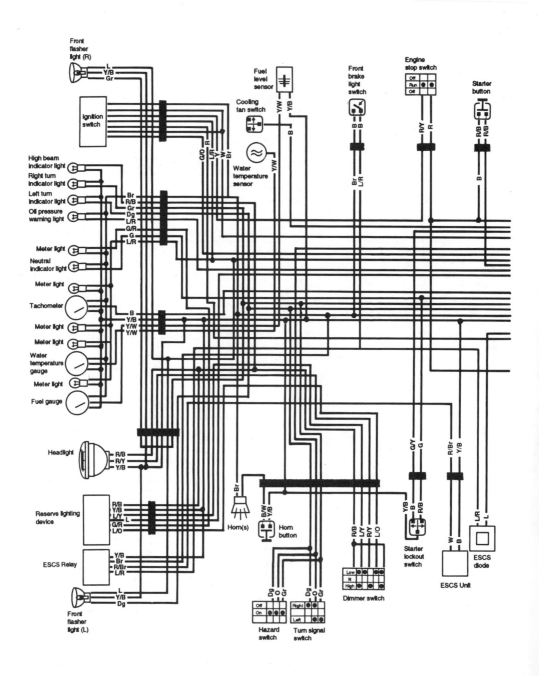

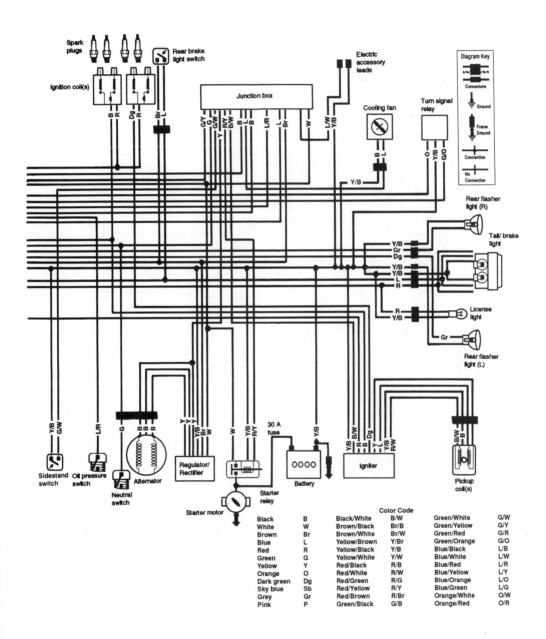

Color Code					
Black	B	Black/White	B/W	Green/White	G/W
White	W	Brown/Black	Br/B	Green/Yellow	G/Y
Brown	Br	Brown/White	Br/W	Green/Red	G/R
Blue	L	Yellow/Brown	Y/Br	Green/Orange	G/O
Red	R	Yellow/Black	Y/B	Blue/Black	L/B
Green	G	Yellow/White	Y/W	Blue/White	L/W
Yellow	Y	Red/Black	R/B	Blue/Red	L/R
Orange	O	Red/White	R/W	Blue/Yellow	L/Y
Dark green	Dg	Red/Green	R/G	Blue/Orange	L/O
Sky blue	Sb	Red/Yellow	R/Y	Blue/Green	L/G
Grey	Gr	Red/Brown	R/Br	Orange/White	O/W
Pink	P	Green/Black	G/B	Orange/Red	O/R

16

ZX600 C2, C3, C4, C5, C6 (U.S. AND CANADA)

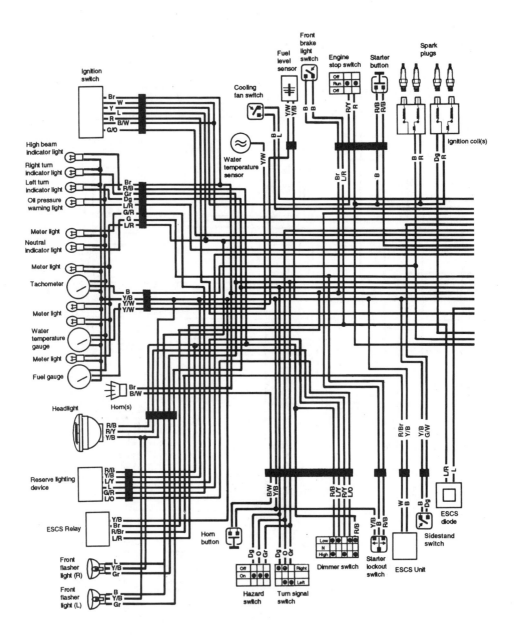

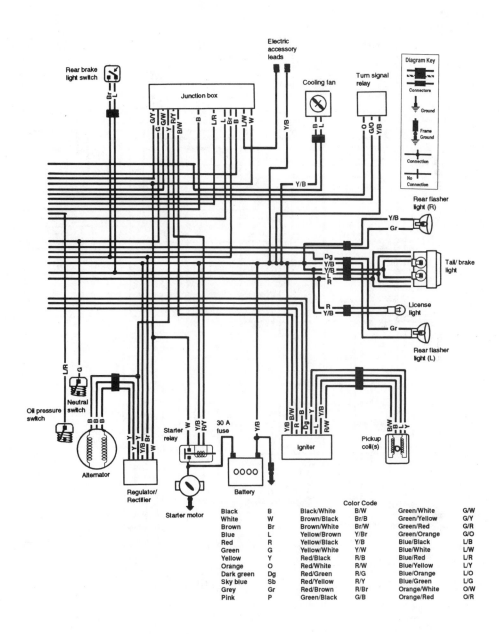

Rear brake light switch

Junction box

Electric accessory leads

Cooling fan

Turn signal relay

Diagram Key

Connectors

Ground

Frame Ground

Connection

No Connection

Rear flasher light (R)

Tail/ brake light

License light

Rear flasher light (L)

Oil pressure switch

Neutral switch

Alternator

Starter relay

30 A fuse

Battery

Igniter

Pickup coil(s)

Regulator/ Rectifier

Starter motor

Color Code								
Black	B	Black/White	B/W	Green/White	G/W
White	W	Brown/Black	Br/B	Green/Yellow	G/Y
Brown	Br	Brown/White	Br/W	Green/Red	G/R
Blue	L	Yellow/Brown	Y/Br	Green/Orange	G/O
Red	R	Yellow/Black	Y/B	Blue/Black	L/B
Green	G	Yellow/White	Y/W	Blue/White	L/W
Yellow	Y	Red/Black	R/B	Blue/Red	L/R
Orange	O	Red/White	R/W	Blue/Yellow	L/Y
Dark green	Dg	Red/Green	R/G	Blue/Orange	L/O
Sky blue	Sb	Red/Yellow	R/Y	Blue/Green	L/G
Grey	Gr	Red/Brown	R/Br	Orange/White	O/W
Pink	P	Green/Black	G/B	Orange/Red	O/R

ZX500 A1, A2, A3
ZX600 A1, A2, A3, A4 (EXCEPT U.S. AND CANADA)

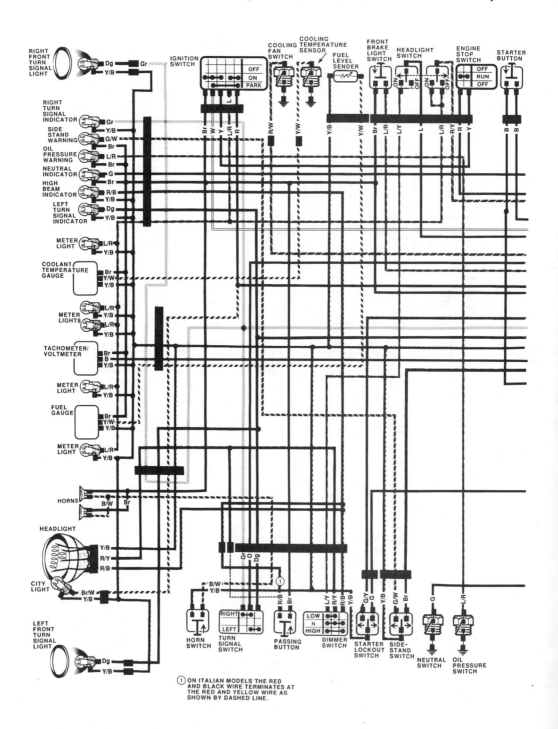

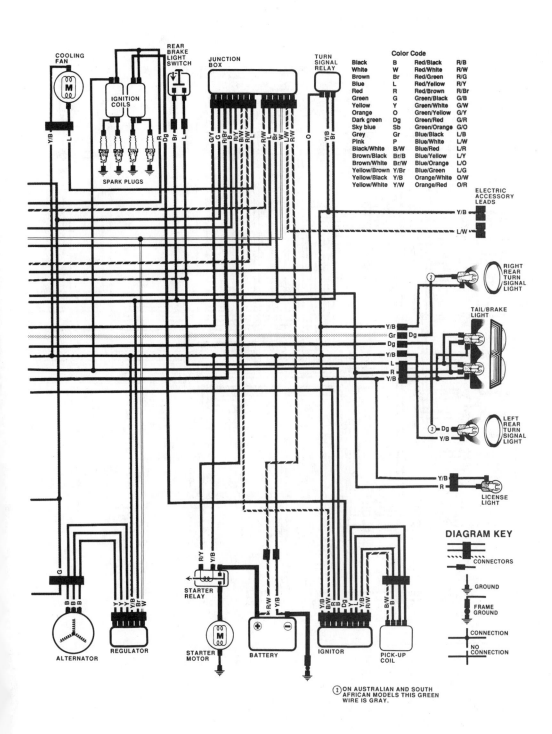

Color Code

Black	B	Red/Black	R/B
White	W	Red/White	R/W
Brown	Br	Red/Green	R/G
Blue	L	Red/Yellow	R/Y
Red	R	Red/Brown	R/Br
Green	G	Green/Black	G/B
Yellow	Y	Green/White	G/W
Orange	O	Green/Yellow	G/Y
Dark green	Dg	Green/Red	G/R
Sky blue	Sb	Green/Orange	G/O
Grey	Gr	Blue/Black	L/B
Pink	P	Blue/White	L/W
Black/White	B/W	Blue/Red	L/R
Brown/Black	Br/B	Blue/Yellow	L/Y
Brown/White	Br/W	Blue/Orange	L/O
Yellow/Brown	Y/Br	Blue/Green	L/G
Yellow/Black	Y/B	Orange/White	O/W
Yellow/White	Y/W	Orange/Red	O/R

DIAGRAM KEY

CONNECTORS

GROUND

FRAME GROUND

CONNECTION

NO CONNECTION

② ON AUSTRALIAN AND SOUTH AFRICAN MODELS THIS GREEN WIRE IS GRAY.

16

ZX600 A5 (EXCEPT U.S. AND CANADA)

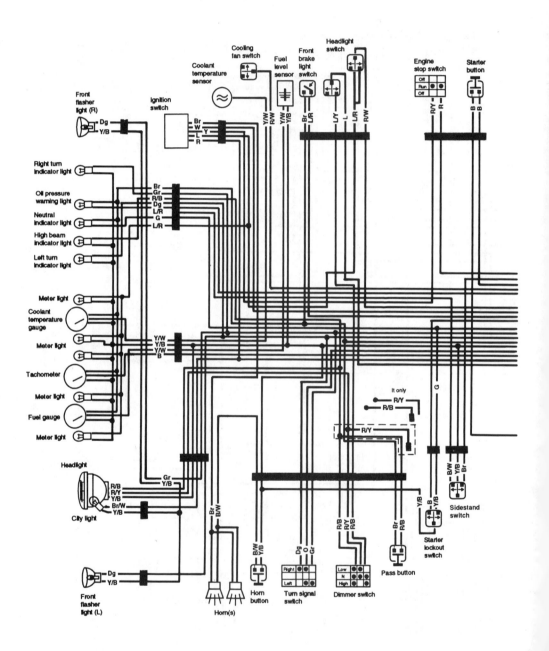

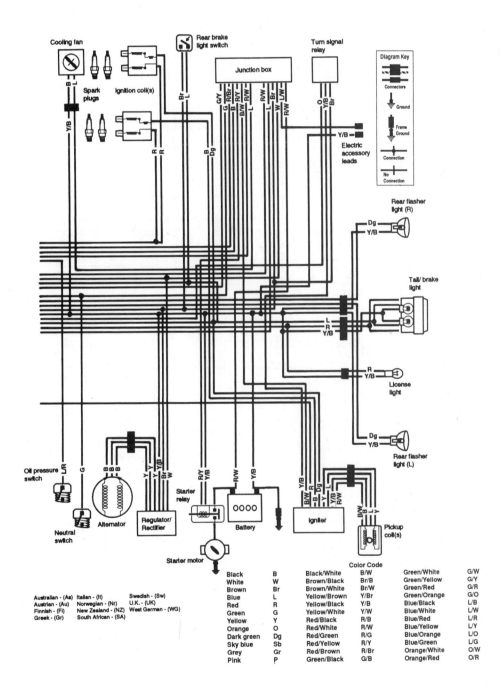

Cooling fan

Spark plugs

Ignition coil(s)

Rear brake light switch

Junction box

Turn signal relay

Diagram Key

Connectors

Ground

Frame Ground

Connection

No Connection

Electric accessory leads

Rear flasher light (R)

Tail/ brake light

License light

Rear flasher light (L)

Oil pressure switch

Neutral switch

Alternator

Regulator/ Rectifier

Starter relay

Battery

Igniter

Pickup coil(s)

Starter motor

Color Code					
Black	B	Black/White	B/W	Green/White	G/W
White	W	Brown/Black	Br/B	Green/Yellow	G/Y
Brown	Br	Brown/White	Br/W	Green/Red	G/R
Blue	L	Yellow/Brown	Y/Br	Green/Orange	G/O
Red	R	Yellow/Black	Y/B	Blue/Black	L/B
Green	G	Yellow/White	Y/W	Blue/White	L/W
Yellow	Y	Red/Black	R/B	Blue/Red	L/R
Orange	O	Red/White	R/W	Blue/Yellow	L/Y
Dark green	Dg	Red/Green	R/G	Blue/Orange	L/O
Sky blue	Sb	Red/Yellow	R/Y	Blue/Green	L/G
Grey	Gr	Red/Brown	R/Br	Orange/White	O/W
Pink	P	Green/Black	G/B	Orange/Red	O/R

Australian - (As) Italian - (It) Swedish - (Sw)
Austrian - (Au) Norwegian - (Nr) U.K. - (UK)
Finnish - (Fi) New Zealand - (NZ) West German - (WG)
Greek - (Gr) South African - (SA)

16

ZX500 B1
ZX600 C1 (EXCEPT U.S. AND CANADA)

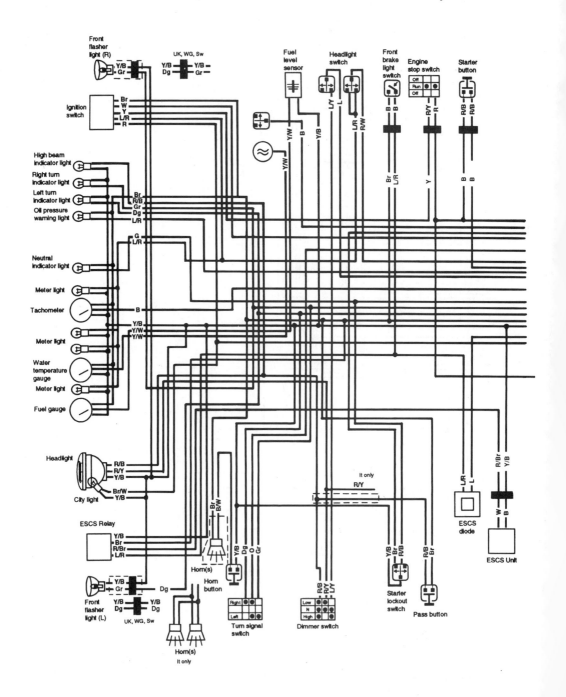

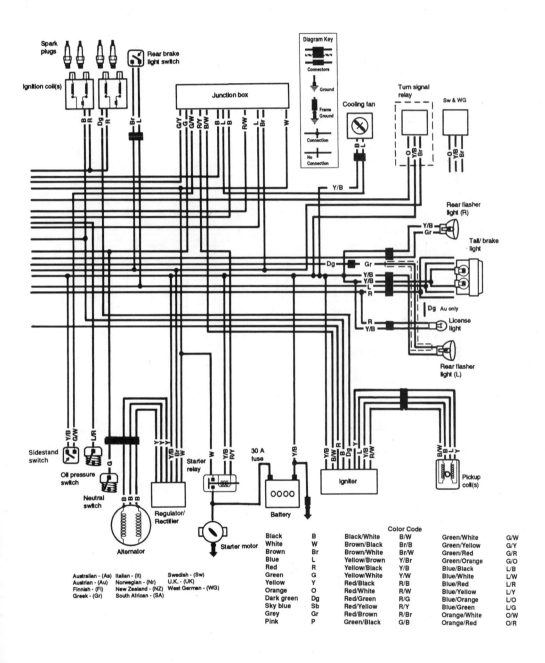

				Color Code			
Black	B	Black/White	B/W		Green/White	G/W
White	W	Brown/Black	Br/B		Green/Yellow	G/Y
Brown	Br	Brown/White	Br/W		Green/Red	G/R
Blue	L	Yellow/Brown	Y/Br		Green/Orange	G/O
Red	R	Yellow/Black	Y/B		Blue/Black	L/B
Green	G	Yellow/White	Y/W		Blue/White	L/W
Yellow	Y	Red/Black	R/B		Blue/Red	L/R
Orange	O	Red/White	R/W		Blue/Yellow	L/Y
Dark green	Dg	Red/Green	R/G		Blue/Orange	L/O
Sky blue	Sb	Red/Yellow	R/Y		Blue/Green	L/G
Grey	Gr	Red/Brown	R/Br		Orange/White	O/W
Pink	P	Green/Black	G/B		Orange/Red	O/R

Australian - (As) Italian - (It)   Swedish - (Sw)
Austrian - (Au)   Norwegian - (Nr)   U.K. - (UK)
Finnish - (Fi)   New Zealand - (NZ)   West German - (WG)
Greek - (Gr)   South African - (SA)

16

ZX500 B2, B3
ZX600 C2, C3, C4, C5 (EXCEPT U.S. AND CANADA)

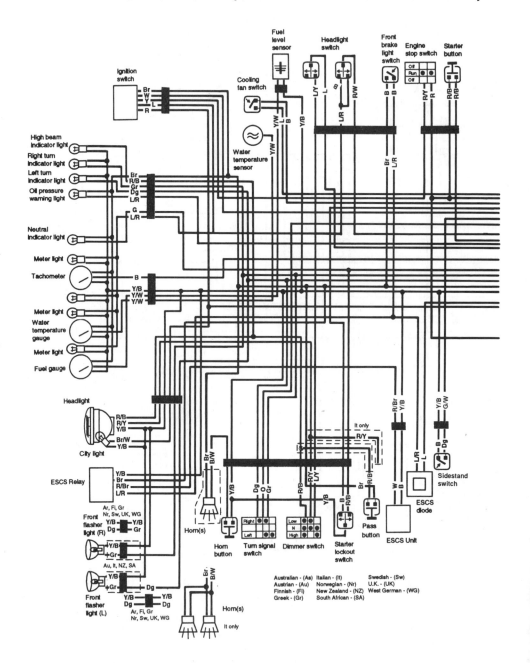

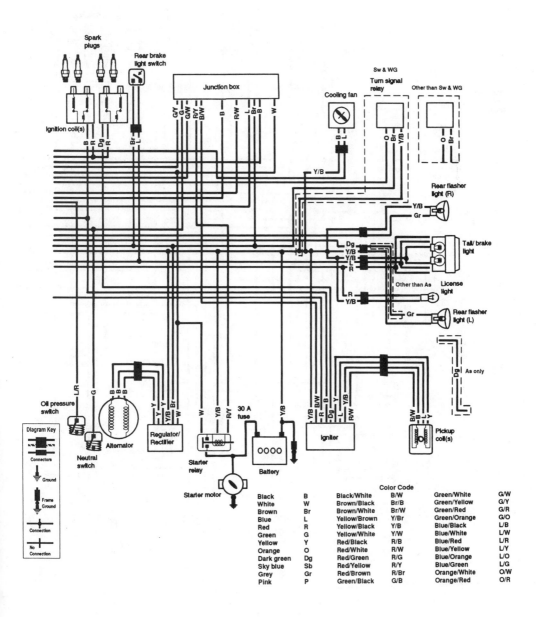

Color Code						
Black	B	Black/White	B/W	Green/White	G/W
White	W	Brown/Black	Br/B	Green/Yellow	G/Y
Brown	Br	Brown/White	Br/W	Green/Red	G/R
Blue	L	Yellow/Brown	Y/Br	Green/Orange	G/O
Red	R	Yellow/Black	Y/B	Blue/Black	L/B
Green	G	Yellow/White	Y/W	Blue/White	L/W
Yellow	Y	Red/Black	R/B	Blue/Red	L/R
Orange	O	Red/White	R/W	Blue/Yellow	L/Y
Dark green	Dg	Red/Green	R/G	Blue/Orange	L/O
Sky blue	Sb	Red/Yellow	R/Y	Blue/Green	L/G
Grey	Gr	Red/Brown	R/Br	Orange/White	O/W
Pink	P	Green/Black	G/B	Orange/Red	O/R

16

ZX600 C7, C8, C9, C10 (U.S. AND CANADA)

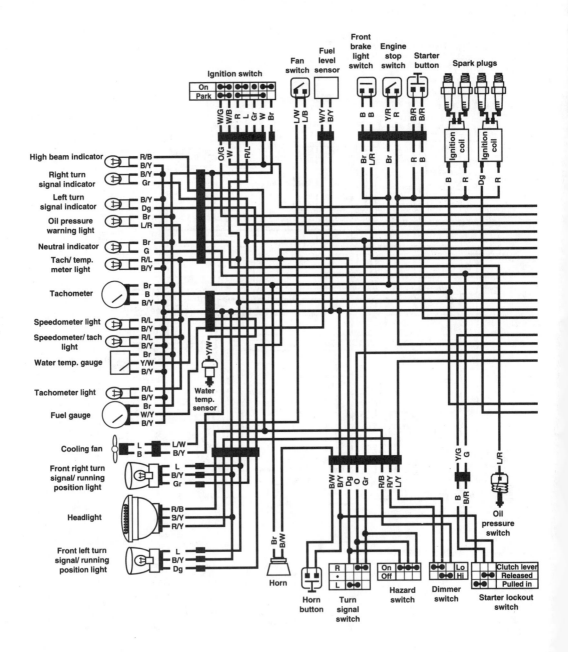

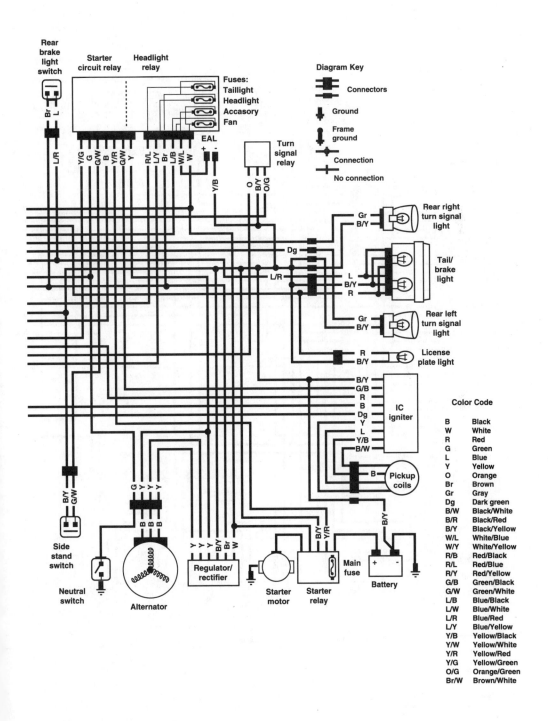

16

ZX600 C6, C7, C8, C9, C10 (EXCEPT U.S. AND CANADA)

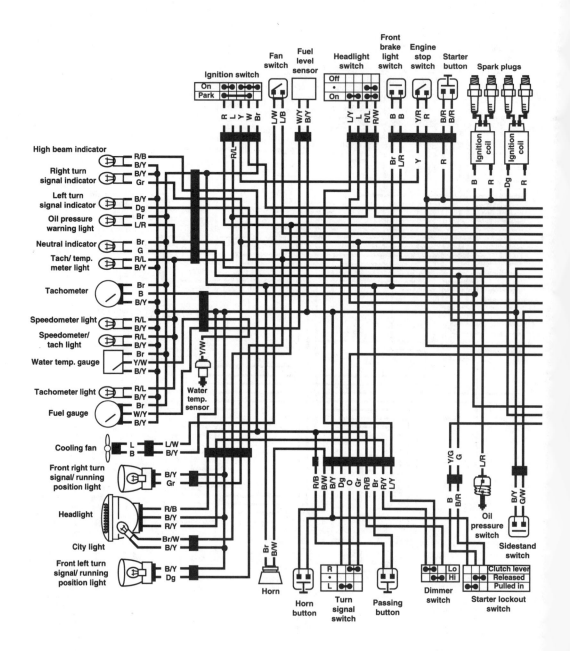

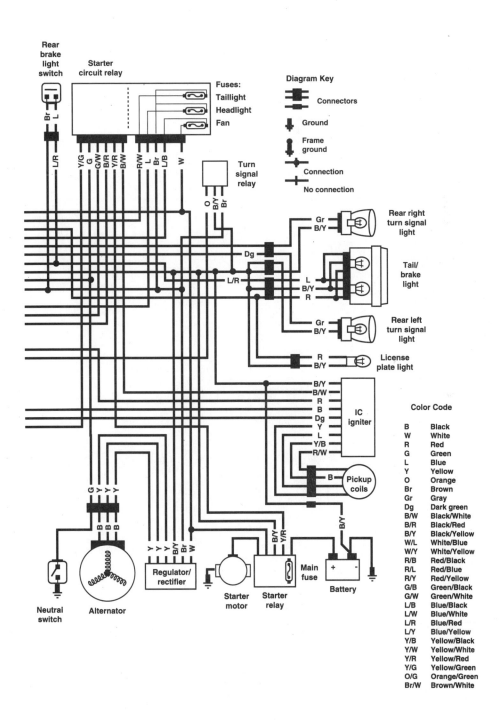

16

NOTES

NOTES

NOTES

NOTES

MAINTENANCE LOG

Service Performed	Mileage Reading				
Oil change (example)	2,836	5,782	8,601		